PRAISE FOR MARK MOBIUS'S
PASSPORT TO PROFITS

"Fascinating stuff....The Mobius genius emerges."
—*Kiplinger's Personal Finance Magazine*

> Mobius Rule No. 2: Taking risks is what you get paid for.

"One of the world's most insightful international investors tells why the crisis in emerging financial markets has created an extraordinary buying opportunity."
—**Burton G. Malkiel, author of**
***A Random Walk Down Wall Street* and**
Global Bargain Hunting

> Mobius Rule No. 57: When everyone else is dying to get in, get out.

"Mark Mobius is a delightful traveling companion, and his wisdom is tested. I'm glad it's Mark dealing with the sinister folk at the airport in Lagos, Nigeria, and not me."
—**Andrew Tobias, host of**
Adam Smith's Money Game

> Mobius Rule No. 58: When everyone else is screaming to get out, get in.

more . . .

"Combines great analytical skills, hard work, perseverance, and plain common sense...highly readable."
—**Mark Faber**

Mobius Rule No. 76: If the whole world is down on a country for exaggerated, short-term reasons, shift it from a hold to a buy.

"Mobius's knowledge of emerging markets should prove valuable to investors....He makes a convincing argument for investing in a well-managed emerging markets fund, demonstrating the potential values to be found in these markets as well as the potential losses involved in assuming the risk."
—*Library Journal*

PASSPORT TO PROFITS

Why the Next Investment Windfalls Will Be Found Abroad—and How to Grab Your Share

MARK MOBIUS

WITH STEPHEN FENICHELL

WARNER BOOKS

A Time Warner Company

Copyright © 1999 by Mark Mobius
All rights reserved.

Warner Books, Inc., 1271 Avenue of the Americas, New York, NY 10020
Visit our Web site at www.twbookmark.com

 A Time Warner Company

Printed in the United States of America
Originally published in hardcover by Warner Books, Inc.
First Trade Printing: July 2000
10 9 8 7 6 5 4 3 2 1

The Library of Congress has cataloged the hardcover edition as follows:

Mobius, Mark.
    Passport to profits: why the next investment windfalls will be found abroad—and how to grab your share / Mark Mobius with Stephen Fenichell.
        p. cm.
     ISBN 0-446-52251-1
     1. Investments, Foreign. I. Fenichell, Stephen. II. Title.
HG4538.M585   1999
332.67'3—DC21   98-38868
                                                          CIP

ISBN 0-446-67605-5 (pbk.)

Book design by Giorgetta Bell McRee
Cover photography by Kelly Campbell
Cover design by Flamur Tonuzi

ACKNOWLEDGEMENTS

"Where is Steve's luggage?" This became the refrain as we moved from Siberia to the Urals, from Istanbul to Rio to the rest of the world. Steve Fenichell became so engrossed in this book that he often forgot about his luggage and our schedule. It's a tribute to Steve that he was able to concentrate on his writing and research tasks while, at the same time, keeping up with our grueling travel plan. Not only is he a great writer, he's a wonderful traveling companion who asked questions during company visits that added depth and insight to our research.

In addition to Steve, a tribute must go to Doe Coover, my agent, who really made this project a reality with her practical advice and upbeat attitude. Also to Rick Horgan, our editor at Warner Books, who gave us important insights into how to tailor such a book to both the specialist and general reader.

Chuck Johnson, President of Templeton, and Charlie Johnson, Chairman of Franklin Resources, are the greatest people to work for. Their long view, sense of humor, and patient understanding of the vicissitudes of emerging markets investing provide the bedrock of our work.

Finally, and most important, gratitude and thanks must go to the Templeton staff members who contributed their experiences and insights: Roman Filatov, Alexis Zarechnak, Dominic Gualtieri, and Ivan Darmanian in Russia (Roman's adventures in Russia could be another book); Sven Richter and Ochieng Okeyo in South Africa (whose trip to Nigeria provided amusing and hair-raising anecodotes); Grzegorz Konieczny and Nick Fitzwilliams in Warsaw, Poland; Shwan Taha then in Dubai (now in Istanbul, Turkey); Chetan Sehgal and R. Shankar in Mumbai, India; Tom Wu, Allan Lam, and Eddie Chow in Hong Kong; Dennis Lim, Ong Tek Khoan, and Jim Root in Singapore;

Rafael Gowland and Patricio Demaria in Buenos Aires; Chris Freund and Nguyen Xuan Minh in Ho Chih Minh City, Vietnam (now in Singapore); Jack Lin and Jerry Lou in Shanghai; Gustavo Stenzel and Bernardo Carneiro in Rio de Janeiro; and Seiichi Ono in Tokyo.

Special thanks also to Zita Ng in Singapore, who always ensures that I appear in that part of the world, on time, where I'm supposed to be!

CONTENTS

Preface ix

PART ONE: The Boom (Eastern Europe)
CHAPTER ONE: Hope and Growth 3
CHAPTER TWO: Baltic Boom 60
CHAPTER THREE: All the Riches in Russia 105

PART TWO: The Bust (Asia)
CHAPTER FOUR: Hong Kong 161
CHAPTER FIVE: Hong Kong II "Catching a Falling Knife" ..192
CHAPTER SIX: Ground Subzero: Thailand 232

PART THREE: Beating the Odds (Latin America)
CHAPTER SEVEN: The Next Domino? (Brazil) 281

PART FOUR: The Final Frontier (Africa)
CHAPTER EIGHT: Nigeria 331
CHAPTER NINE: South Africa 352

CONCLUSION: Winners and Losers.............................385

Appendix 420

PREFACE

The views expressed in this book are solely my own, and do not represent the views of my employer. In reading this book, you should keep in mind that specific company information—including performance, share prices, and similar information—is by necessity historical and used only to illustrate my points. Things change rapidly in the investment world and these are no exceptions.

Although it is my aim to have provided a useful perspective on emerging markets and emerging market investing, you should also keep in mind a few basic investment principles. One is that all investing involves risk. Another is that the greater potential for investment reward is invariably accompanied by higher degrees of risk. Emerging markets investing is no different.

Certainly, as I have explained, there is the potential for great rewards for the patient long-term investor. But one must also be able to accept the significant risks, which I have also outlined. Keep in mind: any quotation of investment results is historical. Even the most experienced investor cannot guarantee future investment results.

I hope this book *is* a passport to profits, but also a guide to how you can survive what can sometimes be an emerging markets jungle.

PART ONE

◆

The Boom
(Eastern Europe)

BALTIC STATES and RUSSIA

*Boldface capital words are countries Mobius visited

**Boldface lowercase words are cities Mobius visited

Chapter One

♦

HOPE AND GROWTH

The Name Is Mobius. *Mark Mobius.*

As Jack Reaves, our skilled American pilot, smoothly brought the thirteen-seat Gulfstream IV jet in for a landing, I restlessly pressed a tiny brass button marked "TV" on the suede armrest beneath my window.

With a discreet whir, a mahogany-paneled TV set slid up from the dim recesses of a built-in cabinet, and began automatically displaying a computer-generated "air show" depicting the graphic image of a small aircraft—this aircraft—winging its way across a simulated slice of sea marked "Gulf of Finland."

A digital readout indicating our altitude—*rapidly decreasing*—and time to destination—*two minutes fifty-five seconds*—had all five members of our Templeton Emerging Markets support team poking around in the spaces surrounding their seats, scurrying to gather up their papers and books in preparation for making a quick getaway just as soon as our feet hit the tarmac.

Our most recent flight, from Abu Dhabi (the money center of the United Arab Emirates) to Estonia on the Baltic Sea, hadn't been all that grueling, from my point of view. But I couldn't help noticing that young Dennis Chan, a specialist in custodial rela-tions from our Hong Kong office, had been catching a little shut-eye in the minutes prior to landing. I don't usually suffer from jet lag, probably because I tend to be in such perpetual motion that my body doesn't get enough time to reset its internal clock to a "home base" before being wrenched off into another time zone.

Glancing up from a wedge of faxes the thickness of a small city phone book—representing one morning's communications relayed to Abu Dhabi from our Singapore office—I caught a brief glimpse out my Plexiglas porthole of the dense fir forests surrounding Tallinn, the capital of Estonia, scheduled to be stop number one on our upcoming tour of the Baltic Republics. Within seconds, we would be landing in one of the very few countries I'd managed to miss during nearly forty years of incessant globe-trotting. As so often happens just prior to landing in any new country, I found myself experiencing a pleasurable twinge of anticipation. Sometimes I wonder if I travel to run money, or run money to travel.

So Why the Baltics?

The easy answer is that all three tiny Baltic Republics—Latvia, Lithuania, and Estonia—were booming during the summer of 1997. The largest single factor propelling this Baltic Boom appeared to be the remarkable run-up occurring in Russia directly to the south. In 1997, the Russian stock market had shot up, in percentage terms, more than any other stock market in the world: over 200 percent. In the following year, 1998, the Russian stock market dropped by over 50 percent, making it the world's worst performing stock market at that time—*c'est la vie*.

The fledgling Baltic markets (whose daily turnover could still scarcely compete with five seconds of active trading on New York's Big Board) had pulled down comparably staggering returns during the same period. But the simple fact that the newly established Baltic Republics, only recently freed from the Soviet yoke, qualified as a financial flavor of the month would not have been enough to draw me here, under most circumstances. I don't pay all that much attention to hot stocks, or hot markets, preferring to leave them to the hotshots. I was more interested in gaining indirect exposure to the Russian and Polish markets by investing in adjacent economies, which, for better or worse, were inextricably linked to their more populous and powerful neighbors.

I'd come to the Baltics to do what I do just about every working day of my life: scope out new regions, countries, and companies in a nonstop financial safari focused on bagging bargains. My idea of a bargain is, by the way, not very complicated.

I buy stocks in companies with good growth potential over a five-year period.

Period. End of story. Or, in another sense, beginning of story. Because the process I put myself and my staff through in order to identify and acquire the "right" stocks—right for the moment, right for me, right for my investors—can be complex, not to mention time-consuming. My often idiosyncratic methods, developed over a quarter-century of stock-picking, demand that I spend a whole lot of time in the air, so that I can spend even more time on the ground.

So Why This Book? And Why Now?

Here's the direct answer:

"To get the word out to investors who might want to venture into the emerging markets."

One of the great treats of being a successful fund-manager is that people (who often recognize my Yul Brynneresque shaved head and noble visage from TV talk shows) are constantly cornering me in hotel lobbies and airport lounges, pumping me for scoops. Of course, even if I felt like passing on the occasional "hot tip"—which I definitely do not—ethical and legal considerations would strictly forbid me from doing so.

So what's my blueprint, my road map, they ask, my method of picking the right regions, the right countries, the right companies at the right time?

How did I know to throttle down on Thailand before the baht crashed, to gear up in Russia just as it was preparing for liftoff, and to pull back in Russia before that market crashed?

"Oh, it's a long story." I shrug, hoping that will discourage them from asking for more.

But sometimes, some people actually *want* to hear the whole story—especially during those long flight delays—from the buried treasures I've dug up in some of the most unlikely places, from the Chilean mining-and-transport company Antofagasta, whose hidden asset turned out to be copper mines worth more than its railroad, to total turkeys like the Turkish utility looted by a locally powerful clan, who took the book on investor rights and tossed it in the trash—to date, with total impunity.

True, as we swooped in on Tallinn airport in tiny Estonia, I'd good reason to celebrate my recent tenth anniversary at the helm of the world's first listed emerging markets mutual fund. While our flagship Templeton Emerging Markets Fund (the first New York Stock Exchange–listed emerging markets fund) had scored an average 23.3 percent annual gain over the decade ending March 31, 1997, the average U.S. equity fund had achieved a barely respectable 11.4 percent average annual gain over the same period. Suffice it to say, 1998 was a less than stellar year for emerging markets *performance* but a wonderful year of *opportunity* because stocks were fabulously cheap.

We'd beaten the indexes, we'd beaten the averages, we'd beaten the advanced, dynamic First World industrial economies by buying up shares in companies few people had ever heard of, in countries even sophisticated investors had long been inclined to dismiss with a snobby sniff. In the roughly ten years since the legendary Sir John Templeton took the twofold risk (one, of betting on emerging markets, and two, hiring me) to run his pioneering emerging markets fund, I'd put in enough time on commercial flights to earn myself a frequent-flier first-class flight to the moon.

I'd toured rubber plantations in Thailand and road-tested bikes over the pothole-ridden roads of rural China.

I'd choked on roasted camel's meat, sheep's eyeball, guinea pig and dined (surprisingly well) on scorpions on toast.

I'd hobnobbed with princes, potentates, and pashas, and been swindled in souks so labyrinthine I'm still amazed I ever found my way out.

I'd taken bone-jolting rides on mountain roads that would have turned my hair gray if I had any left to turn.

All to find *undervalued companies* before other investors do.

I think you could safely say that I'm driven.

And I hope by the end of this book, you'll feel driven, I hope, to take a few leaves out of it.

Ticket to Ride

These days, I spend at least 250 out of every 365 days either on the road, or in the air. For most people forced to endure it, homelessness is the ultimate sacrifice. But it's taken me many years of hard work to achieve the high status of full-time nomad—an endangered species I've long admired for their fierce independence, their refusal to abide by conventional norms, their desperate desire for freedom. Though some people probably pity me for having no home, no family, no domestic life to speak of, my somewhat eccentric lifestyle offers untold opportunities for variety, stimulation, and creativity.

It's only been in the last few years, by the way, that with safety in mind our Franklin/Templeton Group has forced me to use a $20 million thirteen-seat Gulfstream IV private jet. This allows me to avoid unsafe airlines and frees me and my free-floating Templeton team from the countless hassles, inefficiencies, and rigidities of commercial travel, particularly after logging so many flight hours on TAP (the Portuguese airline, whose initials facetiously stand for "Take Another Plane"), to the Turkish airline THY (They Hate You), and Belgium's Sabena (Such A Bloody Experience Never Again). Actually, they're all wonderful airlines.

Sure, I've read studies that purport to show that private jets can be more economical for corporations than commercial flights. But more to the point, I'm a little too familiar with the safety statistics relating to commercial flying in some of the regions of the world we routinely visit. In particular, I'm thinking about Russia, China, and certain parts of Latin America. No offense, but with the amount of flying I do, the numbers are not in my favor.

So I genuinely appreciate the opportunity afforded me to fly in a plane that I can feel fairly sure offers a stronger safety record than the local airline. It's never easy assessing what a single life may be worth, but since I typically have four to five staffers aboard, the cost-benefit analysis improves considerably in favor of the personal plane.

If it makes any of you jetless feel any better, our aircraft was acquired at a cut price by Templeton, where we make a religion of hunting down bargains. Its first owner, whose designers were responsible for the flashy custom decor, was a Saudi jeweler whose clientele was heavily weighted toward Arab sheiks. The interior could easily be mistaken for the boudoir of an Arabian princess, complete with gold-plated fixtures, polished brass fittings, suede wall coverings, and what I've been reliably informed (I received the news with a shudder) is genuine iguana skin upholstery. Personally, I wouldn't mind ripping it all out and replacing it with plywood filing cabinets, because we use the plane mainly as a flying office. But a full-scale renovation turns out to be—somewhat ironically—too expensive even to contemplate.

Apart from the occasional overnight flight, I spend nearly every night of my restless life in hotels. I select these temporary "homes away from home" more on the basis of offering an up-to-date fitness center than any other single amenity. Until just a few years ago, I owned apartments around the world, in Washington, D.C., Hong Kong, Singapore, and Shanghai, primarily for investment purposes.

But I found before long that even when stopping by old stomping grounds, I preferred the anonymity, convenience (and twenty-four-hour fax services) of business hotels. As for my remaining personal investments, I've long since stopped thinking too much about them, except to leave most of my money tied up in our own funds, where at least I've some idea where it's being put to work and for whom. Frankly, I'm too busy to figure out what else to do with my money. Odd as this may sound, I don't have much room for money in my life—I'm much too busy handling other people's to spend or tend to my own. As I recently remarked to an old friend, I've never had a problem being different. In fact, I'd call my long-standing desire to be different the key to my record of success as an investor.

Material Disclosure: I should probably set the record straight right here and now by disclosing (we fund managers are as much fiends for disclosure as our lawyers and compliance officers) a material fact:

There is no simple secret, no single blueprint, no rigid road map, that will guarantee you—or me—long-term success as a global investor.

But there are, of course, plenty of good, solid lessons to be learned from observing the methods of research and analysis employed by a long-term investor in these famously turbulent markets.

I am, first and foremost, a firm believer in getting out and kicking the tires—in some cases, literally. My idea of a perfect day is one spent visiting six or eight companies without breaking for lunch. We might tour a factory, check out a new distribution center, ask a few questions, get a few answers. And my idea of a perfect night on the town is to have dinner (after a jog or a stint at the gym) with my ever-rotating Templeton team going over what we've seen and heard, comparing notes, hashing out plans for the (long-term) future.

So, short of taking you on the road with me, I'll try and do the next best thing: give you a feeling for what I do and why, by revealing daily scenes of my working life and every now and then, when the situation warrants, stepping back to fill in the broad brushstrokes.

Emerging Markets: When? How? Why? Why Not?

In 1986, when I first began investing in what were then called less developed countries (LDCs) as a fund manager, the term "emerging market" had only recently been coined by the International Finance Corporation (IFC), a subsidiary of the World Bank. At the time, the term represented more wishful fantasy than reality, because many of these markets, stranded on the shoals of an outmoded socialism, were submerging faster than they were emerging.

FELT

As one by one the LDCs of what was formerly known as the Third World converted—usually by fits and starts—to a market economy, they were obliged to set up capital markets, the first phase of which is usually a "stock" market, although that is something of a misnomer, because stock markets often trade in all forms of securities and financial instruments, from bonds to futures and options, as well as commodities, not to mention various funny and fancy hybrids in between.

Before I'm willing to risk any funds under our management in one of these spanking-new capital markets, we insist that it share a few basic characteristics with mature (First World) markets. I've defined these minimum requirements by an easy acronym: FELT.

FELT stands for:
F—Fair
E—Efficient
L—Liquid
T—Transparent.

Putting on My Felt Hat, Puttin' on the Ritz

Whenever I enter any newly emerged market, I ask myself four basic questions:
1) Is it Fair?
2) Is it Efficient?
3) Is it Liquid?
4) Is it Transparent?
(By "transparent" investors mean: is it easy to find out what's really going on in this market? As in who's buying and selling what stocks, at what price?)
If the market meets our FELT criteria, we get excited about it.

If it doesn't, we approach with great care.

The current IFC definition of an emerging market is: "A market growing in size and sophistication in contrast to a market that is relatively small, inactive, and gives little appearance of change."

When I started out in this game, with only around $100 million in the kitty (in contrast to today's $14 billion and climbing), only five Asian countries—Hong Kong, Malaysia, the Philippines, Singapore, and Thailand—fit the bill, under that definition. Of those five, tiny Hong Kong—where I'd lived, on and off, for over twenty years—was our pivot, our linchpin.

I knew, or imagined I knew, Hong Kong's uncanny ways like the Chinese medical meridians on the back of my palm. I felt safe investing there. But when we first began investing heavily there in October 1987, the last great American stock market crash was just sending shock waves around the world, bringing down world markets, many of which were just starting to recover from the 1970s slump, brought on by the global oil crisis.

By the time the tidal wave hit Asia, the head of the Hong Kong Stock Exchange closed the place down for three days. By the time it reopened, we'd lost roughly a third of our total investment on paper. This profoundly unsettling experience (which featured me personally persuading many a spooked investor to sit tight and ride out the wave) taught me and my then-tiny Templeton Emerging Markets team an unforgettable lesson about the inherent risk of putting too many eggs in one basket.

This traumatic financial upheaval drove home—like a nail—our number one Mobius Rule:

> ## Mobius Rule No. 1: Your best protection is diversification.

The Basket Boom

Fortunately, diversification has become easier with more opportunities to choose from.

Fortunately, today there are many more baskets, and far fewer basket cases.

Ten years ago, when Templeton launched one of the first emerging markets mutual funds, no other U.S.-based mutual funds invested significant portions of their portfolios overseas. But today (according to Lipper Analytical Services), over 900 mutual funds invest heavily in foreign securities. And over 100 do what I do—invest exclusively in so-called emerging markets.

Some Statistics

Around eight years ago, total private investment in so-called LDCs was well under $30 billion, while official and public (government sector) development aid funds amounted to well over $65 billion.

By 1998, the tables had turned: private investment in emerging markets had increased nearly tenfold to roughly $250 billion, while public sector aid had dwindled to $50 billion.

In 1990, net financial aid from First World countries to emerging markets was four times the flow of private capital.

By 1998 those tables had also dramatically turned: now the flow of private capital had increased to fully *five times* the size of government aid.

In these numbers can be traced a wholesale global transition from sclerotic statist—that is, state-controlled—to dynamic free-market economies.

An even better yardstick by which to measure the growing importance of emerging markets: in the early 1970s, U.S. stock markets comprised an overwhelming 66 percent of the world's total stock market value.

By 1998, that share had dropped to 38 percent, while foreign markets soared to a whopping 62 percent. Ten years ago, total market capitalization of emerging markets was around $184 billion, or 5 percent of the world's total equity market capitalization.

By now, that figure has risen to nearly one trillion dollars, or

just about 15 percent of the world's total equity market capitalization.

These shocking—to many longtime investors, used to thinking
only in First World terms—statistics mean that investors today
have many more choices and ways to expose their portfolios to
these high-growth emerging markets than any of us did ten, five,
or even two years ago. That's the upside.

Now for the downside.

It really isn't so bad.

With so many choices, choosing the right investment vehicle
becomes even harder.

So Many Eggs, So Many Baskets

At Templeton, we generally utilize a number of strategies in our
never-ending quest for diversification.

With a global fund, we seek to limit exposure by permitting
only a set percentage of capital to be invested in any one region.

With a regional fund, we limit our exposure to any one country.

With a country fund, we'll limit exposure by restricting the
percentage of the portfolio we can invest in any one sector or
company.

And in general, our mutual fund diversification strategies also
result in our not being overly dependent on the fate of any one
stock issue or security.

Note: as a small investor, you should consider adopting similar hedging strategies, or invest in funds that do.

A Note on Fund Types

Global funds give investors exposure to a number of regions.

Regional funds invest in a number of countries in the same region.

Regional funds rise and fall with the fortunes of a region, and
typically take the form of either pan-Asian, East European, or

Latin American funds. These funds buy baskets of stocks throughout a region, permitting investors to make a bet on the region of their choice.

Country funds invest in a single country.

Country funds, incidentally, can give investors spectacular growth if they buy at the bottom. But they can also show substantial losses if a country's entire stock market tanks.

For example: while our Russia Fund could rack up close to a 200 percent return in a single year, our global funds, which included Russian shares, did not and could not show nearly as spectacular returns. Then again, neither did they offer nearly the same risk of spectacular losses. In mid-1998, as the Russian stock market dove by nearly 40 percent in one week, our closed-end Russia Fund shares dropped sharply in value. Although—and this was a result of sound market strategies—we had lightened up on our investments sufficiently by then and kept nearly 30 percent of our fund's assets in cash, because we felt that the booming Russian stock market had become grossly overvalued. Hence, even as the market tumbled, we were able to protect our shareholder value by hedging our bets.

Closed-End Funds

Closed-end funds raise a fixed amount of money by selling a limited number of shares. These funds invest their money like mutual funds but trade on the market like stocks. Which means that sometimes they can behave a little strangely. The value of the stock tracks the underlying portfolio, for example, but still may trade above or below the portfolio's worth at any given moment. Unlike an open-ended fund, investors in closed-end funds can't redeem their shares at will. Most of the first round of emerging markets funds were closed-ended, because the funds' sponsors wanted to avoid having fund managers feel pressure to sell stocks at low prices during market downturns, because they had to raise cash to buy back shares submitted for redemption.

The strange behavior of closed-end funds—they can trade at deep discounts or steep premiums to the NAV, or net asset value (that's the total worth, or market capitalization, of the assets in the fund minus liabilities at a given time), of the stocks in their portfolio—can create opportunities for investors. Playing premiums (which can remain high even after the share value collapses) is a common strategy among sophisticated investors.

Open-Ended Funds

Open-ended funds can expand infinitely to meet demand—although some managers close them down when they get too big and unwieldy to efficiently manage—and they can sell as many shares as the market will bear. Investors enjoy commensurate freedom too, to buy and sell shares, because they can easily pull money out by selling or redeeming shares—that's basically a way of selling the shares back to the fund manager—as opposed to selling them in the open market, the way you would do with a closed-end fund.

Owning an open-ended fund can be great except during sharp market corrections, where the unwelcome prospect of redemptions can exert a negative effect on long-term performance, by putting pressure on fund managers to focus on short-term as opposed to long-term gains.

That's why open-ended funds are often more attractive investments during market lows—because the fund manager has the luxury of putting the inflow of money to work at very low prices.

Closed-end funds can sometimes be a better bet during market highs.

A Few Things *You* Can Do

First, buy a map, globe, or atlas.

Whether you're thinking about putting together your own portfolio of emerging markets stocks, or buying into one of the many global or emerging markets mutual funds, a critical first step is to get yourself a good globe, atlas, CD-ROM, or paper map of the world. This is a critical first step. (For a great freebie, the next time you're on a plane, tear out the route map in the back of your in-flight magazine, because airline route maps tend to be excellent.)

Now get out that map or globe, or pop that CD-ROM into your D drive, and take a good, long hard look at it. You may not have done this at any great length since the sixth grade, but time spent in studying a world map can never be wasted, and can be critical to your success as a global investor.

The first thing you'll probably notice is the relatively small size of the so-called First World compared to the vast swatches of land covering what used to be called the Third World, otherwise known as the less developed countries, or LDCs for short. Of course, for most of the past few hundred years, a handful of small, highly developed West European countries—Great Britain, France, and Germany, for the most part—dominated the rest of the globe, with the notable exception of North America— although Canada was a British Crown colony.

The legacy of that often brutal period of colonialization and imperialist expansion is still very much with us, because the "other half" of the world, once freed from the imperialist yoke, reacted against Western capitalist "exploitation" by adopting a variety of socialist models and forms of development in what turned out to be a futile attempt to free itself from the economic and psychological burdens of colonial status.

For hundreds of years, First World industrialized countries had exploited their colonies as sources of cheap raw materials. What the Third World had in abundance was natural resources: oil, metals, timber, commodity cash crops. What it lacked was infrastructure, both public and private: roads, factories, rail-roads.

What little infrastructure the LDCs did have mainly served as a transportation backbone skewed sharply toward exporting raw materials from the colonies back to their home markets: railroads built by the colonists ran, for example, from mines to the nearest port, where the raw materials could be shipped out for processing—simultaneously transferring, not incidentally, to the home industries the lion's share of the profits. Those industries often turned around and sold the finished products back to their own colonies at a hefty rate of return.

Following independence from their mother countries (which for most former colonies took place in the late 1950s and early 1960s), the First World sought to help out the Third World by lavishing large amounts of foreign aid on them. Academic experts in Third World development—I was educated as one as a graduate student at MIT—theorized that you could figure out where best to situate a factory, a road, a dam, or a railroad, give the local leadership the money to build them, and presto! You had development.

They turned out to be wrong. Very wrong. The problem with such thinking was that it was too strongly influenced by the then fashionable notions of centralized planning that had been popular in the socialist world since the Russian Revolution, but had only captured the imagination of the Western academic elite during and immediately after the two world wars.

A comparatively high degree of centralized planning, conducted in the context of military mobilization, had enabled the great industrialized powers of the West to wage highly destructive wars with maximum efficiency: destroying each other's industrial plants, and killing untold numbers of combatants and civilians.

Once those wars were concluded, the awesome technologies developed to fight and win those wars, from airplanes to radar to nuclear energy—would and could (or so it was naïvely believed) be turned to good use in an age of world peace to bring the globe into a new era of long-term prosperity and harmony.

Well, then came the Cold War, dashing many of those dazzling and naïve visions. But in fact, centralized planning and the introduction of modern technology did help many an underdeveloped country jump-start the rudiments of an industrial economy. But the failures of centralized planning were also momentous. By the 1970s, with world markets reeling from the effects of stagflation brought about by oil price shocks, the statist economies of the Third World and the moribund economies behind the Iron Curtain had begun to spring leaks, leading to wholesale inefficiencies, while propping up rapacious dictators from Asia to Africa to Eastern Europe.

Now add to that unfortunate situation the often brutal imposition, immediately after World War II, of the Communist system on the subjugated countries of Eastern Europe by a brazenly imperialist Soviet Union, which hoped to prop up as many autocratic and dictatorial regimes as the Western powers, and you had a recipe for catastrophe. What's surprising, in retrospect, is not that the entire worldwide socialist system crumbled, but that it lasted so long.

Today, having at long last freed themselves of the yoke of colonialism—and, in the case of Eastern Europe, Russian imperialism—and having then relinquished the self-imposed yoke of socialism, nearly all of the world's major emerging markets—at Templeton we now invest in nearly forty countries that meet that definition—are located in four distinct regions beyond the tiny, tidy horizons of the industrialized, developed First World:

1) Asia
2) Eastern and Southern Europe
3) Latin America
4) Africa and the Middle East

The Wall Street Journal recently devised a list of world markets ranked according to degree of investor risk, with Level 1— "Countries Most Similar to the U.S."—arrayed as follows, in alphabetical order: Australia, Canada, Denmark, France, Germany, Ireland, the Netherlands, New Zealand, Sweden, Switzerland, the United Kingdom.

Okay, forget all about Level 1. That's the First World. For our purposes, off the charts.

Let's turn to Level 2—"Other Developed Countries"—in which the *Journal* includes: Austria, Belgium, Finland, Hong Kong, Italy, Japan, Norway, Singapore, Spain.

Two of particular interest are:

1) Spain—although it along with neighboring Portugal is no longer any great shakes for bargain-hunters—and

2) Hong Kong, because even though its market is highly developed, it is rapidly becoming the major market for the world's greatest emerging market, China.

Among the "Mature Emerging Markets" the *Journal* includes: Argentina, Brazil, Chile, Greece, Korea, Malaysia, Mexico, Philippines, Portugal, South Africa, Thailand.

These are considered "mature" emerging markets not because they are immune to the extreme volatility common to all emerging markets—because believe me, they're not—but because they offer a wide range of investment opportunities, some degree of transparency in the operation of their markets, and comparatively advanced systems of investor protection, including securities regulation and treatment of minority shareholders.

I say "fairly," "relatively," and "comparatively" because all of these countries are still far from North American and West European standards, in spirit as well as geography. No one—and I mean no one—should be operating under any illusions that investing in these countries is anywhere near as safe, secure, or—let's face it—tame as putting your money to work in the world's most advanced industrialized countries.

Among the world's "Newly Emerging Markets," the *Journal* includes: China, Colombia, Czech Republic, Hungary, India, Indonesia, Israel, Poland, Sri Lanka, Taiwan, Venezuela.

All of these nations comprise key markets in our portfolio, and should be examined closely for opportunities by any prospective emerging markets investor with the stomach to handle the risks. And last if not least, for the truly adventurous, the *Journal*'s "Final Frontier" includes: Egypt, Jordan, Morocco, Nigeria, Pakistan, Peru, Russia, Turkey, Zimbabwe.

For what it's worth (in some cases, *a lot*), we've done extremely well in Turkey. For my money—or for that matter, yours—I'd not be inclined to lump it in with the far less developed markets in Pakistan, Zimbabwe, Morocco, Nigeria, or Egypt.

On the other hand, every "Final Frontier" market can be a place to make lots of money. Why? Because the level of risk is commensurately higher. Which brings us right to:

> ## Mobius Rule No. 2: Taking risks is what you get paid for.

The Big Five

So let's spread out that map or spin that globe again, or boot up that CD-ROM.

Today, China, India, Indonesia, Brazil, and Russia are all considered viable emerging markets, by anyone's yardstick. Not only are they emerging, but according to a recent report by the World Bank, all five are slated to become "the economic powerhouses of the next quarter-century."

Let's take a quick look at that list again: China, India, Indonesia, Brazil, and Russia.

Just a decade ago, even five years ago, all five could have easily wound up on a list of the world's financial disaster zones. But today, the World Bank forecasts that growth in these rapidly developing countries will surge to an average of 5.4 percent a year through 2006, beating by a wide margin the comparatively tepid performance of the under 3 percent growth rates turned in by the advanced industrial economies. And of course, the crash in Indonesia and other Asian countries in 1997–98, as well as the economic collapse of Russia in mid-1998, proved that real dangers remain.

The lion's share of this growth is projected to come from rising fortunes in the economies of Eastern Europe and the former Soviet Union—today known as the CIS countries, which stands for Commonwealth of Independent States.

Although output declined sharply in the years immediately following the collapse of Communism, these economies are starting to soar again—like Atlas rockets, or perhaps I should say Scud missiles. Despite recent setbacks in Russia, the potential for recovery cannot be dismissed. The coming prominence of the five largest emerging market nations, the World Bank predicts, will very soon "redraw the economic map of the world over the next quarter-century."

Taking the Plunge

So what does that mean for you, the aspiring global investor?

Well, the same thing, actually, that it does for me:

All five future economic powerhouses should be given big

Magic Marker slashes (or if you're inclined to military-style strategizing, pushpins) on your wall-sized Mercator projection.

All of the future Big Five should be places you should be taking a closer look at, to see if you can find companies in them you'd like to invest in.

Apart from the Big Five, the high growth rates enjoyed by nearly all emerging markets today—there are, of course, notable exceptions that prove each rule—suggest the following:

Mobius Rule No. 3: If you want to gain exposure to the world's fastest-growing economies, you've got to take the plunge into emerging markets.

Why? In a word: growth.

Between 1987 and 1997, the economies of three major emerging markets—China, India, and Malaysia—grew by well over 118 percent.

Over the same period, the economies of three major First World countries—the U.S., the U.K., and Japan—grew by a comparatively insipid just under 58 percent.

On an annualized basis, in 1988 the average GDP (gross domestic product) of the world's emerging market countries hovered around 5 percent.

At the same time, the average GDP of the developed countries was a little over 4 percent.

A decade later, the growth gap between the world's emerging and developed markets had widened even further:

Emerging markets average: 6.6 percent.

Mature markets average: 2.9 percent.

The economic problems in late 1987 and through 1988 pushed those averages down in emerging markets, but a wide gap remained.

Investors take note: these stupendous growth rates should not be taken as proof that stock markets in the emerging markets will continue to shoot up indefinitely, in tandem with their high-growth economies.

If anything, the Asian Contagion of 1997–98, much like the Latin American Tequila Effect of three years before, demonstrates that most if not all emerging markets are liable to take more than a few tumbles and stumbles on the road to wealth and prosperity before attaining anything close to the stability of the world's more mature markets. On the other hand, it's that very volatility which, if managed appropriately, can generate well-above-average returns over the long haul.

We've all got to face up to:

> **Mobius Rule No. 4:** High volatility is a characteristic in *all* markets—even the most mature ones.

The reason for this is really quite simple: all markets, being based more in mass psychology than objective reality, have a tendency to overshoot and undershoot economic growth rates. Judging the influence of irrational emotion is, by the way, the way we make most of our money.

> **Mobius Rule No. 5:** If you factor emotion out of the equation, and base your strategy on long-term fundamentals, you can win when markets *fall* and when markets *rise*.

Such overshootings and undershootings tend to cancel each other out over time, by the way. Which means that stock markets do eventually reflect economic growth in the long haul.

But also like all markets, emerging markets tend to be cyclical. That's a nice way of saying: sometimes they go boom, sometimes they go bust.

Risk and Reward

The best way to take the edge off this volatility, I've found, is to faithfully follow the time-honored value-oriented and sometimes contrarian strategy first pioneered by our founding father, Sir John Templeton, often called "the godfather" of emerging markets investing.

At Templeton, we try to:

1) Search the world for the best investment bargains;
2) Focus on the long, not the short term;
3) Use common sense; and
4) When we see unrecognized value, we are willing to be contrarian, "buying when others are despondently selling, and selling when others are greedily buying."

That last eloquent phrase, by the way, is a quote from Sir John himself, who thirty years ago plunged in where most others refused to go, into a shaky, uncertain emerging market called Japan.

By Way of Background

A century ago, Scottish and British investment trusts—the U.K. term for mutual funds—lost their shirts and made king's ransoms by investing in that century's great emerging market: America. British and Scottish pooled funds underwrote the headlong expansion of American railroads—and American civilization—into the then wild, wild West, paying for ranchers to buy cattle and feed to feed them, and for whole towns to be built on once-desolate plains.

The West was won, they say, by the Colt .45 revolver. But it was also won (and sometimes lost) by a little-known, brave band of risk-tolerant investors from the then global center of financial capital: Great Britain.

And Today . . .

At Templeton Asset Management Inc. (a subsidiary of the U.S.-based Franklin/Templeton Group), our Emerging Markets Team currently controls billions under management. This is invested in some forty countries on behalf of over forty funds and private client portfolios, ranging from regional (Eastern Europe, Latin America) to country-based (Russia) to global emerging markets funds.

Investment philosophies aside, every one of our funds and nearly every one of our clients—government entities, corporations, nonprofit foundations—has its own rules and quirks. An employee pension account, for example, might direct us to be fully invested at all times. That means that we can't keep any cash in that fund—only securities. A doctors' fund, on the other hand, might place certain restrictions on its investments: a prohibition against investing in tobacco or alcohol, for example. Personally, I try to leave the complexity and constraints of complying with these rules to our compliance personnel, leaving myself more time to focus on the Big Picture.

The BP

Properly framing the BP involves, first and foremost, guiding a staff of sixty-odd analysts and other professionals based in ten Templeton offices around the world, from Hong Kong and Singapore to Johannesburg, Mumbai (Bombay), Shanghai, Istanbul, Buenos Aires, Warsaw, Rio de Janeiro, and Moscow, through a laborious process of determining which regions, countries, and companies seem promising, not in five months' time, but five years.

Which brings us to:

> **Mobius Rule No. 6: Wait five years, and call me in the morning.**

Before investing anyone's nickel, the first question we ask ourselves is: "Where do we see this company heading in five years?"

If the answer comes back: "straight down the tubes" or "belly-up" we train our sights elsewhere. But if the outlook looks positive, we zoom in (literally) to take a closer look.

What I Bring to the Party

A key part of my contribution to this process is the maintenance of a broader, more global, more historical outlook on current events than many of our young analysts, who—due to being "area specialists" or sometimes to sheer youthful exuberance—occasionally harbor a perfectly natural tendency to hype companies they're hot on, usually in their home regions.

Not that hot is necessarily a bad thing. But after listening to or reading their pitches and prognostications, I've got to sit back, take the long view, and examine their analyses from a cooler, more mature, more dispassionate perspective.

What I do, and encourage our staff to do also, is:

1) Relentlessly focus on the long, not the short term. And

2) Compare companies, regions, and countries around the world without fear or prejudice.

On our long flights, and during late nights up in my hotel room, I frequently find myself weighing companies in Latin America against companies in Africa, Eastern Europe against Asia, countries balancing national economies within regions against one another, and regions against each other, perpetually striving to find the right mix, to strike the right balance that will, we hope, provide top-notch long-term performance.

I spend a fair amount of my time pondering any number of supposed imponderables:

1) The macroeconomic trends that funnel and channel this ever-higher-velocity flow of money that goes whirring around the world these days, at a rate only limited by the prevailing speed of data transmission over high-speed fiber-optic cable.

2) How, why, and when the so-called emerging markets first began to explode, and

3) How long the present global trends—a durable peace, a resulting decrease in international tensions, the prevailing emphasis on butter, not guns—can continue unchecked.

I'm always on the lookout for the next Big Crash, because the great paradox of "value investing" is that we make most of our money *after* as opposed to *before* the fall. Personally, I don't mind the inevitable crashes and downturns, because:

1) I'm always mentally prepared for them, and

2) Even if they affect our short-term performance, I've been through enough of them to know that they don't last forever and that they offer us our best bet at bagging bargains.

Whether it's the Asian Contagion or the Latin American Tequila Effect, it's important to keep in mind that you're going to find the most and the best bargains during hard times.

Which only goes to prove Mobius Rule No. 7: Despite what Dickens said:

> **Mobius Rule No. 7: Bad times can be good times.**

Or, as a colleague of mine recently put it: "For us, bad news is good news."

The Crunch Method

A certain school of thought lately fashionable in some parts of the global financial world holds that since at least 85 percent—the numbers vary—of a particular company's fortunes are linked to macroeconomic fluctuations in national and regional markets, all you need to do to achieve success as a global investor is plug a set of financial data into a sophisticated computer model, and presto!—you buy or sell according to what your software tells you.

Though I couldn't disagree more strongly, the advantages of this method are painfully obvious to someone in my peripatetic position. As opposed to the high-overhead, hands-on, look-see Mobius Method, the Numbers Cruncher certainly saves everyone involved a lot of time and money. Not to mention fuss and bother. You don't need to hop a plane—much less a private one—and soar off into the great unknown. You don't need to schmooze with management. You don't need to tour the plant, kick the tires, see whether the cameras have shutters, or that the cars come with doors. You can forget about popping melatonin for jet lag. Hang out with your wife and kids on weekends. In short, get a life.

My personal reaction to this theory and method is that it's a fine theory, in theory.

But the acid test of any theory comes in practice, and in the real world, as measured by performance year in and year out, my own experience tells me that the greatest problem with data-driven investing lies not with the models themselves (which are often quite sophisticated) but with the quality of the data available to insert into them. It was the early computer geeks who, after all, coined the cute phrase GIGO—a sardonic acronym for "garbage in/garbage out."

My Mobius Trip

Personally, I'd much rather see with my own jaded, crusted eyes what's going on at the plant. I *like* knowing whether the workers look well fed and happy or not, whether management seems to be managing change with panache or seems overwhelmed by the tide of world events.

If I've learned anything while racking up 30 million miles of flight time, and sitting through well over twenty-five hundred days on the road and in the air, it's:

> Mobius Rule No. 8: Lies can be as revealing as pure, honest truth—provided you know what cues to be looking and listening for.

(That's because the way they throw you a line of nonsense to conceal the truth can tell you as much as the truth itself, if you're tuned in to the signals con artists use to fool some people, some of the time.)

Personally, I don't believe that I, or for that matter our shareholders, would be thrilled to find out that we relied strictly on theoretical models or macroeconomic indicators and variables to make our investment decisions. Even if that saved them money in the short term, I don't believe that such an approach provides maximum returns over the long haul.

The reason?

> **Mobius Rule No. 9:** By the time most of the data prepared by multinational institutions and governments becomes available, it's already been factored into the stock price.

One great advantage of getting to know the people who run the show, and are on the hook when things go wrong—as opposed to merely scanning their numbers—is that you might have enough faith in them to buy or hold on to shares when the stock price is down in the dumps.

> **Mobius Rule No. 10:** Buy "good" stocks at "bad" times, and "bad" stocks at "good" times.

> **Mobius Rule No. 11:** Times that people think are bad are often good.

> **Mobius Rule No. 12:** Stocks people think are bad are often good.

The Mobius Method

Please don't get me wrong: the fundamental and technical analyses of stocks remain critical weapons in our intellectual and analytical arsenal. But what I personally bring to the party tends to be much more intuitive. (By fundamental analysis, by the way, I refer to the judgment of "fundamental" factors like profit outlook, price-to-earnings—P/E—or book-value ratios, and the like. By technical analysis I mean the study of charts and other broad market movements to make investment decisions.)

My Mobius Method kicks in the moment I hop off the plane onto the tarmac of a new country, and stroll through the airport concourse, observing—for example—as we pass through customs the level of hassle to which a foreigner is subjected before being allowed to enter.

> **Mobius Rule No. 13: Countries that make it easy for travelers to enter tend to be friendly to foreign investment.**

This purely personal process gathers intensity as we head into town (the state of roads and highways is often a useful yardstick of economic efficiency) and check into the hotel, take a walk around the neighborhood, talk to cab drivers, shop in stores, get stuck in traffic.

Reality Check

While halted at a stop sign in Seoul, South Korea, a few years ago, I watched a young, not particularly prosperous cabbie whispering conspiratorially into a cellular phone. At that moment, I woke up to the promise of digital telecommunications in developing countries—where in many areas it's easier and cheaper to develop a wireless phone network than a costly, cumbersome, obsolete fixed-line one. That's known as "leapfrogging technology" and it's one of the main reasons that former LDCs can achieve growth rates far higher than countries with a more broadly installed technological base.

And it was while standing, several years later, in an electronics store in New York that I first saw a sign indicating that the cellular phone company was subsidizing the price of these phones. *"With activation,"* it read, *"*$49.95. *Without activation:* $249.95.*"*

Which told me that growing competition in cellular phone service was forcing some companies to virtually give away these costly phones. What would be next, the whole store? This moment of revelation prompted me to reevaluate my mobile phone company holdings worldwide. Too many starry-eyed investors appeared to be ignoring the possible negative consequences of fierce telecom competition in the not-too-distant future.

Sixth Sense

My antennae start to quiver even more finely the closer I get to a company on our "watch list." Before I've shaken the manager's hand, I've checked out his office, the view out his window, his furniture, his carpet, his clothes, all for signs of mastery of a situation, or of being mastered by it. The main things that I want to know about management are, in no particular order:

1) How capable are these executives at managing change?

2) Are they committed to protecting their assets, and the status quo, or do they have a handle on what is going to be needed to keep this company out in front?

3) Are they on top of the trend, or beaten down by it—and showing it through all sorts of subtle signals? A frayed jacket sleeve. A facial tick. A subtle frown or a raised eyebrow when obliged to respond to a certain carefully posed (nonleading!) yet awkward question.

4) What is their position on shareholder rights, and protecting shareholder value? In too many countries around the world, these concepts remain alien to the corporate culture. If so, I know enough to keep my distance, even if the company looks promising in other respects.

5) Are they honest? Can we determine the ethics of management? Are they going to cheat us, as has happened in a number of countries, including Brazil, Hungary, Turkey, and India? (The list, sad to say, goes on and on . . .)

I like to scrutinize the people at the helm of every company we invest in.

In a world where statistics and numbers can be shaky indicators of future performance, we've learned through experience:

Mobius Rule No. 14: The quality of management is paramount.

That's why we like to make company visits, so that we can get to know the top people, and analyze their motivations, their goals, their aspirations, and above all, their problems and challenges.

Investment by Analogy

With every country and company we visit, I try to leverage my own personal global experience to help us draw meaningful comparisons between similarly positioned companies operating in the same industries in different parts of the world.

Let's say we pay a call (pun intended) on a telecom company undergoing the process of privatization in Estonia.

We'll look at their numbers and their balance sheet in light of the numbers and balance sheet of a similarly sized, similarly situated telecom company in, let's say, Brazil.

Since these companies are not necessarily evolving along the same time lines, I try to draw these analogies not at identical points in time, but at similar stages in a comprehensive development process. The axis might be privatization, GDP growth, the company's extension into new markets, or development of new products, processes, and services.

If I know, for example, that a diamond exploration firm in South Africa has been trying out an experimental slurry process in opening up a new field, I'll ask a Canadian company looking for diamonds in Siberia whether they've considered that same process too. If not, why not?

From the quality and tone, as well as the content, of management's responses (presuming they're leveling with me, but sometimes even if they're not) I end up learning more about both companies, as well as about their industry, and often their country.

I like to use these sessions with managers to pose general questions about the problems they're dealing with, about their successes and failures, to help me put together a clearer picture of the general trends in their national and regional economies.

Risk Is Real

Investing in emerging markets is not, they say, for the faint of heart.

I'd like to add that it takes nerves of steel more than the brains of an Einstein, or even a Warren Buffett. But I would be irresponsible if I didn't disclose right up front that emerging markets often operate (when they function at all) quite differently from markets in the advanced industrialized countries.

In many emerging markets, financial figures can be hard to come by, and famously unreliable (if not incomprehensible) even if available to investors.

Issues of accountability and shareholder responsibility can be alien concepts.

Liquidity—the ability to easily buy and sell stock—or the lack of it, can be a chronic problem.

Simple settlement of seemingly straightforward trades can sometimes be hazardous to your financial health.

Not long ago, I was sitting in a broker's office in Botswana when I said, in passing, "You know, once we've settled our business, I'd love to take a look at the stock exchange."

My friend smiled broadly and, sweeping his arms wide, said: "Well, that's not very difficult, it's right over there." He pointed to the other side of his spacious office. He was not only the leading broker, he was the president of the stock exchange!

In another, even tinier African country—I won't mention names for fear of offending the locals—the stock exchange was run out of a coffee shop. (Remember that Lloyd's of London started in a coffee shop.)

Over the years, I've become all too familiar with the significant risks that investors face in emerging markets. In no particular order of magnitude, they are:

1) Political risk: The possibility that revolutions or political turmoil in a country—possibly even leading to nationalization or expropriation of assets—could wipe out the value of an investment.

2) Currency risk: The impact on an investment of fluctuations in a national currency.

3) Corporate risk: Decline in shareholder value based on poor or even dishonest management.

4) Broker risk: Unscrupulous or dishonest brokers who fleece investors in order to improve their own balance sheets.

5) Settlement risk: Problems experienced in trying to settle transactions, and in obtaining, registering, and paying for securities.

6) Custodial risk: Exposure to local safekeeping agents (popularly known as custodians) who may not provide adequate security for clients' shares.

7) Operational risk: Arising from inadequate auditing and bookkeeping standards.

8) Market risk: Exposure to extreme fluctuations in market values.

So I've disclosed all the risks I can think of.

Still interested?

Really?

So why, you might well ask after reviewing that list, should anyone bother with these messy, risky, strange situations?

Because if you want to hit the financial home runs of the future, you'll need to pay attention to what goes on outside the U.S. and Western Europe. Despite their acknowledged volatility, even the most prudent investor in search of diversification and asset allocation should, I believe, be willing to risk a minimum of one quarter of their total portfolio in global and emerging markets, whether that investment be made in individual stocks or in an ever growing list of global and international mutual funds.

To back up this view, a recent study by MSCI (Morgan Stanley Capital International) completed in early 1998 compared the returns of their EAFE Index (which reflects the performance of markets in Western and Eastern Europe, Australasia, and the Far East) with the Standard & Poor's 500 over sixteen ten-year periods. Starting with the ten years ending in 1981 and concluding with the ten years ending in 1996, the EAFE either matched or beat the S&P 500 during fourteen of those sixteen decade-long periods.

ADRs

While mutual funds provide a dazzling (and dizzying) array of investment philosophies and opportunities, more and more foreign companies (some still quite obscure) are selling shares on U.S. exchanges in a format known as an ADR (American Depository Deceipt).

Buying an American Depository Receipt is the easiest way to play individual stocks for U.S. investors, because the purchase involves no special brokers, and no special transaction costs. ADRs are listed on the U.S. domestic exchanges (mainly the New York Stock Exchange) just like any other domestically listed stock. You can open up your daily newspaper and find the price of Telebras (the Brazilian phone company) for example, just as easily as you can track the price of shares in GM. You can also call your local broker and buy an ADR as easily as you can any domestic stock. Most of the foreign companies that have gone to the trouble of creating ADR programs are the blue chips of their respective regions.

Companies that have been listed on American exchanges must conform to certain minimum accounting standards and requirements not necessarily met by all foreign companies.

Still other global and international companies are tapping into international markets by issuing GDRs (global depository receipts), freely available on all major international exchanges, particularly in London.

There are different types of DRs (both A—for "American"—and G, or "Global"):

1) Unsponsored—issued by depositories without a formal agreement with the companies.

2) Sponsored Level 1—traded over the counter (OTC) and on foreign exchanges.

3) Sponsored Levels 2 and 3—traded on U.S. exchanges but required to comply with various SEC (U.S. Securities and Exchange Commission) registration and reporting requirements. Sponsored Levels 2 and 3 DRs are the most widely available, and considered the most secure global investments because companies offering DRs on U.S. exchanges are required to issue profit and loss statements (P&Ls) and balance sheets audited according to U.S. GAAP, which stands for "generally accepted accounting principles"—widely considered the most transparent and stringent accounting standards in the world. An amended version called International Accounting Standards (IAS) is fast becoming a universal accounting standard.

4) 144A DRs—private placement. Available to U.S. institutional investors only, avoiding various SEC registration and reporting requirements.

5) Reg S—private placement. Available to non-U.S. investors in compliance with U.S. SEC Regulation S (very rare, of minimal interest to the small investor).

A U.S. investor can buy a GDR listed in London and/or any other exchange as long as it is registered with the SEC or is part of the 144A or Regulation S program. But transaction costs, due to currency exchange requirements, tend to make GDRs a less appealing investment to U.S. investors than ADRs, which as I've said, trade like U.S. shares.

Volume Discount

While I freely concede that ADRs and GDRs can make wonderful investments, it's important to note that some ADRs tend to trade at a premium to their equivalent shares listed on the company's domestic exchanges. This higher price tends to reflect the higher costs associated with the need to meet comparatively stringent U.S. SEC reporting and registration requirements, as well as the costs incurred in balancing the books according to GAAP. In addition, there is sometimes a so-called foreign share premium levied on sales of shares to nonresidents, but that would apply to domestic shares sold to foreigners as well as to DRs.

As a fund manager, I should probably further disclose right up front my strong personal bias in support of the view that mutual funds can achieve *volumes of scale* and *ease of access* far outweighing our management costs, and permitting broader and more sophisticated diversification and hedging strategies than individual investors attempting to pick stocks on their own.

And by buying large blocks of stock, we can exert greater leverage on managements, who occasionally feel compelled to play an age-old game I call "fleecing the foreigner."

Getting De-Fleeced

As a small investor, once you get caught in this sort of squeeze play, your only choice (basically) is to get out. By contrast, we—and by "we" I refer to all mutual fund managers—may decide, on the other hand, to hang in there and fight City Hall—whether that be in a domestic or international court, at a company shareholder meeting, or by organizing our fellow minority investors into alliances to persuade (translation: force) management to accede to our demands.

Trading Risk

In 1993, we bought a sizable chunk of shares of a promising-looking Indian company. Three years later, once the stock had risen to what we considered a peak price, we decided to sell it. No problem, right? Wrong. Much to our chagrin, we couldn't sell it because the shares had never been properly registered. In a strict legal sense, the shares weren't ours, even though we had paid in full for them.

So what did we do? We spent hundreds of hours—not to mention thousands of dollars in legal fees—before we found out what had gone wrong.

In India, the company controlled the registration of all the shares sold. And in this case, the company repeatedly missed deadlines to register our shares. When our lawyers contacted them, they blamed a disorganized postal system. But our suspicion was that they were trying to manipulate the market price by withholding the registration of shares, which would have the effect of contracting the number of shares in the market, thereby artificially driving up the price. If they wanted the price to go down, all they had to do was register the shares and let them be sold in the open market.

In Russia, companies also often control the registration of ownership of securities. Companies can refuse to register shareholders they don't like, or think may be biased against management. Ownership, in certain cases, can be disqualified at the stroke of a pen (sometimes a poison pen), which means that an entire investment can effectively be confiscated by management.

Water Water Everywhere yet Not a Drop to Drink

> Mobius Rule No. 15: Buy wet (liquid) stocks in wet (liquid) countries, not dry (illiquid) stocks in dry (illiquid) countries.

Before deciding to invest in any region, country, or company, you have to first take into account the ephemeral yet critical issue of liquidity. Which quite simply means an investor's ability to buy and sell a stock.

A related issue is activity, which is an investor's term for turnover.

If liquidity, activity, and turnover are too low in a particular country, or in a particular stock, we don't buy. Or we make token or minimal purchases, just to test the waters, and to see how the system operates. The problem with low liquidity and low activity is not only that they make it more difficult to buy and sell stock, but that an illiquid market makes the spreads between the bid and asking price too wide.

That's bad even for the small investor. But with a big fund, where hundreds of gaping price spreads can seriously affect performance, killer price spreads are to be avoided like the plague.

Our pricing department must consider a midpoint to arrive at its "fair market" price. So if the spread is wide enough to drive a truck through, the moment I've acquired a stock, I've lost money, on paper and in theory. I hate it when that happens.

And Now for the Good News

On the upside, investing in a low liquidity–low activity market can generate phenomenal returns because the purchase of just a few stocks by a few investors can drive the price of those shares through the roof.

Of course, following the same pattern, a major sell-off in an illiquid market can cause prices to drop catastrophically.

One emerging markets broker recently acknowledged in *The Wall Street Journal* that he occasionally gets "panic-stricken fund managers ringing me up asking why ABC is down 10 percent, when all that has happened is that Mr. Smith has come into the market and sold a few shares to pay his gas bill."

Investing in an illiquid market can be the proof of an adage I'm not, for obvious reasons, particularly keen on: an emerging market is a market that you can't *emerge* from when it *submerges*.

In Bob We Trust

Picking the right broker is always a key issue, but in an emerging market, it can be critical. You need a broker who knows the local lay of the land, who knows the prevailing conditions like the palm of his hand, so he can steer you around the worst obstacles.

Often, the major international brokers can seem like the safest bet, but they may not know much about local conditions.

On the other hand, some small unscrupulous local firms will simply up and take off with your cash.

Even more common than outright theft is the reprehensible practice known as "front running," when your "trusty" broker takes an order for shares and then "gets out in front" of you by scooping up the same shares for himself, in the expectation that your order will drive up the price. An alternative strategy is that he buys, then sells to you. Of course, this sneaky-Pete move lets him sell his shares at a profit at a later date—or even a later hour.

"You'd be amazed," a London broker was recently quoted in *The Wall Street Journal*, "at how often I'm told that Templeton or Fidelity is buying. The brokers use codes. If they tell you 'The Bald Eagle has landed,' you know it's Mark Mobius."

Operational Risk

Let's face it: in many emerging markets, accounting and book-keeping standards and methods tend to leave a few things to be desired. Every country's culture, legal system, and society strongly influence how they handle accounts.

Koreans, for example, tend to be very strict on themselves, and have an extremely detailed accounting system which reflects that strictness. The itemizations can drive you crazy because they don't group items the way we do.

In South America, the accounting systems tend to be extremely sophisticated, because companies have to account for inflation by constantly updating asset values.

In general, anywhere outside the U.S., Canada, and Great Britain, quarterly statements tend to be an endangered species.

In Russia, the accounting system evolved according to socialist as opposed to capitalist imperatives, which meant that meeting production quotas meant more, to take just one example, than proper depreciation of assets. A confiscatory taxation system gives companies a strong incentive to understate earnings, which is why (based on personal and anecdotal experience) I believe that the Russian economy is growing at a far faster rate than official figures indicate. Stock market evaluations reflect the true economy (including a buoyant black market and barter economies), which is why you can have a skyrocketing stock market in an officially stagnating economy.

Our analysts go to great lengths to sort out these variances, so that we can concentrate on real earnings and real cash flow. But analyzing emerging market P&L (profit and loss) statements can be a guessing game—and sometimes even a shell game. That's why we consider it so important to visit the company and size up the situation visually, physically, and viscerally. If you can't do that, and if you don't have easy access to a Gulfstream, it's important to take P&Ls with a shaker of salt, and concentrate on fundamentals like market share.

Let's Look on the Bright Side

The upbeat scenario is that over time emerging market accounting will have to improve.

Why?

Because more transparent accounting practices are the key to gaining more foreign investment.

As more and more offshore money pours into emerging markets, companies have learned the hard way that it pays to have their books audited according to IAS.

Many major institutional investors—and I certainly don't blame them—wouldn't put a plugged nickel, much less a real dime, into a company that isn't audited according to IAS.

So even in Russia, where I've heard CFOs growl and howl about being forced to spend "half a million dollars" to have their accounts audited according to international standards, they're finally getting the message that that half a million dollars invested in a reliable P&L can pay vast dividends in the form of foreign investment inflow.

Market Risk

If you find that occasional 10 percent monthly swing in the Dow unsettles your stomach, try Turkey: 50 percent fluctuations in a month are not uncommon.

But don't fly off to Hong Kong for a safer ride: the stock market there is historically three to four times as volatile as the U.S.

How to avoid being sideswiped by these risks?

> **Mobius Rule No. 1 (once again, with rhythm): Your best protection is diversification.**

Along with:

> **Mobius Rule No. 16: Patience is more than its own (just) reward.**

Five-Year Plan

If anyone tells me "I want to make a killing in under two years in emerging markets," I tell them to take their money elsewhere. The wild, almost manic-depressive swings in emerging markets make market timing difficult, and if your timing is terrible, costly. The only way to consistently stay ahead of the game is to adopt a long-term view, when appropriate with a strong contrarian spin.

When we look at the balance sheet of a company, we might be willing to pay a high P/E (price-to-earnings) ratio if we think that the company will achieve the high growth needed to obtain what might become a low multiple in five years' time.

More than any other single lesson I've learned, it's:

> ### Mobius Rule No. 17: Long-term planning pays.

The reason for this is astoundingly simple: all markets are fundamentally cyclical. Like people—because they're composed of the aggregate decisions people make—they're given to extended bouts of irrational fear and panic and equally irrational exuberance.

In all fairness to emerging markets, if their extreme volatility makes them seem a little bit manic-depressive, I think of them as immature markets.

Like adolescents, they tend to get a little bit carried away at times. But, and I can't repeat this enough: it is by riding these wild mood swings like a surfer taking a wave that you can make money, hand over fist. An entirely rational market, after all, is a market that would barely budge at all.

> ### Mobius Rule No. 18: The time of maximum pessimism is the best time to buy.

> ### Mobius Rule No. 19: The time of maximum optimism is the best time to sell.

Seems counterintuitive, right? Well it is, and therefore it requires a positively stoic ability to let your mind rule over your passions. Which brings us unerringly to:

> ### Mobius Rule No. 20: If you can see the light at the end of the tunnel, it's too late to buy (or sell).

The Importance of Being Contrary

"If you buy the same securities as other people, you'll get the same results as other people."—Sir John Templeton

How on earth, you might ask, when all the "smart money" was running scared out of Thailand at the height of Asian Contagion, could it have possibly made sense to buy there?

For the right answer to a very good question, let's take another look at a pet phrase from Sir John Templeton, that great investor: "To buy when others are despondently selling and to sell when others are greedily buying requires the greatest fortitude but pays the greatest rewards."

Now, the emphasis here is on the value placed on an asset by sentiment, as opposed to pure, dispassionate reason.

Despondency and greed are emotions. They aren't about thinking, but feeling. Now, you may feel in your gut that a stock is going to go up, but you're better off testing that hunch against the hard-core reality of a corporate balance sheet.

Of course, in the short term, the "smart money" tends to be right: when the Thai baht drops by 50 percent in two months, you've got a full-fledged disaster on your hands. But if you sell then, your decision will be based on sentiment and emotion, not on a rational assessment of long-term fundamentals.

Of the decisions made by the herd, a certain percentage will be based on reason, and a far greater proportion will be based on emotion.

So turn the picture upside down:

> **Mobius Rule No. 21: You earn dividends by discounting a market's "emotional quotient" (E.Q.).**

Fear and Greed

A few years ago, my brother's wife bought into one of our global emerging markets funds. Her market timing was a trifle iffy, in that she bought in at the height of the 1993 emerging markets boom, because everyone else did.

That boom, unfortunately, was quickly followed by the great 1994 emerging markets bust, brought on by the great Mexican peso crisis, which led to the Tequila Effect, which made Latin American markets take a tumble.

Now, when my sister-in-law took a look at her monthly financial statements, she got an idea into her head that because the value of the assets she had purchased had declined, she had lost money.

Well, of course she had, except that she hadn't lost anything, unless for some reason she was compelled to sell at that point. In fact, this was the time of greatest opportunity for her, as well as for me, because for every dollar she invested in our fund during the bust, she was getting more assets for her money.

But for a while there, since she hadn't yet cottoned on to that fact, you could have cut the atmosphere in her and my brother's house with a knife on the night I stopped by for dinner.

My sister-in-law, being the fine woman she is, didn't hide what she thought under a bushel basket. "It went *down,*" she moaned, the first time I saw her after the big drop, in hushed tones, as if the neighbors might hear and think the less of us for our disgrace.

I begged her to have faith, and to take advantage (if she still had the stomach for it) of the marvelous discounts at which she could now buy more shares in my falling fund.

She looked at me as if I'd lost my marbles. How could any sane person, she asked, buy into a falling—she might even have said failing—fund?

Because, I explained, "If you buy low now, that gives you an opportunity to sell high later."

Obvious, in its own way, but it's astonishing how many investors do precisely the opposite. Suffice it to say, my sister-in-law bought low and sold high.

Templeton's Law

The same basic rule can be stated in an even simpler way:

> **Mobius Rule No. 22: Buy stocks whose prices are going *down*, not *up*.**

Sounds nuts, right?

Wrong. My sister-in-law certainly thought so, but if you can't take the heat, as they say, stay out of the kitchen.

The Asian Spin Cycle

A case in point: in 1991, we launched an Indonesian fund for sale to Japanese investors. Our launch of the fund just happened to coincide with the then peak of the Indonesian market, just prior to a major market meltdown. Of course, none of us knew that at the time. All I knew was that I smelled a bubble aching to burst because stock prices were sailing skyward like helium balloons. At the time, because I was in Japan, I asked a Japanese fund manager his strategy for picking stocks.

"I select stocks," he solemnly said, "that are going up."

This is, of course, a brilliant strategy in a bull market.

But in a bear market, it's a prescription for ending up with your backside in a sling. In any event, when we started examining the hard numbers—the P/E ratios—of the leading Indonesian stocks, the prices being asked relative to the company histories made the whole country look very expensive, particularly in relation to other, rival markets in the region. We were in a real pickle, because here were our Japanese investors, who had entrusted us with millions of dollars to make a killing in Indonesia, and I was having trouble finding a bargain in the bunch.

What we did was sit tight.

"Hurry up!" our investors kept calling and faxing and e-mailing me. "Get invested 100 percent! If you're not 100 percent invested you're not earning your fee!"

I took the heat, and didn't budge one inch from my squatting position. Shortly thereafter, the bottom fell out of the market, and it didn't take two minutes for those same investors to start calling me up, suddenly singing a different tune: "Stop buying stock! Start selling stock! Stay heavy in cash!"

I didn't breathe a word, not even my four favorites: "I told you so."

Nobody ever thanked us, by the way, for saving their skins. But even more to the point, our shareholders began putting pressure on us to *stop* buying just when it made sense to *start* buying. They were frantic about us losing their money, but I had to keep telling them, doing my best to keep my exasperation in check:

"These short-term losses are only *paper losses*. The only way to *make* money is by buying now."

Their problem, of course, was a lack of a proper long-term perspective.

Mobius Rule No. 23: If a market is down 20 percent or more from a recent peak and value can be seen, start loading up.

Ground Zero

The Holy Grail of global investors is known as "Ground Zero."

This can also be thought of as: "A market that doesn't exist yet."

This may sound existential, but in reality—provided there is one—a Ground Zero market is a market that nobody knows about yet, and that is guaranteed—at any moment now—to take off into the ozone layer, stratosphere, orbit, the outer limits, or what have you.

Now here is a classic case of the "getting in on the ground floor of something big" mentality, preferably when nobody else is looking and the coast is clear. This only happens once or twice in a blue moon, of course, but that's precisely what makes it a global investor's wet dream.

Not surprisingly, given the prevalence of emerging markets funds (and, I should add, of emerging markets gurus), it's getting harder and harder to achieve the blissful innocence of Ground Zero.

Though the cult of Ground Zero could be seen as the logical extension of the contrarian's golden rule—*Buy When Everyone Else Ain't*—it's also perfectly possible to take this inescapable logic to such extremes that it's no longer healthy for anyone's pocketbook.

"You can't beat getting in at Ground Zero," crowed one well-regarded fund manager I know, "because the only way to go is up!"

But that's just not true. The horrible fact is that Ground Zero, as its nuclear name implies, can be a very dangerous place. Some people—and I will not name names—seem to think that emerging markets only emerge upward. As we veterans know, they can also submerge—if only temporarily.

Growth

Over more than a decade of emerging markets investing, I've found that being a genial yet cynical optimist is the best posture to earn long-term dividends in emerging markets.

Why?

Despite all the stops and false starts, booms and busts, bubbles and crashes, over the long haul, the same logic seems to apply:

> ## Mobius Rule No. 24:
> ### Time heals most ills.

Particularly with regard to emerging markets. And those gradually rising values represent, I believe, reality—as opposed to rank speculation.

My fundamental optimism is based on two long-term trends:

1) The often painful and wrenching conversion to a market economy being undergone by nearly all emerging markets by this point in history.

2) The recent global achievement of something approaching genuine world peace.

The only way we're ever going to see a true lasting peace in this world is by promoting investment flows between countries so that people—even regional antagonists—over time become mutually obligated to each other.

The best hope for a lasting peace in the Middle East is to see the Arab countries and Israel make money instead of war together. If the song of the 1960s was "Make Love, Not War," the siren song at the turn of the next century has to be: "Make Money, Not War." A quantum leap in human productivity, of course, is the true meaning of the term "peace dividend."

The other great vital forces I see at work all around me as I travel the world, spurring the growth of emerging markets, are: the prevalence of more and better food and more and better health care.

This means that people are healthier and live longer. Once widespread fears of a planet-strangling Malthusian population explosion have mainly receded—except in a few regions, such as sub-Saharan Africa—as demographic experts have come to agree that population growth rates tend to abate as economic growth rates increase.

If people live better and have more confidence that their children will live to adulthood, they tend to have fewer children. As women gain more control over their lives, they tend to naturally moderate the number of children they're willing to bear. Longer life spans also mean more opportunities for education. Which means that literacy rates rise. Which ultimately leads (particularly in an information-driven society) inevitably to productivity growth, which is the real key to lasting global growth.

Mass Communications

Universal trends in mass communications mean that it's getting harder for people to live outside the global economy. Families sitting in China watching *Dallas* or *Santa Barbara* on China's 96 million TV sets are going to wonder why they're not living the way Americans do, and they're going to put pressure on their leaders to give them what they don't have.

They see a kitchen on TV that's the size of their whole house, and start wondering how to get one too. They want the same things, and they want them now.

Leapfrogging Technology

Emerging market countries, for all their many problems, are in luck in one critical sense: they don't have to reinvent the wheel, or the telephone, or the photocopying machine, or the laser printer to realize the rewards these marvels of modern technology can bring. In practical terms, this means that formerly poor countries can move straight from the bush-telegraph to the digital age without having to pass through the costly, fixed-wire analog phase.

Some countries are already communicating by satellite and digital PCS (Personal Communication Systems) technology before a fixed-copper twisted-pair cable needs ever be laid through virgin bush. Other countries—we'll see a few in the next chapter—are setting up stock exchanges that don't need trading floors because all trading is electronic and brokers can enter buy and sell orders on their office computers. The productivity enhancements gained by computers and other technological innovations can be obtained in the blink of an eye.

Such technology transfers (once the cause of such anxiety on the part of the West during the late and not lamented Cold War) are of far greater help to the Third World than the massive handouts for prestige infrastructure projects favored by the foreign aid freaks of the 1960s and 1970s.

Foreign Aid That's Not a Band-Aid

Ironically, getting emerging markets managers hooked on steady inflows of private investment—as opposed to hooked on foreign

aid—was the best thing that ever happened to both managements *and* investors. Why?

Because international investors tend to penalize managements
who don't take shareholder rights seriously, or who don't deliver
shareholder value.

One of the most overwhelmingly positive trends affecting the
climate of global investing today is the widespread growth of
what investors call an "equity culture." Which simply means
that as more and more companies begin to rely on investment
from shareholders—as opposed to infusions of capital from
banks, or from governments—the more responsibility they have
to take for protecting those shareholders' interests. All over the
world, for example, companies that started out as small family
firms have grown into global colossi. And as more and more
non–First World companies begin to operate internationally,
global competition has forced them to be as efficient as the dynamic firms of the First World.

Foreign investors keep managements honest, in more ways
than one. By insisting that an American-style ethos of openness,
transparency, and disclosure becomes the standard of doing
business, foreign investors actually protect not only their own
but other investors' funds.

The Market Economy

The other great changes I see affecting the world business climate as I travel have come about as a result of what you might
call the three "shuns"—or "-tions":

1) globalization

2) deregulation

3) privatization (integration and conversion to a market economy).

All of these trends are, in fact, the results of a world economy
which, mainly as a result of the greater ease and speed of global
travel and communications, has left enterprise managers with
little choice but to imitate the free-market model and compete
on a broader, less local scale.

Although many weaker firms have fallen by the wayside, all over the world firms that have learned to compete on the global playing field are emerging stronger than ever before from the crucible of competition. The impact of technology, particularly information and communications technology, must not be underestimated. As banks, for example, around the world invest more in computers, the results have increasingly been showing up on the bottom line. And one of the few advantages that the former Third World enjoys over its First World competitors is that emerging-markets-based firms can invest in the latest technologies—and management methods—without having to continue to amortize the old outmoded systems.

Lower Tariffs, More Competition

From the rise of regional trading blocks such as the European Union, NAFTA (North American Free Trade Agreement), and MERCOSUR (the Southern Cone Common Market) in South America to the establishment of the World Trade Organization (WTO), tariff barriers to free trade have been falling right and left, ushering in an era of a global free market. The dismantling of many of these trade barriers followed the Latin American debt crisis of the 1980s, which is an excellent example of how financial crises can so often be blessings in disguise because they bring about much-needed change. With companies all over the world having to compete in their home countries as well as abroad, they've become better competitors by increasing their productive efficiency. These newfound efficiencies and strategies have coincided with the rapid spread of an equity shareholder culture around the world to bring more value to investors and stakeholders.

Take a Walk on the Cynical Side

Still, despite all such rosy scenarios, it's critical to keep in mind that there are and will continue to be many potholes and bumps

on the road ahead. You must be a cynic as well as an optimist—
I often characterize myself as a "cynical optimist"—because
brokers, pundits, survey researchers, managers, and even other
investors are always dying to throw you a line, which if you're
gullible enough, you're likely to swallow hook, line, and sinker.

People, particularly small and novice investors, love nothing
better than falling in love with a good stock story, particularly
one with a happy ending. A woman I know bought stock in a
globally active sewing machine company because she heard on
the radio that the CEO was of Chinese descent and that as China
expanded, the market for sewing machines would be enormous.

As yet, that investment hasn't panned out, because though it's
a fine theory (in theory) it overlooks the fact that once a country gets richer and there are more women working, fewer and
fewer of them will find the time or feel the need to sew their own
clothes.

Reason Regionally as Well as Rationally

Let's take another look at that map, or globe, or computer
screen with the map display on it. If you could overlay a transparent sheet with a graph of market lows and highs over time,
you would see that with few exceptions, regional boundaries still
very much define emerging markets.

In an age when jet travel and electronic commerce would seem
to dominate an increasingly global economy, it's surprising how
strong regional boundaries are. Regional economies in the less-
industrialized, underwired parts of the world are obviously more
closely knit together by geography and overland trading links
than the more high-tech corners of the globe.

For better or for worse, when the Mexico peso crisis hit the
sombrero in 1994, the entire Latin American region suffered
from what global investors quickly dubbed the Tequila Effect. In
the same vein, when international currency traders began to
seize on weaknesses in the ASEAN (Association of South East
Asian Nations) countries—Indonesia, Malaysia, and Thailand

primarily—the ripple effect that coursed through the region was called Currency Contagion and the Asian Financial Flu.

In both regions, certain countries (Hong Kong in Asia, Chile in Latin America) stood to some degree above the fray. But every global investor contemplating where to put whatever funds are at their disposal should first ponder the pluses and minuses of Asia vs. Africa, and Latin America vs. Eastern Europe. This is the best way to hedge your bets, because you can be pretty sure that if Asia is down, Latin America or Eastern Europe will be doing just fine.

Of course, as briefly occurred during the last bout of currency contagion, all emerging markets were roiled by the fear of competitive currency devaluations, and low-cost exports flooding the globe. So what do you do then?

Sit tight. Don't worry, be happy. As long as the fundamentals are on the money, they'll bounce back again, usually stronger than ever before.

Regional Benchmarks

At Templeton, once we arrive at a scenario for a region that we feel comfortable with, we set a benchmark (composed of an average of corporate price-to-earnings ratios) against which to judge a country's or company's performance within the region. In effect, we set a rate of return we'd like to see from that country or company over the next five years.

For some examples, as of 1998, the average P/E of U.S. blue chip stocks (Source: Morgan Stanley Capital International [MSCI]) was 22.

The German average P/E: 25

France: 24

Canada: 23

Now, for a stark contrast, let's take a look at:

The Brazil, India, and Poland average P/E: 15

Mexico: 17

Turkey: 11

Of course, one key caveat is that good companies and affluent countries rate high P/Es for a good reason: the world's major markets contain a high proportion of the world's best-performing companies.

But a low regional or national P/E can also make a very attractive bet for an investor willing to wager that a country's transition to a market economy will help a company's transition to competing in the global economy, which in turn will mean greater efficiencies and higher productivity, with correspondingly higher earnings.

Interest Rates

Once we've got a regional scenario under control, I take a close look at local interest rates. If the rate of interest on a savings account is 10 percent, I want the stock market to be selling at an average of 10 times earnings (P/E) to compete with keeping your money in a savings account. If bank interest rates are 5 percent, I consider a P/E of 20 tolerable, if less than ideal. And if bank interest rates are running at 3 percent, I consider a P/E of around 30 a minimum requirement for investing.

Once we've plugged all these scenarios into place, we might plunge into the dicier business of culling through our list of intriguing stocks from each country, sorted by sector. When we've got our watch list of stocks compiled, we decide which ones we'd like to take a closer look at. Then we get on the plane and go.

A Privatization Primer

It sounds like the driest of bureaucratic abstractions. Just say it— "privatization"—and those Latinate syllables literally drag on your tongue. But privatization is much more than an abstraction. It's a revolutionary trend sweeping the world for a number of very good reasons, not the least of which is that it is the only way for long-dormant value to be pried out of moribund state industries, which have been black holes for capital, instead of generators of it. This has proven true not only in former Communist and socialist countries, and not only in emerging markets, but in the First World as well. Great Britain and more recently France have made fortunes by privatizing their national phone companies, while achieving better service into the bargain.

Privatization is the engine driving the lion's share of the world's emerging markets today. For example, during the first half of 1997, Latin American stock funds produced some of the world's highest annualized returns. The reason?

Stock markets in Brazil, Argentina, Mexico, Venezuela, Colombia, Chile, and Peru were all fired up by a wave of privatizations.

Meanwhile, in Brazil, the big news was the wholesale shifting from the public to the private sector of several key companies, including Telebras (the national phone company), Electrobras (the national electrical utility), and Petrobras (the state petroleum company)—although for the time being, the government was keeping crown jewel Petrobras pretty much to itself.

Five years ago, the state-owned Telebras was charging 70 cents for a monthly telephone line. In 1998, they were pulling in $10 a month for the same service, if not better.

Taming Brazil's 2,500 percent annual inflation rate took some of the element of the surreal out of everyday life in the world's eighth largest economy. In just two years, according to the *New York Times,* direct foreign investment in the country, once a basket case, soared from $1 billion to $16.5 billion, due mainly to the privatization of vast, ossified, state-owned companies in the mining, electrical power, and telecommunications sectors.

Getting in on the Ground Floor

> ### Mobius Rule No. 25: Privatization primes the pump.

Getting in early on newly privatized companies is the best way to benefit from the resulting unlocking of value.

Of course, gauging these situations can often be tricky, because some countries (and some central governments) rig the process to benefit insiders, while others simply bungle it in less venal ways that can result in horrendous rip-offs of shareholder value.

To the institutional investor, visiting companies in the early stages of privatization—generally before the shares become listed on international exchanges—is the next best thing to knowing the future. A comparable step for a small investor is buying an ADR early on in the privatization process, the moment they become available through a reliable broker.

That these state-owned companies were ever permitted to become so bloated before, in some cases, withering away was mainly a result of misguided policies widely adopted after the Communist revolution in the Soviet Union, and in the post–World War II period elsewhere, even in the First World.

Everywhere, progressive thinkers turned to nationalization of basic industries as a politically palatable panacea for redressing social inequality. The theory being, of course, that the profits generated by these industries wouldn't be siphoned off by the few, but freely distributed to the many. We now know that precisely the opposite occurred: the enterprises simply became inefficient and padded, and failed to modernize themselves (particularly in terms of implementing technological innovation) according to the strong motive force of free competition.

The results, half a century later, have clearly been catastrophic.

Of course, it's easy to speak from 20/20 hindsight, but from our perspective today, it's surprising the depths of ignorance and naïveté that made so many otherwise intelligent people believe that a centralized bureaucracy might be a socially superior vehicle for managing the production and distribution of goods and services than a private firm that must compete with rivals to deliver the same services or make the same products.

Twenty-five years ago, I wrote a book advising Western companies and managers about how best to establish trade links with Communist China. In my own consulting and industrial research business, operating out of Hong Kong, I'd developed contacts that afforded me some limited experience in dealing with the Communist Chinese.

My Chinese experience (though I was only permitted to peer through a crack in the door) constituted my first exposure to the sheer absurdity and epic waste engendered by the wholesale adoption of statist policies.

Today, the Chinese Communist Party, in a startling turn-around, has been forced to give way to the global tidal wave of privatization. In the fall of 1997, China announced at its Fifteenth Party Congress in Beijing that some 10,000 out of 13,000 languishing medium and large state enterprises (out of a total 118,000 national-, provincial-, and municipal-owned enterprises) would ultimately be converted to private ownership.

Though in a splendid exercise of old-style Marxist verbal legerdemain, the Congress cloaked their ideological retreat in what the *New York Times* called "semantic gymnastics" by styling their version of "privatization" a form of "public ownership." Yes, in the same way that AT&T and IBM are "publicly owned" because their shares are owned by members of the public! (Some Sri Lankan officials once tried to perform semantic gymnastics by calling privatization "peoplization"!)

Of course, it's no secret that the blanket term "privatization" has provided a golden cover for corrupt managers and politicians to enrich themselves in nearly every country where such policies have been adopted. Or, in many cases, rammed through reluctant and resistant legislatures and sluggish central bureaucracies. In Russia, the privatization program—key to economic reform—has suffered frequent setbacks caused by scandals involving backdoor deals between corrupt managers and greedy government officials, the lines between whom have long been blurred, and are becoming positively invisible as the old system gives way to a new hybrid.

The fiery debates touched off by privatization in every country (even in the U.S., where Republican plans to privatize large chunks of public land have drawn intense fire from liberal Democrats who consider them handouts to the private sector) all boil down to a single point:

Who gets the biggest piece of the action?

Who stands to profit?

The government?

Outside or foreign investors?

The managers of the failing industries themselves?
The people?
The workers?
The investment bankers?
In Russia, controversial "loans for shares" programs meant that deep-pocketed banks would lend the government cash in exchange for shares in companies undergoing privatization. Privatization became a way of acquiring valuable assets for little more than a greased palm in the right place.

All that said, privatization remains the only method available to governments saddled with unprofitable state industries to obtain the level of investment necessary to turn these crippled colossi around. Though the fairy tale of the sleeping frog being kissed by the princess and turning into a prince might be a somewhat romantic analogy, privatization can be miraculous in its ability to pry long-lost treasures out of rusty industrial boxes, to which the state had long ago misplaced the key. The key being incentive, of course. More than money, incentive is the royal road to riches.

Profitable investing in emerging markets demands a close study of the privatization process, because the difference between a good and a bad investment can be simply a matter of timing—buying at the right moment in the privatization curve. From George Soros—who plunked down $1 billion as half of a nearly $2 billion bid by a consortium in Russia for a quarter share of the massive Svyazinvest telecommunications holding company—to the small investor who buys a few ADRs in Telebras, getting in early on the privatization curve is the key to riding the wave of the future.

MOBIUS RULES

1: Your best protection is diversification.
2: Taking risks is what you get paid for.
3: If you want to gain exposure to the world's fastest-growing economies, you've got to take the plunge into emerging markets.

4: High volatility is a characteristic of all markets—even the more mature ones.

5: If you factor emotion out of the equation, and base your strategy on long-term fundamentals, you can win when markets *fall* and when markets *rise*.

6: Wait five years, and call me in the morning.

7: Bad times can be good times.

8: Lies can be as revealing as pure, honest truth—provided you know what cues to be looking and listening for.

9: By the time most of the data prepared by multinational institutions and governments becomes available, it's already been factored into the stock price.

10: Buy "good" stocks at "bad" times, and "bad" stocks at "good" times.

11: Times that people think are bad are often good.

12: Stocks that people think are bad are often good.

13: Countries that make it easy for travelers to enter tend to be friendly to foreign investment.

14: The quality of management is paramount.

15: Buy wet (liquid) stocks in wet (liquid) countries, not dry (illiquid) stocks in dry (illiquid) countries.

16: Patience is more than its own (just) reward.

17: Long-term planning pays.

18: The time of maximum pessimism is the best time to buy.

19: The time of maximum optimism is the best time to sell.

20: If you can see the light at the end of the tunnel, it's too late to buy (or sell).

21: You earn dividends by discounting a market's "emotional quotient" (E.Q.).

22: Buy stocks whose prices are going *down,* not *up.*

23: If a market is down 20 percent or more from a recent peak and value can be seen, start loading up.

24: Time heals most ills.

25: Privatization primes the pump.

Chapter Two

◆

BALTIC BOOM

Mobius Map

While still in a holding pattern over Estonia, I spent the last few minutes before landing drawing a mental map of the market I was about to enter—like a general sitting up late at night in his tent, studying the strategic terrain of the territory he hopes to conquer by noon the next day. Our digital air show showed Estonia occupying a small (42,000 square kilometers) hump of flat land lying directly south of Finland across a narrow arm of the Baltic Sea known as the Gulf of Finland.

Directly on its eastern border lies Russia.

Directly to the south you find Latvia, and below that Lithuania.

Along Lithuania's southern border, the thin sliver of the Kaliningrad region juts out like an arm into the Baltic Sea. Until World War II it was part of Prussia, and now the Russians refuse to give it up because it's one of their only warm water ports left, and a base for their now-withering navy.

Preliminary Assessment

Geography, they say, is destiny.

Nothing proves this point more clearly than the remarkable

resurgence by mid-1997 of this tiny nation (roughly the size of Vermont and New Hampshire combined) of 1.5 million people as a model of a well-managed conversion from a state-run to a market economy.

At a time when many of its East European neighbors were internally divided and ambivalent about how to proceed, when to proceed, and even whether to proceed with the push to reform, plucky Estonia bravely plunged ahead of the pack.

After seven years of independence and market competition, Estonia has witnessed a massive economic restructuring that keeps its growth engine running full speed ahead.

"While the rest of Europe dithers over market reforms," the staunchly pro-capitalist *Forbes* magazine has written approvingly, "Estonia proves that there is no substitute for youth—and a free market." To this sexy mélange of youth and freedom (and hope and growth) I would add a few key geographic and cultural factors:

1) The country's proximity to Finland, a bastion of technological innovation and economic deregulation, and

2) Its long history as a trading and mercantile center with direct links to: Russia, Poland, Germany, and the Scandinavian countries.

If this were a multiple-choice test, and I asked you: "Which of the above countries has contributed most to Estonia's present prosperity?" I think you know what the answer would be.

That's right: "All of the above."

To geography, I'd add: smarts.

Decisive policymaking by the young reformist government voted into power in August 1991 (in the wake of the failed coup against Soviet Premier Mikhail Gorbachev) played a critical role in this little country's stunningly successful conversion to the free market. Mart Laar, the courageous young man who had gained fame as a student leader of protests against Soviet rule, was elected prime minister at thirty-two.

Within ninety days of his administration's ascent to power, a new constitution was established dissolving the old Soviet central bank, and chucking the soft Russian ruble in favor of the hard kroon (pronounced "crown"), which the Young Turks of

Tallinn resolved to peg to the steel-tough German mark, regardless of the consequences.

The positive effects of these rapid reform measures were instantaneous.

Within a year of Estonia's peaceful transition to independence, or what the Czechs called the "Velvet Revolution," more than half of the country's forty-two commercial banks had collapsed. Which sounds like a catastrophe—and for a short time it was—but Estonia only emerged stronger from the depths of this fiscal crisis because most of those banks were just deadwood anyway.

With the detritus of a half-century of stolid Soviet rule now deposited on what Trotsky termed "the dustbin of history," the way was now paved for new, stronger, innovative institutions to move in and fill the vacuum. Hansabank, founded in 1991, in just five years boldly leapfrogged over the competition, by dint of strong technological and managerial talent, to become the biggest bank in the Baltics.

One of the first decrees issued to the newly liberated Estonians was the levying of a simple flat tax—26 percent on both corporations and individuals. Combined with the conversion to a freely convertible currency, with no currency controls to intimidate foreign investors, Estonia promptly announced to the world's global market-makers: "We're hospitable to foreign capital."

Note: global capital likes nothing less than having its freedom restricted. The new capitalist mantra: "Don't tread on my money." Which leads us inextricably to:

Mobius Rule No. 26: Low-tax economies tend to be good places to place your investment dollars.

Now, five years later, Estonia was well on the road not just to recovery, but to out-and-out prosperity. You might even call it a speedway. Because Estonia and its little neighbors facing the

Baltic Sea were in the summer of 1997 in the midst of a full-fledged, flyaway boom.

Boom Towns

I've started our around-the-world tour in tiny Estonia, because:

1) It's a classic "gateway" country—a conduit to other, larger countries.

2) It recently converted from a planned to a market economy.

3) It's a classic boom country, at least until the next bust.

You could say that all booms are alike, in the sense that it's awfully hard to make money during them, especially at their peak, unless you get in early enough to beat the boom.

Gateway Countries

On my mental map, gateway countries are nearly always worthwhile investment targets. They tend to be culturally flexible, open to innovation, and readily adaptable to change.

A few gateway countries: Hong Kong, Switzerland, the Netherlands, Singapore, Mauritius.

All are small, and comfortably rich off the fat skimmed from the trade among and between their larger, stronger neighbors.

Something to look for in a gateway country is its origin as a trading port and/or mercantile center. This puts them at a distinct cultural advantage to more insular, and less cosmopolitan, regions of the world that developed as agricultural or industrial zones.

Because trading cultures have a way of being cross-fertilized by every country and continent to which they maintain commercial contact, this makes them breeding grounds for new ideas, new ways of doing business, new models, new trends.

Gateway countries derive much of their wealth from low-cost trade, financial transactions, and high-value-added industries.

Economists call them "entrepôt" countries, which is French for "between the posts."

"Between the posts" countries tend to be small and feisty, because they have to be. Lacking in natural resources—except, typically, harbors—they learn to rely on grit and smarts instead of guts and brawn.

They learn to survive by their wits. They learn to stay neutral and nimble and above the fray. They'd rather sell you the shirt off their back than fight you in a dark alley. They'd rather make loans to finance a neighbor's army or navy than go on a rampage themselves.

On the Ground

My first impression of Estonia was that it was small. The airport was small, but efficient. The capital was neat and compact like many other small cities, from Zurich to Boston. The stock market was small. Most of the companies we visited were small—at least as measured by market cap—which is the total value placed on the company by the stock market. But like many such small places, it seemed to thrive from this "economy of scale." Orthodox economists tend to see beauty in largeness.

But the unorthodox economist E. F. Schumacher decided differently: "Small Is Beautiful." Not to mention productive. (Of course, large can be beautiful too.)

Radio, Radio

From the customs officials to our taxi driver to the businessmen and -women we met with, nearly everyone spoke English. This may sound trivial, until you consider that English has become the lingua franca of global business and finance. A Mexican banker once told me that the Americans had everything: a business language (English) and a language of romance (Spanish).

Countries where the English language is widely spoken possess a distinct competitive advantage over countries where it is still largely an alien tongue.

Cultural Characteristics

In the taxi on the way in from the airport, I was struck by the German-sounding language I was hearing on the radio station our driver tuned in to as we sped along thickly wooded, well-paved roads into the central city. I was interested in this because I'm half German by birth (my father was German, my mother Puerto Rican) and am a German citizen by choice. A German passport, by the way, makes my world travels easier and safer.

But my investor's ear was tuned to the German tradition of hard work and productivity that has made Teutonic countries admired and feared over the centuries—in particular, in this century. In a short article on Estonia, one American business magazine had praised the "Young Turks of Tallinn" as "scions of stoic Lutheran culture," who could be counted upon to steer through the tough spots of free-market competition and come out ahead.

All three Baltic capital cities were originally founded as trading ports by German merchants who later linked them into the German-dominated Hanseatic League, a prosperous confederation of merchant city-states whose roots lay deeper than the more recently imposed Russian veneer. Still, vestiges of Russian domination were everywhere, from the Russian radio stations to the large numbers of Russian immigrants, who still make up 20 percent of the Estonian population. Their presence, I gathered, is not entirely welcome. One day, over lunch, I asked a young Estonian banker about this hot button issue, and he got a little hot under his starched striped Gucci collar.

"The Russians are welcome to apply for citizenship," he replied, "but most of them haven't bothered because they want to remain Russian!"

All over Estonia, we encountered considerable anti-Russian feeling. But when we spoke candidly with businesspeople about their hopes and concerns, we learned that financial dependence on Russian markets and contacts was still extensive. For many if not most of the companies we visited, Russia remains their dominant customer and trading partner. So the romantic idea that the Balts will be able anytime soon to entirely free themselves from the Russian yoke struck me as a little far-fetched.

As a prospective investor, I could scarcely regard this as a total loss.

As David Hale, chief economist with the Zurich Group in Chicago, quite rightly points out: "All the Estonians need to do now is take what has been for one thousand years a geopolitical liability [proximity to Russia] and turn it into an asset. They could be the world's beachhead to Russia."

Beachhead to Russia

I liked the sound of that. As one of the first fund managers to heavily invest in Russia, we needed all the beachheads we could get to Russia, because gaining exposure to Russia's markets without gaining exposure to its problems—of which, more later—seemed like a good bet.

Hotel As Metaphor

The Olümpia Hotel, a modern concrete-box high-rise adjacent to Tallinn's lovingly restored medieval Old Town, looked great from a distance.

But as is often the case with Soviet-style buildings, the closer you get to it, the uglier it becomes. Fortunately for us, it had been extensively renovated since its dowdy days, when it served as Tallinn's main Stalinist-style Soviet Intourist hotel. Even this minor detail was significant in assessing this rapidly emerging market, as this one building's rapid conversion to a world-class business facility had been accomplished with a high degree of taste and panache.

It wasn't too much of a stretch, I decided, to regard this little corner of Tallinn as a metaphor for, and microcosm of, the relatively smooth, swift conversion of the larger Estonian economy to market-driven success. As if to drive this point home, the state-owned Olümpia was in the process of privatization itself.

On the day we checked in, an auction of a preliminary share issue was held in the spanking-new first-floor conference room, itself a sleek symbol of capitalism triumphant. It might have been something we could be interested in, but we needed a more detailed look at the financial statements.

Signs of the Times

After checking in, I was taken aback to discover that my well-furnished, modern room lacked air-conditioning. When I asked if any of the rooms were air-conditioned, the bellman paused delicately before replying: "Yes, but they're very expensive."

"How much?" I demanded, as much from curiosity as frugality.

"Twice the price of a single room."

"What's the price of a single room?"

"Fifty-five dollars."

"In that case, I'll take the room with the air-conditioning."

Our elite, all-suite, air-cooled thirteenth floor was dubbed the "Jewelry Floor."

Each suite was named after a precious stone. As the head of our party, I rated the Diamond Suite (although the Ruby and Emerald suites taken by my colleagues were no different). Since I was deeply involved in ordering furniture—by the ton, with prices to match—for our new offices in Hong Kong, I took a few minutes out to examine the superbly designed blond wood Scandinavian-style furniture, made right there in Estonia. It looked Finnish. It felt Finnish. Even more to the point, it underlined Estonia's cultural and commercial ties to Finland, which lies just a few hours' ferry ride (and even shorter flight) across the Gulf of Finland from tiny Tallinn.

The Healthy Heart

After making a mental note to find out how much it would cost to ship a container load of this sleek stuff to Hong Kong by slow

boat to China, I hopped the lift up to the new fitness center on
the top floor. Though it might not sound as important as technical analysis, maintaining one's physical health can be one of the
most important factors to surviving the high-stress investment
world.

> **Mobius Rule No. 27: Success as a global investor is
> closely linked to optimism.**

Sometimes, especially with jet lag, I can get depressed after
checking into a hotel after a long multi-time-zone flight. I've
found that regular workouts, typically a combination of aero-
bics and weight training, help spark a chemical reaction that re-
stores my natural and fundamental long-term optimism. And
keep me mentally alert for my meetings the next day.

Surveying the Territory

From my lofty perch on a stationary bicycle located some 200
feet above ground, I could easily make out through the gathering fog clusters of castles and ramparted, crenellated walls,
punctuated by bulbous brick towers, all encircling a steep hill,
crowned by a stout fortress. I later learned that this hill is
known as Tompea, an Estonian corruption of the German word
"Domberg," which means "Cathedral Hill." The castle is the
seat of the Estonian parliament.

Further off to my right, just past Tompea Hill, I could make
out the squat superstructure of a large oceangoing container
ship, the legacy of a typical top-down decision made by Moscow
to turn Tallinn into the largest grain-trading port in their vast
empire. After the war, other large-scale light and heavy industries, from fish processing to meat-packing, had moved in. We'd
seen the shattered hulks of these factories on the shabby outskirts of town on our way in from the center. Now, five decades

later, the city was reverting to its original role as a trading, financial, and mercantile center.

The ships and the factories would stay, of course. But the future of this town, and the nation surrounding it, was clearly demarcated by the glistening bulk of the newly built Hansabank headquarters, which dominated a fast-growing "little Wall Street" section of the city.

Before drifting off to sleep that night, I picked up a copy of *City Paper*, a surprisingly well-written English-language publication serving the three Baltic Republics, which I found placed on top of my bedside table, right alongside the hotel's night-light.

> **Mobius Rule No. 28: Reading local papers and watching local newscasts can provide valuable insights unavailable anywhere else into the mentality of local markets.**

"As is common among emerging markets elsewhere," an article entitled "Market Mania" started out, "much of the trading in the Baltics still lies in the realm of raw speculation.

"In deciding whether to buy given stocks [one local analyst] observes that most investors and even many analysts and brokers are often acting more on *raw emotion* than anything else. As a result, the real talent is not necessarily the ability to identify good companies, but the ability to anticipate which stock the masses of overly emotional investors will rush to next—making sure that you get there and buy it first."

You read it here first.

The Phone Company

First thing Monday morning, we met with the deputy CEO of the Estonian Telephone Company Ltd., the newly privatized national phone company, in a conference room conveniently located on the first floor of the Hotel Olümpia.

Note: In the early states of privatization, the great state-owned dinosaurs, typically utilities and telecom companies, tend to be first on the block. They may not seem sexy. But in emerging markets, getting in early on these big babies is the quickest way to surefire profits.

Deputy CEO Heinar Leismann, who looked to be in his mid-fifties, radiated a distinguished appearance in a well-worn tweed jacket. He looked more like a history professor than a hard-bitten executive. He took a casual stance in front of an easel out-fitted with a giant pad of white paper, pages of which he carefully flipped as, with Magic Marker in hand, he scrawled illustrations to back up his main talking points.

Mobius Rule No. 29: Clothes may not make the man, but they can provide clues to the personality.

As with most other people I have met in the former Iron Curtain countries, I found myself wondering: where were *you* before the curtain rose?

For some reason, I placed Leismann at Tallinn University, conducting seminars on telecom policy.

His presentation began with the following rather dry observation: "We didn't start thinking seriously about the future of telecommunications in Estonia until the late 1980s, when Estonia was not yet free. Our telephone system was overseen by the Estonian Ministry of Posts and Communications, of which I was vice minister."

Okay, he'd been a bureaucrat.

Just before liberation—August 1991—the state-owned Estonian Telephone Company had still been functioning under strict directives from Moscow. But as the Soviet system began to crumble, the newly liberated Mr. Leismann and his colleagues at the Ministry of Posts and Communications had begun scouting the brave new world of greater telephony, on the lookout for a likely strategic partner.

Strategic Partners

Under the classic privatization model adopted all over the former Communist Eastern Europe (including Russia), state-owned companies seeking to go private are told by their governments—which still own them—to go hunting for a strong strategic partner.

These are typically First World companies in the same industry as the company undergoing privatization.

The rationale is to provide the resulting joint venture with the technical and managerial benefits provided by the strategic partner, so that these more often than not antiquated, clunky juggernauts can be turned into lean, mean high-tech machines.

Strategic Investors

The oft-heard phrase "strategic investor" was no sweeter music to my ears than the dread term "underwriters"—those are the investment bankers who manage the issuing of new shares on behalf of new companies, and they like to set higher prices than I like to pay.

In general terms, my experience with strategic investors has not been terribly positive.

Why?

Because while a portfolio investor like us is looking to make *money*, a strategic investor is looking to gain *control*.

E.T. Call Home

In most national privatization programs, the national telecom company is among the first firms to be taken private. That's because the revenue to be raised by selling off the telecom operation can be quite hefty, while the investment required to upgrade the system to international standards is typically so great that only a well-heeled, deep-pocketed strategic partner is going to be up to the task of jump-starting these creaky jalopies and kicking them into high gear.

In Estonia's case, the MPC (Ministry of Posts and Communications) hoped for a partner willing to help them upgrade their entire domestic phone system, not just the urban network. This was a potential fly in the ointment, because though it was clearly more profitable to serve the more densely populated urban areas, for political reasons, the company could hardly ignore the sizable slice of citizenry who lived out in the countryside, many of whom had been on waiting lists for decades hoping one day to be granted the privilege of having their own phone.

Now let's look a little more closely at this decision, because it's critical to any foreign investor, large or small.

Q: Why is the company often placed under a legal obligation to find a strategic partner?

A: Because, just as the management of any private company looking to sell it would want to buff it up to fetch the highest price, the government's goals tend to be:

1) To maximize the proceeds from privatization.

2) To curry political favor by improving services.

What usually happens is that the new company gets saddled with the political imperatives of the old company. So the government tells the strategic investor:

Let's make a deal. We're going to give you an opportunity to make one heck of a lot of money. But in exchange for this opportunity (which we're going to guarantee for a period of time by extending the monopoly enjoyed by the present company's state-owned predecessor) we've put down a few nonnegotiable demands:

1) You're not going to be able to provide service only to the people who can pay a lot.

2) You're going to have to serve everyone, even if that involves taking a few losses.

If all goes well, a well-handled privatization can be a win-win situation for everyone involved, from managers to customers to underwriters (investment bankers) to you and me—foreign investors in general.

The reason that privatizations (provided you get in on them early enough) tend to make good investments is that a combination of higher investment—from the people who buy the shares *and* from the strategic partner, if there is one—with improved management almost invariably leads to higher productivity. I said *almost* invariably—not always.

Whenever you buy a stock in a company, you're placing a bet on that company's long-term prospects. The price of that stock is really just the average of a range of potential buyers' and sellers' opinions of what the shares are going to be worth in the future.

Let's take, for example, an obscure telephone company in Estonia. Like nearly every other public sector telecom company in the LDCs (Less Developed Countries), its penetration rate was woefully low. Its waiting list for telephones was endless; its prices too high for the average citizen; poor phone services, in fact, were one of those mundane realities that engendered so much resentment that their lack hastened the socialist system's collapse.

In the First World industrialized countries, we tend to take universal phone service—or 100 percent market penetration— practically for granted. But one of the widest chasms dividing the emerging from the developed worlds is easy access to electronic telecommunications, analog and digital.

Privatization offers cash-strapped developing nations:

1) A way to get cash out of their antiquated phone networks, which would take millions to bring up to speed. And

2) A way to close the telecom gap as quickly and efficiently as possible, at next to no cost to the taxpayer.

Mobius Rule No. 30: *Low* telecom penetration rates represent *high* potential growth.

(Investors *like* telecom companies that start out near the bottom, because that only enhances their upside potential.)

Okay now, back to Leismann.

"Our first problem in seeking a foreign partner," Leismann continued, "was that our currency at the time was still the Russian ruble. As late as 1991, the first question we all had to ask ourselves was: what will the people in Moscow say? Estonia, you see, wasn't yet free."

Sizing Up Management

One of the most critical factors in judging any company, telecom, utility, industrial, or what-have-you, is the quality of management.

So one of the first things we look for, not surprisingly, is any sign of shady dealings or ethical misconduct. We had no concerns in this regard with present company, but if we find or learn of even a hint or wisp of impropriety, we stop there. Usually, local brokers—assuming they're on the up-and-up themselves—know all the rumors, and consider themselves ethically if not legally bound to disclose what they know about any company they recommend.

> **Mobius Rule No. 31: Always inquire about the probity and honesty of management before anything else.**

(We've learned that one the hard way.)

The Vision Thing

Number two on my personal check list is the "vision thing": the skills and imagination of management. The best way to check out the management is, as I have said, to meet with them personally. But if you can't do that, the next best thing is their annual report, or if they have one, the company's World Wide Web site.

A snag: only the largest emerging markets companies, particularly those with ADR programs, publish their reports in English as well as their native tongue. But as I travel the globe, and I see

English increasingly taking over as the international language of business, we're also seeing more and more reports written in two languages: that of the country the company is based in, and English.

You can also sometimes write to the investor relations person at the company if you have any questions, on the basis of reading the annual report. In the case of companies undergoing privatization, and of countries making the transition to a market economy, the critical question for us (and for all potential long-term investors) becomes: how capable is management of handling the seismic shift from statist to free-market policies?

If in the bad old days management's major concern was serving the needs of an entrenched political elite, today the management is trying to cope with customer and market demand. And today's savvy customers are demanding services that not long ago they were used to begging and pleading for—usually to no avail.

From a Bureaucracy into a Company

From the moment that Leismann and his team began putting out feelers to attract overseas suitors, they received no end of attractive offers. All sorts of large foreign phone companies were positively drooling to help the Estonians open international gateways and split the profits from the resulting high volume of international traffic.

Why? Because it didn't take a rocket scientist to see that with such an appallingly low penetration rate, all you had to do was supply a reasonable percentage of the thousands of Estonians languishing on waiting lists for years with a phone of their own, at a reasonable rate, and you would be in the money for a long time to come.

Also, Estonia was one of those former socialist countries that was taking to capitalism as if it had never gone out of style.

In the Czech Republic, I once spoke to a telephone company executive who told me that before the collapse of Communism, the waiting list had been so long for telephones that people inherited their place in line, and that people would actually leave their children and heirs their place in line in their wills! In many emerging markets, phone lines are so scarce that the phone companies auction them off to the highest bidder.

By the end of 1992, the Estonians had signed an agreement with a newly formed company, Baltic Telecoms A.B. Now this was in itself a 50-50 joint venture between Telecom Finland (Finland's national telephone company) and the Swedish telecom company Telia.

Frankly, I could imagine no better strategic fit for Estonia's newly privatized entity than the Finns and the Swedes. Finland lies squarely on the cutting edge of telecommunications technology today, while the Swedes are also notoriously efficient telecom providers.

An Excellent Connection

One of Estonian Telephone's regional advantages: Finnish backing.

Finland happens to be one of the most technically advanced places on earth.

As an April 1997 article in *Business Week* asserted: "While the rest of the world tinkers and putters, Finland has infused cutting-edge technology into every corner of its economy."

Did you know, for example, that Finland, with only 5 million people, has the highest penetration of wireless phones in the world?

The numbers are staggering: 33 percent vs. 17 percent in the U.S.

Not to mention the highest rate of Internet usage. Its phone network is 100 percent digital.

So it doesn't take an Einstein (or a Warren Buffett) to see that all you have to do is marry Finnish and Swedish telecom technology with millions of ill-served and long-suffering Estonian customers, and you have a magic trick on your hands.

The lion's share of the credit for this astoundingly high penetration rate goes, by the way, to a recent wave of deregulation throughout the Finnish economy. Until not too long ago, Finland was like a lot of its neighboring Scandinavian countries: one of the most tightly regulated places on earth. For decades, tight regulatory environments were the "progressive" path to social success.

But all over the world, from London to Bombay (Mumbai), deregulation of telecom and utility services is very much the name of the game.

> ## Mobius Rule No. 32: Keep on the lookout for industries that once were heavily regulated and are now being deregulated.

1) Telecom
2) Power, energy, gas, and light (public utilities)
3) Financial services

For decades they were laggards and slugs, now they're cutting-edge companies.

In fact, Finland is one of the world leaders in a new technology that may very soon make both phone and natural gas companies very sexy: a marriage of phone and utility lines.

One of Finland's large power companies is wiring each household to monitor electricity costs in real time. This innovation has profound implications for a potential convergence of the power-energy and the telecom sectors. Elsewhere, utilities are experimenting with transmitting digital signals—data and voice transmission—over their utility lines. Any company with a direct line into people's homes is going to be worth a second look.

> ## Mobius Rule No. 33: Don't be put to sleep by utilities. Be woken up by them!

The Estonian government, in accordance with what has by now become a standard privatization procedure, kept a controlling interest in the new venture—51 percent.

The reason? In a word: politics.

All over the world, privatization remains remarkably controversial. Despite the fact that it nearly always works like a charm, stridently nationalist and demagogic politicians like nothing better than to fulminate against the "handing over" of strategic assets to those demons of our time, "furriners," at what are usually described as "fire sale prices."

Notwithstanding that we "darned furriners" are usually being asked to fork over the lion's share of the cash to upgrade these aging monsters. In the case of the Eesti phone company, the Finnish and Swedish strategic partners were putting up all of the cash, in exchange for . . . a 49 percent piece of the action.

The Estonians were putting up their antiquated fixed-line analog network, which was going to have to be extensively upgraded anyway.

On the face of it, Estonian Telephone didn't sound like much of a bargain for the Finns or the Swedes, or for that matter, other passive or portfolio investors (like us) once the shares that the government still held came to market. The Swedes and the Finns were putting up millions of dollars, while the Estonians were putting up a whole lot of rusty old metal.

So what gives?

What the Estonians were really bringing to the party was themselves: 1.5 million customers, who the Finns and Swedes knew perfectly well were going to be so thrilled to be offered telephone services at all—particularly state-of-the-art ones—that they would not only be jumping for joy for at least the next ten years, but would be willing to pay Estonian Telephone handsomely for the privilege.

Strictly for accounting purposes, Coopers & Lybrand had valued that asset—the funky, antiquated phone network, most of which was soon to be obsolete anyway, because it wasn't digital—at 800 million Estonian kroons (U.S. $60 million).

I made a note to have my staff translate that into dollars, because since the dollar has become the world's reserve currency, we have to teach ourselves to constantly think in dollar terms. For the moment, and for my purposes, the precise dollar figure didn't matter as much as the methods employed by C&L to arrive at it.

Curious as to just how C&L came up with that figure, I interrupted Leismann to ask: "How did they arrive at that number?"

I liked Leismann. But his answer was disconcertingly vague.

"They spent some three months here studying it," he hesitantly replied, "looking at land and equipment."

Which was not, as you might expect, quite the level of precision I had been looking for.

NAV

After years of investing in emerging market companies, I've learned to discount P&L (profit and loss) statements and balance sheets, in favor of more ephemeral issues like earnings and market share. But by far the most important single consideration in judging whether a company is over- or undervalued in the marketplace is its NAV (net asset value).

When you're buying stock in a company, what are you really buying?

All sorts of intangibles, to be sure, like goodwill and management skill, and a brand name, and all that. But at the end of the day, what you're really buying is more nuts and bolts: hard assets. Assets, of course, don't always have to be *things*. They can be receivables—money owed—or even debt owed to creditors. They can even be goodwill. But whatever those assets are, it's important to know what they are, because the easiest way to determine the legitimate value of a share of stock is to take the value of all those assets and divide them by the number of shares outstanding.

> Mobius Rule No. 34: If the net asset value (NAV) divided by the number of shares gives you a dollar figure *higher* than the share price, then you *could* consider it an undervalued stock.

(By the same token, if the number you come up with is lower than the stock price, then the stock is probably no bargain.)

In attempting to determine the NAV of a company, we first look to the accountants hired by the company to give us a figure to work with. We can then use that, for what it's worth, to make extrapolations of the value of these assets in comparison with, in this case, other newly privatized phone companies around the world.

To evaluate earnings, we use yardsticks like "income per line" or "income per subscriber" as one of a number of means of judging the overall efficiency of the system.

Let's take, for example, one of our most successful investments of all time: Telebras, Brazil's gigantic, monolithic telecom company (stock that jumped over 200 percent in 1997 alone as it neared full privatization—read: breakup). We know that ordinary analog lines that once rented for under a dollar per month are now going for ten dollars a month, which is bringing in more than enough revenue to build yet more lines, which makes for a powerful engine of growth.

As the number of lines exponentially expands along with the rates, profits keep pace right along with them.

Playing Privatization Monopoly

So the newly formed Estonian Telephone Company was formally launched as of January 1, 1993, as a monopoly with a ticking clock. Such governmental granting of limited monopoly powers is quite common in privatization scenarios, because the government needs to give the new company an incentive to make the heavy investments in service upgrading that are needed to bring the system up to speed.

A monopoly with a limited duration is also quite common under privatization, because it is a central tenet of liberal government policies to gradually open up the market to competition, in the hope of eventually giving the customer the choice among several operators, thereby improving service and price. In other words, granting a monopoly in perpetuity would be like granting the company a license to print money forever. But when to let the monopoly run out becomes a delicate balancing act (and for investors, a complex guessing game) between a number of carrots and sticks.

A government will tell the company, for example: if you meet these service targets, we'll let the monopoly continue until a new deadline.

In the case of the Estonian Telephone Company, the government granted the company a full monopoly on domestic and long-distance service for eight years, until the year 2000, by which time the free market was supposed to kick in.

Personally, when scanning the numbers, I considered that window of opportunity a tad too narrow in which to turn an ocean liner around. This somewhat subjective judgment, of course, had a negative effect on my decision to buy the stock. My problem with the limited monopoly was not just philosophical but practical: it seemed like too short a payback period.

A warning bell inaudibly rang in the room, accompanied by the popping up of a (minor) red flag.

While Leismann was alluding to a target of installing 25,000 new digital phone lines per year, I was now thinking that once the company had its strategic partners in place—the Swedes and the Finns, backed up by their own government—and they had all their ducks in a row, they would probably be in pretty good shape to face the future. Under that best-case scenario, the company would be good enough—well enough managed, top-notch technology, and so on—to compete fairly in the open market with the majors. Because once you opened up the market to full and free competition, that meant that any one of the big players—Telecom Italia, for example, or even AT&T—might just decide to sweep into tiny Estonia and take on Estonian Telephone, in a fight to the Finnish.

The question was: could they get their act together in time? If not, once competition hit, they might well be history.

But here's where the scenario-izing got a little more complex, because even if the majors did decide to play hardball on Estonian Telephone's home turf, the way they might decide to approach it would be to buy Estonian Telephone—or a very big piece of it—rather than go head-to-head with it. If that scenario were to be played out, the stock would become a strong buy, because it would be a takeover target, and takeover targets tend to suddenly surge in price.

In the meantime, the Estonian economy was heating up so fast that Leismann and crew were feeling hard-pressed to keep up with the pace. Leismann openly expressed mounting frustration at the position taken by some of his largest customers (particularly banks) who were demanding, as he confided with a wry, self-deprecating smile, "levels of telecom services not yet in operation in Germany."

"Like what?" I asked, intrigued. "Digital ATM lines?"

"Ah, well," Leismann responded, with another cagey smile, as if reluctant to divulge family secrets, "all I can say is some kinds of tricky services!"

Once again, this level of precision was not quite what I would have hoped for.

On the other hand, one of the hazards of meeting with top management is that they can often have a very good grasp of the broad brushstrokes, and a somewhat hazier handle on the details.

But demands for "tricky services" were, unfortunately for him, the least of Leismann's worries.

"Like it or not"—and I had a feeling he didn't like it one bit—Leismann candidly conceded, "by the year 2000 we will have competition here."

So then the monopoly bloom would be off the rose. The gloomy tone with which he pronounced the word "competition" was one indication that this particular management—which I assumed was dominated by holdovers from the old Ministry of Posts and Telegraphs—was hardly looking forward to the advent of competition with comfort and joy.

So what, I asked him plainly, were his contingency plans for the future?

"That is an open question," the man in charge replied with a shrug. "If we don't prepare quickly, the future presents problems. It's easy to say this and that in presenting business plans. We know, and you know, that you can explain and tell and write what you like, but it's only when competition looms one knows for sure what will truly happen."

Politics, Schmolitics

Unfortunately, Mr. Leismann's best-laid plan to sell off a portion of the government's remaining share in the company to private investors had gotten stalled somewhere up there in the castle high on Tompea Hill, in the Estonian parliament. "Privatization of telecommunications," Leismann said with another of his re-signed, philosophical shrugs, "is very controversial in Estonia."

It seems that after they made a resounding success of their joint venture with the Finns and the Swedes, the politicians were now en-gaging in a little Monday morning quarterbacking, and turning up the heat on management for its now seven-year-old decision to sell off 49 percent of the domestic phone system to "foreign interests."

Whenever people want to attack privatization, they always talk about governments and countries "selling their birthrights for a mess of pottage," employing the biblical analogy. But that really isn't fair. Because it's more like selling a half share of your decaying old jalopy to your best friend so you can both invest in a new engine, and maybe even a new pair of taillights.

Of course, it's easy for politicians with 20-20 hindsight to carp and grumble about how cheap these initial asset sales were.

But here's the real point for you and me: if those assets weren't dirt cheap, why on earth would we ever buy them? If they were priced on the same asset-value basis at AT&T or MCI, or British Telecom, why wouldn't we just go off and buy MCI, AT&T, or British Telecom?

Unfortunately, one problem with privatizations is that the politi-cians still play a role in them, usually by drafting the legislation under which the process is initiated and then implemented.

"Most of our parliament members have heard that 'monop-oly' is a bad word," Leismann observed mildly. "And, with all due respect, that is all that they know."

Future Shock

"Maybe I will not say nothing more right now," Leismann abruptly concluded, cutting off what was beginning to feel like an awkward discussion.

"Future ideas I can explain as well. Most important from the company's point of view is the future—the fate we will suffer under competition. Only one thing is clear," he concluded with a philosophical shrug: "That nothing is clear yet."

Company Assessment

Here was a company undergoing privatization which had not yet listed its shares publicly. That was a positive, because the earlier you can get in to size up these companies before they go to market, the better off you'll be.

Another upside was that telephone companies around the world are hot stocks right now, because of a technical trend we've seen spreading worldwide: the vaunted, oft-celebrated Information Superhighway.

But on the downside, this very heat tends to diminish these telecom stocks in my eyes, because they're too hot to be cheap. And as I'm constantly reminding my analysts: "It's not enough for a stock to be good, it's got to be good *and* cheap."

Sometimes I throw in, for emphasis: "Dirt cheap!"

Sometimes, I'll even tighten up the criteria further: "It's got to be a *good* stock that's *cheap* because most people think it's a *lousy* stock. Find me good stocks that *look lousy*," I tell my analysts. "And then we'll see if they're worth it."

Note: one problem with privatizations having done so well recently is that it's getting harder and harder to find cheap ones.

The Estonian government, for example, once it moved these shares to market (particularly in light of the political pressures described above), might well feel compelled to price their assets at the high end, so as to deflect any criticism that they'd gone soft on foreigners.

Now the problem with that is that if you don't go a little soft on the foreigners, we'll find a government that will. It may not sound nice to say it, but that's just the way it is.

I mean, we can stick our money in a second flat just about any darn place in the world, so why would we stick it in Estonia, of all places, unless we think we're going to make a killing on it?

A further problem with privatizations is that, as they become more the norm around the world, governments have gotten wise to the fact that they can jump through the roof right off the bat. That puts them under pressure to:

1) Maximize the profits from privatization.

Which sometimes conflicts with another goal:

2) Draw outside investor interest.

Now in most privatizations, the company and the government bureau handling the sale will turn to its strategic partner and also to its underwriter—the investment banks which actually bid for the right to handle the sale, and garner the fat fees—for advice on proper pricing.

This creates an assortment of problems and questions for the potential foreign investor, one of which is that an underwriter (that's an international investment bank that helps bring the new share issue to market by setting a fair market price for the shares) gets the gig by promising the government and the company that they can get the highest possible price for the shares when they float them into the market.

Which is all very well for the company, and the government, if that high price can be sustained over time. But what sometimes happens if the underwriter sets too high a price for the shares is that potential investors stay away in droves, and so the new share issue falls flat on its face.

Now even if the new share issue does great straight out of the gate, in a flurry of hype and great expectations, the share price may drop within a couple of weeks, or months, once the initial wave of broker-driven and hype-driven enthusiasm has waned.

So now the question becomes: what's the real fair-market price for these assets?

Going Mobile

Our next meeting was with the head of the Estonian Mobile Telephone Company, which just happened to be part owned by Estonian Telephone Company. This made a good deal of sense, because the government saw no reason to deprive the big fixed-line analog company of some of the benefits (low costs and high profits, to name just a few) of wireless digital transmission.

The difference in personality types was striking.

While Mr. Leismann radiated a world-weary, rather beaten-down, almost depressed air, Mr. Tonu Tee, the general director of the Estonian Mobile Telephone Company, could not have seemed more trendy and upbeat if he'd tried.

Tonu Tee was a slender young guy in a well-tailored dark suit with slicked-back hair. He looked like a guy going places.

His mobile phone company was still teeny-tiny, but its growth rates were nothing to sneeze at. In 1991, they had had 155 subscribers. By 1997, they had 80,000, with 100,000 projected for the end of the upcoming year.

They were incredibly productive, with low overhead and labor costs. They operated the whole system with just 170 employees, and managed to pull in a stunning return on equity of a lip-smacking 24 percent.

In neighboring Finland, Mr. Tee observed—as I've recently noted—that the mobile phone penetration rate had recently hit a worldwide high of 33 percent (or one third) of total households. Using this yardstick, with the Estonian rate currently hovering at around 6 percent, he felt he had plenty of room to grow, particularly in happy harmony with his Finnish partners.

Curious about Tee's formula for success, I asked him for it. He had the winning formula right on the tip of his tongue.

"Better service," he replied crisply, sounding a bit like one of his own advertisements. "More motivated employees. We are not working nine to five. We are more like Japan."

On top of that, with regard to raising their public profile, they had a great slogan, which he willingly repeated with a sly smile: "Always With You!"

Though I couldn't share, for some reason, his unbridled enthusiasm for "Always With You," I was right up there with him—up to a point.

So what was there not to like with Estonian Mobile Telephone Company?

It was not listed on the stock exchange.

If it was, it would probably be expensive.

Telephone companies all over the world had lately become

pretty expensive. And the most expensive kind of telephone companies were mobile phone companies.

Conclusion: a great company. But not an opportunity at this point in time.

The Energy Company

After telecoms, public utilities usually comprise the next wave of state-owned companies to be privatized. They tend to be vast and unproductive, and need serious money to be upgraded into profitability. But on the upside, once they've got their infrastructure in place, their costs tend to be low—fuel, or in the case of hydroelectric power, just maintenance. And overhead.

Utilities may not be sexy, but they can be sleepers.

The big questions to ask with any utility:

1) How subject is it to regulation?

2) If it *is* subject to regulation (and most of them are), how onerous is it?

3) If they're *not* subject to government regulation, chances are that's because they're no longer a monopoly. And if they're no longer a monopoly, the overriding question becomes: can they stand the heat of competition?

From the flag-draped lobby of our hotel (which sported glossy pictures of various famed political bigwigs like Vaclav Havel, the poet-playwright-president of the Czech Republic, who'd presumably stayed on our exclusive Jewelry Floor), our intrepid Templeton team—drawing the occasional curious glance at our dark suits, black shoes, and black leather briefcases containing notebook computers slung over our shoulders—set purposefully forth up a few blocks to a nondescript low-slung modern building faced with Soviet-era white tiles, a few of which were coming loose in long adhesive strips. Was that a symbol of something, or what?

Here was the bulky, hulking headquarters of Estonian Gas, a bulky, hulking company which, like the phone company, was looking to haul itself, kicking and screaming, into the twenty-first century. The Estonian Gas building had been blessed (or

cursed) with the standard Soviet-style massive cavernous echo-
ing lobby, all the better to display World War II corporate
memorabilia and monuments to various long-deceased or put-
out-to-pasture commissars.

Now, even the statues of the commissars had been put out to
pasture (or deep-sixed in the local landfill) to be replaced, in this
case, by a series of insipid Estonian landscapes.

A wide wooden central staircase led up to successive floors.
The elevator, no bigger than a water closet, seemed to me
painfully slow, and mainly for show.

We met the general director, Aarne Saar, and his finance director.

The sleekly appointed modern conference room was nearly
filled with a large plastic-laminate table. On it sat bottles of the
obligatory morning mineral water, with bubbles and without.

This still being the A.M., coffee and tea and biscuits were also
being served by a shyly smiling young woman who acted as our
interpreter.

Saar was another one of these distinguished-looking, scholarly
types, of approximately the same age as Heinar Leismann, with
a steely gaze behind gold-rimmed glasses. He conducted the
meeting as if it were a seminar on "Twentieth Century Gas."

Saar knew the big picture when it came to delivering Estonian
gas. But after spending a few minutes filling us in on the broad
brushstrokes, he left the details to his finance director, whose obvious desire to be exceedingly precise in her answers made me
wonder if she wouldn't unwittingly reveal to us more than she
intended to do.

In 1991, with the coming of independence from Russia, the
Estonian state had been faced with the problem of what to do
with its sprawling natural gas network, which was in part
owned and operated by the Soviet natural gas giant Gazprom
(which since privatization has grown into the largest, most powerful company in Russia, whose chairman would become Yeltsin's
prime minister).

After taking over the transmission pipelines from Gazprom,
the Estonians had cut a deal—you might rightly call it an ami-
cable divorce—with them by granting them a third share in the
new company in exchange for their pipeline network. An addi-

tional 39 percent of the total shares was now held by the Estonian state. The remaining 28 percent of the shares would soon be sold off to minority shareholders.

The first takers of the private shares—in accordance with the principles of classic privatization—were a pair of strategic investors:

1) The German natural gas giant Ruhrgas (which bought 15 percent); and

2) Gaz de France, one of Ruhrgas's key European competitors (5 percent).

An additional 8 percent had been purchased by various investment funds.

Now, Estonian Gas, which was still one-third-owned by Gazprom, was being asked to operate as a stand-alone venture in a competitive semi-open market. In Estonia (as elsewhere) the local gas company's competition wasn't going to be other gas companies, but other energy companies, primarily those selling oil and coal.

In Estonia, the oil was cheap black crude from Russia and local Estonian oil distilled from oil shale. And then, of course, there was the cheapest, lowest-down, dirtiest fossil fuel of them all: coal.

So how to boost sales?

Fortunately for the new company, the Estonian parliament was prepared to give them a boost, by drafting an energy law—still pending—a component of which was likely to be a pollution tax that would raise taxes on the rival dirtier fuels.

This was not only good news for the Estonian environment, which like all former Soviet satellites was in need of some serious upgrading. It was also good news for Estonian Gas, and for its shareholders.

Like natural gas in most parts of the world, the gas itself was cheaper than rival fuels. But to get it into your home or business required an up-front investment to pay for installation for the necessary equipment, which over time would—or so the subscriber hoped—be amortized in lower monthly home-heating and cooking bills.

The main reason, Saar insisted, that their basic supplies of natural gas were so abundant and cheap was that they were still working off favorable long-term contracts signed with Gazprom.

Now of course it was his job to put a positive spin on that Gazprom connection.

But as I saw it, though it was a sweet deal now, over time that Gazprom connection—which was more like a headlock—could be oppressive, because they would be in effect forced to purchase all their supplies from one provider.

Sure, things with Gazprom may be great now. But what if, at some future date, once those favorable contracts had elapsed, they turned around and turned off the smiles and started turning up the screws?

Where was Estonian Gas then?

Without saying why I was interested, I wondered out loud if they had any contingency plans in place to develop an independent source of gas other than Gazprom.

Saar's elaborate shrug and vague allusion to a future Gazprom project to import Norwegian oil spoke volumes to me.

Though a strategy of looking for secondary suppliers made sense in the long term, Saar conceded, he insisted that "all other sources of energy are at present more expensive than Gazprom." I took this to mean that his old owner and master, the mighty Gazprom, was still calling the shots.

So if they faced the prospect of one day getting squeezed on supplies, I was curious how they planned to boost business. In this new, presumably cutthroat deregulated energy environment, with oil and coal still much cheaper, what was the biggest barrier, I wondered, to getting prospective customers to switch over to gas from coal or oil shale?

"The client needs to be convinced," Saar replied, "that it's worth the investment in equipment installed in the home. We've spent a lot of time upgrading our metering systems. In Soviet times, we only had a central metering system. This was notoriously unreliable. There were no meters in individual households."

No household meters!

If you happened to be hunting for a simple, single example of the fundamental absurdity of the top-down, command economy, that had to be it: pumping energy without limit to consumers—you could hardly call them customers.

The only reason that they even had central metering in the towns was that it was *interesting,* strictly from a production standpoint, to have the central bureaucracy have some vague notion of total consumption. Individual subscriber usage? Under the old system, that was basically irrelevant.

Now the customer was going to have to pay for the gas. What a mind-boggling change!

No wonder some people were hopping mad.

And no wonder, Gazprom or not, I was suddenly getting just the slightest bit interested.

Numbers Racket

Having dropped—unwittingly—that minor bombshell, Saar politely excused himself and turned the meeting over to his finance director, a redheaded middle-aged woman with thick pointed glasses and a dark heavy dress, who had a habit of pursing her lips and scrunching up her eyebrows, as if deep in thought, before responding to a question. She reminded me a little of the elderly female KGB agent in the classic James Bond film *To Russia with Love.*

Women's Lib?

All over the former Soviet Union, and the former Iron Curtain countries, corporate finance directors are women. I asked a Russian friend about this, who advised me not to draw any false conclusions from it.

"This is not a sign that women enjoyed any great position of power under Communism," he said. "In fact, precisely the opposite was the case. In an economy based not on finance, but on production, all prestige and power were vested in the men who managed production. It was all very well to let women handle the money, because money was meaningless. A knowledge of finance was considered a plebeian, lowbrow occupation."

In other words, despite their rhetoric to the contrary, the Communists were just as likely to be male chauvinist pigs as we decadent capitalists. I found that something of a relief.

Candid Assessment

Estonian Gas was interesting, but since we didn't yet know its stock price on the open market, we could hardly assess it against other, similar gas companies elsewhere in the world. But what blew me away was that all they had to do was start installing meters and charging customers, and they had one hell of a business going for themselves.

Add to that the fact that next door in Finland, the gas companies were using their gas pipeline routes to also lay data transmission lines, and you had a potentially interesting situation. There's a company called Williams International that's doing this in the U.S., arousing considerable investor interest. The Finnish connection meant that the possibility of something similar happening here was not all so far-fetched.

The major downside to utility companies in general, as I've noted, is that they tend to be overly regulated by the government. This shouldn't be so surprising, because politicians all over the world have never been able to ignore the fact that people don't much like paying their gas and electrical bills. For some reason, people feel that running their stoves and heating their houses is some sort of God-given right.

But on the upside, once you've got those lines (gas and electric) installed, people have little choice but to pay up once they realize that if they don't, the company can—and will—cut the juice.

Another upside: Estonian Gas's strategic partners, Gaz de France and Ruhrgas, were major players. They weren't likely to see their investments go sour, and might even be willing to go head-to-head with Gazprom to offer supplies at reasonable rates.

I liked this company. I made a note to keep an eye out for its IPO (initial public offering).

On our way out the door, I casually noted to the finance director that Estonian Gas shares were not yet listed on any exchange, and I wondered if she could tell me of any plans to sell shares to the public.

"After the state has sold the shares it's planning to sell, we plan to go to the Tallinn Stock Exchange," she said.

"Isn't that funny," I replied. "We plan to go there too."

The Stock Exchange

"As you can see, we have no trading floor. Just offices with computers," said the young, attractive, very chipper Helo Meigas, the charming chairman of the management board of the one-year-old TSE—the Tallinn Stock Exchange.

Meigas spoke lightly accented English and seemed very much a product of the new post-Soviet, postindustrial era. In a recent issue of *Forbes*, Helo, just thirty-one, had been held up as a poster girl of the current crop of "young, graduate-school-educated Estonians with an appreciation for democracy and a knack for capitalism." To which I would have added: "an appreciation of technology, and a knack for implementing it."

Our visit to the local stock exchange was not, by the way, just a courtesy or social call.

> **Mobius Rule No. 35: Never, ever invest in a country without checking out its stock exchange first.**

An emerging market is, by definition, one in which the market is new.

By "market," we generally mean the stock exchange, because that's where the market gets made. That's where the transactions take place.

You can, by the way, tell an awful lot about a stock market by actually paying a visit. And if you're in the slightest bit financially inclined, it's often an interesting enough "sight" to make it a brief stop on your next foreign tour.

Here is a simple question I ask myself when entering a new stock exchange: is it a club or a computer room?

For all the charm of clubs, I prefer computers. They make my life easier, and are less liable to create headaches of the sort that less-than-arm's-length transactions commonly conducted in smoke-filled back rooms do.

For example, the members of the New York Stock Exchange, or for that matter the Paris Bourse, would have been aghast to get a gander at the "trading floor" of the Tallinn Stock Exchange. It offered nothing more impressive to the eye than a small, simple suite of rooms, smoked-glass (instead of smoke-filled) offices, off a sterile, wall-to-wall-carpeted hall.

The place was as silent as a morgue. And considerably less dramatic. There was no shouting or waving of hands, no passing of bits of paper by floor runners, no ringing of bells. It struck me as a miniature version of the newly restructured Hong Kong Stock Exchange, another eerie "dematerialized" place where the designers seriously considered playing tapes of old-style feverish face-to-face trading (with all those confetti-like confections of ticker-tape paper) so that the brokers wouldn't get too nostalgic for their anachronistic, cozy club.

"It is an entirely paperless system," Meigas pointed out proudly, gesturing with one hand across a row of desks topped with quietly blinking computer screens, "dematerialized and de-centralized." By which she meant that there were no stock certificates, virtually no paper records, and that all transactions were conducted electronically.

From its founding (May 31, 1991) up to the beginning of 1998, the market cap of the exchange had risen from zero to $1.4 billion.

Daily turnover was approximately $5 million.

Still, by the way, exceedingly small by institutional standards. Some days, our own trading floor in Hong Kong handles more trades than that—just for own account.

The place cleared, on average, 500 transactions a day, though on a particularly active day, they might close as many as 700.

"We started out with two objectives," Helo told us. "Our first goal was to insert more liquidity into the market and to put adequate disclosure mechanisms in place."

Here were our FELT questions: Remember?

Was it Fair? Efficient? Liquid? Transparent?

Curious as to the answer to FELT number one (fairness), I asked Meigas about a report I'd heard in the press, in which a government official (Vahur Lokk, a securities manager at the Estonian Ministry of Finance) was quoted in a local Baltic periodical in 1997 as saying that "up to two thirds of the transactions conducted on the Estonian exchange were products of insider trading." Such loose controls are not uncommon in the early stages of emerging markets formation.

Without batting an eyelash, Meigas coolly replied: "We are still not up to date with regard to many regulatory areas. We have no takeover code, for example, as yet. Minority shareholder rights are not yet sufficiently protected. The market is still very much self-regulated. Legislation in the areas is at present inadequate. The rules on insider trading have not yet been well defined."

Clearly, there was some room for improvement in the fairness department.

But Helo (hello there!) Meigas made it clear they were working on it, because a stock market that isn't fair isn't going to flourish in the current climate.

Was it efficient?

That was obvious just from looking at it, and watching it work. Absolutely. Terribly so. On its own terms, it was in fact far more efficient—because it was dematerialized—than the NYSE, or the Paris Bourse, though the Paris Bourse is going paperless soon, as well.

Was it liquid?

Well, yes, in a manner of speaking, but not nearly enough for our purposes.

The most actively traded stocks were those of a few banks and other recently privatized corporations. One stock, Hansabank, was the bellwether stock, and accounted for a third of its market cap. They needed fresh blood; new privatizations coming down the pike.

So in order to really be interesting to us, it had a ways to go in the liquidity department.

But it was clearly on the right road, and the good thing about booms is that they bring more money in, and the good thing about bringing more money in is that it improves liquidity and activity.

Another thing about illiquid, small markets: the entry of a major player (like us) could cause it to shoot through the roof. Just place what for us would be a modest order, and it was likely to go haywire.

Was it transparent?

"We try to find mechanisms to enforce and regulate the market," Helo Meigas replied to my question as to transparency. Now remember: transparency is the degree to which an investor is provided with reliable and up-to-date information about transactions. Key to maintaining transparency is something called a "central share registry," which functions as an impartial clearinghouse for information about trading.

> Mobius Rule No. 36: The best way to determine transparency is to inquire about a central share registry. If there isn't one, in most cases a market can't be considered fully transparent.

"A central depository keeps every account," Meigas crisply replied, "to inform the market of major shareholder acquisitions. We have the contractual right to print out major acquisitions for distribution to our members. All transactions are cleared through the central bank. We also fund the central depository. All of which means that the market is fairly transparent. Ninety-eight percent of total turnover is handled through the exchange. If the party to the transaction is a member of the exchange, the transaction must be reported to the system."

Note, the neighboring Russian stock market, for all its astounding successes, still lacked a central depository, so that no single organization was responsible for keeping track of all trades. The resulting lack of transparency has been a hindrance not only to real structural reform, but to the investment of capital by outsiders. To put it bluntly, fewer people are likely to bet on a horse race they know to be rigged.

In closing, Meigas noted that they hoped to double the number of companies listed to forty before very long.

"But it's hard to find a company comparable to Hansabank, which represents one third of our total market cap of $1.4 billion."

That, for what it was worth—around $460 million—just happened to be our next stop.

The Bank

"I hate to even think about my net worth," observed young Rain Lohmus, one of the original nine founders of Estonia's astounding Hansabank, "because it would spoil my appetite for work."

Spoiled appetite or not, Lohmus's net worth (as measured in a stock that had soared in value in less than two years a mouth-watering 800 percent) was currently estimated at $15 million.

But what struck me most favorably about his comment (which one of my analysts had flagged for me back in Warsaw) was its healthy emphasis on the value of work over money. An example of the Baltics' fabled "stoic Lutheran culture."

I like bank stocks.

All over the world, banks are yielding excellent results from the long-delayed impact of better technology. New methods of servicing clients using automated teller machines, new communications systems, more powerful computers, and other technological great leaps forward are boosting bank profitability worldwide.

In the case of newer banks, the ability to leapfrog over older banks saddled with costly, cumbersome branch systems and bloated staffs permits even greater profitability. Estonia's Hansabank was a splendid case in point.

If Tallinn's stock market was the stock exchange of the future, Hansabank was the universal bank of the future. (A universal bank, by the way, is one that is permitted by law to act like a bank, a broker, a holder of stocks in companies, and an insurer, a multiple threat at present outlawed in the U.S. by the much-derided Glass-Steagall Act, a legacy of the Great Depression.)

A sure sign of this was that the bank's official language was English—the language of global finance. In emerging markets, investing in banks provides the advantage of investing indirectly in an entire economy. Since banks are often primary engines of local economic growth, buying their stock is the equivalent of buying stock in every company they invest in. Double your pleasure, double your fund.

Hansabank's sparkling glass-walled headquarters was sleekness incarnate. The skin of the building was sheer glass and steel; the interior offices were gleaming white, cool and crisp as a Merimekko sheet. Everything about Hansabank was consciously and deliberately futuristic.

The only part pointing at all toward the past was the tall, wide picture windows of the top-floor boardroom, which offered sweeping wraparound views of Tallinn stretching all the way out into the sparkling blue Gulf of Finland.

Established in 1991 by nine foresightful individuals described by CEO Juri Mois as "prominent in Estonian business life," Hansabank was born as the smallest bank in the Baltics and was now by far the largest, with assets topping $800 million, with a market cap, as I've said, now set at a staggering $460 million.

Out of fifty-six Baltic banks, Hansabank Group had garnered over 12 percent of the total regional market. Inside Estonia, their share of the market currently verged on 30 percent. Even more impressive, their return on equity had exceeded 50 percent per year every year since they were founded.

For any bank, or for that matter any company, that was remarkable.

"All of the other Baltic banks are old, restructured Soviet-era banks," said Hansabank's young, energetic Juri Mois dismissively, a touch of pity lacing his precise, perfect English.

"There was no real banking under the Soviet system. Banks were basically crude credit mechanisms, established to funnel funds to factories to buy materials."

While most other Baltic banks were dinosaurs (comparable in a way to Heinar Leismann's phone system) heading straight down the road to extinction, the young upstart Hansabank had "no burdensome branch network," Mois explained, with a modest shrug.

Like most modern bankers, Mois could easily have done without branches, which he derisively described as "places to park customer accounts. Branches are expensive to operate, and expensive to close down. Our competitors have hundreds of branches. We've got twenty-five of them, modern and well-equipped ones. Which means that if we dropped our loan interest rate by 2 percent," he speculated cheerfully, "we would be the only bank making a profit in Estonia."

Explanatory note: because he had such comparatively low overhead, if he dropped his rates to attract customers he could still make a small profit while driving his competitors out of business.

Though the chuckle was amiable, a competitive edge was distinctly detectable. First Estonia, then the Baltics, then Russia and Poland. What was next? The world?

The bank had recently opened five branches in Latvia, and their recent takeover and restructuring of a Latvian bank had been, according to Mois, "a positive experience."

"If growth is not possible to achieve or sustain in our domestic market, we will go outside, possibly to Russia, or even Ukraine," he said, sounding a bit like a general planning his upcoming summer campaign.

"At present, 10 percent of savings on our balance sheet represents telephone banking from Russia and Ukraine. Our people all speak fluent Russian. This society is comprehensible to Russians. This is a good trading place for Russians. Westerners like us because it feels Western here. Russians like us because they also feel at home here."

Mois spoke with real feeling as to the potential for small states abutting great nations to prosper as mercantile centers, facilitating trade links among the rich and more famous nation states on their borders. He was talking, of course, about gateway countries, although he wasn't using the term.

"Of the list of the largest banks in the world, fifteen are Dutch," he said, with what I took to be almost a conspiratorial grin. This was clearly an exaggeration, but I got the point he was driving at:

the Dutch, like the Estonians, were smart, small, hardworking, and perfectly positioned to take full advantage of—whoops! I meant to say "work with"—their larger, more powerful neighbors.

Mois was particularly upbeat on the Estonian potential for growth in trade with Russia. Here I leaned forward, because that was a large part of why I was here: to see about buying stocks that would give us exposure to Russia's upside, without exposing us to Russia's downside.

When I asked him which sectors of the local economy were booming the most, he unhesitatingly replied: "Anything having to do with trade to Russia. For example, sea transportation is growing 50 percent per year. It's impossible to stop this trade from flowing—it's in the Baltic blood. Despite politicians' attempts to do otherwise."

Striking a somewhat more restrained note, he conceded that a large part of Hansabank's parabolic growth had been a function of riding the wave of a rapidly expanding local economy.

And what, I wondered, if—perhaps I should have said "when"—the Baltic Boom burst?

"Of course, we ask ourselves this question all the time," he replied soberly. "Could this present boom be merely overheating? Is our experience the beginning of a big success, or the beginning of a big decline?"

Personally, I couldn't have said it better myself.

But with a touch of quiet bravado, he added: "Analysts have warned us that we can't sustain our current rate of growth forever, but we don't listen to them. For the past six years, we've been doubling our assets annually. After talking to the analysts, we set a target of tripling of assets every year."

He concluded his presentation with a stunning statement: "Our short history is our biggest asset."

Company Assessment

Though Hansabank's stock price was at the time too rich for my blood, what I learned from meeting with Juri Mois at his spanking-new headquarters was probably priceless.

His assessment of Hansabank's regional prospects fit in with my own thoughts about the value of buying early into gateway countries as they develop into regional mercantile and financial centers. Hansabank's stunning growth spurt confirmed our strong conviction that bank stocks are good bets—provided you get in early enough—and that they are awfully strong at "bagging bank baggage"—my term for shedding outmoded branches and systems.

Regional Assessment

My strategic reason for coming to the Baltic Republics had been simple:

Diversification.

Remember Mobius Rule No. 1: "Your best protection is diversification"?

We'll, I'd been following it.

But in light of the fact that:

1) The markets were still small, which means not very liquid, and

2) They were expensive,

We had to cut to Plan B, which is our code word for: Boom Plan.

The Big Question:

How do you find bargains during a boom?

Mobius Rule No. 37: Look for companies not yet privatized, or fully privatized.

And:

Mobius Rule No. 38: Look for second-tier companies with small market caps and big growth potential.

An Estonian example: rated by sheer sexiness, the Estonian Mobile Telephone Company had the most appeal, followed by Hansabank, followed by the Estonian Telephone Company, followed by Estonian Gas. But fortunately, apart from sex appeal, I'd have rated Estonian Gas the best bet, because it's not sexy, because they're installing gas meters, because they might have a data highway soon to rival a phone company.

Plan B Part Two:

> **Mobius Rule No. 39: Wait for the panic.**
> **Then, calmly, buy.**

Why?
Because you're being paid to take a risk that the short-term sentiment is greatly exaggerated.

> **Mobius Rule No. 40: In the perception gap between**
> **emotion and reason, you'll find**
> **your buy window.**

Market Metaphors

Sometimes I regard emerging markets as somewhat like clay pigeons, hurled out in the sky by the swinging arm of free-market policies, on a trajectory into open space. Will they rise, fall, or take a weird turn? And like the man with the gun, you try to take aim and hope to hit the mark at the right point in the trajectory, at a low point just before it takes off into the stratosphere.

An emerging market is also like a cannon shot—the explosion being the release of long-pent-up value. Except for one thing: you can't always hit the right market at just the right time, all of the time. That's called market timing, and in my opinion, it's damned near impossible.

I left the Baltics with a twinge of regret, because we had by no means gotten in on the ground floor. We'd missed the fabled Ground Zero by a long shot.

But if the truth be told, it really doesn't matter.

Because you can find bargains in booms as well as busts.

It's just a little harder.

Remember when a declining America was all the rage, and historians were comparing the U.S. economy to Rome's before the fall? Not long ago, the Japanese were thought to have all the cards, and the keys to the future, while the Americans were the wave of the past.

Fast-forward ten years. Now, the Japanese have discovered they aren't infallible because they too can suffer busts, as well as booms. Now, the Americans are looking smart. But not so fast— every boom contains the seeds of the next bust.

That's the way the world works, and personally, I find it very exciting.

As we left the booming Baltics, we flew straight to equally booming Russia.

On the plane, we learned that the Southeast Asian markets, those once-seemingly-invincible "Tiger Economies," were collapsing, falling one after another like dominos, proof that even if the "domino theory" didn't work to project the pattern of Communist incursions, it does a pretty good job of explaining the links between markets in regions.

But Hong Kong, the smart money said, was impregnable, backed by U.S. $80 billion in hard currency reserves, and the money might of fast-growing China. Hong Kong would never fall, they said, just as the British said about Singapore in 1940 until the Japanese took it in two days.

Then, of course, Hong Kong started to drop through the basement, and everyone started to freak out.

Did we?

Let's just say that even as we checked out companies in Russia, I was faxing and phoning Hong Kong and Thailand to beat the band, hoping to take maximum advantage of the free-for-all there.

MORE MOBIUS RULES

26: Low-tax economies tend to be good places to place your investment dollars.

27: Success as a global investor is closely linked to optimism.

28: Reading local papers and watching local newscasts can provide valuable insights unavailable anywhere else into the mentality of local markets.

29: Clothes may not make the man, but they can provide clues to the personality.

30: *Low* telecom penetration rates represent *high* potential growth.

31: Always inquire about the probity and honesty of management before anything else.

32: Keep on the lookout for industries that once were heavily regulated and are now being deregulated.

33: Don't be put to sleep by utilities. Be woken up by them!

34: If the net asset value (NAV) divided by the number of shares gives you a dollar figure *higher* than the share price, then you *could* consider it an undervalued stock.

35: Never, ever invest in a country without checking out its stock exchange first.

36: The best way to determine transparency is to inquire about a central share registry. If there isn't one, in most cases a market can't be considered fully transparent.

37: Look for companies not yet privatized, or fully privatized.

38: Look for second-tier companies with small market caps and big growth potential.

39: Wait for the panic. Then, calmly, buy.

40: In the perception gap between emotion and reason, you'll find your buy window.

Chapter Three

◆

ALL THE RICHES IN RUSSIA

On the morning in August 1997 that we flew from St. Petersburg, the old imperial capital of Russia, to Nizhniy Novgorod, an industrial city on the Volga River, the thirty-six-year-old privatization chief of St. Petersburg was shot dead while riding in the back of his government-issue Volvo sedan, by a sniper who opened fire with an AK-47 from the attic of a building on the Nevsky Prospect, the city's main street. The hit man had excellent aim and possibly an X-ray scope, because the bullet penetrated the car top, while the vice governor's wife, sitting beside him, was hardly hurt.

Though many bankers and businessmen had been gunned down gangland style in the years since Communism's collapse, this brutal contract-style killing of the popular young vice governor Mikhail Manevich was the first assassination of a high-level politician in post-Communist Russia. This incident savagely and dramatically underscored the mounting bitterness—and brutally high stakes—of the scandal-ridden privatization process in Russia.

Like cocaine barons guarding their turf with assault weapons, the St. Petersburg Mafia had apparently concluded that young Mr. Manevich had to go, and go violently—to serve as an example to any uppity bureaucrats who might consider emulating his example—because his plans threatened them with getting a thinner slice of the rich privatization pie.

At first glance, the power struggle of which this hit was merely a local skirmish appeared to be a clear-cut case of Mafia thugs seeking to steal the state's crown jewels—or buy them for a song—while bumping off honest reformers intent on distributing the profits of privatization to the highest bidder, and indirectly to the public at large.

But as Winston Churchill once said of Russia itself, the behind-the-scenes struggle remained "a riddle wrapped in a mystery inside an enigma." That statement has been proven, time and again, all the more apt in these last chaotic years of post-Communist independence.

Riddle/Enigma/Mystery

"A riddle wrapped in a mystery inside an enigma" perfectly described the murky world of Russian investing. This was perhaps the only country on earth where the stock market could have shot up 200 percent in a single year even as official statistics indicated a stagnant, no-growth economy.

I had reason to believe that the official statistics were severely distorted. While the economy officially stagnated, a shadow economy, consisting of barter and other noncash, off-the-books arrangements, was growing by leaps and bounds. But a fair amount of this robust activity was not finding its way onto the official economic reports. It was possible to infer some measure of its existence through statistics indicating higher energy consumption, and higher freight charges being racked up by the railroads, all of which indicated that more goods were being produced and moved through the production pipeline.

Why was so much soft—or funny—money being kept off the books?

1) A terrible tax system, for one thing, which provided strong incentives for companies and individuals not to report earnings on official documents, because they stood a good chance of being seized by desperate tax collectors under pressure to raise revenues to keep a floundering central government afloat.

2) A punitive and costly social burden—in itself a form of tax,

payable in services as opposed to money—which forced companies to provide housing, medical care, vacation resorts, and the
like to their employees. These costs were dragging Russian business back into the quagmire.

Without some serious fiscal reform, the runaway stock market
boom Russia was presently enjoying was guaranteed to run out
of steam—as, within a year, it did.

The Big Problem: until the tax system could be changed, encouraging earnings to be reported, none of that income was ever
likely to find its way into the hands of shareholders.

Tax Surrealism

Even Prime Minister Viktor Chernomyrdin—just weeks before
he was dismissed in a cabinet shake-up by President Boris Yeltsin
only to be reinstated six months later but dismissed again in a
perpetual game of musical chairs—denounced what he called
this state of "tax surrealism." And he knew what he was talking
about from personal experience, since as the former chairman of
Gazprom—a state-owned mega-monopoly that had grown since
the collapse of the Soviet state into the largest private company
in Russia—he'd been responsible for forking over more than its
fair share of taxes. (He was also widely rumored to be the richest man in Russia.)

In 1997, Gazprom had seen more than a third of its profits
disappear into the government tax maw. And that was actually a
special case, because Gazprom had paid what it owed in full. In
that same year, the central government only collected about half of
the taxes it had planned to take in, a sorry state of affairs so egre-
gious that the IMF had suspended a partial payment on a nearly
$10 billion loan until the federal government got its house in order.

The Russian tax code contained, according to our calculations,
over 200 separate taxes, many of them contradictory.

Our analytical team estimated that the average tax burden imposed on Russian companies ran up to 80 percent of real profits.

For global investors, it was becoming increasingly difficult to continue to invest in Russian companies strictly on hope—hope of higher reported earnings, hope of meaningful tax reform.

If Russian companies could not even safely report the earnings they'd honestly made, how could we ever expect any profits being legitimately generated by their operations to ever find their way into investors' pockets? And in particular, *foreign* investors' pockets?

Privatization, Russian Style

The real reason that Russian privatization officials were being gunned down in the streets was that despite the innumerable and seemingly insurmountable problems plaguing the national economy, the value of assets hived off to the public at bargain-basement prices in the early years of the market conversion had skyrocketed in recent years.

Just as the mounting street value of illegal drugs, which rises exponentially with each step of the demand chain, causes desperate people to beg, borrow, steal, and kill to get their hands on them, so the rising value of these once-dirt-cheap assets was causing some scary people to draw blood to gain control of them.

At one of our more successful investments, the Krasnoyarsk Aluminum Company in Siberia, an elite battalion of assault troops had surrounded the facility and attempted to take it and its managers hostage during one particularly hard-fought battle over disputed shareholder rights.

Investing in Russia had become like entering a rich gold field studded with land mines: laced with veins of rich treasure, and riddled with pockets of pure poison.

Contract Killing

In this context, the killing of St. Petersburg privatization chief Mikhail Manevich on the ancient streets of his home city could be considered a defining moment in the process of Russia's bitterly contested conversion to a viable market economy. Boris Yeltsin's then–deputy chief of staff publicly proclaimed

Manevich's murder as caused by a "bullet aimed straight at the heart of reform."

First Deputy Prime Minister Anatoly Chubais—shortly to be dismissed himself—vowed at Manevich's funeral to "get those who pulled the trigger and those who paid with their stinking stolen money. We're not leaving them a choice. It's us or them. There's no middle way!"

Ironically, the young man comforting Mr. Manevich's grieving wife at the funeral, former federal privatization chief Alfred Kokh, had been ousted just days before by a furious Boris Yeltsin, amid a chorus of allegations that he had conspired with a group of Kremlin-connected bankers to rig the auction of a one-quarter interest in Svyazinvest, a giant telecom holding company granted wide monopoly powers by the Yeltsin regime.

To make matters worse, Kokh had also recently presided over the auction of a sizable chunk of the eagerly sought-after Norilsk Nickel, the world's largest nickel producer, to the same group of financiers! And the winner had been . . . a consortium led by the Kremlin-connected Oneximbank, one of Russia's most powerful financial institutions, whose chairman, thirty-seven-year-old Vladimir Potanin, a former deputy prime minister himself, was a close ally of First Deputy Prime Minister Anatoly Chubais, since dismissed from his post by Yeltsin.

Shortly thereafter, the Moscow prosecutor's office disclosed that it was investigating Kokh's acceptance of a $100,000 "book advance" funneled to him through a Swiss intermediary, who happened to work for a Swiss Oneximbank subsidiary. The subject of the book had become a hot topic, under the circumstances: privatization. Although the charges of payoffs by Oneximbank were never proved, the circumstances certainly suggested that Boris Yeltsin's reformist government suffered from, at the very least, a few image problems. The scandal deepened and widened when it ultimately emerged that First Deputy Prime Minister Anatoly Chubais himself, along with a group of his fellow reformers, had accepted book advances of roughly $90,000 each to write their own joint book on privatization.

And who might the publisher dishing out the dough be? Why, none other than Segodniya Press, owned by Oneximbank.

The Oligarchy

A murky Moscow oligarchy—composed of a small group of powerful bankers, widely rumored to control up to one half of the Russian economy—had bankrolled Boris Yelstin's 1996 re-election campaign. Now that he was safely back in office, the markers were being called in. So who were these so-called oligarchs? Most had in an earlier era enjoyed cozy connections to the old Communist hierarchy. Rumors swirled around some of them that their initial seed money had been provided to them by the KGB and/or other powerful elements of the old system, which had never really died, but had simply been reconstituted as a monopoly.

Many of these oligarchs had hugely profited during the early 1990s, when a cash-strapped central government had lent them—ostensibly for safekeeping until a privatization plan was announced—some of the richest pieces of the privatization pie. Vast caches of oil and mineral reserves, primarily, had been turned over to these banks in exchange for the commodity the government most desperately needed: cold cash.

For the oligarchs, this had turned out to be a very good deal. You might even say, a sweetheart deal, since when it came time for privatization they knew the inner workings of those companies and how to win the privatization bid.

Oneximbank

One of the most powerful, mysterious, and feared oligarchs (due to his close links to the reformist wing of the Yelstin administration) was the then thirty-seven-year-old Vladimir Potanin, whose octopus-like Oneximbank was rumored to have emerged from the wreckage of the sprawling Soviet Foreign Trade Ministry, in whose covert corridors Potanin had once worked.

In the case of Norilsk Nickel (another Kokh-managed auction in which Oneximbank had mysteriously come out on top), Oneximbank had acquired its chunk of shares in the freewheeling early 1990s under one of those controversial "loans for shares" schemes. To render the privatization process even more insider-controlled, the group handling the sale of the shares—on behalf of the government—and the outfit that bought them were one and the same: Oneximbank.

During the weeks leading up to both hotly contested share auctions, we'd been approached by a number of groups to join them on making bids for Svyazinvest and Norilsk Nickel. But under such tightly controlled conditions, it had become entirely impossible—not to mention financially and morally unjustifiable—for rank outsiders like us to even bother to bid. It was at least some small consolation to learn that the American financier George Soros and Oneximbank (the lead partners in the Cyprus-based consortium that won the Svyazinvest auction) had paid a pretty price for their shares.

Particularly when the outfit in question was derisively described in the peach pages of *The Financial Times* as a "virtual company" with a staff of less than 100, with its chief assets being "a pile of questionable operating licenses, stakes in dozens of strong-minded companies, and no cash revenues apart from dividends."

Confidence Games

All this high-profile infighting, wheeling and dealing, and allegations of corruption were causing the Yeltsin administration to rapidly lose face with the international investment community. It certainly didn't help matters when the International Monetary Fund declined to extend the next $670 million installment in its $11 billion loan to Russia because of its failure to initiate meaningful tax reform—a weakness of will that would come back to haunt the country when the inevitable crash came.

Further tarnishing the new Yelstin-appointed "clean team's" image, the Control Risks Group, a British consulting firm, announced that Russia had won the dubious distinction of being voted "the most corrupt country in the world," narrowly edging out rivals Nigeria and Uzbekistan in the minds of Western fund managers. As the *New York Times* acidly commented, "it was a stinging rebuke to the image of Russian reform."

Oligarch

In the long run, the burning question of whether the run-up in Russia would sustain itself, or would soon start to totter like a house of cards, depended on whether Boris Yeltsin and his band of young, ardent free-marketeers would be willing and able to break the power of the robber barons, and lay the groundwork for restructuring the Russian economy.

Or whether—as some savvy observers sadly suspected—the reformers themselves had been so co-opted by one faction within the larger oligarchy (which itself was rapidly splintering) that any crackdown would come in the form of public whippings, conducted largely for show.

As we would see in 1998, the reformers would soon fall prey to a new purge, as a long-shaky economy collapsed in earnest.

A New Leaf?

One brief hint of fresh air, and a possible sign that Russia's moral compass might be gradually turning in the right direction, occurred just a few weeks after the controversial Norilsk and Svyazinvest auctions, when Vladimir Potanin, Oneximbank's controversial chairman, executed an embarrassing about-face while attempting to secure total control of Norilsk Nickel, the world's largest nickel producer.

When Oneximbank's name had been pulled out of the hat by the soon-to-be-replaced Mr. Kokh as the winner of the Norilsk Nickel auction, this not unexpected development had been taken as bad news for the shaky cause of minority shareholder rights in Russia.

Like many Russian companies, Norilsk Nickel, a decaying colossus based in the Siberian Arctic, was a vast enterprise with virtually unlimited upside potential—and a virtually unlimited downside. Like many Russian companies, it was in desperate need of vast infusions of foreign funds if it was ever to have the slightest hope of becoming a viable, profit-making institution, much less a viable competitor in world markets. And like many other Russian companies, Norilsk was owned by a bitterly divided pool of shareholders, some of whom held "preferred" shares, while others held "common" shares.

Prefer the Preferred?

In Russia, preferred shares are often sharply discounted against common shares in the marketplace, because they often don't come with voting rights attached. It's not uncommon for foreign investors to be permitted to *only* buy preferred shares, because entrenched managements don't much cotton to a bunch of foreigners with newfangled ideas about reengineering and restructuring coming in and questioning their judgment.

Or, worst of all, telling them that they should fire workers, sell the gymnasium, and consider revamping that money-losing resort property on the Black Sea reserved for the recreation of senior managers only.

> **Mobius Rule No. 41: When buying shares in foreign companies it's important to read the fine print, and know the quality of rights conferred by ownership of the shares.**

Profit from the Spread

For a small investor with no interest in voting shares, the spread in price between the discounted preferred shares and the common shares offered a rare opportunity for arbitrage—which means taking advantage of the spread between two fluctuating prices for the same thing. In this case, for example, shares in Norilsk Nickel.

According to the company charter, NN's preferred shares were supposed to be converted into common shares after the state's stake in the company was sold to the public.

But when the new management—controlled by Vladimir Potanin's Oneximbank—announced its intention to convert the shares, they didn't state a conversion date.

Suspecting that something strange might be going on—that the preferred shares might never be converted to common—the market promptly placed an increasingly steep discount—as high as 30 percent—on the preferred shares.

Which presented a nice slice of arbitrage to any daring investor willing to:

1) Take the risk that the shares never would be converted,

2) Forget about voting rights, and

3) Bet that the price of the preferred would eventually rise to that of the common shares.

Share Dilution?

Share dilution takes place when a company issues new shares and doesn't see to it that they are sold at a fair-market price.

If shares are distributed to insiders or favorites at less than the going rate, that's a classic case of share dilution.

So when Oneximbank announced a new offer of Norilsk Nickel *common* shares, as a means of raising some $625 million in the capital markets, Western shareholders of the *preferred* Norilsk shares were a bit put out to learn that they were to be excluded from the rights offering.

This meant, in effect, that the value of the foreign-owned preferred shares was likely to be diluted. This obviously didn't sit well with foreign investors, such as ourselves.

We owned some 400,000 Norilsk Nickel preferred shares worth roughly $2.5 million, and were of course concerned that our investment would be endangered by this proposed shell game.

But what could we do? With Oneximbank firmly in the saddle, it wouldn't have been easy for the rest of us to gather enough votes to stage a full-fledged minority shareholder revolt.

The new common shares were slated to be sold for just over $5. The current common share market price was around $12.50.

Which meant a quick $7.50 per share windfall to the Russian domestic buyers and owners of the new common shares, a large number of which were held by...you guessed it, Oneximbank. In more mature markets, this move would have been nixed by any court in the land, as an unconscionable dilution of share value.

To make matters worse, the prospectus at no point gave the slightest hint of management's plans for the money: $600 million.

Even more disconcerting than this specific case of corporate hanky-panky was the fact that no clause in this plan in any way contravened any statute of Russian securities law. Which meant that if they went ahead and trashed our interests, we could expect to get no relief from the local courts.

In Russia, it's not uncommon for management to take a large pool of company funds and simply siphon them off, either into their own pockets, or into a cluster of shadowy subsidiaries, in which they happen to emerge as controlling shareholders.

One veteran investor in Russia I know claims that the only way to make money in Russian investing is to pick the winning team in any management squabble—some of which have become deadlier than Russian roulette.

But—miracle of miracles—at the very last minute, during a proxy vote at the next Norilsk Nickel shareholder meeting, Oneximbank shocked everyone by voting to kill its own plan. So what prompted this sudden change of heart?

Another Young Turk of Moscow, head of a fast-growing brokerage company, had forcefully persuaded Oneximbank chairman Potanin that to execute such a brazen attack on shareholder rights would have a negative effect not only on Norilsk Nickel's future as a vehicle for international investment, but on his own bank's reputation among foreign investors.

This argument proved surprisingly persuasive, mainly because both Oneximbank and Norilsk—not to mention any number of Oneximbank subsidiaries—hoped to tap into Western capital markets for many years to come.

A New New Leaf

Within a month of the takeover, Oneximbank took over the revenue flow of the company, and was able to settle some $200 million in back wages on the workers, who under the previous management—the state—had been waiting six months to get paid.

Oneximbank, with its deep pockets, was then able to settle nearly $2 billion in back debts, and struck a deal with the local *oblast* (provincial administration) to unload the lion's share of its social burden, in exchange for paying—and that meant actually forking over—a tax on its profits. The new management also came up with another $2 billion to embark on a long-needed restructuring, money they were able to come up with without fleecing the foreigners.

The saga of Norilsk Nickel shows that even if the initial auction was less than fair by Western standards, the company—and the shareholders—stood to benefit from the takeover anyway.

The moral of the story, from our point of view, was that in some cases two or three wrongs could in fact make a right.

Like much of Russia's privatization program, the Norilsk Nickel takeover involved self-dealing, punctuated with occasional bouts of legality—but in this case, it also worked—if not like a charm, then at least like a battered old Model-T Ford.

Cheaper by the Dozen

So what could possibly have possessed a band of crazy outside investors to risk Russia at all, particularly at a time when such wild and woolly scenarios seemed more like the rule than the exception?

The easy answer?

Cheap assets.

Which was the same reason, by the way, that Russia's momentous privatization program had turned so vicious, intense, and in some cases lethal:

Cheap assets could over time be worth fortunes.

To give just two examples, even after the staggering run-up of stock prices, Russian oil was still being priced on the Russian stock market (calculated as a ratio of market capitalization to known oil reserves) at 75 cents a barrel, as compared to close to $12 for American oil companies.

Much the same could be said of Moscow City Telephone, a hot Russian telecom stock valued at $870 per access line, compared to $1,000 a line in the U.S. and $3,000 per line in another comparably fast-growing emerging market, Brazil.

Back in 1993, when we first went into Russia, the government had just been embarking on its headlong plunge down the cliff of private enterprise. Like some economic short-order cook, it had simply waved its magic wand and presto! some 14,000 state-owned juggernauts had been swept private before you could say "Boris Yeltsin."

In the early 1990s, Russia's massive industrial infrastructure was being valued by the fledgling stock market at just $10 billion—a tiny fraction of its true value, even in dormant form.

Newly privatized oil companies, when their known reserves were calculated against aggregate share price, were seeing their market caps (the total value of all the company's shares as a function of their market price) set by the fledgling stock market at pennies per barrel.

In retrospect, these prices were way out of line with global reality.

But this wasn't New Jersey, or even Saudi Arabia; this was scary, risk-rich Russia.

Without the powerful inducement of acquiring assets at fire sale prices, few foreigners would have been brave enough or foolhardy enough to put a dime in the place.

Fortunately, for every well-publicized incident of brazen and blatant abuse of shareholder rights, there were two or three cases where shareholders were treated just as honestly and openly as General Motors shareholders.

> **Mobius Rule No. 42: Often the macro picture contradicts the micro picture.**

(In this case, the macro picture was that the place was dirty, low-down, and dishonest. But the micro picture presented isolated pockets of real opportunity.)

Mobius Rule No. 43: By correcting the gap between the macro and micro views, you can get a jump ahead of the crowd.

Ground Zero

When we first began tentatively sniffing around Russia, the macro picture could not have been more bearish, unless a full-fledged civil war had broken out.

1) A besieged Boris Yelstin had barely staved off a counter-coup by shelling the parliament.

2) The place was a hotbed of hard-core Communist resistance.

3) Inflation was skyrocketing.

4) Industrial output had hit rock bottom.

5) Capital flight was endemic. Any Russian with a few rubles to his or her name had smuggled their money out of the country, and shoved it in some offshore safe haven, far removed from the long arm of the Moscow tax man.

6) There were no stock exchanges.

7) There were no balance sheets.

8) There were no earnings reports, because . . .

9) There were no earnings.

10) The country was deep into what became known as the Great Contraction, when the country's GDP (gross domestic product) plunged by nearly half in five years.

Q: So what attracted us high-risk-freaks, like bees to honey?

A: There was stock to be bought, for nickels and dimes to the share.

1) Companies were being privatized right and left, big ones, small ones, good ones, bad ones, sometimes as many as a dozen a week.

2) Assets were being auctioned off like excess inventory, for

pennies on the dollar—or old rubles to new rubles—to sometimes not even the highest but often the *only* bidder.

3) Entire companies—oil and ore giants, telecom, energy—could be had for peanuts.

Q: So why was the Russian state so determined to conduct a fire sale of its potentially valuable assets?

1) They—the government—desperately needed money.

2) A lot of individuals—mostly managers—also desperately needed money. (So they were skimming and scamming and getting rich in the chaos.) Which made a lot of ordinary people done out of these deals very angry.

But there was also another, more legitimate reason that things were so cheap in Russia back then: no one could be sure which way the wind would blow: toward a viable conversion to a market economy, or toward a civil war between would-be capitalists and ardent counterrevolutionaries.

The ultimate big winners of the second Russian Revolution (to convert to a market economy) were by no means clear.

So we "furriners," in effect, had to *get paid* to take the plunge.

Fortunately, those of us willing to take the risk came out smelling like roses. At least, for a while.

Until the expected and probably inevitable deluge.

A Fair Exchange

> **Mobius Rule No. 44: When getting in at close to Ground Zero *anywhere*, the first thing to look for is: a viable stock exchange.**

When we first set foot in Russia, registration of shares was a problem.

"Who registers the shares?" we would ask, toward the end of nearly every company visit.

"Oh, we do," the company official would smilingly reply.

"But what's our guarantee that if you don't like our face, that you won't just go and erase our name from the registry?"

"Trust us," came the reply. Butter wouldn't melt in their mouth.

Personally, the lack of central share registry made me very nervous.

Back in 1994, the Russian Stock Exchange was so primitive that trading began at around 3:00 P.M., give or take an hour or so, when a BMW would pull up to the stock exchange building in Moscow to unload a few million bucks' worth of cold cash.

Brokers would sit at long tables waiting for workers and ordinary citizens who'd been given share vouchers—which could be exchanged for shares in newly privatized Russian companies—to bring them in by the bushel, and sell them for a song.

At around 6:00 in the evening, the BMW would return to collect the vouchers that the brokers had bought on the cheap from the gullible workers and citizens. As one veteran of the scene recently recalled, "It really was over the counter."

Fast-forward two years.

By 1996, the RTS (Russian Trading System), an electronic link between brokers and dealers established under the aegis of the U.S. Agency for International Development (USAID), was trading an average turnover of $14.2 million daily in 1996.

Which wasn't too bad, considering that the vast majority of Russian stocks were still so thinly traded that we had to wait days, or even weeks, to execute a trade.

A Central National Depository Registry

Still, the Russian stock market had quite a ways to go before it could be considered safe and secure by American standards.

The U.S. SEC strongly suggests (US SEC 17 [f]) that American investors should only invest in foreign securities placed in a depository and registry whose capitalization is above $200 million. Although the SEC later relaxed this rule, only one registry in the country reportedly met that minimum requirement, and it was owned by (guess who?): Oneximbank.

Russia desperately needed to establish a central share registry and depository where all Russian shares could be registered and deposited in a *dematerialized*—that is, paperless—form. In other words, stored as digital data, as opposed to paper stock certificates, which can more easily be manipulated, as in burned, trashed, or lost. For investors to even have to *think* about the possibility of shares not being correctly registered was a powerful turnoff. Why not go elsewhere?

So Boom or Bust?

Now, five years after we purchased our first Russian stock, the Russian Bear Boom had entered its second year in high gear. So the same questions now arose that hover ominously over all runaway booms, at all times, anywhere in the world:
1) Is this the peak before the decline?
2) Or the early stages of a prolonged wild party?

Some Good News

There were, on the macro level, a few things to feel good about. And to give us confidence that despite all our misgivings, some real sustainable growth was taking place that would justify those rising share prices.

After plunging 43 percent since 1989—the year the Berlin Wall came crashing down on their heads and the Iron Curtain opened like a Venetian blind—the Russian domestic economy in 1997 actually reported a marginal gain in GDP of a not exactly staggering .4 percent.

This may not sound like a lot to you, but given the amount of money being made that never got booked, it was mighty impressive. Particularly since the GDP had risen for two consecutive quarters, the first such back-to-back upswings in five years. It could be, for all we knew, the beginning of a Great Expansion. Or just a minor blip on the screen.

There had been some impressive—and little noticed—improvements in the results of that tidal wave of privatization. Despite the fact that the program had been highly corrupt, and much criticized for being riddled with errors, it had accomplished many of its initial goals.

According to recent Russian government statistics (confirmed by the American embassy in Moscow), by year-end 1998, 75 percent of manufacturing enterprises had been privatized, while 85 percent of manufacturing output was being generated by privatized companies.

More than 80 percent of industrial workers were currently employed either in privatized or quasi-privatized firms.

Even more critically, the huge industrial overcapacity that had plagued Russia during the Communist era had been largely squeezed out of the now heavily privatized economy. A burgeoning service industry had been created from scratch, with large and small banks, advertising agencies, small and large shops, thriving on the new opportunities.

Under the old system, the prevailing wisdom had been: "He who doesn't steal from the state is stealing from his own children."

Another common pearl of worker's wisdom: "We pretend to work, and they pretend to pay us."

Taken together, it's not hard to understand why the Soviet system collapsed. In fact, the truly astonishing thing is that it took so long to buckle under its own "internal contradictions."

After just a few years of free-market policies, employee morale had sharply improved.

"It's become more difficult to steal from new owners than to steal from the state," a Russian oil and gas analyst recently told *The Wall Street Journal*. This fellow personally attributed the 1.3 percent rise in oil production in 1998, not very much but still the first increase since 1988, to the fact that: "Management has become more motivated."

In his own industry, newly invigorated, financially incentivized managers were "overhauling oil wells, installing new technology, and investing more wisely."

Thank God a few things were going right.

Cultural Uplift

From the standpoint of cultural values, the country was in the midst of a major turnaround. A once-insular country, which out of ideological distaste had shunned foreign trade, was now a major player in international commerce. Since 1989, the contribution of Russia's massive trade surplus—that's right, trade surplus—to its output had risen by a factor of five.

And Now for Some Bad News

Still, judging by my own personal experience, in too many of these promptly privatized firms, the same old sad socialist sacks were still running the show.

Which meant, more often than not, running their companies straight into the ground.

Five years of high-pressure, full-speed-ahead privatization and economic "shock therapy" had failed to bring fresh blood into the ranks of too many senior managements.

If anything, the prospect of getting rich off privatization had encouraged many an over-the-hill manager to stay put, hoping to cash in his chips before hitting the dacha. As a result, threatened and paranoid managers tended to adopt, in desperation, a passive survival mentality.

This lose-lose strategy involved:

1) lowering output,
2) cutting employment and wages, and
3) running up massive arrears to suppliers and the federal budget.

Something, sooner or later, would have to give.

The Second Tier

At the crack of dawn on the same morning that the privatization minister of St. Petersburg was shot dead in the street, we hightailed it to Nizhniy Novgorod—the former home base of then–Deputy

Prime Minister Boris Nemtsov, and a reputed hotbed of reformist zeal.

We'd done very well, thank you, by our basket of blue chip
Russian stocks. But the ones we owned were getting expensive.

Our strategy in Russia in the second year of its boom was the
same one that I employ during all booms anywhere and everywhere: move down the list from the big, large-cap stocks, which
have gotten expensive, and look into the second-tier, smaller-cap
stocks.

> **Mobius Rule No. 45:** Take a good, hard look at your
> portfolio. Find all the stocks that have gone up 100
> percent or more in one year or less, where the
> earnings have not risen as much and the five-year
> projection is not good. And consider dumping them.

What? Am I nuts?

Why sell stocks that are your crown jewels?

Because your "crown jewel stocks" can be your most dangerous stocks.

Sure, you feel loyal to them because they've done well by you,
and you by them. But watch out. They can be deadly.

Let's take a quick look at our situation.

Here we were, the proud owners of a splendid collection of
Russian blue chips, nearly every one of which had gone right through
the roof. Not altogether surprising, in a market that had tripled in
value in a mere eighteen months. We had a good chunk of:

1) The oil giant Lukoil (up 184 percent in one year).

2) Vimpelcom, Russia's number two cellular phone company
(up 154 percent).

3) Trade House G.U.M. (up 132 percent in one year), the
wonderful old department store in Moscow housed in a dramatic location right off Red Square.

4) Rostelekom, the huge phone monopoly, and St. Petersburg
City Telephone Network, two of the brightest telecom investments available, both well up in the triple digits in the past year.

So we'd hit all the sectors, and picked up the cream of the crop.

I should have been happy, proud as punch.

Instead, I was running scared.

> **Mobius Rule No. 46: You don't maintain high performance by holding on to old blue chips that are no longer blue.**

> **Mobius Rule No. 47: Find the next batch of blue chips *before* they turn blue.**

The fine, seasoned stocks in our portfolio weren't priceless oils, guaranteed to appreciate forever. They were more like prime steaks, capable of going bad if you held on to them for too long.

Small Is Not Always Beautiful

As I advised our Russia Fund shareholders after our second successful year in operation: "It's difficult to imagine just how *big* Russia is. If you fly eastward from Moscow, it takes nine hours to reach Vladivostok, on Russia's Pacific coast."

Like the U.S., Brazil, and China, Russia's *size* is intrinsic to its *character.*

Even after being shorn of many of its Soviet-era and tsarist imperial possessions (and pretensions), Russia is still the largest country on earth, as measured by land mass. It covers eleven time zones, stretches nearly halfway across the globe, and contains just about every conceivable form of landscape on earth, from snowy mountains to hot sandy deserts, from lush lowlands to dry grasslands, from endless tracts of tundra to lush forests.

Its natural resources are staggering:

1) It's the world's largest producer of palladium, accounting for around 70 percent of the world supply.

2) The second largest producer of platinum after South Africa.

3) The second largest producer of diamonds after South Africa.

4) One of the largest producers of nickel, gold, oil, and natural gas in the world.

On the upside, a big country is a place where companies can grow to fit the landscape. Where the maximum domestic markets are huge, companies don't have to rely so much on export-driven strategies to succeed. They don't have to rely on a global strategy to succeed. If they can become category killers in their own country, they're halfway there. And having conquered their own territory (assuming that it's big and diversified enough), moving on to the rest of the world doesn't seem like such a quantum leap.

On the downside, large countries' problems are often tailored to their size. They're not nimble. They're not quick. Unlike a small car, or a small country, a big market can't easily turn, or be turned around, on a dime.

> Mobius Rule No. 48: In a big country, it takes time for new ideas to be absorbed to the farthest corners, to congeal and permeate the cultural permafrost.

Big ideas, for example, like competition.

Like other big countries before it—China, most strikingly—for centuries Russia regarded itself as the center of the known universe. Such insular attitudes breed contempt, born out of fear, toward the rest of the world. Insular attitudes are recipes for stagnation. The only way to shake them up is through culture-contact shock treatment: trade, war, or conquest.

Russia's Pacific Rim

We experienced a vivid example of this hard-core cultural schiz-ophrenia during one of our first swings through the country, when we spent a few days scoping out Vladivostok, an industrial port city on the Sea of Japan.

This decaying metropolis lies about as far from Moscow—cul-turally as well as physically—as Moscow lies from New York. Though the region had clearly benefited from its proximity to the Pacific Rim (as we drove through the city, I saw construction sites covered with logos of developers from South Korea and other Asian countries), it was also a prime example of the tragic Soviet propensity to turn port cities and trading centers into in-dustrial nightmares, often for purely political reasons.

Like Tallinn, and even like St. Petersburg, Vladivostok still had many more factories than it should ever have been asked to support, especially for what was always at heart a port town.

As such, it suffered from industrial overcapacity, the bane of the bloated Soviet system. As we tooled around town, dropping in on receptive and unreceptive managements in turn, we found ourselves sometimes treated like invaders from, if not outer space, at least the outer limits, and at other times, like long-lost cousins bearing gifts from rich and exotic lands.

A Haven for the Culturally Confused

At an air transport company whose business had fallen off 40 percent during the previous year, we were greeted with a scowl by a thick-eyebrowed, heavyset managing director, who promptly put me at ease by asking: "Are your capitalist plans to destroy the Russian economy proceeding on schedule?"

It was a question which, quite frankly, I wasn't prepared to answer with anything more than a stutter.

In this man's mind's eye, we were still the enemy, still fighting the Cold War, except by more covert means. Were we CIA agents? I'd have bet my boots he thought so. Our new weapons were financial instruments, and our stated intentions—to invest and share the benefits with them—were merely cover for our true goal: the undermining of the great, proud Russian state and its people.

You run into this attitude, by the way, all over the former Third World. It's not too surprising for the poor to envy the rich. But what's striking in Russia is how this defensive attitude has managed to survive in a country that was, until recently, one of the greatest military and industrial powers on earth—hardly your traditional "Third World" backwater.

Watch out whenever these xenophobic attitudes crop up, whether they're openly expressed in meetings, or more covertly expressed in thinly veiled hostility.

Mobius Rule No. 49: A bad attitude is a major red flag. It's meant to turn you off. Let it.

This guy didn't even pretend to listen to my attempt to explain that we weren't spies out to wreck the vestiges of his crumbling empire. Instead, after a few grunts of incomprehension, he stood up and brusquely refused to answer any more questions about the operation of his company, or its clearly desperate financial condition. With a peremptory wave of his hand, he signaled the end of our meeting.

He didn't realize that he needed us more than we needed him. But to have drawn any general conclusions from his behavior would have been dead wrong. Did his attitude suggest that Vladivostok was, as a rule, hostile to foreign investment, being so far from Moscow? Well, no.

The TV Producer

The very next day, we visited a company that was similarly struggling, with less than 10 percent of its potential capacity being utilized. A producer of radio and TV components, just three years before it had been struggling to keep up with orders, because it had enjoyed a solid share of the Russian domestic market.

But no longer. Nowadays, with fierce competition from cheaper Asian imports (many originating in countries located not far from Vladivostok by plane) this company's electronics business was distinctly endangered.

But the electronic component manufacturer's attitude was 180 degrees the reverse of the scowling, paranoid air transport chief.

The company had established ties with U.S., South Korean, and European firms, and although these alliances had not produced much business—let alone hard cash—the managing director radiated hope, optimism, and confidence.

He was excited, he said, about a contract he hoped to sign soon with a South Korean company that might increase production by 50 percent. His business, on objective terms, had not been nearly as hard hit by the conversion to market realities as the air transport company, which hardly had to face up to foreign competition at all.

Because his business was more fundamentally linked to the global economy, the electronic components manufacturer had been forced to engage with the new global realities. *Objectively*, in some ways, he was worse off than his neighbor the local air transport company.

But *subjectively*, he was miles ahead of the curve.

Another, equally important lesson to be learned from not so random encounters is:

> **Mobius Rule No. 50: A strictly "objective" or technical analysis of a company's situation can be misleading. A visit on the ground can make the difference.**

Back to the Map

Before landing at Nizhniy Novgorod, on the Volga River east of Moscow—known as Gorky during the Soviet era—let's take another quick look at that map again. The Volga is the longest river in Europe, a slow-moving, wide, easily navigable stream that made Nizhniy a lively port city as far back as the thirteenth century.

By the turn of the nineteenth century, Nizhniy was already a bustling industrial center, and the site of an annual international trade fair housed in a cluster of sprawling, ornate brick buildings hugging the riverbank that have only recently been restored. Under the Soviets, the city was closed to foreigners, renamed Gorky after the Russian writer Maxim Gorky (who had the good sense to disapprove of such Stalinist silliness), and trans-formed into a "secret strategic city" known primarily for its weapons factories.

Quickly to become Russia's third largest urban area after Moscow and St. Petersburg, Gorky became more widely known in the West as the cultural backwater to which the dissident physicist Andrei Sakharov was exiled until 1986, when he was freed from this form of house arrest under pres-sure from Western powers. In 1990, the city was reopened to foreigners, the International Trade Fair was revived, and the old name was restored. In Russian, it means "Lower New City."

The most famous local boy to have made good is Boris Nemtsov, the telegenic, energetic young first deputy prime min-ister installed by Yeltsin as his right-hand man—with the em-battled Anatoly Chubais on his left—to aid in the cause of reform. During his tenure as governor of the local *oblast* (province), Nemtsov had fervently sown the seeds of reform in his home region with such distinction that Yeltsin had plucked him from provincial obscurity and installed him in the highest corridors at the Kremlin.

We'd drawn a red line on our map around Nizhniy Novgorod because we had it on good authority that there were plenty of people in high places here who spoke our language—the lan-guage of foreign investment. People who understood that we might be coming to *help*, not to hurt them.

The town had always been known as a showcase of ideologi-cal transformation: under the Soviets, it was supposed to provide an inspiring civic lesson concerning the virtues and unlimited potential of "The New Soviet Man." Now, under the capitalist regime, it was once again being touted as a capitalist showcase, as indeed it had been back in the late nineteenth century, before the arrival of communism.

Our first stop was the kremlin. Not Moscow's Kremlin, mind you, but a smaller, spartan version on a hill high above the old river town. In Russian, *kremlin* simply means "fort." Nizhniy's gray, gloomy kremlin sat high on a grassy, forested hill overlooking the broad, slow-moving Volga. Much as we admired its stolid architecture—thick stone walls dating back to the sixteenth century, and its eleven ramparted masonry towers peering down into an open green central courtyard—we didn't tarry long before calling on the local offices of the administration of the *oblast*, a Russian term meaning roughly "state" or "province."

In the stark, very large office of Andrew Zotikov, chairman of the Regional Promotional Agency, founded by Boris Nemtsov himself to function as an intermediary between foreign investors and local factories, we encountered a delegation of gray-suited, middle-aged men who did not, to our vast relief, in any way resemble Stalinist thugs.

Chairman Zotikov was a vigorous-looking man just beginning to gray at the temples, who wore the look of someone with a passion for getting things done. He repeatedly massaged an unlit cigarette in his right palm, as if preparing to light it. But he never lit it, perhaps out of politeness to his foreign visitors, who don't tend to be quite so oblivious to thick clouds of billowing cigarette smoke as the average Russian, who seems to thrive in a nicotine haze.

In fluid English, Mr. Zotikov explained that his nimble little regional agency had been keeping its hand in industry, as an active investment partner in a number of local companies. His agency had, for example, been pushing a project to produce buses. The buses were intended to be not only a potentially profitable product for the company that made them, but a boon to the whole region, which was in dire need of a more modern mass-transit system.

Public–Private Partnerships

As I listened, I was struck by the idea that a municipal or regional government would have had the guts to have gotten so involved with jump-starting a local business, right down to the dreary details. It had apparently:

1) Prescribed and/or designed the product, and

2) Was expecting this product to be sold nationally if not worldwide, while

3) Meeting the infrastructure needs of the region.

Here was an emergent form of capitalism that combined some aspects of traditional capitalism and aspects of socialism. Reminiscent of the Japanese MITI (Ministry of Trade and Industry)—the government agency that oversees the Japanese industrial system—and of other public-private partnerships I've seen in Brazil, the government here was taking a strong lead in guiding and managing private investment.

This was hardly Adam Smith's invisible hand, but that didn't mean it was bullheaded. Though American-style capitalism is certainly all the rage, that doesn't mean that regional variants might not be successful models for some countries to follow. In the U.S., free-marketeers have generally dismissed the idea of industrial policy as a fantasy cooked up by economists who might otherwise find themselves out of a job. But in other emerging countries, such as Korea or Taiwan, where the culture itself is more about consensus decision-making than rugged corporate individualism, industrial policies have worked wonders to stimulate local investment and jump-start local industries. In today's more zealously free-market era, such partnerships are widely falling out of favor.

"Our goal," Zotikov continued amiably, "is to attract foreign portfolio investment to our second- and third-tier industrial companies—companies that have not yet taken an active role in the stock market, but might be ready to do so, if properly prepared."

Though it has been highly touted as a hotbed of reformist zeal, the city of Boris Nemtsov and his protégé Sergei Kiriyenko—soon to be nominated prime minister by Boris Yeltsin—had its problems, among them the standard-issue post-Soviet detritus of idle weapons factories, strapped pensioners, and once-proud, now resentful workers.

Corporate Culture

"If they were properly prepared."

Hearing that phrase made me think back to a recent lunch in Vilnius, the capital of Lithuania, with the young and very smart finance minister of that country. When commenting upon the Russian privatization program, he'd said, shaking his head: "They took those companies private, with no preparation whatsoever."

He certainly had a point. During the peak of the program in 1993, an average of twenty small and large firms were privatized *every two weeks,* setting a pace that had even the most adrenaline-rich foreign investors gasping for relief.

This was far and away the largest privatization program ever attempted (only to be outstripped, in a couple of years' time, by a Chinese plan to privatize even more companies, although the details are still being worked out).

That was, I was shortly to learn, simply the Russian way.

Russians are born revolutionaries.

They are impulsive by nature. But as I remarked to the Lithuanian finance minister, "They're smart impulsive, not dumb impulsive."

That's why I felt they were worth betting on.

For all the quantitative economic analysis and modeling and technical issues that could be brought to bear on the problem, the real reason that I and so many other investors were willing to venture so much in Russia was an intuitive assessment of:

Cultural characteristics.

Survival Instinct

Shortly after setting up our Russia Fund, I had a brief conversation with one of the chief executive officers of a company called

Iridium, an American company backed by Motorola and a few other electronics giants, which is presently sending hundreds of tiny satellites into orbit for communications purposes. At the time, Iridium had twenty-five satellites in space already, and were hungry to launch more, because the demand for satellite transponder space was rapidly outstripping supply.

So there they were down at Cape Canaveral, waiting for an American crew to launch a couple of satellites. And those cautious Americans kept aborting the launches, on the grounds of prudence and caution. They'd say the weather's not right, the sunspots were bad, the cloud cover was too thick, whatever came into their heads to take a wait-and-see attitude.

The old can-do American culture that won the West and two world wars has since suffered from an obsession with legal liability and risk-aversion.

In the meantime, while the Americans dallied and dawdled, a rival Russian crew launched a whole raft of satellites into orbit. "The hell with the weather, let's get those tin cans up there," they'd say. And when they heard that the Americans had scratched a launch, they'd laugh. "Those Americans are wimps."

Of course, if you're thinking of hitching a ride on a Russian space station versus an American one, I'd probably pick the American, for its safety record.

This impulsive element in the Russian character stems, I believe, from a culture steeped in the ethic of human survival. They live in a harsh environment, and have lived through a harsh history: invaded by Napoleon, invaded by Germany, oppressed by the tsars, murdered by Stalin, put to sleep by Brezhnev, extorted by the Mafia. That was how they were able to sustain such incredible losses during World War I and keep fighting—until the Germans hatched the ingenious plan to send Lenin into Russia on a closed train, to sap their will to win.

Mobius Rule No. 51: When investing in any country, it's important to assess its cultural characteristics.

They can be simplifications and generalizations. I wouldn't buy stock solely on such subjective analysis. In the case of Russia, however, reflecting on these psychological and cultural issues helped give me the confidence to invest, when I most needed it. And the confidence to pull back and keep a third of our holdings in cash, when I saw that things were not going ahead according to plan.

The Car Company

In 1941, after repeated bombing and shelling by Nazi invaders, the nine-year-old automotive works in Gorky lay shattered beyond recognition. But within a year after VE Day, in late 1945, the sprawling complex was producing a splendid new car popularly known as the Pobeda, which meant: "Victory."

In 1953 the Pobeda's successor, the Volga, named after the river, rolled off the assembly line. It quickly became the motorized transportation of the mid-level Soviet minister, appealing to those ranked not quite high enough to rate a plush ZIL. In 1959, Soviet premier Nikita Khrushchev, on an official visit to the U.S., was offended when a group of American farmers offered to produce enough food to feed the Soviet Union.

"And in return, we'll send you cars," Khrushchev replied, no doubt to save face.

Not entirely sure whether this was merely a quip or a nonnegotiable directive from above, one of Khrushchev's aides promptly dispatched a note to Gorky. For a time, rumors were flying that a special fleet of Volgas was awaiting shipment to the U.S. presumably to compete with the products of Detroit's Big Three.

That, of course, never happened. But the quality of the original Volga sedan was good enough for the idea not to have been dismissed out of hand. The Volga sold well in Europe, running up against Volvo and even Mercedes-Benz. As one proud Russian owner of a Volga 21 recently wrote, "The gear change consists of two parallel levers on the steering column, so finely balanced that I can shift gears with my index finger without taking my hand from the wheel."

Clearly, this was a car any Russian could be proud of. At a price roughly equivalent to ten times the average manager's salary, a Volga was a status symbol in the closed Soviet market. But during the sleepy years of *zastoi*—Russian for "stagnation"—after Nikita Khrushchev was replaced by the sleepwalking Leonid Brezhnev, the sad saga of the "brand-new" Volga 24 mirrored the more widespread decline in the larger Soviet system.

While the spiffy Volga 21 took just three years to move from design to production, the Volga 24 took eight years from drawing board to open road. As one Russian writer, Ivan Paderin (chairman of the Volga 21 Owners Club in Moscow), sadly noted, "It hardly needs saying just how outdated the Volga 24 was by the time it entered production."

By the time we reached the plant where the Volgas were made, the huge sprawling place had clearly run out of gas. And in the sorry saga of this company—and its more recent revival—could be seen a model of the Soviet experience, from triumph to tragedy to absurdity.

Nevertheless, a half century after the plant's construction in 1932 (originally completed according to blueprints provided by that virulent anti-Communist, Henry Ford), the company employed over a quarter of a million workers, who enjoyed extensive social services, including free housing, 120 kindergartens, 10,000 cattle at a company-owned ranch—which provided workers with food at subsidized prices. It owned a sanatorium in Sochi, a popular resort on the Black Sea, and an 1,100-bed first-rate medical hospital. Life was good in the worker's paradise, because no one felt the weight of this vast social burden on their own shoulders.

There was, in fact, only one problem: the place was gradually sinking into quicksand.

Efficiency was nonexistent. Waste was rampant. Production costs were so high that no one had any real sense of how to calculate them. Quality was suffering. Steadily, the once-proud Volga sedan was losing its once-profitable export markets. While the West innovated, the Russian automotive industry stood still, mired in the triumphs of a Stalinist past.

A New Leaf

But there were a few signs of new hope in the air. Now, with Russians used to paying high prices for shoddy cars, there was ample room for improvement. The market, for one, was growing by leaps and bounds: during the first six months of 1997, car production in Russia had shot up 13 percent higher than during the same period of the previous year.

This stood to be the best year for the Russian car industry since the collapse of Communism. Still, even *The Economist,* which had described the Russian car industry as "overmanned, undercapitalized, antiquated, and criminalized," had characterized this company, the country's second-ranking carmaker, as "the only Russian auto company that could be regarded as well managed, by Western standards."

Which was more than could be said for Russia's largest car manufacturer, which despite the fact that it currently accounted for 70 percent of production and 60 percent of domestic sales was widely considered "too intractable a mess for saving in anything like its present form." Which quite obviously meant that no matter how many cars it made, it was sinking deeper into the quicksand.

Site Inspection

After visiting the carmaker we moved on to another Soviet dinosaur, a steel pipe manufacturer.

As our dark sedan (a Vol*vo,* not a Vol*ga*) pulled up to the front gates, we were waved on by a brace of uniformed security guards in full battle dress, wielding assault weapons, a not-uncommon site in Russian industrial installations during these turbulent times. The place was the size of a small city, with acre upon acre of dusty, grimy buildings that looked as if they hadn't been cleaned, much less remodeled, since 1932.

We trooped up dozens of dusty, dirty, linoleum-lined stairs to the third floor of the executive office building, where after hitting a broad landing paneled in vinyl wood-look wallpaper, we were escorted down a long, dingy hallway to the huge office of the finance director.

It was decorated in masculine Soviet style, simultaneously austere and plush, grand in scale, but tattered and frayed around the edges. There was a vast laminate conference table, black vinyl chairs, cheap plastic fake-wood paneling, and thick wall-to-wall carpeting that had seen better decades. And yes, come to think of it, it was bright Communist red.

The finance director handed out cards emblazoned with the symbol of a rampant red deer which identified him in English as a "director on economics [sic]" and a "corresponding member of RAEN," which I assumed was the Russian society of economics. He was also, according to the same card, an "assistant professor of economic science."

But to me, with his dark heavy jowls and distinctively Slavic thick beetle brows, he looked a little like Leonid Brezhnev. He was of the heavyset type, and wore a fat flashy gold watch and the requisite rumpled gray suit. His impassive demeanor was that of the stock Soviet heavy in Hollywood films. Heroic wooden plaques lined the walls of his office, which featured bronze bas-reliefs of heavy cars and trucks. This was evidently one of the last bastions of heavy industry, Soviet-style.

What struck me first about our immediate environment was how cocoon-like it seemed. Whatever windows might have been present were so shrouded in thick drapes as to shut out all natural light, muffling most sounds from the world beyond. Like so many executive offices in Russia this office had an entrance with double doors, both padded.

The vast factory that stretched out for miles and miles beyond these thick walls seemed like an abstraction, a fantasy, a mirage. The only concrete connection to the outside world was the dinning sound of sheet metal being stamped, from far, far away, at a distinct remove from our more abstract discussion. It occurred to me that we were here to talk about money, not production, and that in their scheme of things, the connection between the two remained rather remote.

His first question for us was fairly straightforward, under the circumstances.

"I wonder," he wondered, "if you were to purchase a block of shares directly from the company, would you be interested in making some sort of arrangement that would require you to hold shares for a certain period of time?"

I wasn't quite sure what he was driving at, but I took a wild stab at hitting this curveball.

"The nature of our investment would be longer-term than the typical investment, because we look at a five-year time frame. But our rules would not allow us to *guarantee* that we would hold shares for a set period of time, because we have to keep our instruments liquid."

Why, I was curious, did he care so much how long we held our shares? As long as we bought and sold them in the secondary-share market, it shouldn't affect his position in the slightest. Unless, of course, he and his fellow managers were facing a creeping takeover. If so, they would need allies who would agree to hold shares in abeyance, or perhaps vote with them if push came to shove, as a way of preventing their possible ouster.

"To what extent," he kept pressing, looking for some sort of commitment from us, "would you be willing to work with management, assuming that we would assist you in acquiring a large block of shares?"

In Russia, buying shares involves considerably more than picking up the phone and calling a broker and placing a buy order.

In Russia, the *real* trick can be getting your hands on the shares themselves.

Getting shares often means rooting them out of dark corners where various people have stashed them, waiting for the right opportunity to cash out. It means, sometimes, going out to lunch with someone who, after the first course, casually mentions that he happens to have a few thousand, or even a few million, shares, in his back pocket.

Of course, once you get your hands on the shares you're looking for, all too often that's when the real fun begins. In our case, since we need to buy big blocks in order for the investment to be worth our while, we frequently buy direct from management, or through private deals conducted off the stock exchange.

What he was proposing, vague as it sounded, was his help in buying a large block of shares, in exchange for "reaching an understanding—formal or informal" that we would not flip them immediately. But why? I had to find out why, before agreeing to anything.

Trying to steer him off his main target, I asked him if the company was considering issuing any new shares. He dismissed the issue of new issues with a wave of his huge hand.

"I would prefer"—he managed to both growl and scowl at the same time—"to discuss that at a later time. Right now, I would prefer to discuss whether such an arrangement could be worked out, in principle."

He was like a dog with a bone.

"Well, in principle," I repeated, "we are limited in the amount of illiquid shares we can purchase." By illiquid, in this case, I meant shares that, for whatever reason, we couldn't sell at the drop of a hat. We don't like to get in unless we can get out—at a moment's notice.

> **Mobius Rule No. 52: In case of fire, maintaining a viable exit strategy is critical to not getting burned.**

To my reply, the finance director smoothly replied: "I will tell you how we might make them liquid. We are currently working with an underwriter interested in participating with us in an ADR program. This is basically how we see the development of a new, more liquid market for our shares.

"I think," he mused, "that we can find a lot of common ground in working on a secondary issue for the shares. If a prestigious investor were to participate, we think that this would boost our image."

Now I thought I knew what the big man was driving at.

We call this being a "rabbit." If a company can get me to pay a certain price for a big block of shares, that serves to legitimize that price, particularly since I have a well-deserved reputation as a value investor, who likes nothing less than to overpay for a share of stock, if I can help it.

He roughly estimated that this issue of new shares should total about $100 million. This was around one third of the company's market cap, which currently stood at $350 million and change.

"We could probably think about taking up to half of that," I said quietly.

His eyes did not exactly bug out, but I could tell by the elaborate casualness of his response—a silent shrug—that the scope of our purchasing power had impressed him.

Having put out the preliminary feelers, he now started talking turkey.

"Par value is 1,000 rubles," he said. "The market price is now $90 per share. We can arrange for you to acquire shares at a deep discount, possibly as much as 20 percent from market price. But if you want the assistance of the administration in buying a large block of shares, we must be talking about a block on the order of at least $10 to $20 million."

"That would be no problem," I said. "Our rules would permit us to buy up to 10 percent of the company."

"If you were to purchase up to 10 percent of the company"— the financial director stood his ground—"we would be concerned that if you sold your stock in the market all at one time, that could have a negative effect on the market."

Oh, that again.

"Or a positive effect," I corrected him. "It all depends on the price."

But he was more concerned with power than price.

"This is true," he conceded. "But only as long as you are operating in tandem with the company. If each party is acting only out of its own self-interest, it is possible for each party to undermine each other. We are interested in working with shareholders who are willing to combine their own self-interest with that of the company."

Translation: we are only interested in shareholders willing to vote with management on all outstanding issues.

What he wanted was for us to promise him that if we chose to sell we'd let him know about it first, and let him be the first buyer of choice.

Making Money

We moved on to the more vexing question of whether the company was making any money. Our man stoutly maintained that his profits were up one and a half times that of the previous year. We'd been given what we assumed were accurate figures, contained in a recent press release, stating that the company had turned a profit of $123 million so far that year, with a net profit forecast of $175 million. In the Russian context, that was impressive.

With big orders for pipes from foreign financial oil companies, things were clearly looking up. Boris Nemtsov, the hometown boy made good, had certainly (and we hoped not falsely) raised the demoralized company's hopes by issuing a directive to the government that oil companies should no longer purchase foreign pipes—it was bad for the Russian image—and should instead buy local. And by local, he meant his hometown. It was, of course, no coincidence that the pipes were made in his hometown. Unfortunately, though this played well in local media markets, there was no sign, as yet, that many government ministers were taking his threat very seriously.

It was curious, I thought, that in an officially stagnant economy, the market for steel pipes was doubling. We understood from reliable sources that the Russian market would be buying more than three times the previous year's level. Of course, this was just another nail in the official statistics' coffin. The existence of such a strong and growing shadow economy made corporate P&L statements and assessment of book value a case of groping in the dark.

Awesome Social Burden

"How about social costs?" I wondered, which was of course the real fly in the ointment. "How are you progressing on turning these social operations into profitable enterprises?" I was thinking about that spa on the shores of the Black Sea. Why not make that a moneymaking resort?

The groan that he let out sounded almost stagy, until I realized that it came direct from that massive gut.

"Our social costs are *huge,*" he moaned. "Did you notice all those housing projects along the road to the airport?"

Indeed, I had, and drearier examples of the poverty of public housing I'd rarely laid eyes on.

"Well," he said sadly, "on those houses alone we spent $6 million last year in upkeep, and took in practically nothing. Last year, if all of our housing for the workers had been transferred to the city, we would have paid 160 million rubles less in housing costs. Which would have freed up $25 million in working capital.

"This social sphere is a very serious problem, full of many paradoxes . . ." he sadly concluded, before brightening up: "It will be resolved"—he smiled hopefully—"by the end of the century."

Company Assessment

Despite its huge problems, despite its huge social burden, despite a management that seemed to be, to put it mildly, not entirely in tune with the latest management trends, my gut told me that this was one to keep an eye out for.

It just might be the Russian equivalent of U.S. Steel before its revival, before the turnaround, before the subsequent soaring of stock price.

On the upside, Russia enjoyed very low production costs in some key areas:

1) Zero or close to zero environmental costs.
2) Low energy input costs, although those have gone up slightly.
3) Low labor costs, but productivity a big question mark.

With all three economic inputs below world levels, they should have been producing pipes at a level competitive with Japanese imports.

And now the downside: competition.

Pipes from Japan were selling for half the price. Meanwhile pipes from Mexico and Argentina were entering the world market at lower prices. How was the Russian manufacturer going to compete with them? Boris Nemtsov was going to have to make his government ministers force the oil companies to buy a lot more for the domestic market to make up the difference.

So the bottom line was that while the company should have been turning out the cheapest pipes in the world and storming the developing markets, or at least holding on to their own market share and not losing it to cheap Asian imports, precisely the opposite was happening. Though they were churning out more pipes, they were losing market share, because their prices were too high. The reasons:

1) High social costs.

2) Unrealistic expectations as to how much margin they should make on each car.

To put the worst possible face on it, you had to own up to the possibility that on each meter of pipe it made, the place was actually losing money. The reasons for this would have been any number of gross inefficiencies, out of which the largest looming was probably the social burden.

The Money Tree

By the bye, did you happen to notice that these Russian managers have an insatiable appetite for money? Particularly for capital improvements? The way these guys talk, it reminds me of Senator Everett Dirksen, who said, "A billion here, a billion there, and pretty soon you're talking about real money." According to our source, his company was currently spending $100 million out of their own cash flow each year on "its own development."

Where was all that money going? I didn't know, and neither, I suspected, did he. It was entirely possible, given the sorry state of Russian accounting, that nobody knew, or for that matter, cared. I wouldn't have minded so much if he'd said that that $100 million was going to pension off redundant workers. Or even for new equipment or job training. But while they were very focused on how to take the money in, their plans grew a lot more starry-eyed when it came to detailed plans to put the money to work to make money.

My gut feeling was that these guys were still thinking in terms of the budget from Gosplan—the old Soviet central planning agency in Moscow. Now, instead of Gosplan, and the central financial teat in Moscow, these guys thought they had us deep-pocketed foreign investors to take up the slack. But if in the early stages of the market run-up, foreign investors were happy just to see prices soar on rising expectations, soon we were all going to be looking for real earnings, and real earnings reports, audited according to U.S. GAAP.

It wasn't always going to be that sad old Marxist line: "To each according to his needs, to each according to his ability."

Share Dilution

As it turned out, there was a new issue of shares, but we later learned, after our meeting, that at the previous year's shareholder meeting management had secured for itself the right to issue new shares without further approval of existing shareholders.

Though management assured us repeatedly that they would never issue new shares in any way that would be unfair to existing shareholders, we didn't like the sound of that. Why, if they had no such intention, had they explicitly granted themselves such a right by amending the company charter?

Mobius Rule No. 53: When scrutinizing a company as a potential investment, carefully inspect the company by-laws for the prospect of *share dilution*—one of the easiest moves in the age-old game of "fleecing the minority shareholders."

Arkhangelsk

From Nizhniy, we flew far north toward the Arctic Circle, to the land of the long white summer nights. Arkhangelsk is near where the Soviets based their nuclear submarines for long dives under the polar ice cap.

The tidy town had originally been founded in 1574 by Ivan the Terrible, who hoped to make contact with British traders searching for a northern access route to China. But today, it's a dreary cluster of soiled white-tiled government buildings—set off by a tall banal tower—arranged around a "town green" that looks like a weed-strewn, abandoned lot.

The only decoration in this great town square is a monumental statue of Lenin which with its sweeping white marble coat and face pointedly staring into the future—a future that would make the old boy roll in his mausoleum today—resembled the curving prow of one of those famous Russian ice-cutter ships, blasting through an icy arctic wind.

Dostoyevskian Despair

Our first meeting was with the director general of a company that produced navigation equipment, formerly for the Russian navy.

Now, with swords being turned into plowshares, their main market was commercial fishing boats. Since the company had for years relied on the military to keep it in operation, with the defense industry practically in mothballs, they were struggling to stay afloat.

"Have you been spending much time looking for new customers lately?" I innocently asked the heavyset, thick-jowled director general, who smoked like a chimney.

He shot me a look of complete incomprehension I'll never forget. We might have been able to ascribe our failure of communication to a language problem, except that we were both using interpreters. We not only didn't speak the same language, our larger frames of reference were out of sync.

"Why would we do that?" he asked, in total shock, as if I'd asked him when he stopped beating his wife. The meeting suddenly turned edgy and hostile. "That would be extremely expensive," he curtly continued, "not to mention a complete waste of time."

Okay, okay, I nearly said—sorry I asked. And I'd meant it almost as a pleasantry.

The icy contempt with which he delivered this bromide was, of course, defensive in the extreme. His aide, an older woman, frostily informed me, as if I needed to be told, like a child: "The only goal of financial companies is to work in order to get rich."

Smiling grimly through clenched teeth, I agreed that that was indeed our goal, but that we hoped by so doing to enrich not only ourselves, but our investors, as well as the companies that we invested in.

She continued to scowl, while her boss informed us that he needed around $4 million right away to restructure his plant, purchase new equipment, and develop new products. I think he expected me to write him a check for the full amount right then and there. When I didn't hand over the money, as requested, his aide once again felt compelled to put in her steely two cents.

"Financial companies," she said harshly, as if speaking from direct experience, "do not invest anything in enterprises, but are only opportunistic companies which get rich in murky waters and then disappear."

I think the mixed metaphors were all part of her plan to undermine my confidence.

But then something interesting happened.

Five minutes later, in response to an innocuous question, she practically broke down in tears before delivering the ultimate socialist confession: "Companies like us cannot do anything by ourselves," she said, all that hostility suddenly displaced by profound despair. "And the state does not help us. We are so helpless," she said. "We cannot take care of ourselves when we are hurt."

Much as I took umbrage at their hostility, this confession about their new role was truly pathetic, in the sense of engendering pity.

Endeavoring to help—I would practically have bought stock

on the spot—I wondered whether the respected financial director might be able to provide us with some additional financial information.

Now her demeanor turned frosty again.

"But we have supplied references!" she protested.

"In order to divulge additional information," her boss grimly intervened, as if to call off my attack, "I will need to ask our board of directors, at least ten days in advance of their meeting."

It was obvious that the director general, who looked more like a military general than a corporate director, was not the world's greatest expert on financial minutiae. All he knew was that he needed money, and that we should give it to him, if we were not criminals or capitalist spies.

I asked if they'd made any recent attempts to seek out new investment.

The answer, when it came, was curt and cool: "Nyet."

The basic problem, quite clearly, was that they had grown so used to responding to directives from above that they had not even the glimmering of initiative.

The grand old days of Gosplan were over.

Frankly, I had a feeling they weren't going to make it.

Siberia

"Oh damn!"

I don't often resort to such vulgar expletives, but as our car pulled up in front of the looming bulk of the Octyabrskaya Hotel, I couldn't help but recall with a shudder of horror our last night in Krasnoyarsk: a sleepless ordeal spent on a narrow, thin mattress of very old ticking, in a tiny room without a working phone, with no fax machine in the lobby and indifferent food, and worst of all, they didn't take credit cards, so we had to pay them in cash: rubles, not dollars. Fortunately, exchange services were available at reasonable rates right in the bank branch in the lobby, and at all hours!

By the way, you run into that name Octyabrskaya all over

Russia: it celebrates the October Revolution, when the Bolsheviks came to power back in 1917.

When you see it still on a marquee, you can bet that it's a hotbed of counterrevolutionary (that is, *counter* to the capitalist counterrevolution) zeal. Steer clear.

It was, on the other hand, impolite to complain too bitterly about what were basic Intourist conditions in the Soviet Union pre-glasnost, particularly since this was, after all, Siberia—even in summer, always cool and crisp. In the gulags, the prisoners wore thin cotton uniforms, even in winter, and they could see their breath in their log bunkhouses.

Large pieces of this section of the country had been, over the centuries, constructed with slave penal labor: long before the Stalinist holocaust, during the time of the tsars. Elaborately carved wooden buildings still line the back streets of Krasnoyarsk, a surprisingly pleasant-looking city located on the banks of the Yenisey River, surrounded by endless acres of *taiga* (pine forest) climbing up the lovely Sayan Mountains.

Krasnoyarsk had been a remote rural area until the Soviets, with their penchant for industrializing everything, turned it into not only a major center for defense industry, but a consumer manufacturing center as well.

Now the region—which extends over an area equivalent to that stretching from North Dakota to Texas—turns out one third of the country's aluminum, and almost a quarter of its refrigerators, but also tons of tires, silk fabric, and other white goods.

Under the old system, the Krasnoyarsk region was a center for secret defense industries.

Kras-26 and Kras-45 were underground nuclear cities connected by tunnels rumored to be longer than the total track length of the Moscow Metro.

Today, it is the site of one of the larger regional stock exchanges in Russia.

Other defense plants in and around Krasnoyarsk produced nuclear missiles, solid rocket fuel, space and ground satellite communications equipment, and a number of other high-tech items for the now-defunct Soviet system.

Now the old Kras-45 secret nuclear city has been converted to a plant churning out BASF magnetic tape cartridges for audio and video equipment.

Kras-26 makes Samsung TVs!

A huge $54 million Coca-Cola plant has recently been completed.

And a high-tech company called Iskra, formerly a defense communications facility, in a joint venture with some American firms is producing high-grade digital communications equipment under the brand name Krastelecom.

KrAZ

And then there was Krasnoyarsk Aluminum, an industrial behemoth still struggling to sell its products on world markets.

This sprawling plant was comprised of twenty-three huge (600-meter-long) ancient buildings which, like most industrial facilities in Russia, had seen better days.

KrAZ, as it is known for short, is one of the largest aluminum producers in Russia. It's got a workforce on the floor of around 7,000.

In the early 1990s, they had signed a cooperation agreement with Kaiser Aluminum, which had been helping to modernize KrAZ's production technology to reduce environmentally damaging emissions, to the tune of a $50 million investment on Kaiser's part.

KrAZ, it was generally conceded, was the cream of the crop of Russian smelters. Unfortunately, it suffered from management turmoil.

We'd bought our first shares in KrAZ in early 1996, and gradually beefed up our holdings until by mid-1997 we owned about 2.3 percent of the company.

That might not sound huge, but it made us the only portfolio investor to own more than one half of a percent in the company.

By the time of this last visit, the company had gone through four general directors in the past six months. However, we remained bullish long-term on the company because we believed that its new controlling shareholder, a Russian bank called Rossisky Kredit, had the interests of other shareholders in mind.

We met with the company's current economics director, Mihail Vasiliev, around the standard huge conference table, staring at each other across the standard battery of bottles of mineral water, gas and nongas. Vasiliev was a young man and seemed, under the circumstances, surprisingly calm.

My first question was, not so surprisingly under the circumstances, "Who's in control?"

The last time we pulled up at those same heavily barricaded front gates, we'd just missed the Russian equivalent of the shootout at the O.K. Corral.

This place could have been called the KrAZ Corral.

He smiled thinly.

"Well, in the last three months we have had three meetings of our board of directors, and at the last meeting, Mr. Kolpakov was replaced by Mr. Dsyensky."

"And who is Dsyensky?" I wanted to know.

"Oh, he is a representative of Glencore," he replied, surprised that I didn't know. Glencore is a Swiss-based trading company.

Only a few short months before, KrAZ had been the epicenter of one of those pitched, epic, knockdown, drag-out struggles for control that have been a staple on the Russian business scene ever since the collapse of the Communists. This is an excellent example of a risk faced by foreign investors in foreign countries: divided management.

A House Deeply Divided

The battle royal raging over Russian aluminum had begun in 1994, at the lowest point of the anarchic Dark Ages of the post-Communist period. With the aluminum and metals sector in limbo due to a total breakdown of raw materials supplies, a number of "trading companies" had arrived on the scene to offer their "help" in providing precious raw materials, in exchange for . . . sometimes, the moon.

One such trading company, called TransCIS Metals, was

owned and operated by the notorious Brothers Cherny, collo-
quially known as "The Blacks."

The Blacks had linked up with an outfit called TransWorld
Metals, a U.K.-registered company that had been founded in
1993 by David Rubin, originally of London. The Blacks and
TransWorld had jointly acquired about 20 percent of KrAZ, and
began helping the company to obtain hard-to-get raw materials
(primarily alumina) from abroad.

In the early 1990s, the metals sector in Russia had suffered
from a breakdown of the supply chain. Suppliers, who had
been accustomed to getting paid by Moscow-based ministries,
now didn't know when and/or if they'd get paid at all. As a
consequence of this atmosphere of uncertainty, they'd cut off
supplies. Into this vacuum floated outfits like Glencore and
TransWorld, who promised to keep supplies flowing under so-
called tolling contracts, which gave them equity interests in the
companies they assisted in exchange for advancing raw materials.

Through affiliated offshore companies, the Chernys and
Rubin began snapping up stakes in the two top Russian smelters:
Bratsk and Sayansk.

If they succeeded in gaining control of KrAZ, they were in a
position to corner the market in Russian aluminum.

In late 1994, an investigative article in the Russian newspaper
Izvestia pointed out some of the hazards of doing business in the
hard-hitting Russian aluminum sector.

Ivan Turushev, the general director of KrAZ before Mr.
Kolpakov, had been "attacked and beaten up" that October by
a band of anonymous thugs.

After recovering from the attack, Turushev went public with
a series of accusations alleging that Yuri Kolpakov, his successor as general director, had stolen $14 million from the com-
pany till.

Shortly thereafter, Mr. Kolpakov made the tactical error of
leaving town. During his absence, a battalion of heavily armed
military personnel surrounded the KrAZ factory, and forcibly
entered the Department of Securities, where the share register
was kept.

Remember all that stuff about a central share registry?

Because the register of KrAZ shares were kept on the premises, this sort of skulduggery could be used to manipulate ownership in the company.

The commander of these troops had attempted to execute a sale of KrAZ shares to TransWorld by accessing the company computer, and had actually entered the sale as if it had been transacted on the Russian Stock Exchange.

Since these armed men were allegedly under the command of the federal administration, Mr. Kolpakov could only assume that they were acting on orders placed by someone quite close to President Yeltsin.

When Kolpakov returned to the plant, he managed to persuade the invaders to retreat to neutral territory, and proceeded to commence negotiations. After the troops agreed to back off, he resorted to the expedient of crossing off the company's share register 17 percent of the 20 percent share allegedly owned by TransWorld. These shares, Kolpakov claimed, had been illegally entered by the troops and were therefore illegitimate.

Kolpakov later maintained in a TV interview that his side had prevailed in every court case connected to the shares since then. "We took a patriotic stance," he said. "We did not want to give away the factory to the West."

Kolpakov also enlisted the help of a certain Anatoly Bikov, rumored to be the godfather of the Krasnoyarsk Mafia, in his battle for control with TransWorld.

Talk about a hot sector.

When I first encountered Mr. Kolpakov, on an earlier visit, I had found him distracted and, even worse, condescending.

We spoke briefly of KrAZ's to date futile efforts to transfer his crushing social burden—including fourteen kindergartens—to the municipal authorities. As we were discussing this and that, Kolpakov had announced, out of the blue: "We would like to buy Templeton's shares back."

He obviously wanted all the shares in his court as he battled for control.

I explained that I thought he should feel safer with a passive, portfolio investor like us, as opposed to a strategic investor like the Korean company Daewoo, which already owned a substantial block of KrAZ shares.

For the time being, at least, we dropped what was obviously a sore subject.

Later that evening, in accordance with Russian custom, we accompanied a group of company honchos to a private banquet, following a shareholder meeting.

The banquet was held on a large estate carved into the forest covering the beautiful mountains on the outskirts of town, overlooking the Mana River.

Kolpakov, all sweetness and light, took us on a tour of the company tennis courts, the sauna, the elegantly appointed log cabins, and the vast banquet hall, all executed in Russian Rustic style.

The celebration was attended by a number of local power brokers, including the mayor of Krasnoyarsk, as well as the governor of the Krasnoyarsk region, and the director of the local railroad, whose fees are, interestingly, a significant portion of KrAZ's cost.

Now, a year later, Yuri Kolpakov was gone. Glencore had a seat on the board.

And Rossisky Kredit was the controlling shareholder.

"Is all this management turmoil affecting production?" I asked Vasiliev.

His answer surprised me.

"As a company," he said, "our goal is to try to remain independent of all of our individual shareholders. We insist that no shareholder should have the right to interfere with the management of the company. We try to insure that our prices are competitive. I think that it's good to have representatives of both sides on the board. These are two huge trading companies. Naturally, they will try to jockey for position as long as they're here. So I'm going to try to benefit from the fact that both these groups are interested in us. For example, I have an agreement with TransWorld that will give us raw materials cheaper than the prevailing world price. And we have an agreement with Glencore that will help us lower costs in other important areas."

KrAZ Update

After our visit, KrAZ shares continued to soar, up to around $20 apiece, about double the price we paid for them.

If this upward trend was sustained, this would be a real success for us because it represented a case in which our in-country presence and willingness to meet with and work with management had paid off.

Given the turbulence, investing at all had of course been a calculated risk, but a risk we had felt worth assuming because why were we in Russia at all if it wasn't to take risks?

> **Mobius Rule No. 54: A divided management can be a good thing, as long as the people in charge can figure out how to play both sides against the middle.**

The calmness at KrAZ, after armed assaults and rubouts in the streets, seemed like a symbol of the new, tamer Russia—no longer such a wild, wild West, and probably no longer a place where you could expect triple-digit returns as a matter of course.

> **Mobius Rule No. 55: As things settle down, returns settle down with them.**

I suppose this was a cause for celebration, but I realized that I missed the "bad" old days, when it was wild in the streets, and you never knew what might happen next.

Any day now, Russia would be a place for the Beardstown Ladies Club to invest.

And we would have moved on to darker, more perilous pastures.

Of course, only a few months down the rocky road, the ruble would be devalued, the Russian government would go into default on its debts, and the whole shaky house of cards would collapse into a rubble of rubles. What was my reaction at that point? To pull back and ride out the storm.

Fireworks

Just a few weeks after we flew south from Siberia, Moscow celebrated its 850th anniversary with a massive, multimillion-dollar fireworks show.

I've always loved fireworks, and I make a point of catching a show whenever and wherever I can, from Hong Kong's celebration of its reunion with China to Moscow's celebration of rejoining the union of capitalist republics. So on that gala night I rounded up a few friends and hightailed it over to Moscow University, to see if we could see the rockets going up at close range.

The changes I'd seen in just three years of visiting Moscow were simply staggering.

The city had long been a showcase of Communist splendor, a socialist theme park dedicated to glamorizing the utopian notion of a workers' paradise. Even as the rest of the country starved and decayed, even at the worst ebb of Stalinist purging, Moscow had been kept well scrubbed, clean, pristine, and grandiose.

But following the sudden collapse of the Communist state, Moscow had lost what little luster it had had under the commissars. By the time I first visited in 1993, the place had gone quickly to seed.

But just in time for its 850th, Moscow was on the rebound, with hordes of flashy "New Russians" prowling the streets in their Mercedes-Benzes and BMWs, chattering away on cell phones. Though the wealth being piled up in the city, much of it squandered on vulgar and conspicuous displays of sudden riches, was not reaching its way down the social hierarchy, or out to the countryside, it was rapidly turning Moscow into a showcase again, but this time of capitalism unleashed.

This was no longer even a Potemkin worker's paradise, but a yuppie wet dream—a city of glitzy shopping malls—one bunkerlike structure fronting right on Red Square—and traffic jams, all presided over by the ambitious and effective Moscow Mayor

Yuri Luzhkov, who had been wily enough to keep the lion's share of former state property in municipal hands, thus cashing in on the real estate boom.

The crowds were so thick and jubilant that we couldn't even approach the gates of Moscow University. So instead, we walked into an apartment building and took the elevator up to the top floor, and knocked on the first door at random.

The man who opened it was suspicious of us at first. But after one of our Russian friends—our local broker, a young man still in his twenties who'd started out selling books and was now trading stocks and bonds, and was reputedly worth mega-millions—gently explained the purpose of our mission, this curious pajama-clad citizen generously gestured us in, to gaze out his window at the pyrotechnic display bursting above and below.

It was a tender scene, to be sure. But we couldn't get a clear enough view from there, so our host insisted on taking us all up to the roof of the complex, which afforded us a splendid view of the surging crowds massing below. Here was a complete stranger celebrating this unprecedented occasion with us, in a spirit of goodwill and good feeling. Having grown up and lived through much of the period of intense anti-Communist Red Scares and the Cold War, I never would have dreamed that I would live to enjoy such a sweet moment.

The next day, we attended a midnight concert in Red Square, and gladly listened to Luciano Pavarotti sing to the stars, in front of Lenin's Tomb.

MOBIUS RULES: THE BOOM BOX

All booms are the same: they make me nervous. They're hard places in which to find bargains, and I can never get the fact out of my head that:

Every boom contains the seeds of the next bust.

41: When buying shares in foreign companies it's important to read the fine print, and know the quality of rights conferred by ownership of the shares.

42: Often the macro picture contradicts the micro picture.

43: By correcting the gap between the macro and micro views, you can get a jump ahead of the crowd.

44: When getting in at close to Ground Zero *anywhere,* the first thing to look for is: a viable stock exchange.

45: Take a good, hard look at your portfolio. Find all the stocks that have gone up 100 percent or more in one year or less, where the earnings have not risen as much, and the five-year projection is not good. And consider dumping them.

46: You don't maintain high performance by holding on to old blue chips that are no longer blue.

47: Find the next batch of blue chips *before* they turn blue.

48: In a big country, it takes time for new ideas to be absorbed to the farthest corners, to congeal and permeate the cultural permafrost.

49: A bad attitude is a major red flag. It's meant to turn you off. Let it.

50: A strictly "objective" or technical analysis of a company's situation can be misleading. A visit on the ground can make the difference.

51: When investing in any country, it's important to assess its cultural characteristics.

52: In case of fire, maintaining a viable exit strategy is critical to not getting burned.

53: When scrutinizing a company as a potential investment, carefully inspect the company by-laws for the prospect of *share dilution*—one of the easiest moves in the age-old game of "fleecing the minority shareholders."

54: A divided management can be a good thing, as long as the people in charge can figure out how to play both sides against the middle.

55: As things settle down, returns settle down with them.

PART TWO

◆

The Bust (Asia)

SOUTHEAST ASIA

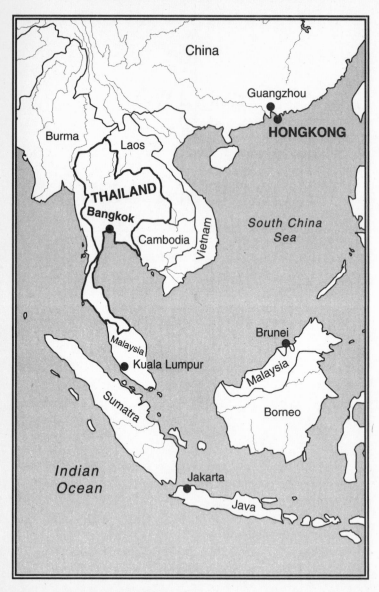

*Boldface capital words are countries Mobius visited

**Boldface lowercase words are cities Mobius visited

Chapter Four

◆

HONG KONG

"People used to think that Hang Seng was a surfing term. But now you've really got to pay attention to international markets."

—DAVID WYSS
CHIEF ECONOMIST
DRI

When the World Bank, the International Monetary Fund, and the International Finance Corporation decided to hold their 1997 annual meeting in Hong Kong, the idea—which must have seemed like a good one at the time—was to celebrate the peaceful handover of Hong Kong to the mainland Chinese in an atmosphere of buoyancy and optimism.

There were, after all, any number of reasons to be bullish on Asia.

1) The Asian tigers—South Korea, Thailand, Taiwan, Indonesia, Malaysia—were riding high.

2) China, the next tiger, was booming to beat the band.

From Kuala Lumpur to Jakarta, from Manila to Shanghai, pricey condos were rising over rice paddies. Water buffalo were grazing peacefully beside Mercedes-Benzes and John Deere bulldozers.

As the world approached the next millennium, the smart money was betting on the dawning of a new age of dominance by the world powers girding the Pacific Rim.

And then.

And then . . .

The Happy Handover

At the stroke of midnight, June 31, 1997, all but a few disgruntled wet blankets of Hong Kong society celebrated the return of the British colony to its motherland.

On the morning of July 1, the short-term survival of the "Hong Kong way of life"—its freewheeling, free-market financial system—seemed as solid as Norman Foster's futuristic, fortress-like Hong Kong & Shanghai Bank headquarters.

In fact, the serenely optimistic view of current and future Hong Kong events was best summed up by Vincent Cheng, executive director of the bank, when he pronounced himself "convinced that Hong Kong will flourish as an international financial center both within China, and as a communications, services, and transport hub of Asia."

This upbeat assessment was cheerfully echoed by Sir Alan Donald, the former British ambassador to China, who had played a leading role in the negotiations leading up to the handover. "China," he steadfastly maintained, "will continue to use Hong Kong as a provider of investment, a quarry for technological, managerial, and marketing know-how, as a point of access to international financial markets, and as a gateway for the overseas Chinese to invest in China."

With a reassuringly wide swath of southern China bordering on Hong Kong showing galloping growth rates in the 20 percent-plus annual range, was there any reason to doubt them? And with China flashing semaphore signals that it was planning to privatize literally thousands of state-owned companies by listing them on the Hong Kong Exchange—as opposed to Shanghai and Shenzhen, on the mainland—Hong Kong's regional financial supremacy appeared to be unconditionally supported by the regime in Beijing.

Any surviving fears of the once widely anticipated "handover hangover" evaporated as Hong Kong's hair-trigger Hang Seng stock index held steady as she goes, for the first weeks and months of Chinese sovereignty.

For my part, I felt reasonably confident that China had little if any interest in killing—or even squeezing too tightly—the goose that laid the golden eggs.

"There's a 25 percent chance of disaster when the Chinese take over," I was widely quoted at the time. "But we see a 75 percent chance of a positive outcome, which far outweighs the downside risk. So we expect money and people to flow from China into Hong Kong after 1997."

But I also added that I was reducing my exposure to Hong Kong stocks from 16 percent of our global portfolio to about 8 percent as a result of our finding better bargains in Southeast Asia.

And the funds flowed in, with a vengeance.

All through the fall, as the Chinese entered their Year of the Tiger, throngs flocked in the streets of Central—the financial district—to line up for hours outside banks and brokerage houses to snap up as many "Chinese red chips"—mainland Chinese companies being sold on the Hong Kong Stock Exchange—as they could.

For the time being, at any rate, Hong Kong's status as the ultimate gateway country seemed enhanced, as opposed to diminished, by being swallowed up by its larger neighbor.

Now, as opposed to being a thorn in China's proud side, Hong Kong was preening itself to assume a new role as China's richest, most advanced, most Westernized city.

Until, That Is, the Fur Flew

In early July, the bottom fell out of the Asian market.

What would soon become known as Asian Contagion had begun.

Before the crisis subsided, the Asian Flu would strike nearly every country in the region, and break the backs of once-proud economies, in countries that had become convinced that there was no downside, only an upside. That they'd figured out the magic formula for success. That they were invincible. That they were unbeatable.

> **Mobius Rule No. 56: When you tap into an attitude in any country that says "we're number one, we're the best, no one can beat us" . . . that's the right time and the right country to SELL.**

When Asian Flu first broke out with a vengeance in Thailand in the summer of 1997, after years of unrestrained lending on speculative real estate projects, the local banks started to look kind of shaky, at least to impartial outside observers.

Here were a few of the warning signs, by which you can sometimes tell if a boom, any boom, is about to go bust:

1) The nation's current account was perilously low. A current account takes into account all the payments a country must make to outsiders, and compares it to all the revenues it's taking in. When the account is out of balance, that's a bad sign. And when the balance skews way toward the net outflow column, that's when global investors start getting antsy.

2) Inflation was rising. That's another bad sign. A major red flag. When the inflation rate starts rising far and fast in any country, that's also a good time to sell.

3) Companies had taken out huge loans in dollars in the belief that they could easily repay them in healthy baht, because the interest rates were lower on dollar-denominated loans than on baht loans. They would take the dollars they borrowed and buy baht at a lower price, and rake in the difference on the interest rate differential. It was a great way to make money as long as the baht remained strong. But any sign that the baht might weaken would surely bring the whole house of currency cards down. In effect, the entire country was gambling on the strength

of its own currency, and now that gamble was looking a little risky.

Why?

Because the big commercial banks—no doubt tipped off by the central bank in Thailand—were beginning to get an idea that perhaps the baht was not so strong as had once been thought. And the problem with currency is that a perception of weakness may bring about actual weakness. The more people got the idea that the baht was in danger of being devalued, the greater the chances that it actually would.

And what would that do?

Well, a devalued baht would make it much harder for all those Thai companies to pay back all those dollar-denominated loans, because they would need to make many more baht to pay back those dollars. That was very bad news for overleveraged companies—which included some of the largest companies in the country—whose debts in some cases would soon start outstripping their assets. Which in turn would make the banks even edgier, and make them less likely to extend or roll over these loans. Because these banks would be looking at big black holes themselves, in the mirror, and would be trying to call any and all loans to keep themselves from going under.

Forex Forever

Into this tense, anxious pool of people biting their nails, waiting for the other shoe to drop, quietly slipped a group of ladies and gentlemen collectively known as "foreign exchange traders," or "forex traders," for short. They were also less kindly known as "currency speculators," a term that they don't like very much, but which has caught on because it catches some of the flavor of what they do.

And what do they do?

They buy and sell various countries' currencies, of course.

Now there was a time, not so very long ago, when most major currencies were fixed to the gold standard—last established under the Bretton Woods agreement after the Second World War.

But in 1971, most of the world's industrial powers allowed currency exchange rates to float—which meant that they would be permitted to seek their own level on world markets, and that currencies could be traded against each other just like any other commodity. Still, currency trading remained a relative backwater on the financial scene until the mid-1980s, when a massive increase in the volume of foreign trade caused more and more money to go whirring around the world, constantly being exchanged for local currency when it stopped to buy some goods or services. To get just some idea of the size of growth in daily turnover in currencies, daily turnover has soared from *$190 billion* in 1986 to an estimated *$1.3 trillion* in 1998.

As this market grew, traders—propped up by large lines of credit extended from banks, brokerage houses, and other financial entities seeking to get into what can be an extremely lucrative activity—began speculating on these fluctuating currency rates, aided by computer programs and models that helped them trade massive amounts of currency in the blink of an eye. Traders put up only a fraction of the currencies they buy and sell in cash—everything else is purchased on margin.

Today, thousands of currency traders sitting at computer screens all over the world—some working for banks, others for brokerage houses, still others for companies and central banks—manipulate with countless buy and sell orders the value of hundreds of currencies, which trade much like stocks, bonds, or any other sort of financial instrument.

Still, the central banks of many countries sometimes try—and often fail—to fix the rates at which their currencies are exchanged on global markets against other currencies, to prop up their own economies. If a government wants to favor exports, it will take steps to let its currency drop, so that its exports become more attractive. If a central bank wants to stimulate imports and strengthen its currency, it will buy large amounts of its own currency on currency markets, seeking to prop up the price.

When a country sets a price at which its currency can be exchanged against another currency, that's called a "peg." Pegs—typically measured against a stable reserve currency like the dollar—became popular in some Asian and Latin American countries seeking to lend stability to turbulent or hyper-inflated economies. And sometimes, when the central bank of a country has enough hard currency in reserve to support the rate of exchange it wants to maintain by buying vast sums of it on the open market, these pegs hold. And sometimes, they don't.

When they don't hold, it's usually because the currency traders no longer believe in the price being asked for it by the central government of a given country. So what do they do? They start selling it short, which means that they make a bet with somebody else that the price of that currency will fall.

Selling Yourself Short

What do I mean by the term "selling short," whether it's a stock or a baht?

I call it "selling something you don't have at a price that you don't want to pay."

What short-sellers do is the following:

1) Borrow stocks, or bonds, or currencies, or what-have-you from their owners.

2) Sell the shares that they've borrowed, hoping that the price will fall.

3) If it does fall, they get to buy the stock, or currency, back at a lower price, and

4) Pocket the difference.

The "shorts"—which is short for short-sellers—are taking the risk, and making a bet, that the price of whatever commodity they're selling will fall by a given amount within a given period of time. Where they can get caught short is if the price of that commodity, instead of falling, goes up—at which point they're forced to come up with the difference. So it's by no means a win-win proposition. Sometimes, short-sellers end up shorting themselves.

But if enough currency traders start feeling in their bones that the Thai baht or Mexican peso is overvalued at the current or prevailing rate and that it's destined to take a dive, all of their actions, taken together, will produce that effect. It's a perfect example of the tendency for markets, being based fundamentally in

psychology—hope and greed—to create self-fulfilling prophe-
cies. Lo and behold, the currency will drop—which gives the
central bank of the country two options:

1) To cave, and let the currency "float freely" to seek its "new
natural level." Or . . .

2) To fight, and start spending their currency reserves to defend the baht or the peso.

In the case of the Thai central bank—the Bank of Thailand—
on July 2, 1997, they decided to abandon the baht's fixed peg to
the dollar (it was actually not a precise peg, but a so-called trading band, or limited range of rates) and let it float on international currency markets. As expected—though not perhaps by
the central bank—the baht collapsed. Over the next few weeks,
in an ill-advised and ultimately futile attempt to bolster the baht,
the Thai central bank spent some $60 billion dollars ($23 billion
of that borrowed) before throwing in the towel.

After that, the baht was on its own. And what it did was sink
like a stone.

The Global Game

And when global investors—banks, institutions, money funds,
individuals—saw what was going on in Thailand, which was
that the vast majority of companies had dollar-denominated
debts greater than their assets, and that the Thai banks and so-
called finance companies that had extended those loans were
going to be in deep trouble, they did just what global investors
always do during a time of crisis: they pulled all their money out
before they lost any more of it.

During the ensuing period of so-called Currency Contagion—
so called because the rapid drop of the baht prompted similarly
shaky currencies to fall, from Malaysia to Indonesia—a whole
lot of very mad people out there (many of them running the
Southeast Asian countries) began stridently denouncing the
"currency traders" and accusing them of engaging in a conspiracy to ruin their once-high-flying Asian tiger economies.

Chief among the proponents of this conspiracy theory was the prime minister of Malaysia, Mahathir Mohamad, who having proudly presided over what for a long time had been known as "The Malaysian Miracle" had no desire to go down in history as the man who had presided over the collapse of said Malaysian Miracle.

He became convinced that the huge drops in his currency, the ringgit, were the result of this malicious conspiracy on the part of a lot of devilish forex traders. A Muslim, he even went so far as to denounce this ring as a "Jewish" conspiracy, in part because the most visible and famous currency trader of them all, Mr. George Soros, just happens to be Jewish.

If this all sounds somewhat unhinged, you may do well to recall that as recently as the 1960s, when the British pound sterling was suffering pretty much the same fate, Prime Minister Harold Wilson fiercely blamed a cabal of Swiss bankers he called "The Gnomes of Zurich" for making his life miserable.

Sticky Thai Rice

With the baht locked into a sickening downward spiral, the Thai banks—which were now sitting on huge loans in baht that were looking a lot less likely to be repaid—promptly cut off all lending, bringing the breakneck economy to a screeching halt. This newfound conservatism was in sharp contrast to previous practice, which had been to lend virtually without restriction to just about anyone, particularly "anyone who was anyone"—that is, with political or social connections to the military, bureaucratic, business, or government elites.

They even had a name for that sort of thing: "crony capitalism."

It was first invented by a clever American journalist to describe the cozy cartels that rose up in the Philippines under the late, not very lamented President Ferdinand Marcos. But today, it's been used to describe the economic system most favored across Southeast Asia, in which cartels and conglomerates with connections to the government and to the army dominate economic affairs.

In Korea, they called these cartels *chaebols*.

In Japan, they call them *keiretsu*.

In Russia, where crony capitalism is definitely all the rage, they call it *semibankirschina*, which means: "rule of the seven bankers."

The entire theory that a high-growth economy was best controlled by a governing elite composed of military and government officials, banks, corporate honchos, and others in favor was often promulgated by those elites, who popularized the term and the concept of "Asian values." That was all very well as long as the governments and economies involved could deliver the goods: high rates of growth. But once the music in this game of musical chairs stopped, the governments—and those officials and cronies who had been raking in so much off the top—suddenly found themselves being denounced as crooks and scoundrels.

It emerged that there was no such thing, really, as Asian values. There were just fair, open, and transparent economies, and unfair, closed, and opaque ones.

Zooming In

So how had did the panic begin? What was really happening? And as an investor caught in the downturn, or someone looking to cash in on the panic, what do you do?

The number one thing that you do: don't panic.

Panic, after all, is an irrational visceral response to a sense of powerlessness and helplessness, which typically comes from a lack of understanding of circumstances. But panics, odd as this may sound, are nothing to be scared of.

As FDR once said, "The only thing to fear is fear itself."

Understanding the origins of the difficulty can help to diminish anxiety.

And in any number of critical ways, all busts start with a boom.

Why?

Because all busts start with a gathering consensus that a market has gone too far, too fast.

The same people that were so in love with the market, and with every stock in it, that they'd sell their grandmothers into slavery to buy more stock, now all of a sudden won't touch a share of stock with a ten-foot pole.

Objectively, this fickle attitude makes absolutely no sense.

But that's failing to take into account the rule of emotion, which tends to force snap judgments.

Emotions make people see only in black and white, good and bad, up and down.

So what was good suddenly becomes bad.

What was white suddenly becomes black.

What was rosy and wonderful is now, all of a sudden, dark and terrifying.

A lovely dream turns into a nightmare, and if you don't watch out: you're toast.

Let's Get Technical

Hoping to avoid getting toasted—or having to get toasted to get over having become toast—some stock market crystal ball gazers perform a mathematical ritual known as technical analysis in the hope of forecasting these big market drops.

I'm something of a fan of technical analysis—which is the study of large price movements across markets—although I tend to personally practice more fundamental analysis, which is the study of companies' price-to-earnings ratios (P/E), profits, earnings, and market share, and other fundamental factors of corporate performance.

But I started out in the financial world, actually, in Hong Kong boning up on technical analysis, as a fledgling "chartist"—which is what stock market types call technical analysts, because they spend so much of their time studying charts. From a technical standpoint, the Thai market had performed what chartists refer to—but only after crossing themselves, saying a few Hail

Marys, and stabbing the nearest vampire with a wooden stake—as a "quadruple top."

Now, that might not sound so bad, but it is. Believe me. For reasons not worth delving into here, when any sort of market—a stock market, a commodities market, a futures market—does a loop-de-loop called a double, triple, or God forbid, a quadruple top, beware.

That way lies trouble, big-time.

On the price charts that technical analysts use, the shape of these curves resembles a mountain range, as the market peaks, drops, and peaks again.

So a triple top is highly unusual.

But a quadruple top like the one pulled off by the Thai stock market is, well, pretty much off the charts. What makes an already dicey situation even more dangerous is when your quadruple top displays a range of *declining* tops, as each peak falls a bit lower than the last.

That, my friend, is your exit signal.

If you see that happening in any country, wave bye-bye.

And when the technical analysts got wind of this, and began to whistle while they worked, all sorts of fundamentalists started hitting the exits. Because even if they only sort of believed in technical analysis, that was all they needed to get spooked.

And when a lot of people get spooked, you've got the spark that touches off the panic.

There's Got to Be a Better Way

Based on bitter personal experience, I've found that there are better ways to exit a market than to start shouting at the top of your lungs and trampling over each other for the fire exits. The better way is to slowly, prudently, and gradually withdraw, at a market high.

Don't wait for the market to drop to get out.

Get out while the going's good.

Of course, knowing when to get in and out is called "market timing," and that's very difficult even for the pros to pull off.

But if you adopt a true contrarian position, that can help you see and foresee the right times to enter and exit, because they are pretty much the opposite times that everyone else does.

So, here goes:

> **Mobius Rule No. 57: When everyone else is dying to get in, get out.**

> **Mobius Rule No. 58: When everyone else is screaming to get out, get in.**

But of course, that takes some foresight, and imagination, and knowledge.

Here are a few key danger signals that will tell you when to get out:

No. 1 Sign: you've got brokers you've never heard of calling you up, out of the blue, and telling you at the top of their lungs that you'd better snap up this stock—or else!

"Or else what?"

To which obvious question they're likely to sputter and stutter before spitting out: "Before you lose this great opportunity! Before you miss the boat! Before you underperform the index!"

No. 2 Sign: the use of melodramatic language to sell shares, as if in a panic, is a sign that things have gotten out of control.

> **Mobius Rule No. 59: If a broker starts giving you the hard sell, never buy.**

If they tell you "everyone's getting in on this one," take a pass.

Currency Risk

The Asian Contagion that swept through the Asian markets like wildfire helped to sow panic in the hearts of even the most stalwart and savvy investors.

On the face of it, that's not too hard to understand. After all:

When a foreign currency declines in value, any stock that you own denominated in that currency is going to decline in value relative to the strength of one of the global reserve currencies, such as the U.S. dollar.

So what to do during a currency crisis?

Well, the first thing to realize is one thing:

1) Despite everyone and anyone ranting about destitution and impoverishment, a devalued currency, particularly if the currency is devalued properly and gradually, is not necessarily a catastrophe for any economy. In fact, it can be the engine for the next cycle of growth.

PPP

Then: 2) Get a handle on the value of the currency in question. We have an easy method of doing this. We call it a PPP chart, which stands for "purchasing power parity."

What we do to figure a particular country or currency's PPP is very simple. We divide the rate of inflation in that country by the rate of inflation in another country. Since most of our investors are trading and thinking in dollars, the easiest way to work up a country's PPP index is to divide the rate of inflation in that country by the rate of inflation in the U.S.

You can tell, at a glance, whether a particular currency is strengthening or weakening against the U.S. dollar, which helps you—and us—keep currency risk in perspective. The reason that the PPP index works so well to determine the strength or weakness of a given currency is that one of the key indicators of weakness in any economy is inflation.

Inside George Soros's Head

So what are those currency traders actually thinking when they "go after" Thailand?

Despite the bad rap that "currency speculators"—they prefer to be called "foreign exchange traders"—get in the press, a wise global investor will always do well to try to think like a foreign exchange trader, if for no better reason than to anticipate their next moves, which tend to function with a level of stealth and guile associated with guerrilla warfare.

What global currency traders spend a great deal of time doing is: probing for weaknesses in a nation's defenses.

High inflation rates are a big sign of weakness, and a form of bait to the wily forex trader.

Current Account Balances

The second thing that forex traders tend to look at is trade balances, or imbalances.

A country's current account factors in imports, exports, payments out, and payments in on a basket of goods and services. If a current account is negative, that's a trade deficit. Some countries take into consideration so-called invisibles, as opposed to just hard trade numbers, to correctly assess, for example, the value of services as opposed to simply trade in hard goods.

Politics

The third thing they look at is the political environment. If something looks odd to them on the political side they'll dump a currency without remorse.

In Thailand, an extremely unpopular prime minister only made matters worse by dallying and dithering when decisions were needed, and by radiating an unseemly Buddhist composure even as his economy went into a tailspin.

In retrospect, it wasn't so hard to figure out why he and his cabinet were all so calm in the face of disaster: personally, most of them were worth billions, not millions. And that's not baht we're talking here, but U.S. greenbacks. This general—many Thai politicians were generals before they got into the political business, because the army in Thailand is traditionally extremely powerful—failed to purge shady power brokers from his cabinet, and couldn't keep from meddling in the positive policies of the few brave-hearted bureaucrats truly committed to financial reform. In short, this guy was a walking disaster, and the very personification of a major risk of global investing: political risk. On the other hand, once the crisis hit, the Thai people got out a big broom and swept these guys out of power, which is one of the reasons these periodic crises are not such a bad thing, because they promote much-needed change.

The Right Stuff

With so many markets dropping like flies, what do you do?

Where do you go? Is there nowhere to run? Nowhere to hide?

Does it make sense to race for the exits?

In a word: no.

If you want to know what I did, I behaved more like a shark going in for the kill than a cat with its hair standing on end. The great thing, of course, was that now all of a sudden, all sorts of stuff we'd been looking at but rejecting as too expensive was now affordable, for the first time in years. Let's take, for example, Hong Kong & Shanghai Bank. A world-class bank, with holdings all around the world, very diversified, with vast reserves and one of the savviest, most solid managements in the business—many of them British and Scots drawn from the ranks of old-time Anglo–Hong Kong families. A splendid investment. But for most of the 1990s, just too, too rich for my blood.

Now, from a high of US$370 (for an ADR) just a few months before, it was dropping fast, by 30 percent as the big Hong Kong bubble began to burst.

At one particularly dire point in the crisis, the Thai stock market had fallen nearly *78 percent* from its peak. Why?

You know perfectly well why. Because all the "smart money" was groaning that Thailand was a terrible mess, and that it would be in a "workout" situation for five years, at least.

And in the short term, of course, they weren't so far off the mark. Though even their short-term analysis, by my reckoning, was somewhat shortsighted, because all those same pundits had said the same thing about Mexico back in 1994, and it took more like two years than five for the Mexican market to bounce back.

Of course, all the pundits were frantically comparing Mexico to Thailand, and delivering all sorts of nifty snap judgments on the global airwaves, to the effect that either:

1) Thailand was worse, much worse than Mexico, or

2) Mexico was much, much worse than Thailand.

The thing that I find interesting about market pundits is that much like those they seek to advise, they always go to extremes: "It's a disaster!" "It's a catastrophe!" "There's blood in the streets!"

Now, if you can, take away all those exclamation points from all those opinions.

Don't you feel better?

More calm? More collected?

Okay, take a deep breath, count to ten—and start thinking about going on a shopping spree. A classic quote often attributed to the first Baron Rothschild is that the best time to buy is when there's "blood in the streets." The second part of that bit of advice, I was recently told, is: "Even when the blood is your own."

Which obviously makes the Baron even more interesting than I thought he was.

I would personally amend that to take the subjective factor into account:

> ## Mobius Rule No. 60: The best time to buy is when *everyone else* is screaming that there's blood in the streets.

Because I'm willing to bet that no matter what happens, you take a look down into that gutter, and all you're likely to see is a gutter full of ketchup.

The Only Thing to Fear Is Fear Itself

When everyone else is getting all pessimistic, that's usually when I turn optimistic.

Let's take the Thai people.

I'd lived in Thailand for a few years, back in the 1960s, and I'd been back quite a few times in the years since. I thought I knew the Thai people pretty well, and I had great respect and admiration for them. In particular, for their capacity to persevere in times of adversity.

Something that people during times of panic tend to forget is that adversity often brings out the best in people. And, by the same token, prosperity often brings out the worst in people.

Within a matter of months, not years, I could see the progress that the Thai people and the formerly stagnant Thai government had made to set things to rights. It takes a major blowout for tectonic plates to shift.

The boiling point came when the embattled prime minister seriously suggested that the economy could be saved by opening up more Thai restaurants and popularizing Thai kick-boxing.

It took just a few serious protests in Bangkok—mounted not by disgruntled leftists and radicals, but sober dark-suited businessmen, middle-class people feeling the pinch and getting hopping mad about it—and there was suddenly a new government, a new more respected prime minister, the king had stepped in and started to exert moral pressure to lessen corruption and self-dealing on the part of the local elites. Would all these "bad" people all of a sudden turn into angels? Of course not, but for a while at least, it would behoove them to keep their noses clean. That, in time, would help revive morale, and bring the market around.

Mobius Rule No. 61: In times of crisis, people on the ground start coming to their senses.

They get it together. They start pulling together. They clean up their acts, and start demanding that people in charge do the same. They start working harder. They start saving more. They stop spending money. This was what Oliver Wendell Holmes meant when he spoke of "the moral equivalent of war."

As a partner in the Bangkok office of the consulting firm McKinsey & Company said during the depths of the crisis: "Even turkeys can fly in a hurricane. But when the wind dies down, it's much more difficult to sustain performance. It's a question of muscle.

"During a downturn," he soberly added, "you need to not just cut fat. It's even more important to start building muscle."

Mobius Rule No. 62: Easy times make people go soft. Hard times get people going.

Which means that sooner rather than later, the situation begins slowly but surely to turn around.

The Down-and-Dirty Details

The first thing to do in times of crisis is go for *liquidity*.

You could call it: "A flight to quality."

It only stands to reason that if I now have a choice between a small *illiquid* stock and a large *liquid* stock, I'll pick a liquid one every time. In fact, the only time that I buy illiquid or less liquid stocks is if I have to—during booms, when liquid stocks get too expensive.

Liquid stocks tend to be the market leaders, large-cap stocks, index stocks, the blue chips. The stocks you can never buy during a boom, but are your first choice at the first sign of a bust.

As sentiment sours, these stocks will begin to come down to more reasonable levels.

In Thailand, I was aching to take a closer look at Siam Cement, one of the country's blue chip companies, partly owned by the Royal Household. This was more than just a cement company, but a diversified group with holdings in building materials, petrochemicals, plastics, and in a number of other basic building block raw chemical materials.

It was getting a bad rap in the press: exports down, plants being closed.

In other words, the perfect time to pay a visit.

When Bad News Is Good News

Was Siam Cement, you might ask, one of those companies that "irresponsibly" took out loans in dollars with the expectation that they could be paid back in baht?

Well, yes. And, I ask you, so what?

The point is, they all did it. The point is, such a strategy seemed sound at the time. In fact, the fact that Siam Cement was widely known to have suffered that exposure made it worth buying. Why? Because these ideas about "exposure to risk" tend to weaken sentiment, which makes them attractive targets.

With the currency devaluation, the beleaguered baht would soon be looking competitive again. Under pressure to increase business through exports, Siam Cement was going to start exporting like crazy, because it could make and sell cement and all of its other products cheaper than its competitors in neighboring countries.

And Thailand, which during some bizarre fit of perverse reasoning had slapped an export tax on cement, had—lo and behold—canceled that tax for the duration. This made Siam Cement even cheaper to the Malaysian market, even cheaper, in some cases, than Malaysian cement.

So, like a kid in a candy store, I was rarin' to start buying up all those juicy blue chips I couldn't have dared to afford before the crash.

Bottoms Up

As the Asian virus raged ominously throughout the continent, the new verbal game being grimly played out in global financial circles became: "Pin the Tail on the Bottom."

One global trader announced that this wasn't a panic, but "a systematic meltdown of testing a new bottom." Say what? Other self-styled experts pronounced this a terrific time for "bottom fishing." Still others spoke loftily about "breaching the quadruple bottom."

Meanwhile, into the breach plunged the intrepid International Monetary Fund, the global institution best equipped to deal with such crises of confidence. It promptly stepped up to the baht with a generous offer: a $17 billion bailout and rescue package, which was dangled like a carrot in order to force the ruling elite to swallow the harsh medicine of financial discipline.

But, in the short term, sentiment was so sour that even the prospect of powerful external forces leveraging the Thai economy back into line did little to raise morale.

A Symbol Soiled

By the time of the World Bank meetings, which convened in the elegant, spectacular new Hong Kong Convention Center (a graceful glass oblong with a swallowtail roof that juts out into Hong Kong's harbor like a bird about to take wing), the building's soaring structure no longer symbolized the bounding success of the region, but its equally bounding excess.

This brave new continent, Asia, that for over a decade could do no wrong—particularly in the eyes of Western investors—had suddenly been bitten by a bad bug. In the anxious flicker of a trader's eye, all bets were off. And as each country along the once-mighty Pacific Rim fell in turn into the trader's targets, a long-discredited description of Asian political behavior used to justify U.S. intervention in Vietnam was dusted off and reapplied to the region's financial markets. Remember the domino theory? Yikes! It had risen again, from an unmarked linguistic grave.

Finger–Pointing

To many a distressed government official and/or central banker, the real culprits were easy to spot:

A devilish conspiracy of international investors and global currency speculators, who had launched an unprovoked, irrational "attack" on Asian countries and their sovereign currencies, backed up by a shadowy alliance of "Western powers." These Western powers, jealous of Asia's boundless success, were determined to lay the high-flying Asian tigers low.

This position was most aggressively taken up by Prime Minister Mahathir Mohamad of Malaysia, who personally held the hedge-fund manager George Soros responsible for the seep slide in the ringgit.

"Villainous acts of sabotage" on the part of "hostile elements bent on unholy actions" was the assessment of the problem pronounced by the Malaysian foreign minister, Abdullah Ahmad Badawi.

To the international financial community, the culprits were equally obvious:

Lax, often corrupt government officials and regulators, who tolerated and often encouraged a cozy culture of self-dealing that led to irrational excess, extravagance, and all the other classic attributes of a runaway boom blossoming into a full-fledged speculative bubble.

To many distressed government officials and central bankers, the solution was also simple:

To control the flows of "hot money" running in and out of countries, and across national borders, and if necessary ban or heavily tax "currency speculation" altogether.

To many foreign investors and outside observers, with less to lose from the prospect of meaningful political and fiscal reform, the solution was equally obvious:

To impose discipline on these out-of-control banks, businesses, and corporations, tighten up credit, raise interest rates, and above all: reform, reform, and reform.

Ominous Atmospherics

As if on cue, Mother Nature appeared on the scene to play an atmosphere-setting role in the darkening Asian drama. In collaboration with countless big- and small-time agro-arsonists, the skies over the continent filled with sooty smoke. The product of thousands of large and tiny forest fires set by farmers and ranchers to clear rain-forested land of trees to plant cash crops—mainly palm oil and rice—these sooty storm clouds were so thick and blinding that airplanes couldn't fly above invisible airports, ferry boats ran aground in midstream, and ordinary citizens choked on fumes far worse than their usual fare in the region's densely packed cities.

This gathering haze was quickly seized upon by some clever pundits as the perfect symbol of the hazy, murky, illiquid, and far from transparent markets common to so many poorly regulated Asian countries. The smoke and mirrors that blinded domestic and international investors to these countries' weaknesses now served, it was said, as a wake-up call for the tired tigers of Asia to get off their high horses, and clean up their acts, or face the awful consequences. The inability of the Indonesian government to force those farmers to stop those fires underlined the sudden powerlessness of those Asian tigers who were supposed to have Confucian-oriented governments.

Confusion rather than Confucian reigned.

The Russian Typhoon

It certainly didn't help Malaysia's already tenuous position in the international rationality sweepstakes when its minister of science, technology, and the environment announced that it had hatched a plan to purchase a largely unproven "Russian technology" that would scrub the hazy skies over the country with cyclones. These artificial typhoons would, he maintained, cause torrential rains—miniature monsoons—that would wash the smoke right out of their air.

Remarkably, the Malaysian cabinet and finance minister promptly approved the plan. A Malaysian company, BioCure, was reported to have signed a memorandum of understanding with a "government-owned Russian party" to produce the cyclone.

The cyclone strategy followed on the heels of other unsuccessful technical fixes Malaysia had brought to bear on the problem: spraying water from tall buildings in Kuala Lumpur, and cloud seeding—in which airplanes sprinkled clouds with a salt solution—to produce rain.

Datuk Law, the Malaysian environmental minister, while declining to disclose the size of the cyclone to be generated, adding "the details I don't have," did hasten to say that he understood that it was to be "quite strong," and that if the Russians didn't make a cyclone, Malaysia wouldn't have to pay for it.

Which is precisely what the Russians were afraid of!

Hunting for Black October

By the October World Bank meeting—which appropriately enough marked the tenth anniversary of the world's last great global stock market crash—flocks of private planes bearing battalions of grim-faced global bankers landed at Hong Kong's congested Kai Tak airport. Due to the inadequacy of the airport—which was shortly to be replaced by the vast new Chek Lap Kok on Lantau Island—they were forced to quickly debark their passengers and wing off to neighboring Taiwan and the Philippines to park.

With Thailand crashing, the Philippines crashing, Malaysia crashing, and Indonesia crashing, the first question on every participant's lips was the same: would Hong Kong be next? While for months since the handover, the complacent refrain had been "business as usual," now you could hear the teeth-grinding anxiety behind the second-most-asked question: "Will the peg hold?"

Peg o' My Heart

The peg in question was a clever monetary device, a fixed link engineered between the Hong Kong and U.S. dollars in a system known as a "currency board."

This brilliant bit of monetary policy had originally been adopted by the Hong Kong Monetary Authority at the inspired suggestion of a little-known economist at GT Management, John Greenwood, during a very bad panic during the summer of 1983.

That had been one of the first times since the Japanese occupation during World War II that longtime Hong Kong residents had been forced to face up to the fact that the Union Jack would not be flying forever above the exclusive Hong Kong Club.

As the prospect of being handed over to Communist China began to sink in, the local and international markets freaked. The result? Abject fear and panic. It was wild in the streets. Hong Kong stocks, in those days, could be picked up for a song.

But the peg, the currency board in the form of the Hong Kong Monetary Authority, worked like a charm. The great thing about it was—and is—that it was so deceptively simple. The potentially unstable Hong Kong dollar was linked to the supposedly rock-solid U.S. dollar by means of a system of currency reserves by which the Hong Kong government promised to swap Hong Kong dollars for their U.S. dollar equivalent at any time, thereby ensuring anyone who kept their holdings in Hong Kong dollars that they could exchange them for U.S. dollars, at will.

Despite opposition from some economists it was used in other countries, such as Argentina and Bulgaria. But while the Argentine and Bulgarian examples were strict currency boards, the Hong Kong board was a looser version, since the HKMA could become involved in influencing interest rates and other activities.

Other countries did not have the huge foreign currency reserves of Hong Kong and they tried to copy the "peg" system.

But what some of those copycats failed to comprehend, to their peril, was that you needed tremendous wherewithal, and political will, to make a peg hold.

The Thais had had a "loose peg" called a "trading link" to the U.S. dollar, which they could not afford to support when it came under attack.

But Hong Kong had more than adequate foreign reserves to keep the peg pegged: some US$80 billion in their central bank. Plus infinite (or almost infinite) credit from China.

But way back when, in the beginning (as Morris Mole of Crédit Lyonnais Securities wittily writes), "The peg was a con, in so far as the Hong Kong government had no [currency] reserves worth poking a stick at."

But over time—and each time that Hong Kong's Hang Seng index snapped like a bullwhip—the peg held firm and fast. And what was once a pious fraud eventually became a hard, fast reality. Even as the World Bankers and their attendant lackeys kowtowed and powwowed to the Beijing regime, the Hong Kong Monetary Authority gradually built up sufficient currency reserves to literally swap every Hong Kong dollar in circulation with a physical U.S. dollar.

And the funny thing was, just like any other form of money, if you had enough of it, you really didn't need to spend it. It was just doing its job lying dormant in Hong Kong's central bank, radiating security, making people feel good about the peg and its prospect of holding firm in the coming storm.

The peg had taken on an awesome psychic significance, because people were nervous in general about the Chinese takeover. True, it had all gone swimmingly, except for a brief PR blunder when Red Army troops looked a little too conspicuous about moving in on the barracks being evacuated by British regiments that had occupied and defended them for the last century and a half.

The ball was now in China's court. The peg had been set at a level that made the Hong Kong dollar look overvalued, compared to the suddenly devalued Asian currencies. This made Hong Kong, which had already grown very expensive (due mainly to the soaring price of real estate, which was itself a function of a government policy to hold a great deal of buildable land in reserve, keeping prices artificially high, thereby benefiting the rich Hong Kong developers), even more horrendously expensive. With office rents and hotel prices sky-high and Asian tourists and businesses suffering, Hong Kong was in for a period of deep, deep uncertainty.

All of which made Hong Kong less competitive than its neighbors with regard to exports. Which made Hong Kong a likely target for the attentions of the currency traders, because they might find themselves inclined to bet that when push came to shove, Hong Kong might feel forced to abandon its peg so they wouldn't get swamped in global markets by cheaper Southeast Asian goods.

That's called "competitive devaluation," which happens when one country devalues its currency so that its rivals' exports won't enjoy a cost advantage.

On the side of those betting on the peg's position was a political consideration: China couldn't afford to let the peg loosen even a hitch.

Because that would send a signal to already shaky markets that the Hong Kong currency, and therefore the Hong Kong stock market, was no longer sound.

The Hong Kong government, now with its eyes on Beijing rather than London, was faced with an unfortunate choice between the greater and lesser of two evils:

Option No. 1: Devalue the currency, abandon the peg, and see its famed stock market crash within nanoseconds.

Option No. 2: Tighten the peg, and watch the property market crash and interest rates rise in an effort to keep investors in Hong Kong dollars.

In the end, they chose to keep the peg and hang on for dear life, despite all the problems that such a policy would entail. They kept the peg pegged by shooting short-term interest rates through the roof, and enduring the resulting economic contraction. Anything, they decided, was better than to lose face, or the confidence of world markets in their fiscal conservatism. But

Hong Kong, no matter which way the government turned, was bound to pay a hefty price.

War of Words

During back-to-back speeches at the World Bank conference, Malaysia's Mahathir called the famous hedge-fund manager George Soros a "moron," and castigated Soros's fellow foreign exchange traders as "a group of ultrarich people."

Boy, what an insult!

"For them," Mahathir bitterly added, "wealth must come from impoverishing others, from taking what others have in order to enrich themselves. Their weapon is their wealth against the poverty of others."

It wouldn't be long before he would assuage his anger at world events by popping his reform-minded deputy prime minister, Anwar Ibrahim, in jail, touching off serious civil unrest.

A Debate Finally Joined

Sitting in the audience, and admittedly enjoying the sheer verbal spectacle, I came to the conclusion that, unpleasant as it must have been for the participants to engage in such vicious personal attacks, it was fundamentally a good and very important thing that the debate had been finally and openly joined between the advocates of tightly controlled, closed economies, and the proponents of open, liberal, free-floating financial systems.

If nothing else, the unprecedently virulent Asian Contagion the world was facing had demonstrated to even the doubting Thomases of the world that globalization was real, and here to stay.

My favorite headline during those turbulent times appeared in *The Financial Times* during a week when the Asian tremors shook up the U.S. financial markets:

"Asian Tail Wags U.S. Dog."

"Was globalization really meant to work like this?" was the

provocative lead of the editorial. "For most of the decade, the world's markets have danced to the tune of American capital. But now a series of small financial earthquakes in Southeast Asia has sent surprisingly large shock waves through the developed world's markets; and the reverberations are becoming increasingly hard to rationalize."

Moral Hazard

Riding in on his white horse, U.S. Treasury Secretary Robert Rubin, a former managing director of Goldman, Sachs, offered his own version of why the current crisis could prove a blessing in disguise. "Capital markets work best," Rubin announced, "when they have comprehensive, timely, and accurate information on economies and policies."

The U.S. free-market solution to the global crisis: increase transparency. Transparency is the quality and clarity of information publicly disseminated about transactions in a given financial system. Increase transparency, and the busts will no longer be as sharp, as long, or as deep and painful.

During the 1994 Mexican peso crisis, Rubin reminded the crowd, Mexico had only worsened its own situation by failing to disclose the extent of its foreign exchange reserves on a regular basis. When Mexico eventually decided to devaluate, and float the peso against the dollar, it came as such a shock to the system that it took longer for the market to recover.

For Richer, for Poorer, in Sickness and in Health

Of course, the ultimate irony of all, at least according to one theory prevalent among the more cynical international investors, was that the central bankers of these countries were rumored to be deliberately driving their own stock and currency values down, so that they could either short their own currencies, and their own stocks, or buy them up dirt cheap in the wake of the resulting devaluation.

I do believe that financial panics are sometimes touched off by central bankers themselves (and people close to them), who have the earliest and most reliable information about a country's economy, well before the private sector.

The Great Man Speaks

At a seminar sponsored by the International Institute for Finance, the former head of the central bank of Taiwan began to harangue the audience, crying out for more currency controls and a stop to the ongoing liberalization of Southeast Asian financial markets. The gist of his argument—which we heard echoed time and again by what I labeled the "control freaks" among the public sector—was that by letting foreign investors in, these countries had left themselves vulnerable to the wily manipulations of the international financial community. The answer was therefore to shut us out, and go back to the good old days when they could play God, and maintain tight control over their little fiefdoms.

The president of the panel spotted me in the audience, and asked me by name if I had any questions to ask the speaker.

I felt a bit nervous being singled out in this way, particularly since I was steaming mad at that central banker's comments, but after a moment's hesitation, I stood up and decided to call the guy's bluff.

"If currency controls are as effective as you suggest," I asked, "then why, when Taiwan suffered a stock market crash in 1987–88, and the index went from 12,000 to 3,000, didn't your controls work then?"

This question was met with a deafening silence in the room, not because anyone was shocked by the sentiment.

The silence came more from the stunning fact that I had dared to question an august central bank governor's received wisdom. Central bank governors, you see, are used to being treated in an atmosphere of utmost deference and respect. They are used to flying around the world extending their hands to the world's financial elite, so that they may kiss the ring, as if every word out of their mouths were gold-plated.

The moderator asked each of the panelists to address this question in turn, but none of them would address it directly. I suspect that this was because they didn't want to offend the revered former central bank governor. The fact that they couldn't answer it in any way that would have satisfied the former Taiwan central bank governor led me to believe that I'd asked the right question.

Chapter Five

◆

HONG KONG: "CATCHING A FALLING KNIFE"

Head and Shoulders

On the sunny summer day in 1967 that I first arrived in Hong Kong, it might have been the Summer of Love in San Francisco, but it was the height of the Cultural Revolution in China. The narrow streets of the tiny, densely packed island colony were filled with roaring masses of young Hong Kong Chinese, brimming with revolutionary ardor imported from across the border, marching through the streets of Central—the financial district—waving plastic-bound copies of Chairman Mao's infamous "Little Red Book."

Bombs were going off in the elevators in office towers—the work of a Commie fifth column. And local rumor had it—I saw no reason to doubt it—that Mao's Red Guards were massing along Hong Kong's practically indefensible border in preparation for a lightning attack. All Chairman Mao had to do—or so it was whispered on every street corner—was bark one command and cut off Hong Kong's water supply, and Hong Kong as we knew it would be history.

Curtains

Having survived a brutal Japanese occupation during World War II, and no shortage of speculative booms and busts in the years since, Hong Kong's future as the last outpost of capitalist excess on the fast-fraying edge of the Communist world was once again looking bleak. The Hang Seng index was scraping the bottom of the barrel. The price of gold (on which many Hong Kong locals fervently speculated) was scouring the sky. But for every local wiseguy willing to bet that this unlikely outpost of capitalist excess perched on the edge of Red China was on its last legs, two or three equally bright bulbs were willing to take that bet and raise it.

Anyone willing to wager in those days that Hong Kong would survive, thrive, and prosper would be a happy camper today. The doomsayers, as usual, were right in the short term, and dead wrong in the long. What outside observers consistently fail to appreciate about Hong Kong is that the place naturally thrives on adversity.

The busy booms and brutal busts of the business cycle have set the rhythms of this old trading town for a century and a half, ever since the British forced the Chinese to cede Hong Kong to them as a colony in exchange for calling a halt to the Opium Wars.

Whether they're out playing the ponies at Happy Valley—that wonderfully efficient and lucrative race course on the edges of the shopping paradise of Causeway Bay—or plunging on their hyperactive stock exchange, Hong Kong locals love to gamble. This gambling instinct saves Hong Kong in times of distress, because real gamblers love nothing better than taking a long shot.

This compulsion to gamble on something—anything—is, by the way, entirely infectious. Before moving to Hong Kong, I'd never speculated on a commodity in my life. But after living in Hong Kong for only a few months, I found myself haunting the halls of the Po Hang Bank, feverishly buying and selling gold bars right along with the rest of Hong Kong's hard-core gold bugs.

Risk Analysis

The essence of Hong Kong is the refinement of risk. In the socialist lexicon, assuming even a reasonable level of risk is called speculation, and is regarded as the root of all evil. But to the committed free-marketeer, speculation is a more morally neutral matter of setting your sights on a target in the near future, and running a real risk of being wrong.

The most lasting lesson I learned during nearly thirty years of living in Hong Kong is the ultimate value of risk. The Hong Kong stock market makes an ideal case in point. It's famously volatile, and requires nerves of steel to ride out its hair-raising roller coasters. But from those dark days of thirty years ago, when a good number of Hong Kong fortunes were made by those willing to see a light at the end of the tunnel, I learned that it usually pays to take the long view. In Hong Kong I also learned that all markets are inherently elastic, and that while what goes up always goes down, the converse is equally true.

Mobius Rule No. 63: What goes down usually goes back up, if you're willing to be patient, and don't hit the panic button.

Mobius Inc.

As fears of an imminent Chinese attack on Hong Kong receded, and the Cultural Revolution rapidly ran out of steam, I established (with some trepidation) a Hong Kong–registered company called Mobius Inc. Having developed a few contacts among Western companies with commercial interests in Asia, I quickly landed some plum assignments managing survey research projects in Japan, Korea, Taiwan, Hong Kong, the Philippines, Vietnam, Thailand, Malaysia, Singapore, Indonesia, Australia, and India.

With the assistance of a small, scrappy, all-young Chinese staff—augmented by a ready pool of freelancers—we helped an American exporter sell toilet soap additives in Indonesia, a Swiss pharmaceutical firm establish a sales operation in Taiwan, and a major international machinery manufacturer make sales to China, at a time when China was still pretty much closed to foreigners lacking high-level contacts to the foreign trade bureaucracy.

We helped Avon determine whether its unique product distribution system could be extended into Asia—it could—and a major dairy manufacturer determine the feasibility of introducing a new type of cheese to Japan—alas, it could not and was not to be.

Upside

For the first time in my life, I was making money. I'd built up a pretty good list of clients, and rented a tiny, inexpensive office on Queen Victoria Street directly across from the old Central Market. On my way home in the evening, I'd dash across the street, buy some fresh fish, take it home and steam it in the Chinese style with chopped leeks and soy sauce . . . delicious! I was starting to advertise. Starting to grow. And to keep my academic hand in, I was a frequent guest lecturer at both the Hong Kong and Chinese universities on the subjects of social and consumer psychology, technical analysis of stock market trends, and survey research.

Downside

But at least half the time I was running around in a state of out-and-out financial terror. Much as I was learning—and I was learning a great deal—about how large businesses were run, I still had to face up to the fact that I knew next to nothing about running a small business. I'd hire people and run up expenses that I had a hard time covering from my fees. And I only made matters worse by putting in low-ball bids to land jobs that ended up paying me too little to cover my costs. Still, by hook and by crook, over a ten-year period, I managed to build up the business. Over time, Mobius Inc. became, if not exactly a cash cow, at least a stable commercial venture.

The Year of the Rat

Hong Kong is built along the lines of a cruise ship: its first-, second-, and third-class decks are strictly segregated according to elevation above sea level. After renting a room from a devoutly Buddhist Chinese woman, and after spending too many sleepless nights inhaling the smell of incense and listening to her chanting, I decided to relocate to the *gweilo* ("white devil") preserve of the Midlevels—a neighborhood of densely packed high-rises clustered just below the rarefied precincts of the Peak.

Despite its prestigious location, the building I moved into turned out to be infested with rats. After returning one night from an assignment in Malaysia, I woke up in a cold sweat, staring down at a fat, hairy, hungry-looking rodent chomping cheerfully away at my toes. I managed to shake the rat loose from its grip. But it ran for cover by scampering brazenly up my chest and right across my face, narrowly missing my mouth.

What They Don't Teach You at Harvard Business School

Since I didn't know the first thing about running a business, I was fortunate to be taught a few concrete lessons by my Chinese staff.

My Chinese lessons began with little things.

"Let's go out and get some lunch," I'd say, without thinking.

"Why would you want to do that?" would come the astonished reply. "Why not get a boxed lunch and eat here? It's cheaper. Why spend the money?"

And so, we would eat a boxed lunch at our desks.

We'd prepare for a trip to, let's say, Kuala Lumpur. "Let's call the travel agency," I'd say, without thinking.

"Why go to a travel agent?" would come the response. "We know a bucket shop." (That's a place where you can buy cut-rate airline tickets.)

And so on, until over time, the pattern of frugality and practicality established itself as an end unto itself. Part of the game.

Part of the fun. It was prestigious, I realized, to save money. And even more prestigious to make it.

Bargain-Hunting

The Chinese can be quite frank, and brutally direct. Despite a widespread impression to the contrary, they're really only indirect when by being direct they'll get themselves into trouble. The Chinese have a distinct aversion to unnecessary arguments, frictions, or to being put at a disadvantage in a commercial transaction. An American might say, as a matter of principle, "I want to be honest with you because I want to help you. I'm your friend and therefore I'm going to tell you that what you are doing is wrong."

A Chinese will ask, "What's the percentage in engaging in this particular conflict? Why should I help him? Why should I be frank with him, because he is just going to hate me for telling him this. It's not going to do *me* any good."

When driving a bargain, the Chinese are exceptionally skilled at giving up bargaining chips they don't give a damn about anyway. "Let them have it," they'll say, pragmatically. "What's the difference? Why not let them win this one? It's no skin off our back."

Under the same circumstances, an American might say, "It's a matter of principle."

But a Chinese would say, "What's a principle worth? Can we eat the principle?"

Handover Hangover

Every one of these culturally critical issues came into play during the years of often tortured negotiations leading up to the resumption of Hong Kong by China. In Hong Kong, the word on the street was that if Margaret Thatcher hadn't in her principled way resolved to raise the touchy subject of the fast-approaching termination of Britain's ninety-nine-year lease on the New Territories, the Chinese leadership would probably have never bothered to demand Hong Kong back, at least not before the turn of the century. But once the British Foreign Service insisted on foolishly reminding the Chinese that come 1997, a large percentage of Hong Kong territory would be rightfully theirs, the Chinese had no choice but to pursue the best deal possible—for them.

Which was to regain Hong Kong, and use it as their window on the West. Their meal ticket, their cash cow, and, just possibly, their ultimate ideological downfall.

Numbers Racket

Over my thirty years in Hong Kong, working closely with Chinese colleagues, I became—in spirit at least—partly Chinese. And becoming partly Chinese helped me enormously in financial matters, because I gradually absorbed the Chinese affinity for numbers. And I slowly began to lose a numbers phobia instilled by a strict math teacher in grammar school, who scared the living daylights out of me by tugging at my (at that time) scorchingly bright red hair.

To the Chinese everything in life is expressible in numbers. That's why the Hong Kong government every year turns a handsome profit auctioning off lucky automobile license plate numbers to the highest bidder.

Snoopy Dog Dog

Just as my industrial research business began to take off, I hit a sharp fork in the road. A savvy American woman named Connie Boucher commissioned me to help her locate a low-cost Hong Kong manufacturer for a line of Snoopy dolls she'd licensed from the cartoonist Charles Schultz. Always happy to help out a client in need, I tracked down a manufacturer for her in no time.

Before long, Connie's line of Snoopy dog dolls had become the 1970s equivalent of the Cabbage Patch Kids. And I, after seeing the sort of money she was making (tragically, Connie recently died; she had been building a fabulous palace on the shores of Lake Tahoe), decided to get in on the act by becoming her Hong Kong sales agent. Soon my Snoopy dog doll business was vastly outstripping—in revenues, if not in personal interest—my fledgling industrial research operation. Something I felt pretty ambivalent about.

Where There's Smoke, There's Fire

I more than happily delegated the doll business to my sharp, aggressive Chinese assistant, Spencer Fu, who was soon running the operation full time. But once our stuffed Snoopy dogs started overrunning our office, I pointedly asked Spencer to stash the overstock at my place while I took off on a long trip to South Korea. On the night I returned, I found myself waking up in the middle of the night in a cold sweat. But this time, rather than rats chewing my lower digits, I was awakened by the sour smell of scorched polyester.

As I dashed out through dark, acrid clouds to the hallway, I grimly realized that the closet in which Spencer had stashed our stuffed animals contained an electric heating coil, which must have ignited the synthetic fur at some point during the night. I managed to put out the fire without having to call the fire department, but my narrow escape from death by doll ignition only heightened my resolve to get out of the doll game for good, before it killed me.

The next morning, as I walked into the office with my eyebrows singed, still smelling of smoke, I gave Spencer a piece of my mind. But instead of the abject apology I'd been expecting, he lit up with an ear-to-ear grin.

"Ah, Mark," he said enviously. "You are a very lucky man. According to Chinese tradition, a man who escapes from a fire is bound to be rich."

That was one superstition I didn't mind buying into. Also, according to Spencer's somewhat idealized version of Chinese tradition, bald men are destined to be wealthy. Since I was halfway by then to losing it all anyway, I decided not to stop at halfway measures. I paid a visit to a Happy Valley Chinese barber and ordered him to take it all off. At first, the exposed skin on my head felt oddly tight, as if stretched. But I enjoyed looking like Mr. Clean.

Aftermath

Much as it hurt to forgo the income, I sold off the Snoopy doll business to Spencer Fu, who has gone on to become the Hong Kong doll magnate I never aspired to be. Meanwhile, I resolved to concentrate my energies on what I really wanted to do: branch out into strategic consulting. I cut my ties to the lucrative dolls, and never looked back.

When I analyze businesses today, one of the first things I look for is management's willingness to *bag baggage*. To cut losses and move on without regrets.

> **Mobius Rule No. 64: Bagging baggage is the first step to freedom.**

High Finance

I would doubtless have gone on happily building up my Asian-business strategic consultancy over the following two decades, if I hadn't happened to stumble into the lucrative sideline of financial consulting in the same way that every other major turn in my life occurred: completely by accident.

One day in 1973, I got a call from an old Hong Kong friend, Eric Hotung, a grandson of the famous Robert Hotung, the first Hong Kong "Chinaman"—as the local Brits used to refer to members of their native population—to be grudgingly permitted to live in the exclusive heights of the Peak.

"I want to know what's going on in the stock market," Eric said, in that inimitable, practical Chinese way. "I want to know what's going to go up and what's going to go down. Can you give me some research?"

I would, I could, and I did.

I approached my new commission as I would have any other market research assignment: by hitting the books. Still a perennial student at heart, I started out studying the technical analysis of price movements, the chartist school. The deeper I delved into this arcane art, the more intrigued I became by its possible predictive potential.

Nineteen seventy-three just happened to mark the peak of one of the longest, most aggressive bull runs in postwar Hong Kong history. So, as a fledgling chartist, I was a bit taken aback to discern one of the best-known technical price formations, the "Head & Shoulders" formation, taking place right there in Hong Kong.

A Head & Shoulders formation occurs when aggregate stock prices run gradually up to a high top, and then plateau off to a second top not quite as high as the previous top. This forms a line on a graph that assumes the shape of a shoulder, a head, and then falls down to the other shoulder. If you see a head and shoulder taking shape on the chart, beware.

An even better idea: sell everything, including your shirt off those shoulders.

Armed with this ominous information, I filled Eric Hotung in on my forebodings. Unfortunately, I neglected to follow my own advice. One too-hot-to-handle stock that Spencer Fu, my old friend and colleague, was particularly enthralled by was called Mosbert Holdings.

Mosbert was a sprawling, ill-defined Malaysian holding company that had made a mysterious entry into Hong Kong, and despite the fact that nobody could figure out where the money came from, had been noisily, busily buying up everything in sight. Companies, buildings—whatever it could get its hands on.

"I bought Mosbert at eight and now it's down to three-and-a-half, half of what I bought it for," Spencer excitedly explained, in a somewhat muddled version of contrarian thinking. "It's a fabulous buying opportunity."

Well, maybe yes, and maybe no. Before taking the plunge, I decided to do some minimum due diligence. I picked up the phone and gave the folks at Mosbert a call. The fellow I spoke to was remarkably unfriendly, and to put it mildly, the last thing from an open book.

"I can't give out any information over the phone," he said brusquely. "And nothing's available in print." As if to drive home that point a little deeper, he hung up on me.

Needless to say, I found this all a bit disconcerting. But Spencer repeatedly assured me that Mosbert was going to be the next great Hong Kong financial miracle. Not to mention, at present prices, the bargain of the century. Against my better judgment, I said, "Let's go for it."

And so, we did. Suffice it to say, the slew of cheaply printed Mosbert shares gracing the wall of the reception area of Templeton's Hong Kong office today are not worth the paper they're printed on. Not only does a high-flying market cover all sins, it covers all scams. Mosbert Holdings turned out to be one of the biggest scams to emerge from a scandal-ridden Hong Kong stock market, which within weeks was collapsing all around us.

Mosbert, of course, went belly-up. Looking back in anger, we had been complete dolts. We should have wondered why the stock was depressed. Because the people on the street who had been driving down Mosbert stock knew a few things that we didn't: that Mosbert was not entirely on the up and up. We should have held on to our wallets when this publicly listed company refused to provide any information to us about its operations and finances.

And with Mosbert on the ropes, the great Hong Kong bull market had buckled to its knees. From a peak approaching 300 (to put matters in perspective, it recently hovered as high as 2,500), the Hang Seng index dropped like a stone to under 100.

At which point—now get this—it settled into a gradual, steady decline lasting until . . . mid-1982!

That's right: it took nearly a decade for the Hong Kong stock market to regain the ground it lost in a couple of rough months at the tail end of 1973. If you look at the drop on the chart, it looks like a ski-jump at the winter Olympics.

But was the lesson to be learned from all this to stay out of volatile markets like Hong Kong?

No way. As far as I was concerned, the lesson to be learned from this disaster was:

If you don't follow what you learn, and don't act on the information that you have gathered, and if you give in too readily to what Alan Greenspan so memorably dubbed the "irrational exuberance" of a runaway bull market, you might end up diving off your own Head & Shoulders.

Déjà Flu All Over Again

Now, a quarter of a century later, as the Hong Kong stock market was once again taking a tumble, I found myself as a guest on the ABC-TV talk show *This Week* straining to explain the laws of financial gravity.

If what goes up must eventually come down, it stands to reason that what goes down will eventually go up.

ABC: Mr. Mobius, what's caused all this? The explanation that we seem to read is that an investment boom in Southeast Asia produced too much capacity, and now you're having some kind of shake-out. That means it's sort of finite and will correct itself, is that the interpretation you would put on this?

MM: Well, the big problem right now is the recognition that finally we have a market economy. A lot of these countries have been used to controlling their exchange rate, controlling their economy from the center, from the central bank. And now, they're beginning to realize that the market is global, and that their countries are being affected by global forces. They have to let these markets free. They have to recognize the market and hear the demands of the market.

ABC: We've heard an interesting theory from some of the governments involved in Southeast Asia, that this is caused by speculators, particularly Jewish speculators. Could you tell us what role speculators played in this, if any? What are speculators?

MM: Well, I think that what people mean by speculators are people who are doing currency transactions, or taking advantage of the potential weakness in a currency. But these people are arbitraging the currencies in a way to take advantage of overvalued currencies. And those currencies would seek those levels over time anyway. I don't think that the currency speculators, if that's what they are, are doing anything more than perhaps precipitating the decline.

ABC: Now, back to the global economy. There's also a theory gaining currency in some quarters in this country that the old rules don't apply anymore, that because of the global economy and other factors, this business of a recession followed by a recovery followed by recession, this so-called business cycle, is out the window . . . New rules, Mr. Mobius?

MM: No, I think we're still going to see booms and busts. And thank God for that, by the way, because that's exactly how we thrive as managers. We want to take advantage of these booms and busts. And the investors have got to be patient, they've got to realize that this is going to be a volatile situation whenever they are getting into stock markets, and it's not going to get less volatile, it'll get more volatile as time goes on.

ABC: Now explain that, Mr. Mobius. What do you mean, "thank God for booms and busts"? As managers, do you mean that you make commissions because we all buy and sell in panics? I'm not going to let you get out of this one.

MM: Well, the nice thing about booms and busts is that it gives us an opportunity as money managers to buy very, very cheaply because the markets overdo it, they overshoot the mark. And that gives us an opportunity. Now of course our investors get very nervous when that happens and we have to soothe them and tell them to be patient. But in the long run it comes out to be a good result.

ABC: But it becomes a problem for the economies of nations, does it not? And that's what people are concerned about now.

MM: It becomes a problem only if the governments allow it to become a problem. If governments would recognize the signals of the markets, and if—for example in Thailand—they had recognized that their inflation was higher than the U.S. and that therefore their currency was overvalued, they should have allowed the currency to freely float. But the governments want to control these currencies, and that's always their big mistake.

The Patron Saint of Hong Kong

Whenever a market anywhere takes a nosedive, it's common for old-timers to wag their fingers and say scoldingly: "You young whippersnappers, you only think that markets go up. Well, aren't you in for a surprise! What goes up must come down. You've never lived through a meltdown! A meltdown teaches you the value of prudence and caution."

But have you ever once heard an old-timer say, "You young whippersnapper, I lived through the recovery of 1995 and let me tell you, that there was some recovery! You can learn a lot from a recovery!"

> **Mobius Rule No. 65: The problem with recoveries is that they don't make good copy.**

> **Mobius Rule No. 66: Market meltdowns make headlines. Market recoveries make money.**

The amount of ink—and stuff and nonsense—spilled over the Mexican meltdown of 1994 and the Tequila Effect that spoiled Latin American markets for a few years—was remarkable. But even more remarkable—though much less remarked upon—is the salient fact that you never, ever see a front-page headline that blares: "Mexican Markets Stage Gradual, Measured Recovery."

For hope at times of crisis, I like to think of people praying to the patron saint of Hong Kong, Milton Friedman, who for thirty years championed Hong Kong as a paragon of dynamic capitalism in action. Thirty years of living through the booms and busts of the Hong Kong business cycle taught me what it means to live in a free market—for all its notable weaknesses, including a predilection toward extreme volatility, soaring booms, and steep busts.

It pays to pay attention to a market like Hong Kong, a market liable to swift and sudden sentimental shifts (a psychiatrist would label it "labile"), because I considered the Hong Kong stock market the paradigmatic global stock market of tomorrow. (At least until the Hong Kong Monetary Authority decided to intervene in the market in 1998.)

Boning Up on Your Fundamentals

At times of distress, there's a tendency to live too much in the moment.

Emotions take place in the moment; rationality looks forward and backward in time.

Panic and fear—as well as greed—bring sentiment into the foreground, and make rationality take an emotional backseat. But examining a subject in the light of history generally helps you take the long view. While caught up in the flux and flow of the severe bout of Asian Financial Flu that roiled all emerging markets during the last half of 1997, I took a certain amount of comfort from the fact that Hong Kong has been a leading center of Asian finance since 1866, when the first securities were traded in the territory. The first Hong Kong Stock Exchange was established in 1891, and has been going strong ever since.

To delve into more recent history, since 1969, when the Hong Kong stock market was first opened to international investors, the exchange's market cap has risen more than 100 times. Over the same period, average daily turnover grew from HK$100 million to HK$13 billion—at an exchange rate pegged to the U.S. dollar at roughly eight to one.

The size and liquidity of the Hong Kong stock market is its big plus, and its big minus. Because when a regional crisis like the latest Asian Contagion hits, it hits hard.

> **Mobius Rule No. 67: A liquid stock market is one that's easy to get out of, not just easy to get in.**

The China Connection

From the late 1970s, when Deng's "Open Door Policy" first opened up the Chinese market to international investment, Hong Kong has accumulated direct investments in China totaling over US$100 billion, representing over half of total direct investment in China.

By 1997, total loans to Chinese enterprises by Hong Kong banks amounted to US$46 billion. For Chinese enterprises—the so-called red chips—seeking to arrange overseas funding, the Hong Kong Stock Exchange had become the first choice to be listed.

By the time of the handover in the summer of 1997, twenty-eight out of thirty-one Chinese enterprises listed on overseas stock exchanges had chosen to list in Hong Kong.

And why was that?

First, because it's the best way to access foreign capital.

Second—and just as important—because the rule of law is so much better established in Hong Kong than in the domestic Chinese markets.

This was, and I hope will remain, the primary and lasting legacy of the much-maligned British and their highly advanced legal system. Chinese companies, and the Chinese government, are smart enough to recognize that if they want to seriously tap into Western markets, the by-the-book Hong Kong market will give foreign investors comfort and confidence. Over time, Shanghai's regulatory system may improve, but it still has a long way to go.

Hong Kong's rapid ascent to the status of "The Wall Street of China" came as something of a surprise to many old China hands, who'd expected the Chinese to insist that the Shanghai Stock Exchange enjoy the lion's share of the prime privatization pipeline. But the Chinese practical side won out over their patriotic side, when the financial powers-that-be realized that Hong Kong is a more mature market, and therefore a more desirable listing location.

Even after taking the temporary troubles of Asia into account, the World Bank estimates that the Chinese Economic Area (mainland China, Hong Kong, and Taiwan) will be larger than the U.S. in purchasing power parity terms by the year 2002.

If this prediction turns out to be accurate, the role of what is now formally known as the SAR (Special Administrative Territory) of Hong Kong will be crucial in providing the financial resources for this astounding growth story.

Hong Kong's Burden

As the Asian Contagion buffeted the world's farthest-flung markets, Hong Kong's greatest problem lay not in China, Malaysia, or even Thailand, but in Hong Kong itself. The place had gotten just too damned expensive. Land cost a fortune, food cost a fortune, apartments cost a fortune, office rents were sky high, salaries astronomical. The result: as other Asian currencies devalued, Hong Kong property prices (on which the entire local economy was based) would have to come down, or Hong Kong would lose what little competitiveness it had left in comparison with Southeast Asian rivals such as Singapore.

Under its new Chinese leadership, Hong Kong faced a tough choice: either lower its exchange rate (abandon the peg) or reduce inflation by some other means. Since property values are the basis of the Hong Kong economy, they were likely to drop, by our estimation, a minimum of 20 percent for the SAR to remain competitive.

In my opinion, if the market were to determine the Hong Kong dollar's "true" value, it would probably have fallen from 8 down to 10 or 11 Hong Kong dollars to the U.S. greenback. But for the Chinese government to abandon the peg only four months after the handover would have undermined public confidence in Chinese stewardship over its prize possession. Which was why they ultimately decided to keep the peg's grip on their dollar, despite the welter of problems that entailed.

Domestically, China was faced with an additional dilemma: not only was the Hong Kong currency overvalued, its own currency, the yuan, had not been devalued in years, and was now looking high-priced in comparison to the devalued Thai baht or the Philippine peso. Malaysia, Indonesia, and Singapore were all headed down the same road to 20 to 50 percent devaluations stacked up against the U.S. dollar.

Making matters even more difficult for the Chinese was that the U.S. government was putting pressure on the Chinese not to devalue the yuan, because the U.S. wanted to lower its enormous trade deficit with China by exporting more goods to China.

The most pressing issue facing all of Asia, however, was China itself.

Not only was China's economy humming along while the others faltered spectacularly, but China was far and away the lowest-cost producer in the region. Everyone, from Korea to Indonesia to Singapore to even Hong Kong, had reason to fear China's capacity to undercut them on exports. And as China moved aggressively to restructure its economy, many Asian countries and companies had reason to hope that China's economic modernization would not be as successful as planned.

All these issues, of a potentially weak property market and a potentially weakening peg, were definitely on the minds of jittery international investors on Friday morning, October 24, as the Pacific Rim awakened to an unexceptional morning session in Tokyo and Sydney, Australia.

As the Japanese markets closed for lunch, the Hong Kong exchange opened sharply lower. By late morning, the Hang Seng rallied briefly before taking a 10 percent nosedive in less than an hour. As Australia and Tokyo got wind of the sell-off in Hong Kong, those markets began to react like cows in a thunderstorm. They began to stampede for the exits.

In a jittery market, the slightest negative signal can be enough to touch off a panic.

In this case, as the afternoon session began in Hong Kong, a wave of panic selling began sending stocks gyrating wildly. Why?

Because Hong Kong had gotten wind of the fact that its problems were having a negative effect on Tokyo and Australia.

George Soros calls this feedback effect "reflexivity."

I prefer to think of it as simply another sign of the fact that markets are naturally self-governing systems.

The panic spread in a wave, like one of those wild effects fans generate in football stadiums following a touchdown. The European markets (which began trading just as the Hong Kong market closed out its afternoon session) opened sharply lower, dropping into the basement by mid-afternoon. American markets promptly followed suit. A few hours later, Latin American indexes took an even worse hit, as traders grew increasingly concerned that currency speculators might soon go after the same weakness they had hammered in Asia: arguably overvalued currencies.

By the end of the day, what had begun as a quaver had turned into a full-scale rout. The great decade-long Asian bubble had just gone ballistically bust.

Red Chip Fever

The *New York Times* was right on the money when it stated: "For investors still willing to try the bumpy ride in Asia, it's hard to think of a sexier pair of words than 'China Telecom.'"

Against this dark backdrop of fiercely tumbling world markets, we strolled into a meeting with the two crown princes of China Telecom, which analysts had dubbed the hottest red chip IPO (initial public offering) to come down the pike since the handover.

Even as Hong Kong's financial secretary was publicly insisting that there was "no political or economic need for us to disband the Hong Kong dollar peg," one of our best and brainiest Hong Kong brokers was blandly assuring us that buying China Telecom was a "no-brainer."

"The issue is oversubscribed by 300 times," he bleated, visibly salivating at the very thought. "It's a hot issue. I'd buy as much as you can get. The gray market is saying you'll double your money in one day. It's putting a 100 percent premium on the market price."

Remember what I said about power brokers: whenever you hear the words "no-brainer" and "hot issue" let a little air out of their tires.

Forty-eight hours later, with the Hang Seng Index doing a

splendid imitation of a lead weight in free-fall, China Telecom was set to open at HK$10.00—a bit below the initial offering price of HK$11.68. The ADRs (American depository receipts), meanwhile, began trading in New York at US$2.50 below its offering price of US$30.50, at US$27.50. The price of the ADR was considered to be roughly equivalent to the Hong Kong shares—it's just that the number of shares folded into a single ADR made the prices look different. I say "roughly" because, as is commonly the case, according to my calculations, the ADRs were priced slightly higher to cover the added costs of the ADR program. If we had bought, we would have bought the shares in Hong Kong, where there is no foreign share premium.

This highly touted $4 billion stock offering had promised to be the bellwether for red chips in the post-handover Hong Kong.

But come the fall, the overheated market in red chips—mainland Chinese companies listed on the Hong Kong exchange—had cooled considerably. By Black October, red chips had dropped 40 percent from their peak in late August.

What to do?

Well, the first thing I did was take the meeting with the top brass at China Telecom.

For All the Money in China

Taken at face value, the numbers looked *great*.

China Telecom was (according to its glossy prospectus, expertly prepared by Goldman, Sachs, the lead underwriters of the initial public offering) "the dominant provider of cellular telecommunications services in Guangdong and Zhejiang provinces [which are] among China's most economically developed provinces [as well as] . . . the two provinces in China with the largest numbers of cellular subscribers."

In other words, *la crème de la crème*, cellularly speaking.

Not only that, but "the telecommunications industry in China has experienced rapid growth in recent years, and the cellular services sector is one of the fast growing sectors within the telecommunications industry."

In short, what was there not to like?

China Telecom's cellular subscriber base had grown at an annual rate of 88.3 percent over the past three years. Mr. Li Ping, China Telecom's vice chairman, was convinced that the existing subscriber base in these provinces could rise from 3 million now to 7 million by the year 2000.

On top of that—as our broker had put it in touting the stock—"you're buying an effective monopoly."

Playing Monopoly

It's quite common for governments to grant monopolies, typically of a limited duration, to cellular and fixed-line phone companies in exchange for a strictly defined amount of investment, to effectively guarantee them a reasonable return on that investment.

But China Telecom was something special: it was connected to the highest levels of the government leadership, by virtue of having been spawned by the PRC (People's Republic of China) Ministry of Posts and Telecommunications, which goes by the acronym MPT.

As Goldman, Sachs pointedly put it: "The company is the primary vehicle for the MPT system to access the international capital markets."

Translation: the Chinese telecom ministry was looking to China Telecom as its meal ticket to the outside world. And to back up what would otherwise have been a hollow promise, the MPT had undertaken to insure that China Telecom would be the only Chinese cellular phone company under its control to be listed on any stock exchange in Hong Kong or outside China. Nor would the MPT "provide cellular services in any province in which China Telecom currently operates, or may operate in the future."

In other words, they were promising a virtual lock on the market.

So far, so good.

We met with Vice Chairman Li Ping, and his senior vice president, Mr. Lu Errui.

Both men were exceedingly well dressed, well spoken, distinguished, obviously highly intelligent gentlemen who looked accustomed to wielding power under the "old system" (Communism) while being simultaneously savvy about operating under the "new system" (capitalism).

China Telecom's number one goal, simply stated, was: "To maximize shareholder value by expanding network capacity, coverage, performance, and functionality."

Their fledgling company's two strongest suits, they modestly explained, were:

1) "The outstanding macro-economic performance" of their assigned territory, which combined two of the richest provinces in China.

2) "The explosive growth of the cellular sector in China, the overwhelming dominance of their market position, and the strong support of the MPT."

Put these two together, and you certainly had what looked like a real gravy train.

Mr. Li explained that by choosing to structure China Telecom as the virtual monopoly provider of cellular services in China's two richest provinces, the MPT had made a deliberate decision to sell off the Chinese "telecom industry's best assets."

Which was, to my mind, a smart move. Because if China Telecom shares sold well in the market, that would set a high value on the rest of the antiquated Chinese telecom system. Which would be like a slam dunk for the MPT.

China Telecom's main competition, a company called Unicom, was comparatively weak. Unicom had been established by a mandate of the State Council in 1993 as the telecom arm of the Ministry of Railroads, Electronics, and Electric Power, which meant that its primary businesses were railways, power provision, and light manufacturing.

Cellular services were a very small part of its operations. All the same, Unicom had been given some pretty lucrative territory, and it had already launched cellular operations in some major Chinese cities—Shanghai, Guangzhou, Tianjin, Shenzhen, and

Xi'an—but its overall share of the cellular market in China was still just a measly 1.7 percent.

China Telecom's market share, by contrast, would start out in the double digits.

"How likely," I asked Mr. Li, "would it be for the State Council"—the overall governing body of the state, with absolute control over the MPT—"to grant any more cellular licenses?"

In other words, "Are you likely to have much competition?"

Li gravely responded: "The MPT has a strong say in setting this regulatory policymaking. If the State Council were to issue a license, the MPT would have to prepare the document."

So it went without saying that the MPT had promised China Telecom shareholders that they were not about to issue any competing licenses.

So the issue of competition was, for the time being at least, moot.

China, Li volunteered, was already the world's third largest cellular market, after the U.S. and Western Europe. And while the total U.S. penetration amounted to 44 million users, or roughly 16.5 percent of the population, his vast country currently had only 10 million cellular subscribers, amounting to a relatively small market penetration.

This allowed ample room for growth—something long-term investors like to see.

The populations of China Telecom's two target provinces were, respectively, 69 million for Guangdong and 43 million for Zhejiang.

Which was where, he emphasized, you could pretty much find all the money in China.

Not only was this guy, I thought to myself, extremely well spoken—in both Chinese and English—but he evidently had a superb command of the politico-commercial landscape in China, which, like its roads, was riddled with potholes. It was hardly surprising that the MPT had appointed Li its liaison to the fickle and fearful financial forces of the West.

It all sounded quite wonderful. Which, of course, should have come as no surprise, since the entire spiel had been exquisitely structured—with the help of Western advisors—to sound symphonic to Western financial ears.

But then Mr. Li casually said something, by the bye, that gave me a moment's pause.

"The minutes-per-usage rate has dropped," Li calmly said, "as business users have been supplanted by residential users."

That was all.

But it echoed what I was hearing elsewhere.

All over the world, the same thing is happening: as cellular services become more of a mass market, the high-end, free-spending business users, who rack up huge phone bills because their tabs are being picked up by their employers, are being supplanted by more frugal residential users. This means that even as the number of subscribers grows exponentially, revenue per subscriber is falling fast. What this portends down the road for China Telecom's profits was anybody's best guess. But from where I was sitting, at least, the long-term picture didn't look very rosy.

The picture had not notably brightened by the time, a year hence, the government announctd its intention to "reform the phone industry," a move deemed likely to end the monoply status of China Telecom.

IPO Mania

Even without all the rocking, rolling, and roiling in Asian markets—which I calmly considered a fleeting epi-phenomenon—buying China Telecom at its high initial offering price was, despite our broker's flamboyant assurances, by no means a no-brainer.

This was also despite the gray market placing a 100 percent premium on the shares—according to rumor—and despite the company's cozy close connections to the august MPT. The gray market, incidentally, is a market in shares that have been allocated to certain subscribers to the initial share issue (IPO) who immediately turn around and sell their share allocation, right out of the gate, to buyers willing to pay a steep premium for the shares.

My little head-mounted antennae were quivering like tuning forks, picking up warning signals.

As best I could figure it, China Telecom's assets when compared to similarly situated cellular companies elsewhere in the world were being valued at a very high price.

Of course, for everyone involved, buying this stock meant placing a bet on the future. For my purposes, I wasn't as concerned about today's price-to-earnings ratio as I was about the P/E five years down the line. But for that P/E to be any kind of bargain in five years' time, CT's growth in revenues—as opposed to subscriber base—would have to be staggering. And even then, growth in numbers or market share wasn't the point. It was growth in profits that mattered.

To their credit, I found Li Ping and his colleagues personally impressive.

And I had not the slightest doubt that under such obviously capable management, China Telecom would flourish in its local market. But I did harbor some doubts about the company's long-term revenue growth prospects. Simply put, as cellular phone service becomes more of a mass medium, prices—and possibly profits—are bound to go down.

The looming question: would increased volume compensate for the drop in revenue per subscriber?

Add to that uncertain mix the feeding frenzy that typically accompanies these red chip IPOs and my gut response was rank skepticism.

IPO Primer

When an IPO is oversubscribed, in this case by a reported 50 or 60 times, this means that more people—institutional investors, primarily—have put in their bids (and in many cases written sizable checks for shares they hoped to buy) than will ever lay hands on them.

China Telecom's underwriters (in this case Goldman, Sachs) had been granted the right by the company to essentially allocate the shares as they saw fit. Which meant that a certain (small) percentage would go to New York in the form of ADRs, and a certain (higher) percentage would be listed in Hong Kong.

IPOs are intrinsically unfair, insofar as both share underwriters and the company are permitted a wide degree of latitude in granting preferential treatment to most favored customers. With a hot IPO like China Telecom—piping hot until the day the bottom dropped out of the Hong Kong stock market—the gray market quickly bids the price way up above the initial share, or opening, price.

The gray market is made up of all sorts of frustrated buyers, who since they haven't been given a share allocation, promise to pay a substantial premium to anyone who did get their hands on some shares over the official market price, if they will sell their shares to them.

This means that anyone who's lucky enough to get a chunk of stock on the first round—a privilege bestowed on them sometimes by random lottery, and at other times because of connections to the underwriters—can simply turn around and flip the stock, minutes after they bought it, into the gray market and make a tidy profit in no seconds flat.

One factor influencing the so-called gray-marketeers is the not unreasonable expectation that the new share issue will soar like a hot-air balloon.

Playing the IPO Game

What I often do in playing IPOs is hang back, and wait and see what happens to the shares in the after-market—that's the open market—in a few weeks, or months. Of course, there's no way to be sure that the price will drop, but once the initial euphoria has ended, it's not uncommon in my experience for IPO prices to dip, or at least drift, once the support limits promised by the first round of buyers have been breached.

In any given share allocation scheme, a certain proportion of the total shares issued is guaranteed to be sold to the general public—to give an impression of fairness. So it's perfectly possible for small investors to play an IPO in precisely the same way that I do.

Flying the Concord

Sometime during the fall of 1994, we paid a visit to a mainland Chinese company which, we had been reliably informed by impeccable sources, was a sure winner: an extremely dynamic young company run by an extremely dynamic young guy named Wong Sai Chung.

Concord Pacific made watches and distributed cosmetics, but what it really trafficked in was the hopes and dreams of Mr. Wong Sai Chung—which were, to say the least, epic in scope.

Mr. Wong's watch factory was in Macau—the tiny former Portuguese colony right near Hong Kong—while his cosmetics plant was across the Pearl River estuary in China's fast-growing Shenzhen free economic zone.

Our Hong Kong brokers were jumping all over themselves with enthusiasm about Concord Pacific, and about its reportedly "well-connected" CEO, and his magnificent plans for the future.

So one fine day we set out from Hong Kong to the Pearl River estuary to pay a visit to both plants, and see what we could see. Which turned out to be not much. Concord Pacific stock was selling for peanuts on the day that we visited its not very impressive looking watch factory in Macau.

When we walked through the door, we expected the place to be humming like a beehive. But all the workers were calmly sitting at their benches, and sitting on their hands, quietly and obediently just sitting and waiting . . . and not working. Not making watches.

Why? we wondered innocently.

Because, we were told, all the electricity had been cut off.

When do you expect the electricity to come on again? we asked.

Oh, in an hour, two hours, an unconcerned floor manager said. We don't know.

How often does this happen?

Oh, quite a lot.

On the upside, the workers seemed to be very neat, very obedient, and very young.

Deciding that it didn't make much sense to sit around with them, waiting for the power to come back on, we hopped a ferry across the Pearl River to Concord Pacific's cosmetics factory on the Chinese side. We walked into this four-story building, at about two in the afternoon, and no one was there. We found ourselves, to our astonishment, staring out at rows of empty benches.

Where was everyone? we asked the one floor manager we were able to track down.

Oh, he said, the electricity does not run during the day, so they only work the night shift.

We couldn't afford to stick around for the night shift to start, so that was the end of that.

Shortly thereafter, Concord Pacific stock shot right through the roof.

Why?

Having apparently decided that a slow build in watches and cosmetics was not up his alley—particularly if your factories are located in areas with erratic electricity—Wong had promptly plunged into property deals. These were astoundingly big trans-actions for an ostensibly green up-and-comer: shopping centers, office projects, residential developments, all over China. And, because it's sexier than watches or cosmetics, Wong was getting into telecommunications.

To be specific, he was aiming his sights at the low-end market. He yearned to be a major player in the fast-growing Chinese mar-ket for pagers, which are a good deal cheaper than cellular phones. Though I knew next to nothing about Mr. Wong personally, it was clear by his deeds, as well as his deals, that he had brains, boldness, and the third element critical to success in China: connections.

In China, the term is *guanxi*, which means "personal con-tacts," not contracts.

But to his credit, Wong also displayed a boldness and daring to do things that other people wouldn't even have tried, much less succeeded at. Now, as we walked along concrete-covered walkways snaking through Hong Kong's tightly packed Central District from our offices at Exchange Place to his offices in the prestigious penthouse of Wheelock House (one of the premium addresses in all of Hong Kong), I found myself pondering an-other, as yet unstated reason for paying this call on Mr. Wong.

A few months before, Wong had acquired a sizable (nearly 20 percent) chunk in a high-flying company called Yaohan

International, which was being run (into the ground) by a flashy, flamboyant Japanese entrepreneur, who'd moved into Hong Kong in a big way.

One of this action-Jackson's first headline-generating acts had been to buy the most lavish private home in all of Hong Kong, a magnificent palace high on the Peak usually shrouded in clouds, which had originally been built by the former chairman of the Hong Kong & Shanghai Bank, who sold it to the man from Yaohan.

Yaohan had at one time been a chain of highly successful department stores in Japan. The company plunged big-time into restaurants (which are famously fine cash cows) and highly leveraged property developments.

He set up a Hong Kong company to hold his Hong Kong restaurant interests, and a second Hong Kong company for his Chinese investments. It wasn't long before the Hong Kong company had become seriously overleveraged, a minor setback to which the CEO's creative solution had been to take the company private—at a price only he considered reasonable. The man seriously proposed to pull off this neat trick by paying next to nothing for the outstanding stock.

We just happened to own a good chunk of Yaohan ourselves. And we balked at his price. As a major shareholder, we were unwilling to discount our shares quite as heavily as he would have liked, and we hoped that other major shareholders, like our Mr. Wong, could be persuaded to hold out for a higher price.

During the short walk across town, it had occurred to me that perhaps during our meeting I might be able to see if Wong was interested in joining forces with us in gaining some leverage with Yaohan.

In return for his shares, we understood that Wong had gained rights to the Yaohan name in China. Which, given the current state of affairs, was a pretty mixed bag.

Concord First Class

"Concord Pacific Holdings, the parent company, is a *very sexy* company," our Hong Kong broker had practically purred, coyly confiding to us some confidential numbers during our briefing before the meeting. "Everyone's in love with this MIT."

"MIT?" I asked, my curiosity piqued by this flagrant adoption of the brand name of my alma mater in Massachusetts.

"Mobile information terminal," our broker said with a smile. "Chinese character paging."

Mr. Wong Sai Chung, chairman and managing director of the Concord Group, was strikingly handsome with a bit of a movie star air, a look he augmented with a high-style haircut and a well-cut basic black no doubt Chinese silk suit.

Although his English was perfectly passable, he insisted upon using an interpreter, no doubt so that not the slightest nuance of his presentation would be lost on us. Not that Wong was big on nuance. He clearly had aspirations to become the Donald Trump of China, who is hardly known as the king of shuttle diplomacy. Wong rapidly outlined for us his "three-pronged" business plan.

No. 1 Prong: Retail—department stores

No. 2 Prong: Property

No. 3 Prong: Telecom

On the retail side, Wong gleefully noted the huge untapped retail market in China, which was growing at an annual rate of 15–20 percent. This was his No. 1 Prong.

"It's the largest retail sector yet to be opened to the outside world," he said modestly.

"Twenty years ago," he fondly recalled, as if reciting from his "Chairman's Message" in the annual report, "we started out with watch manufacturing and a cosmetics distribution business on the Pearl River. But now, the goal is to capture a sizable market of the Chinese retail and department store industry. To do this by ourselves would take ten years, and we would incur large start-up costs, mainly recruitment of good managers. So instead we decided to leverage a good brand name, complemented by our already established shopping malls. We will," he asserted, as if there could be no disputing his bold claim, "realize a major market participation within five years."

What? I wondered.

By leveraging the tarnished Yaohan name?

He had to be kidding. Oh, this guy was aggressive, and impressive. Unfortunately, the only "good brand name" he had to "leverage" was now a basically bankrupt company. There were rumors in Hong Kong that some companies connected to Yaohan might shut their doors. The first sign of panic behavior had been the anxious crowds stampeding into St. Honoré Cake Shops, a company in part owned by Yaohan International, to cash in gift certificates that the shops had sold before they became worthless. Cakes were being snatched from the shelves like cut-rate diamonds. The ironic result was that St. Honoré, which was in no real trouble itself, did a land office business in Christmas cakes.

The next place to be hit by the wave of increasingly rife Yaohan rumors was a chain of amusement arcades called Whimsy, also partly owned by Yaohan.

Once again, panic-stricken customers crowded into these computer-game palaces to use promotional tickets they'd won over the years of jamming coins into the machines, before the place went belly-up. Once again, the problem had been a connection to Yaohan. To the people of Hong Kong, the Yaohan name was clearly jinxed. Could the people of China be so dim and ill-informed to feel very differently?

But here, as I glanced down to read his most recent annual report, Wong was stoutly maintaining that "The Yaohan Group, having established a chain of department stores worldwide with a firm customer following . . . has enjoyed a high reputation as well as brand recognition in China, Hong Kong, and Southeast Asia. . . . We are very positive about the strategic alliance with Yaohan, and believe that it will expedite the process of becoming one of the leading retailers in China."

I'm sure Whimsy and St. Honoré cake stores were not feeling quite so positive about "leveraging" their "strategic alliances" with Yaohan.

But I could hardly blame Wong for the rapid deterioration of conditions at the chain—after all, we'd bought a fair amount of the stock ourselves, and had been, at least so far, powerless to stop the hemorrhage.

"Yaohan International enjoys a great image in China," Wong strenuously insisted, as if to suggest that in far-off China, they hadn't yet gotten wind of the company's problems in Japan and Hong Kong.

"Working with this name and our lengthy experience in China," he bravely went on, "we have found a way to launch hypermarket stores in competition with the French Carrefour and Wal-Mart. With no operating license," he added gleefully, "Carrefour will be unable to obtain a major market share."

"Hypermarkets" are gigantic supermarkets that carry everything and anything, from soup to nuts. Hypermarkets are a little like Wal-Marts, but bigger. Personally, I would never be willing to write off Carrefour, an aggressive French hypermarket company with a very impressive and well-tested high-growth global strategy, out of a battle for market share anywhere. I couldn't resist tweaking Wong's composure a bit, so I openly stated my longtime admiration for Carrefour's corporate strategy.

"Now, Carrefour is one to watch." I leaned forward. "Their strategy is to get the middle and upper part of the lower end markets," I went on. "They've done very well in Brazil, a country where Wal-Mart stumbled, when they started importing golf clubs when Brazilians don't even play golf."

Wong pointedly ignored my flagrant praise of his prime competitor.

But I had another reason for praising Carrefour.

I was curious about his reaction.

His reaction was interesting, because it was basically no reaction at all.

Mobius Rule No. 68: After bagging baggage, the most important thing for management is an *ability to listen*—particularly when it comes to analyzing their own mistakes.

"Our strategic alliance with Yaohan will enable us to bring a successful hypermarket concept to China," was all Mr. Wong would say in response. "This year we opened up three new stores, in Beijing, Shanghai, and Suzhou," he continued, racing ahead. "Because of our getting into Yaohan—at a cost of over

HK$100—we acquired the best image brand name in China. As owners of 19 percent of Yaohan International, we have been given the right to use their brand name throughout China. With the store in Beijing, that one is a 50-50 strategic alliance with Yaohan."

And he just went rolling along, unfazed, praising his Yaohan connection.

"Is there any way," I wondered out loud, "that you can outbid Yaohan in China and Hong Kong and bring it under your wing?"

This was my way of getting into a strategy discussion of the whole Yaohan dilemma.

But Wong dismissed this obviously absurd notion with a quick chop of his hand.

"No interest," he said with a broad, almost cartoon-like grimace reminiscent of a Beijing Opera mask. "The major value is in China."

"How many more hypermarkets do you plan to open in China?" I asked, quickly changing the subject.

"This year three, next year ten," he responded.

"Does Yaohan's bankruptcy in Japan help you by letting you bring in more skilled managers to China from those being laid off in Japan?"

Property Values

CP's No. 2 Prong was property.

This was, in my humble opinion, by far the most impressive sector of his portfolio. Wong had substantial property investments in Thailand—uh-oh—as well as major mega mall, office, and residential developments all over China, plus a prime site in Hong Kong.

The problem was: right now all three markets were heavily overbuilt.

As with all real estate developers, the question was: could we weather the rough times ahead?

"Our studies show that the Hong Kong dollar is overvalued,"

I volunteered. "We believe the property market must go down. What is your strategy if this scenario is correct?"

"We feel that the valuation of the Hong Kong currency is more of a political than an economic issue at this time," he said, a sentiment with which I heartily concurred.

"In the next two to seven years," he elaborated, "I don't believe that Beijing will allow the Hong Kong dollar to be too badly hit. But I also agree that the property sector will have to go down, but no more than 20 percent."

This roughly coincided with our own assessment.

"So how do we do our own business?" he asked rhetorically. "Our China property strategy is to buy in one major city, one major street, one major shopping mall."

This had such a Chinese ring to it, vaguely reminiscent of Chairman Deng's "one country, two systems" formulation for Hong Kong.

"We look at traditional shopping streets in Beijing and Shanghai, the equivalent of Oxford Street in London," he said. This strategy certainly seemed sound. "Prime, prime locations."

In Shanghai, his Concord Plaza, a 3.5-million-square-foot shopping mall, office, and residential development in Nanjing West Road, was located in a prime, central location, adjacent to the proposed Shinwa mass transit subway station.

In Beijing, his Concord Plaza was nearly fully rented, "with a McDonald's already open, and operating a very successful sales outlet."

In Hong Kong, his big condo-mall development was already 50 percent sold out, at an average price of HK$700 per square foot. Even assuming a 20 percent drop in property values, that also left Concord Pacific with expected receipts over the next five years of HK$7 billion.

To be sure, Wong had *guanxi* to spare, as well as strong nerves.

But in every one of his markets—including the hypermarkets—there was at this stage a little more hype than hope.

I was pretty skeptical about his ability to "leverage the brand name"—Yaohan—which was attached to a bankrupt Japanese company already subject to panic attacks in Hong Kong.

I was skeptical as well about his grandiose plans for that so-called highway in the sky. And though I was less skeptical about Wong's property development skills, they were about to be tested in a falling, as opposed to rising market, during which even the major players were going to have trouble riding out the coming storm.

Highway to Heaven

Wong was not just depending on his Yaohan hypermarkets to make his fortune.

His No. 3 Prong was his highly touted "highway in the sky." His MIT: mobile information terminal. In plain English, we'd call it a pager.

"A lot of people," Wong said dismissively, "use our terminals as pagers. But they can also transmit more complex information—stock market quotes, and all sorts of premium information.

"We think of this network," and now his well-chiseled features lit up at the very thought, "as our highway in the sky"—to coin a phrase.

"Chinese people will use this highway in the air to send and receive information."

"I understand," I cut in, unable to resist the urge to bring this airborne discussion back down to earth, "that Motorola has recently decided to close down its wireless telecom service here. They were offering stock prices, racing results, just as you are doing in China. Can you tell me the mistake that they made?"

"Simple answer," he rapidly responded, "to simple question."

I was all ears.

"Hong Kong is very small, it's easy to get up-to-date information. But in China, over 100 million people are playing the stock market, while there are only two stock exchanges, in Shanghai and Shenzhen. Of those 100 million keen to trade, only 10 million are near the location. So they need this information remotely. Mobile phones are very expensive. Our mobile information terminals are very cheap. People pay HK$1,000 for a mobile phone. For an MIT, you can get one for HK$30."

"So you're shooting for that wider economic group," I said. "The middle class." And I couldn't resist: "Like Carrefour."

Wong smoothly ignored that one.

"We are no longer interested in the paging charge itself. We want to charge for stock market results, train schedules, for foreign exchange sales in our department stores and hypermarkets. For these value-added services we charge a fee.

"We have thirty-six networks across the country, with a capacity of up to 4 million subscribers. As of now, in China there are 26 million pager subscribers. By the year 2000, we've projected 50 to 70 million."

One hundred percent growth in two years?

I jotted down those glowing numbers, along with a note to one of my staff to check them out. I was fairly sure that during the China Telecom meeting that morning, Li had said that there were over 2,000 pager providers in China, and over 100 million pager subscribers.

"How many MIT subscribers do you have now?" I asked.

After a long pause: "200,000."

Well, that certainly gave him ample room for growth.

Playing the China Card

At the end of the day, the most important issue to assess in terms of investing in Hong Kong—as well as elsewhere in Asia—was the still-vexing question of the still-forming commercial and economic links between Hong Kong and China.

Simply stated, the question became: would Hong Kong in a few years' time become more like China today, or would China in a few years' time become more like Hong Kong today?

Hong Kong was in the precarious position of being a gateway country that had been just swallowed up by its larger, more powerful neighbor, in much the same way that Latvia, Lithuania, and Estonia had at various times been swallowed up by Mother Russia.

Though I firmly believed that the Chinese were unlikely to be so stupid as to kill the goose that lays the golden eggs, there was still no shortage of potential slips between the cup and the lip. As far as I could read the tea leaves, the overwhelming question behind investing in China, in general, and companies like China Telecom or Concord Pacific in particular, was the future of the privatization drive in China.

A No-No

It's important to note that publicly pronouncing the very word "privatization" is anathema to the Chinese leadership. They're scared to dickens of the ideological connotations and implications of the term, since public ownership of property is obviously a core concept of Communism.

Still, whatever the semantic locutions employed, full-steam-ahead privatization was clearly the only road open to China, if it planned to stay competitive in the twenty-first century.

As *Business Week* has recently and rightly noted: "Beijing's decision to unload its huge state sector is the true denouement of the Cold War—the final triumph of market capitalism over centralized Communist control."

The implications of this move were clearly going to be profound in their potential impact on the global economy.

I think it's not too hard to point the finger at the true root of the fast-spreading Asian Contagion. It lay not in the problems of financial sector overextension in Thailand and Korea, or even in ailing Japan, but in the atmosphere of uncertainty surrounding the future of China's economic restructuring.

The problem was this:

If China's restructuring turned out to be a resounding success, the implications for Asia were far from rosy. Because as Asia's lowest-cost producer, China could easily blow them all out of the water.

Unless that restructuring stimulated domestic demand, in which case part of the anticipated export torrent would be absorbed at home.

This would be a good thing for everyone—China, the U.S., Europe, Asia. But in the short term, it would not be a good thing for the estimated 100 million workers that would have to be laid off in order for the restructuring to go forward.

Nor, in the short term, would it be good for those uncompetitive producers who relied on protectionist policies to protect them from foreign competition.

But if China chose to only protect its producers—in the now-discredited Japanese fashion—and not its consumers, then the scenario for Asia, and indeed for the rest of the world, could be very dicey indeed.

The ultimate issue was whether it chose to follow the crony capitalist path comparable to Korea or Japan, where cozy connections to the government leadership ran the whole show, or whether it chose to follow a more American, more fully free-market route.

Another key point: what would these privatized companies look like? Initial indications were that the government had been considering modeling the red chips of the future on the South Korean model—Chinese *chaebols*—massive conglomerates with interests straddling many industries. But with the *chaebols* now being blamed for many of Korea's economic problems, a new model was being offered as an alternative: Taiwan's more streamlined, single-industry players, which might attract overseas investors likely to be put off by fuzzy-bordered companies that made everything from soup to nuts.

Unfortunately, if recent history were any credible guide, China was saddled with many if not most of the same problems that bedevil Russia: its biggest companies are merely outgrowths and extensions of the old corrupt Communist system, which is far easier to transform into a corrupt crony capitalism than into a legitimate, transparent free market.

Meanwhile, it didn't help matters much that the three largest, state-owned commercial banks in China—the Bank of China, the Industrial and Commercial Bank, and the China Construction Bank—were reportedly "technically insolvent." In layman's as opposed to banker's terms, that meant that their portfolio of bad debts—estimated at 20 percent of all loans—far exceeded the capital base of these banks. If they were forced to declare those bad loans "nonperforming," as they would have been forced to do in, let's say, the United States or Great Britain, the three biggest Chinese banks would fail.

But in practical terms, that was unlikely, because to the government, it was unthinkable.

Bad Beer

Exacerbating the Chinese dilemma, many a red chip company that had so far struck it rich in Hong Kong stock offerings had turned around and squandered the money on speculative investments—often in property—rather than reinvesting the money in building their companies. A case in point was the sad saga of Tsingtao Beer, which many Westerners know because it's widely available in restaurants in the States and Western Europe.

If you've ever had a glass or bottle of it, you know that Tsingtao is an excellent product. But after a hugely successful $110 million 1993 IPO (underwritten by Goldman, Sachs in cooperation with the Bank of China) the money was lent out to failing state enterprises—albeit at high interest rates—instead of being spent on upgrading its antiquated turn-of-the-century plant.

A proposed partnership with the U.S.-based beer giant Anheuser-Busch never took off, while the ill-advised acquisition of two other faltering breweries was hardly the sort of expansion that foreign investors had anticipated when buying Tsingtao shares at a premium price.

In 1996, the Chinese government took the extreme step of tossing out the management that had organized the IPO—judging them to have been corrupt, incompetent, or both. The stock, which hit the ground running three years ago, became a dim shadow of its former self.

A cautionary tale for those eager to make the next great "China play" without taking a good, hard look at the worst-case scenarios.

Body Heat

The intense heat surrounding the coming torrent of red chips was all premised on the hope of so-called asset injections, which would permit these companies to take over cheaply valued mainland Chinese assets. This was then supposed to give these companies the wherewithal to grow and prosper in the fast-moving global economy. In theory, the idea made sense. In practice, many of these asset injections had been injections more of hot air than meat.

The other great unknown was the pricing of these assets, a question rife with political implications. As in Russia, the government was terrified of being castigated for selling off the country's birthright for a mess of pottage.

But if they weren't about to sell off these assets cheaply, who in God's name was going to be interested in buying them?

It was the same conundrum that Russia faced, and had yet to resolve.

Chapter Six

◆

GROUND SUBZERO: THAILAND

In 1990, Dennis Martin, an emerging markets corporate and investment banker with Citibank, paid a private visit to an antiques dealer in Bangkok. "She showed me a drawing of a building," he would later recall to *The Wall Street Journal.* "She said she was going to put up a big office building where her little shop was."

In and of itself, it was an innocuous enough moment. But against the backdrop of what Martin saw going on elsewhere in the country, it was enough to send up a red flag. That some small-time antiques dealer with no track record as a property developer could aspire to become a Bangkok real estate mogul—even a mini one—suggested to Martin (a veteran of the Latin American currency crisis) that events in Thailand were starting to take an ominous turn.

SOS

My own personal epiphany in this regard took place a couple of years later, when at our local broker's suggestion, we spent innumerable hours trying to reach the outskirts of Bangkok. The afternoon's assignment was to scope out (as a prospective investment) a sprawling high-rise "new city" that had recently risen up from out of nowhere, on what just months before had been a verdant vista of rice paddies and hand-hewn canals. If we were *lucky*, our broker breathlessly advised, we *might* be able to persuade this developer to let us pick up a piece of this action. It was, he insisted, a no-brainer.

> **Mobius Rule No. 69: When your broker says "no-brainer," don't forget you've got a brain.**

Playing Monopoly

Like jittery Hong Kong, once-graceful Bangkok had by 1992 become another Pacific Rim boom town, driven relentlessly upward and outward by the soaring price of property. In fact, a prime factor behind Bangkok's boom was the fact that a hefty chunk of Asian money—out of Hong Kong, Singapore, even China—was betting on the booming Thai capital's deriving some direct benefit from a commercial exodus widely expected to flow out of Hong Kong as a result of its handover to China.

Once that exodus failed to materialize—or so the theory went—the bottom dropped out of the property markets in Bangkok, Kuala Lumpur, and Jakarta, all the other Hong Kong wannabes. The ensuing property glut paved the way, some say, for the first bout of Asian Flu.

Gridlock City Circa 1992

While our driver patiently negotiated the bumper-to-bumper traffic that lent the spanking-new elevated superhighway encircling the city center the cramped look of a twenty-four-hour open-air parking lot, I had more time on my hands than I could ever have wanted to gaze restlessly out at the city's manic skyline—which might have been more impressive if it had been clearly visible through the choking tropical haze.

All over Bangkok, in new neighborhoods not even connected to the grid a decade before, vast glass-and-steel office complexes had sprouted up at every street corner and intersection, while at virtually every degree on the horizon, "infrastructure" was going up at a breakneck pace.

Every inch of Bangkok's once graceful ground, which in former years had been laced with canals known as *klongs*, was being rapidly covered in concrete: from new highways and clover leafs to a $5 billion elevated mass transit system being erratically erected (only five years later to be abandoned) by Gordon Wu, Hong Kong's self-styled "Infrastructure King."

Ghost Towns of Tomorrow

Our hot prospect was an "integrated" housing, industrial, and commercial office complex which, from the look of it, resembled nothing more than L. Frank Baum's Emerald City of Oz. It was, fiscally speaking, about as ephemeral, with building upon building standing eerily empty. Its shiny glass towers stood in rows like dominoes about to topple, waiting for the throngs of power-suited yuppies its builder was clearly counting on to pay exorbitant rents to live and work in this white-collar worker's paradise.

Needless to say, the doomed mega-project had been financed by one of Thailand's high-flying "finance companies": pseudo banks slapped together (often by local banks and brokerage houses) as a neat way of circumventing commercial regulations prohibiting loans to enterprises with substandard collateral. In the perverse way of booms, conservative banks that failed to form or fund finance companies saw their stocks suffer, as shareholders regarded them as much too stodgy to cash in on the gold mine afforded by high-risk, speculative property loans.

As *The Wall Street Journal* would five years later scathingly describe this profligate process, Thai finance companies "gorged on cheap foreign credit while lending the money to unproductive projects like golf courses and condominium complexes that were destined to stand empty." Why? Well, as long as these high-risk short-term loans were being repaid, at high rates, the finance companies stood to make out like bandits, or sharks—you take your pick.

But one looming problem that the Thai financial community had failed to foresee, was that at some point in time, the region would run out of people who could afford to live and work in these costly complexes. If I'd ever seen an example of a condo complex destined to stand empty—at least for the foreseeable future—this surefire "hot prospect" was it. Something about the place spooked the hell out of me. It was high time, I reluctantly realized, to reverse course, and start seeking fresh bargains elsewhere.

Hills Like White Elephants

From where I stood—at the center of a vast empty parking lot—the only profits likely to be made off this white elephant would be racked up by real estate scavengers who, one day sooner rather than later, would pick up the whole kit and kaboodle for a song and a prayer. Given the severity of the crisis in the Thai property sector, it was both ironic and poignant that real live (albino) white elephants have for centuries been revered throughout Thailand, and Southeast Asia, as symbols of regal power.

By tradition, every white elephant in Thailand belongs to the king. The Buddha's mother is said to have dreamed of a white elephant touching her side with his trunk, prompting her to conceive. In earlier eras, fierce wars were fought over the ownership of these rare, treasured white elephants, with no quarter asked, or given.

Interestingly enough, today's definition of "white elephant"— a piece of property that costs its owner more to maintain than it's worth—is directly derived from this tradition. In ancient Thailand, if a minister suspected that a minor prince was becoming too powerful, he would bestow a white elephant on him as a gift, knowing that the cost involved in caring for and feeding it would ultimately bankrupt him.

Fortunately for today's good King Bhumibol, the current crop of concrete white elephants—except those invested in by the

Crown Property Bureau—do not belong to the royal household, but to the banks destined to ultimately repossess them. And after they unloaded them at depressed prices, what then? Only the Lord Buddha knew for sure.

What a Difference a Decade Makes

In an interview I gave to TV's *Asia Business News* five years later, in the fall of 1997, I did what I could to get out my global gospel:

> **MM:** Lesson No. 1: *Don't put all your eggs in one basket.* You should not only invest in Thailand. You should not only invest in Hong Kong. You should invest globally. So, make sure that the next time around you have your assets spread around the globe.
>
> Lesson No. 2: You must go to those countries that appear at this time to be the worst off, because in the countries where prices are low, where pessimism prevails now, optimism will prevail in the future. So now is the time to go into these countries that appear to be the worst off, provided, of course, that you are investing in solid companies or you are buying a mutual fund run by managers who are looking for good value. Now, that's very difficult for someone who has lost money in Thailand to do—to put more money in. But although at this time it is a difficult thing to do, that is precisely what you should be doing if you have any money left.

The Royal Road to Recovery

Hoping to steal a leaf out of my own book, I unclipped my lapel mike and hopped the next flight to Bangkok. Now how on earth, you might ask, could we be the slightest bit optimistic about Thailand when all the "smart money" was deserting the place, as if the very ground—which in Bangkok is in fact sinking at a rate of about one inch per year—had contracted the plague?

The main reason that we felt positive was because all of the trends were so negative. This was not just to be stubbornly or rigidly contrarian—because being a true contrarian means not to go slavishly against the grain, but to be always independent in your thinking. It was simply that we and the short-term smart money were operating according to different time frames.

In the short term, the smart money was right on the money. For the near future, possibly even the foreseeable future, Thailand was a mess. A catastrophe. But over time—I reckoned three to four years, maybe five at the outside—precisely because things were going to get so tough, the Thai people would change their behavior dramatically.

Here's how (and why):

1) They would not borrow as much.

2) They would not buy as much.

3) They would save more.

4) They would work harder.

5) They would break their necks to export because they would need dollars.

6) Their industrial output would increase.

And last but not least, not by a long shot:

7) They would demand more from their government by way of reform.

The Broom

Within just a few months of the start of the crisis, Thailand showed some measurable improvement in a couple of key areas. Moral Uplift Plank No. 1: an irate citizenship furiously dumped the gang who couldn't shoot straight, and replaced them with a new, more forceful administration. The crew now in charge, nearly everyone we spoke to agreed, was the most talented to run the country in a long time. That in itself gave me hope for growth.

Tough times bring leaders to the fore. An apt analogy would be Franklin Roosevelt's famous first 100 days, when the New Deal was ushered in to save the country from collapse.

1) Only in times of crisis will people change their destructive behavior patterns.

2) Only when there's a consensus that something is broke will anyone take the trouble to see that it gets fixed.

Lightening Up, with a Heavy Heart

Many Bangkok blue chips enjoyed pride of place in our portfolio as jewels in our crown. But one look at that white elephant on the outskirts of Bangkok made me ready to become a belated believer in the virtues of fiscal austerity. So it was time to "lighten up" on Thailand, but that didn't mean that I planned to flee the country, or dump all our stocks in a month. That would have been a panicky, fear-driven move, and moreover, I had to keep in mind that there could be some bargains in that wreckage.

Clearly, it had come time to reassess our holdings, before we got stuck holding too many bags. Time, in short, to buy some stocks, sell some stocks, reasonably, rationally, prudently, cautiously. With, I hoped, a dispassionate attitude worthy of a Thai monk. Someone asked me how I was purchasing Thai stocks. My reply: "Like porcupines make love . . . with great care!"

Macro Mirage

Looking at the macro picture, near-term, things could not have been much worse. Of course, from my point of view, that was not altogether a bad thing, because we trade in perceptions as much as reality. When we're hunting for bargains, we look for stocks that look lousy, but are in fact simply being misjudged. By the end of 1997, the Thai stock index had declined 70 percent from its all-time peak. In 1993, at the height of the Southeast Asian boom, the total market cap of the Thai stock market had been $133 billion. By early 1998, it had declined to a dismal $22 billion.

From my point of view, even with the index down in the dumpster, there had to be more than a few treasures that were being tarred with the same brush.

The SET (Stock Exchange of Thailand) index's calamitous drop clearly indicated that the "average" investor in Thailand currently regarded Thai stocks as poor bets.

Of course, if we'd been looking at the same group of stocks from the same short-term perspective, we too would probably have cut our losses and run. But as we saw it, the market was once again overshooting the mark, and opening up for us a rare window of opportunity for increasing our positions in many companies formerly too rich for our blood.

Given the magnitude of the market's decline, you did have to wonder: could the index go down to zero? In my opinion, the answer was: not very likely. This was not, I'm afraid, due as much to sound fundamentals as to the sheer volume of money being pumped into the country. The initial $17 billion injected by the IMF to shore up the country's foreign currency reserves was, we assumed, just the first installment of a program that would in time stabilize the currency. It was not nearly enough money to shore the country's ailing financial system, but was mainly a stopgap measure, to plug the holes in the dikes to staunch the flow of funds leaking out.

The chance that the Thai index would decline an additional 50 percent before stabilizing, much less recovering, had of course to be considered. But when stacked up against the far greater likelihood of a gradual if erratic recovery, I held out for the chance of recovery—sooner, rather than later. This issue was of more than academic concern to us, because we'd been sniffing and snooping around and shifting stocks in Thailand since the market took its first big 40 percent drop. And since we'd been buying stocks aggressively on the way down, that meant that as the market kept dropping, we were losing money hand over fist—on paper, at least.

Where, I was asked time and again during the crisis, did I see the greatest bargains?

Without hesitation, I'd reply: "Thailand."

Loss Leaders

If you're savvy enough to buy stocks on the way down instead of on the way up, you need to be willing to rack up losses in the short term. But at certain strategic points in time:

> **Mobius Rule No. 70: You've sometimes got to do *worse* than the market index in order to *beat* the index in the future.**

Although we generally discourage market timing, during extreme meltdowns a few cardinal rules do apply.

One is that a market in free fall will tend to hit bottom, and then rebound as much as 30 percent before collapsing again.

Why? Because markets generally pick up to a point where spooked investors who've been holding off on selling because they want to keep their losses to a minimum are ready to take their hits and move on.

Buster Rabbit

When buying stocks during a bust, you need to make sure that you're picking long-term recovery prospects, not culling over corpses shortly to be found not on an "action" list but a "watch" list. A related problem in Thailand was that the liberalization of the economy prescribed by the IMF—assuming the new powers-that-be succeeded in ramming it through—would inevitably create competition.

For some companies, competition can be a good thing. And for others that have been coddled by government contracts or other forms of favoritism, competition can be their death knell. It can also kill off companies with an overly parochial perspective, not prepared to duke it out with the big boys on the international scene. Other possible victims of the new cutthroat climate would be companies that had thrived under the old protectionist environment, and would fail to keep up once the economy was opened up to all comers. For "all comers," of course, read: foreigners.

On the top of any such watch list in Thailand I would place companies one might call overly "politically connected"—by which I mean companies known to have enjoyed excessively cozy connections to the old regime—because a few of them would be likely to pay a hefty price for their old sins under a coming climate characterized by an obsession with cleaning house.

One of the first things I did as the Thai market started to crash was to ask my staff to compile a list of those companies that had flourished under crony capitalism, because if the global markets and the IMF had their way, those companies would be forced to compete on a more level playing field come the very near future.

Sitting on Top of the World

The big boys, by the way—by which I mean major multinationals—did not get to be big by being nice. They love nothing more than to jump into countries at times of distress, and snap up whatever assets they can pick up for a song. Call them vultures, or call them smart—the result of this commercial Darwinism is the same: survival of the fittest.

Chapter 11?

"Buddhism does not favor the collapse of bankrupt companies since that causes hardship for employees and shareholders."

—FODOR'S *EXPLORING THAILAND*

Buddhist precepts notwithstanding, the fact remained that up until the present crisis, Thailand lacked a viable bankruptcy law.

This, incidentally, can cause far more "hardship for employees and shareholders" than an orderly reorganization under a code that everyone can agree on.

Thailand's old bankruptcy law, originally drafted in 1940, urgently needed updating to reflect the current economic situation, which was as distressed as a pair of old jeans. The existing law provided little incentive for creditors and companies to seek alternatives in restructuring a defaulting company other than letting it go down the tubes.

A creditor, for example, who extended a loan knowing that a firm was about to go under would forfeit certain rights under the law. This, not surprisingly, made banks and financial institutions rather reluctant to extend credit to firms facing serious cash flow problems.

Under the old law, every incentive was firmly in place for banks and finance companies to leave even their best customers twisting in the wind. Under the old law, bankruptcies could take up to a decade to adjudicate. Under the new law, specific timetables were built in, providing incentives for all sides to hash out their differences, and settle their outstanding issues promptly.

But whether or not Thailand adopted its version of Chapter 11, one fact would still loom large over any investor's equation about buying stock in a shaky company: on the list of creditors in any bankruptcy, in *any* country, shareholders' rights to collect whatever crumbs fall off the table are at the bottom of the list. Owning shares in a bankrupt company is therefore equivalent to owning shares in a defunct dirt mine.

Panning for Gold in the Sewer

Prowling through Bangkok's strong-smelling back streets and alleys—and chugging along congested highways lined with half-empty skyscrapers—looking for bargains was a bit like panning for gold in a stream of worthless sand. A better analogy might be hunting for diamonds in a bucket of zircons, because while there were quite a few superficially attractive companies out there, too many—if you dug a little deeper or read the fine P&L

print—were deceptively attractive, as opposed to genuinely undervalued.

The big booby traps, as I saw them, which tend to make trouble during any bust:

1) Excessively high levels of dollar-denominated debt.

2) Management shock: higher-ups prone to deep denial and/or
suffering from what I like to call "deer frozen by oncoming
headlights" syndrome.

For example, of the 480 companies listed on the Bangkok
Stock Exchange, about forty had already gone belly-up by year's
end 1997. An equal number of sick companies had seen trading
in their shares suspended, out of fear that if they were traded,
they too would fail. By our calculations, we expected at least another twenty companies to go under before the situation stabi-
lized. We had to keep our eyes out for weak companies, and for
companies exposed to those companies which wouldn't survive.
Although we don't mind losing money in the short term, we
don't like it when stocks we own go up in a puff of smoke—and
mirrors.

High Finance

Let's take the financial sector first. Why? Because I always do.

> **Mobius Rule No. 71: If you watch a bank like a
> hawk, you'll see in the patterns of their lending
> practices a blueprint of the macro picture.**

During a downturn, banks are always the first to take the hit,
and usually the first to recover. Banks, as lenders to individuals
and businesses who either can or cannot pay them back, are the
canaries in the coal mine of any economy. Coal miners used to
carry canaries (in cages) down into deep mines, as early-warning
signals of any impending escape of toxic gas. Since canaries are
more sensitive to gas than humans, they'd keel over at the first

whiff of gas, long before any coal miner would succumb. Banks, despite their often bloated size, are highly sensitive gauges of any economy, assuming you know how to read the dials. Investors call them "proxies" for the economy at large.

In times of uncertainty, banks make excellent catchall stocks, because if you buy a piece of a bank, you're buying a piece of every loan on their books, which subsumes the whole economy. Let's say you learn that a bank is pulling back in a certain sector. That's a sign of weakness in that sector; you'll know to hold back yourself. But if you find out that a bank is suddenly extending itself to service a certain sector at a time of widespread distress, that means they've found some bright spots in an otherwise dismal picture.

Bankers tend to get a bad rap, whenever things turn really sour, for:

1) "stuffing,"
2) "ramming," or
3) "shoveling"

money down countries' and companies' throats, as if they were force-feeding geese to make foie gras. I hate to burst any bubbles, but in the real world, it doesn't work that way. A better, clearer image would be less dietary, and more hydraulic.

Think of the international banker as a guy with a monkey wrench who mans the valves through which money flows, like oil in a pipeline. When times are good, he opens the valves. When times turn bad, he tightens up or even shuts down the valves. With the flow of money frozen, he starts hunting down everyone and anyone capable of funneling some of that money back into the tank. Because the mere fact that that money has changed hands doesn't, in his view, mean that it's no longer "his" until the loan has been fully paid off.

In the sad, sordid saga of Southeast Asia in the late 1990s, international bankers poured some $400 billion into the region— excluding substantial loans to Hong Kong and Singapore—before abruptly shutting off the valves, throwing the debt engine into reverse, and leaving the poor rejected countries gasping for air. "There was a huge euphoria about Asia and Southeast Asia," a spokesman for Germany's big Commerzbank admitted to the *New York Times*. "It was *the* place to be."

Until, as always happens eventually, it was just about the last place on earth to be caught dead in. It's always the same, but every time the pundits scream as if the bankers have done something wrong. They haven't. They've just been bankers, whose core business is a lot like musical chairs: everything's just jim-dandy, until the music stops.

The problem is always that when the going is good, it tends to be great. And just like the little girl in the nursery rhyme, when it gets bad, it gets horrid. International "flight capital" is poured in at the first sign of strength, and yanked out at the first sight of weakness. What disturbed even the most hard-core free-marketeers in the financial community about the Asian Contagion was the deadly speed with which this money tap could be turned on and off, and what is more, turned into a kind of financial vacuum cleaner, sucking its victims dry. When the taps get turned off, it's like a deep freeze: no one can budge until the guy with the wrench turns the tap on again.

Goin' Bottom-Fishing

One key point to always keep in the forefront of your mind while suffering through the bust end of the boom-and-bust business cycle is:

> **Mobius Rule No. 72: The first country to get hit, and hit hard, is typically the first one to recover.**

A corollary to that: the country hardest hit is forced to confront the deepest root causes of its problems, and will therefore be forced to improve its behavior most dramatically in order to attract now-edgy global investors.

Economic recoveries are no different from any other form of recovery: they follow a classic trajectory of high high, low low, and gradual, steady upturn.

Thailand was like an alcoholic (or any other form of addict) in that it had gone on a binge—which in this case had been to gorge itself on cheap credit—and was now going to have to go cold turkey. So did it pay to sit on the sidelines in Asia and do nothing and wait for the storm to blow over? In my opinion, it always pays to take direct action.

Twilight Zone

A dramatically different scene greeted us on our ride into the congested city center from the airport just before the sad, dismal Christmas of 1997 than we'd seen on our last ride through busy Bangkok only a year before, when even a midnight ride in from the airport could take two hours and change due to heavy traffic. But now, even at well past midnight, as a metered cab carried us down dark, half-deserted streets toward the city center and our hotel, I was astounded to feel and hear the car actually rev up its engines as it rounded a curve. For years, you grew used to the sound of engines idling in Bangkok, as they waited for traffic to sluggishly move, and tempers to fray.

Right here, in the traffic patterns, I found a first reason for optimism: the bust had cleared the lanes, both physically and psychologically.

To my way of thinking, this was the reason that busts can be healthy, because they force people to take stock and reexamine their previous assumptions, and to consider new ways of handling problems. A little less traffic in downtown Bangkok, even most Bangkok citizens would have agreed, was not entirely a bad thing. Not that I was ignoring the high human price being paid for the slowdown. But I remained firmly convinced that in every bust lie the seeds of the next boom, and here was just another sign that this was true.

It may have been just my imagination, but I could have sworn that there were more motorcycle taxis out and about on the streets that night. On Thai cycle taxis, the passenger rides on the same seat as the driver, clutching the helmeted driver from behind. I later heard a report that thousands of metered cabs were sitting idle in a vast parking lot way out of town, waiting for the day in the not too distant future when Bangkok's stressed-out people could afford to ride them again.

The eerie quiet that wrapped the sidewalks in a mood of gloom seemed all the more surreal as we swept by hundreds of twenty- and thirty-story concrete corpses: the half-completed shells of office buildings, with cranes frozen as if in suspended animation above them. There's always something strange about a city frozen in time, whether it be Pompeii circa A.D. 79, buried by volcanic Vesuvius, or Bangkok circa 1998, slammed on ice by the imposition of strict lending limits.

Most eerily impressive were the thousands of apparently pointless concrete columns of Gordon Wu's now-canceled Bangkok Elevated Rail and Transport System (BERTS), which looked like some twenty-first-century prefab Stonehenge.

After checking into a luxury suite at a four-star hotel—which, due to the decline of the baht, cost less than a Motel 6 single room in the U.S.—I could see out my window a ludicrously tall tower called Biayoke II, which loomed more than half-finished above a lesser shaft predictably known as Biayoke I. Biayoke II, rumor had it, might never be completed because it had been put up so quickly that it didn't stand quite perpendicular, making it hard to run the elevators.

Whether this rumor was accurate or not didn't really matter to me as much as the fact that such rumors were running rampant all over Bangkok.

> **Mobius Rule No. 73: At times of great stress, rumors are reliable keys to popular sentiment.**

In fact, the only market functioning at full throttle in Bangkok was the market in rumors, which I make a point of listening to religiously, for signs that the mood in the street is turning one way or another, like sudden shifts in the prevailing wind.

To me, the real meaning of this particular rumor was that it spoke to widespread fears that these vast office towers were likely to stand for years, until the banks and companies that financed them succeeded in repossessing them from their developers, so that they could be sold off to the highest bidder—most likely for pennies on the dollar. Or, perhaps I should say, blips on the baht.

Foreign Influence

So here, staring us right in the face from behind every billboard in town, loomed the crux of the problem: although pots of foreign money lent out at irresistibly easy terms had built these monstrosities in the first place, when it came time for the same white elephants to be sold off, Thai law prevented us foreigners from buying them.

This was due to a pernicious clause in the Thai legal code—inserted to assuage narrow nationalistic interests—preventing foreigners from owning property of any kind—except for the smallest condominium.

The law was structured so that if a Thai woman married a non-Thai man, her family could not legally leave her any property, because it might then fall into foreign hands.

In practical terms, this meant that Thailand's most pressing problem—a ludicrously overleveraged property sector—could not be solved until this silly law was revised. But here was another example of the way that a severe crisis—if it lasts long enough to put the fear of free markets in politicians' and bureaucrats' hearts—can do more good than harm. Because when push came to shove, as I had no doubt that it would, the new "reform" government would have no other choice but to rescind that clause, if it had any desire to dig itself out of its economic black hole. And that, over the long haul, would be a saving grace for the Thai economy.

As I told just about every Thai banker and businessman who would listen to me, there was a time not long ago when the Americans were selling all their trophy properties—Pebble Beach golf course, Rockefeller Center—to the Japanese. This created a fierce nationalist backlash at the time. But who's laughing all the way to the bank now? The former owners of those trophy properties, who have been able to invest that money more productively elsewhere.

You Can't Take It with You

You Jong Keun, the governor of South Korea's impoverished North Cholla province—a former Rutgers economics professor who became a key economic advisor to newly elected Korean President Kim Dae Jung—ran into this very same problem when trying to persuade his fellow Koreans that it was in their best interest, under current circumstances, to relax laws prohibiting foreign land ownership.

"Are you planning to let foreigners buy our land?" they would quiz him suspiciously.

"Yes," You would patiently say (as quoted in the *New York Times*).

"Because even if they buy it, they can't take it anywhere. It's going to stay right here on this peninsula."

This sentiment was echoed by one of Thailand's most respected businessmen, Dhanin Chearavanont, who at fifty-seven has almost single-handedly turned a traditional agribusiness of feed mills and slaughterhouses into a vast empire of fast food restaurants, discount superstores, telecom and cable TV franchises. The listed company, known as the CP (Charoen Pokphand) Group, has been one of our best Thai performers, and is the largest company in the country.

When asked what the country should do first to ease itself out of crisis mode, the mogul responded: "The government should relax restrictions on foreign investors and invite them to invest in Thailand. By doing so, there is a good possibility that we can fill up all those surplus condominiums and office buildings. The government is still too conservative in terms of allowing foreigners to do business and own property in Thailand. We are simply too protective."

A Free Market Dispenses

"What ought to be manifestly clear by now," thundered *The Wall Street Journal* in an editorial at the peak of the currency crisis, "is that the market is a force of nature that is as unstoppable as the tides, and as impersonal."

At the mercy of impersonal market forces, nine Bangkok real estate executives, confronted with the prospect of losing their jobs, decided to open a car wash.

"It was embarrassing at first," one of the ex-hotshots told the Bangkok daily *The Nation*, but the payoff—"a living wage for all the partners plus the satisfaction of taking control of our destiny"—made the humiliation eminently worth it.

Another Thai stock and real estate high-flier worth several billion baht until his condominium complex collapsed under the combined weight of high debt and slow sales set up a sandwich shop on a heavily trafficked corner in downtown Bangkok.

When asked why he had decided to sell sandwiches instead of hying himself off to a Buddhist monastery—a favorite exit strategy for failed politicians and tycoons—he replied: "I don't know anything better to do at this moment than sell sandwiches, and it's a good career to support the staff."

King Bhumibol, who turned seventy at the height of the crisis, struck the same humble note during his annual birthday address to his people. He pledged that the country would emerge from the present economic crisis by "developing a self-sustained agricultural economy and using more domestically produced goods.

"It doesn't matter," he said, "whether we are a 'tiger economy' as long as our economy supports the people."

What he meant could be found in any Thai children's primer: in times of trouble, head back to the land.

Back to the Land

"In the field there is rice. In the river there is fish."
—OPENING LINE TO THAI CHILDREN'S PRIMER

What the king was saying openly was being echoed all across Thailand, as this traditionally agricultural country began to ask itself some soul-searching questions about its need—and ability—to transform itself into a high-tech tiger economy. One of the lasting lessons coming out of the crisis was that the government's deliberate selection of most favored industries to back had been an ill-advised attempt to manipulate the marketplace. Fortunately, the seeds of renewal, literally and figuratively, lay strewn in the fields and the rice paddies of rural Thailand.

The crisis laid bare another harsh fact that had been conveniently forgotten—or brushed over—during the go-go years.

There are in fact two Thailands: a rich urban culture with the highest per capita sales of Volvos in the world, and a poor rural society with over 10 million people living under the poverty line earning just $300 a year. As the Thai industrial boom gathered steam, millions of poor peasant farmers—and their sons and daughters—flooded into the cities to work in the factories.

But the real hope of pulling the Thai economy out of its tailspin lay in its extraordinary wealth of agricultural exports, most notably rice (considered the most fragrant and flavorful in the world) and tapioca, used worldwide in a wide range of food products and animal feeds.

As had been the story elsewhere in Asia, the Thai public had been for the most part willing to look the other way at corruption and collusion in high places, as long as the government delivered the goods in the form of rising wages and a steadily rising standard of living. But once the economy started to stall, popular outrage at the blatancy and level of high-ranking corruption flared into the open, and touched off a trend toward a fresh examination about the direction in which Thailand was headed.

Political Reform

For years, the country's deeply divided parliament—split into factions owing debts to various powerful constituencies in society—had dithered and dallied and failed to even move to a vote on the hot-button issue of ratifying a new constitution. Before the crisis, the unpopular General Chavalit—the incompetent prime minister who had been forced to resign for his role in worsening the crisis—had denounced the very idea of a new constitution as "Communistic."

But when the economy collapsed, the constitution, once considered dead, suddenly showed new signs of life.

"We are not out of the woods economically," said the legislator who chaired the constitutional committee, "so to reject the draft constitution would have been to add kindling to the fire." And so, in a surprisingly short span of time, the Thai people got a new constitution.

Now you know and I know that no mere piece of paper, no matter how strongly worded, was likely to erase at one fell swoop the incestuous ties between corrupt politicians, tycoons, and the military that had been greasing the wheels of a rotten system for decades. But what was most striking was the degree of backing the new constitution received from two elements in the national power structure not known for their leftist leanings: the monarchy and the military.

My Thai Time

Thirty years ago, at the peak of the Vietnam War, I spent a couple of years working in Thailand under contract to a research outfit studying the impact on the local economy and culture of the out-of-control Vietnam War spending. During the war, much of Thailand was turned into a base from which to bomb the North Vietnamese into, as Richard Nixon threatened, "the Stone Age." Many Thais were not overly opposed to this scorched-earth strategy, since the Vietnamese had been their traditional enemies for centuries.

The Pentagon had installed a sprawling combination air-sea base at Sattahip, and another in Ubon, in the remote northeastern region of Thailand, the most arid, poorest part of the country. This meant, in effect, that the U.S. government paid for the infrastructure buildup of rural Thailand, so that these road networks could be used to ferry troops from north to south, along the Vietnamese border. Back in Bangkok, a whole neighborhood along Petchburi Road had degenerated into a slummy, sleazy red light district for GIs on leave. Guys would come in, eighteen and twenty years old, with two to three thousand bucks in their pocket and only three days to spend it.

Some were convinced that they might not live to see another girl, and that this was their last chance to have a good time. Flowing into the city to meet this surging demand were thousands of poor young lasses from way "up country," who would from time to time fall in love with the GIs, and occasionally have babies with them. More rarely, these flaring wartime romances would end up in marriage, common law or otherwise.

The Vietnam War kick-started the Thai economy out of decades of somnolence.

But like all booms, this one definitely had its dark sides. Syphilis and gonorrhea, to take two social scourges, ran in epidemic proportions. On the upside, the jewelry industry, which had always been a traditional Thai staple, enjoyed a growth spurt, with so many GIs buying jewelry for their Thai girlfriends.

The Thai economy was still almost entirely agricultural, based on rice, fish, a little palm oil, and tapioca. What little trade took place was dominated by the ethnic Chinese, who late in the last century had emigrated to Thailand in great numbers, encouraged by the enlightened policies of the then King of Thailand, Rama IV, who was destined to be immortalized—Thais would say disgracefully parodied—by my look-alike Yul Brynner in *The King and I.*

What little dynamism existed in this slowly slumbering economy was injected by these Chinese immigrants, who in contrast to practice elsewhere in Asia were forcefully integrated into Thai society. The king had welcomed the Chinese with open arms, but only under certain conditions: they had to marry Thais, to adopt Thai names, and consider themselves Thai in all ways except religion (they were permitted to keep their Confucian customs, while the Thais remained fervently Buddhist).

The result has been a curious amalgam of Chinese and Thai culture, which in recent years has strengthened the burgeoning social, political, and commercial links among and between Thailand, China, Hong Kong, and Taiwan.

Today, these old well-established Chinese families dominate the country's foreign trade and financial sectors. Of the fifteen commercial banks in Bangkok, the vast majority are owned and controlled by ethnic Chinese. And of those banks, the majority grew out of the trade financial houses of the pre-industrial era, since grown into regional financial powerhouses, and now into—some of them at least—towering houses of cards. The reason, by the way, that there were only fifteen banks operating in Thailand was that the government had not granted a commercial banking license in forty years, creating what the *New York Times* described as "a family-directed plutocracy that rivaled the Finance Ministry in power."

Even in the late 1960s, Bangkok had still been a small town, mainly built of small wooden houses lining lovely but filthy canals. There was no Thai Stock Exchange, but there was a tiny Bangkok Stock Exchange, run by an American named Willis Byrd, which despite its grand name was really no more than a private office, with stock prices chalked up by hand on a blackboard. All the big business wheeler-dealers were agricultural traders and hustlers, including a Mr. Chokchai—nicknamed "The Beef King of Thailand"—a wealthy rice farmer who'd gone to Texas on a visit, and on a whim shipped a herd of Texas longhorns back home to Thailand, where they flourished enough to set off a bona fide beef boom.

With all the money he made on his cattle—by selling tons to the steak-crazy U.S. military—he built one of the very first high-rise office towers in downtown Bangkok. At the time, it stood out like a sore thumb, and everyone considered it a total boondoggle. Of course, looking back, the Beef King was simply ahead of his time, not to mention home on the range.

Back to Bangkok

When I returned to Bangkok as a portfolio investor for Templeton in the late 1980s, the market was still pretty low, slow, and sleepy. And, of course, extremely illiquid—there were only a handful of stocks to buy, and even fewer worth buying. Still, we bought all the blue chips, the big-cap stocks: Siam Cement, Thai Farmers Bank, Bangkok Bank, Siam Commercial Bank. Over the next ten years the values of those stocks steadily climbed into the ozone layer: some by tenfold or more. So we did awfully well in Thailand during the early phase of the boom.

By the late 1980s, the economy was starting to heat up. The first thing we observed was a big jump in exports, beginning with commodities and raw materials, like rubber, tapioca, and rice. The only way to make a play on the agricultural economy was indirectly, by for example buying into a warehouse company, which we did, and did very well by. We also made some timely investments in a company called Thai Wah, which is the largest producer of tapioca in the country.

But Thai Wah, an ethnic Chinese–owned company, was a prime example of what happened in Thailand in the space of only a very few years, because from a tapioca company they turned themselves into a real estate and property company. And of course, after ten years of feverish land speculation, tapioca production had dwindled into a tiny part of their operations, while they had become just another overleveraged Sino-Thai-owned property company.

So what the king was saying in his birthday speech was that in Thailand—as opposed to, say, famine-ridden North Korea, when all else fails you can always survive on the land.

I could still well recall thirty years ago visiting a Thai friend on his family farm out in the countryside. His wizened old grandfather took us on a tour of the rice paddies. We heard a scurrying sound. Without batting an eyelash, his stooped-over grandpa stooped over even further and with a triumphant smile pulled a big juicy rat by the tail out of a hole in the rice paddy ridge.

"We eat this tonight," he said, "delicious." This was, by the way, not a poor man.

Thai Farmers Bank

"We are becoming more or less a colony," sighed Narong Srisa-An, vice chairman of the executive board of Thai Farmers Bank.

The recently imposed strict provisions of the IMF bailout were clearly getting to him, as a Thai national, although he was of ethnic Chinese descent. Thai Farmers Bank (TFB) had been established in 1945 by the Lamsam family, a third-generation Sino-Thai family, and had since grown to become the third largest bank in Thailand, the seventh largest in Southeast Asia, and one of the most conservative in the region.

In 1996, the prestigious periodical *Far Eastern Economic Review* declared TFB one of its Companies of the Year in a review of 200 leading companies. The bank had been singled out for this distinction on the basis of five qualifications: 1) quality of service, 2) response to client demands, 3) vision of management, 4) financial stability, and 5) ability to become a prototype for other organizations.

What a difference a year makes! Just a few days before our visit, Banyong Lamsam, TFB's chairman, had startled everyone by projecting NPL (nonperforming loan) rates for the Thai banking industry as a whole to hit 20 percent during the coming year, while freely conceding that TFB's own NPL level might well hit 18 percent by mid-1998.

Those figures were startling, because if his projections proved accurate, there was a distinct possibility that TFB—along with the rest of the industry—could see its equity capital wiped out by a tidal wave of bad loans during the coming year—ironically, the Year of the Tiger.

To cope with this problem, the banks were being asked to increase their ratios of equity to debt, a fiscally prudent step that all the same was putting all the banks under severe strain to raise new capital. In the case of Thai Farmers Bank, a new rights issue was rumored to be coming just around the corner. Of this, the Lamsam family—which still owned around a third of the bank—was expected to take around 20 percent, which would result in a substantial injection of fresh capital. But—and this was a big but—given projected NPLs at twenty percent of the total loan portfolio, would that be enough? It was, in financial terms, a real cliffhanger.

We were already substantial shareholders in Thai Farmers Bank, and as such we presumably would be entitled to participate in this rights offering. Question: did we dare?

New Rights Issues

My basic rule of thumb on new rights issues and offerings for current shareholders, is this:

If the new rights issue is being offered at above the market price, you should not participate. They're putting more money into the company than the market is willing to pay, and you should be deriving some benefit from that. But if the price is less than the market price, you should participate, because you're getting a better deal as an existing shareholder than an outsider.

Strategic Investors

What ended up taking place was a "private placement" of 376 million shares to a group of "unidentified strategic partners," which added $857 million to the bank's coffers. None of the new shares were offered to existing shareholders, though in a statement to the press, the bank implied that "holders of existing shares wouldn't see their rights diluted."

That, at least, was good news.

With NPLs hitting in some instances 40 percent of total portfolios, the general opinion in the global markets was that Thai Farmers Bank would soon be going to the markets for more. But the fact that the bank was able to close the books on this new share offering was a sign of health—and wealth—not shared by many of its rivals in Thailand.

Penthouse View

Narong's floor-to-ceiling picture windows gave a sweeping view of beleaguered Bangkok. But the view that caught our attention was a smaller one, displayed on the TV screen on his desk. As we spoke, the new finance minister was holding a press conference, at which he was making a long-expected announcement of the fate of fifty-eight insolvent "finance firms"—out of a total of ninety-three—which had been suspended since the summer.

Tarrin, the new finance minister, was rumored to be a tough, savvy guy, although he acknowledged at the press conference that he had suffered through many "long, sleepless nights" hoping to come up with a viable alternative to the abrupt closing of these failing firms. But he and his "dream team" of technocrats, prodded by the IMF, had their eyes on the global markets. And they were looking to him to be merciless in swinging the regulatory ax, and letting it fall heavily on the necks of the guilty.

Wham!

The Finance Ministry's prompt, tough, and decisive action—fifty-six out of fifty-eight saw their doors slammed shut that day—was greeted with a generous round of applause by financial commentators worldwide. An even more important endorsement of this first evidence of biting the bullet was that—however briefly—the Thai stock market rebounded.

But inside Thailand itself, the closings came as a great shock to the system—of crony capitalism. Many of the failed finance companies had been founded in recent years by a few dozen Sino-Thai families, who also controlled significant segments of the country's financial industry. In many cases—too many cases—these powerful families had used their banks and finance companies as virtual piggy banks to fund pet projects, including elegant, now-empty Bangkok high-rises.

Show Me the Money

The only way out was clear to all, even if the locals didn't want to face up to it: more foreign ownership, and sooner, rather than later. That meant everything: buildings, banks, companies, land. As we made our rounds of companies, the new government was still testing the waters, pussyfooting around, floating trial balloons about letting foreigners own banks and property for "limited periods of time" before they would somehow have to sell the goods back to Thai nationals. If this sort of halfway proposal was considered satisfactory, they had a few things coming to them. But I had a feeling that what was really going on was that they were softening up the opposition, preparatory to the day when the floodgates would open, and the foreign money would start flowing back in—at this point, under somewhat different terms.

Although I was well aware that some Thais bitterly resented outsiders dictating their economic policies, I was somewhat taken aback to hear the sophisticated Narong singing this popular Thai tune—although the world-weary tone of resignation with which he accompanied his statement lent it a thin veil of black humor. And from his point of view, some of the new provisions simply seemed gratuitously irksome.

A tapioca farmer, for example, planted just one crop per year, so traditionally the bank lent him money every six months, so he would get a cash infusion at the right time, when he needed to buy seed and fertilizer. This system, in sync with seasonal cycles, had been "in place for forty-three years," Narong sweetly—but with a bitter taste—explained. But now the IMF was forcing him and all the other Thai bankers to throw these farm loans "all into one box, as if they were the same." This would wreak havoc, he maintained, on one of the bank's bedrocks: farm financing.

"But I am in no position to negotiate." Narong shrugged, his face betraying only the slightest hint of chagrin. "I am the one to comply."

The main issue for TFB in keeping with the IMF "tough love" prescription for fiscal health involved a more critical matter than next year's tapioca harvests. Under the latest provisions, his bank would be forced to boost its capital-to-asset ratio from a current 8.5 percent level to 12 percent of the total loan portfolio.

"In March," he said equably, "we'll have to submit to our shareholders at our general meeting our plan to raise capital above 12 percent. We are not really in bad shape at all," he stressed. This was the first sign of distress I could detect in an otherwise seamless presentation. "We are not in any way in trouble. We merely like to set a very high standard."

Of course, I murmured sympathetically into my tea.

Why Was This Man Smiling?

Narong was an avuncular, jolly chap—who no doubt played a superb round of golf and was a pleasure to run into at banking conferences. His sometimes serene, at other times lighthearted demeanor reminded me of the much-caricatured "Laughing Buddha."

In Thailand, by the way, that would have counted as a compliment, not an insult. Despite his Sino-Thai heritage, the behavior streak that Narong was displaying had a distinctly Thai character. The Thais call such composure *chai gen*—which means "cool heart." To have *chai gen* is to emulate the Lord Buddha, and to show oneself free of earthly concerns.

"Oh, we have already scaled down considerably," he said, sipping tea from an elegant Chinese porcelain cup. The one detectable sign of agitation was a faint drumming of his well-manicured nails against a delicate polished walnut table, which stood upon a thick, luxurious Persian carpet. "Everybody is scaling down these days," he said breezily, as if rocketing down the whitewater of financial free fall was just a day at Phuket Beach.

Personally, I admired his show of *chai gen* since I aspire to have it myself. It was gratifying to see someone keep such a cool head—and heart—under a tough environment. Of course, another person observing the same breezy behavior might have thought he was in . . . deep denial.

Confidence Games

Of the fifteen commercial banks in Thailand, most were considered pretty shaky.

One, Bangkok Metropolitan, had already been seized by government regulators. This was widely considered a good thing, as long as the central Bank of Thailand didn't just go and inject capital into the bank, leaving the taxpayers to foot the bill, before forcing the major shareholders to write down their assets. The financial world was keeping a close eye on the Thai government's treatment of Bangkok Metropolitan for signs of resurgent crony capitalism. Since the bank's major shareholders were the politically powerful Sino-Thai Techapaibul family, it was incumbent upon the new Thai government to not treat the family with the slightest sign of kid gloves.

In the end, the new Finance Ministry did its duty by forcing one of the nation's most powerful families to bear the brunt of the asset reevaluations, thereby showing the world that crony capitalism was on the run in Thailand. The government was also, for better or for worse, bowing to the recently resurgent will of the international financial community, backed up by the IMF, which had made banking reform a linchpin of its $17 billion bailout package. By mid-1998, the score would be:

Crony Capitalism: 0
Global Capitalism: 4
Foreign Interests: 2

As the government moved to close three more insolvent family-owned banks, two other banks fell into foreign hands, one to the Dutch banking behemoth ABN-Amro, and the other to the Development Bank of Singapore.

As one of the heads of the government agency charged with overseeing the disposition of bad banking assets later observed, "This marks the end of an era of family banking in Thailand. Whether the families like it or not, Thailand now needs professionals at the helm."

An alternative to folding or seizing a bad bank is the foreign investor bailout—usually dressed up as a merger, although everyone involved recognizes it as essentially a takeover. Such a scenario quickly engulfed a second shaky contender, First Bangkok City Bank, which was looking like it might be swallowed up—er, I mean bailed out—by Citibank.

First Bangkok City Bank

The difference in atmosphere—real and emotional—between Narong's sunny, airy office, which sat high above the stress and strains of daily life, and the dark, gloomy basement cubicle in which we encountered an American-trained vice president at First Bangkok City Bank, could not have been more striking.

One was all sweetness and light; the other, all darkness and despair.

First Bangkok City Bank—which if it was lucky would soon lose the "First Bangkok" to become just another branch of Citibank—had, to its credit, not built a flashy new building. This one was old, tatty, and ratty. The young American-born official we met with, who originally hailed from the New York area, looked like an Asian Don Johnson, complete with carefully cultivated stubble.

When times were fairly good, as they had been up to now, FBCB—the seventh largest bank in Thailand—had enjoyed an enviable dominance of a discrete niche in the Thai market: financing small- to medium-sized trading companies. This had been its traditional bailiwick, and it had prospered by sticking to its last, although the bank had long labored under a reputation for being, as one of our broker's reports baldly put it, "one of the most poorly managed family-owned banks in Thailand."

Back in 1986, the bank had suffered the ignominious fate of being bailed out by the Bank of Thailand, which must have been embarrassing, to say the least. At which point its chairman—Khun Chareon—popularly known as "The Whiskey King," although he also holds the local distribution rights to Carlsberg Beer—had personally pledged to ensure the bank's long-term strength. An immensely wealthy gentleman with wide-ranging interests, Khun had lately been suffering difficulties of his own. His vest-pocket personal finance company had been among the insolvent ones shut down that morning by Finance Minister Tarrin. Not that he was personally hurting, but I had no doubt that his far-flung business empire was at least feeling the pinch.

A few weeks before our visit, the Whiskey King had announced a plan to personally inject 5 billion baht into FBCB, to help it over its current slump. But as the situation both at the bank and throughout the country deteriorated by the day, that began to look like no more than a drop in the bucket, or perhaps I should say beer mug.

The crisis of confidence that first struck the rapidly weakening finance companies had quickly moved, in a predictable rapid-fire chain reaction, to infect the smaller, mid-sized banks. In August, panicked depositors had pulled 21 billion baht out of the bank, for fear that they'd never see their money again if it failed. In September, the bank lost 9 billion. In October, 7 billion. If the bank had been a patient undergoing surgery, we would have been summoning the priest to read the last rites. Instead, Citibank, which had a long and apparently warm relationship with the Whiskey King, stepped in to see if it could pick up the pieces, at the right price. Although it was being called in as a supposed "white knight" to "the rescue," I would have hardly characterized the move as altruistic. According to our young source inside the bank, not only did Citibank and the Whiskey King enjoy a long, close, and evidently warm relationship, but the two operations were a damned fine fit.

"What makes us a tasty morsel for Citibank is that we're a niche market. We're primarily a wholesale operation, and they're mainly a retail bank." Which meant that the two sides complemented each other: a combination, presumably, would be strong in both retail and wholesale. Wholesale banking is directed at corporate customers; retail banking to individuals. So far, at least, it looked like a marriage made in heaven.

But the problem, he grimly explained, was that their particular niche—trade finance—was getting "really hammered right now." Many of their oldest and best customers were in a tight spot, because they couldn't get credit from anyone to buy raw materials, what with all their suppliers insisting on getting paid in dollars, not baht, and all of that up front. Companies that couldn't depend on credit lines to finance their operations were now teetering on the edge of disaster.

Making matters worse for the sellers was that the buyers of these trade goods were taking advantage of the situation by putting the squeeze on their suppliers. They were telling customers, "Hey, I'm not paying you in dollars anymore, I'm paying in baht." Which meant that the prices the manufacturers were fetching for their products—the ones they could make—were going for half their old price in U.S. dollars.

All of which meant that the longer Citibank waited to make its move, the less that the target bank would be worth. The NPL level, already well in the flashing-red-light danger zone, would have soared so high by then, according to current projections, that the net worth might have been dragged down to zero—or below.

Less Than Zero

Grimly, our young source roughly calculated their rising tide of nonperforming loans at 18 percent and soaring fast. By the end of 1998, they were projecting 25 percent NPLs. Although this was roughly in line with the industry average, in their case it was catastrophic because they lacked an adequate capital base to stay afloat. Stronger banks like Bangkok Bank could afford to roll with these punches, but FBCB was like a punch-drunk boxer trying to fight with the flu.

"That basically wipes out your capital," I said, stressing the obvious.

There was a long, pregnant pause.

"I don't like to say stuff like that," he replied, with a hoarse dry laugh. "I can say that we're making provisions to keep up with the new criteria. We were injecting 600 million baht into the bank every quarter, now we've upped that to a billion."

"How's your loan-deposit ratio these days?" I felt terrible asking him.

Another long pause, followed by a dark, sardonic chuckle.

"I don't even want to discuss that." He grinned sheepishly. "It's embarrassing. We've had to borrow heavily from the interbank loan fund—at over 20 percent."

"Are your NPLs covered by the new provisions?"

"Yes, but just barely."

"Do you have a lot of uncompleted buildings in your loan portfolio?"

That question produced yet another dry laugh, followed by a discreet cough.

"If we went up to the roof of this building," he ventured, "I could show you three unfinished hotels, three shopping centers, and at least five office buildings."

"So what will you do with them?"

"We'll take them over and hold them until the market rebounds."

The reason that all this property was frozen in limbo, he explained, was that no one was willing to take a loss on their books. "I've been sitting across from guys who have an unfinished building," he said, "and they need a billion baht to top off. I say, 'Why don't you just sell it?' And they say, 'Because I need to make a profit. Even if it's just 100,000 baht.'" That was about $25,000 at current rates of exchange. "So I say," he went on, "'Why don't you guys stop thinking about making a profit and start thinking about how much of a hit you can take?'"

"Denial," I mumbled almost inaudibly to myself—to coin a phrase—"is not just a river in Egypt."

Okay. You Tell Me: Buy, Sell, or Hold?

At the time of our meeting with the young banker, we had been given to understand that Citibank was pondering planning to buy FBCB at somewhere around 12 or 14 baht per share. That was still something like 75 percent down from its peak. But within a few days of our meeting, we began hearing rumors—admittedly unsubstantiated—that Citibank was revising its estimates downward, and was talking about paying more like 3 baht a share. That was obviously quite a comedown for poor old FBCB. As current shareholders, the question we faced was this: the longer it took for the deal to go down, the worse things would get for FBCB, and the better they would get for Citibank. This clearly made it to their advantage to wait. It could end up like a game of chicken. And if they ended up kiboshing the deal altogether, there was a fair chance that the bank was a goner, and our stock would end up as toilet paper.

Would there be a general offer? Possibly. So, the dilemma we were in was: assuming that they were planning to buy at 3, should we stay in the game at 14? The upside potential was that Citibank's purchase would cause the stock to shoot up—probably. But how high?

Follow-up

In the end, Citibank balked at paying anything at all, concerned about having to swallow all those nonperforming loans. A few weeks after our visits, Citibank officially "suspended" its agreement to buy into First Bangkok City "pending review." Which to my mind was a nice way of saying:

The deal was dead.

This killed off one of the most promising paths to recovery for the ugly ducklings of Thailand's faltering banking sector: selling out to foreigners. Even they were turning tail when they got a good hard look at the numbers. A few weeks before Citibank pulled out of its deal, the big Dutch ING banking group also killed its agreement to take a sizable stake in another weak bank, Siam City, after SC failed to raise sufficient new capital from existing shareholders to help cushion its rising tide of NPLs.

The reason that these foreign banks were pulling out of the market?

The ownership rules for foreigners, although being revised, were still too restrictive.

The government had made a great concession of permitting foreign entities to own a controlling, 51 percent interest in a Thai bank—and that was considered a great breakthrough.

But the foreign bank was still not permitted to increase its share holding above that 51 percent, and after ten years—and this was the real deal-breaker—the foreign controlling bank could no longer participate in share offerings, thereby diluting its stake.

In the end, the government of Thailand was forced to nationalize First Bangkok City Bank, Siam City Bank, and Bangkok Bank of Commerce, and that was just the beginning of a wave of seizures. The government didn't plan to hold on to these three hot potatoes for long, but was hoping to restructure and then sell them. No matter how good a face they put on these government takeovers, they were a major embarrassing failure for the new administration.

They still hadn't mustered up the political will to let foreigners be treated like anyone else in Thailand. And for that, they were paying a hefty price for their pride.

Bangkok Bank

Before the Thai crash, Bangkok Bank had been the largest commercial bank in Thailand, and the fourth largest in Southeast Asia. But now . . . it was hard to say.

Established in 1944 by a group of local Sino-Thai businessmen headed by Chin Sophonpanich, a Chinese immigrant whose two sons currently controlled the bank, BB had long been Thailand's bluest blue chip. Over the years, we'd made a small fortune on BB stock. But now, it was looking dicey.

As we sat cooling our heels outside the office of one of the bank's senior officers, I noted with scarcely concealed interest that the tables in his private reception area were piled high with stacks of paper, stretching nearly to a very high ceiling. These looked to me like loan reports. I had a sinking—or possibly a rising—feeling that headquarters had called in all of the bank's loans for a central review.

This was, from where I was sitting, both a good and bad sign.

It was a good sign because it showed a tightening up of management controls, a prudent move under the current environment.

But it was a bad sign because it revealed that the guys at the top were running scared.

They were worried enough about the spread of bad loans to have stepped in themselves, and begun keeping a close eye on what their guys in the field had been up to. If I had to bet, I would have said that a lot of those loans were shaping up as NPLs, which meant that so many heads might roll in the field that the rice paddies might end up rife with them.

Through the thick teak doors of the executive office, we could hear loud—for scrupulously polite Bangkok—shouting and carrying on. I'm not one to eavesdrop, and in fact we couldn't hear a word of what was being shouted, only the tone and pitch with which it was being emoted. The meeting was obviously quite heated, and, I surmised, probably not much different in tone and temperature from any number of other meetings between bankers and customers taking place all over Thailand. But this one was a doozy, as well as clearly of major import, because only with the biggest loans would the senior official of this major bank be bothered to deal personally.

But once the door opened, we were greeted with an astonishing sight: a typical Thai social scene, featuring an elegantly dressed older gentleman in a beautifully cut suit *wai-ing* (clasping palms together in a praying sign, the traditional polity of Thai greeting and parting) to the bank officer, who politely pressed his hands together in front of his chest in response while also bowing from the waist—a sign of deep and abiding respect.

In private, the feathers had been flying. But in public, you couldn't have guessed that what had gone on had been anything more pressing than a social call. We were later given to understand that this unfortunate gentleman—who obviously will remain anonymous—was a major timber baron, who had become more than a little hot under the collar when the bank, under pressure to call his loan, demanded that he either had to pay back the money they'd lent him or they would have to take his teak logs.

The timber baron's teak logs had been put up as collateral for the loan. But being a bit hard-pressed at the moment himself, the teak baron was having a little trouble meeting his payments. The upshot of that meeting was that he was forced to agree to relinquish his teak, which meant that he would make no profit whatsoever on his timber harvest. I felt sort of sorry for him, although I found it hard to imagine that he had yet sunk to the point where he would have to unload his fleet of Mercedes at the Bazaar of the Formerly Rich, an empty lot on the outskirts of town where every Sunday afternoon since the meltdown, former high-fliers unloaded luxury goods at unheard-of fire sale prices.

Tea and Sympathy

The senior officer graciously ushered us into a group of deep, soft leather sofas, while a capable bevy of assistants tactfully plied us with delicately aromatic tea in china cups so thin they were translucent. The difference between this big bank and all of its competitors was that, despite a rising tide of NPLs, it was still sitting high on the hog. It still dominated the domestic Thai market with a huge market share, and over 300 branches. It still controlled a substantial proportion of the country's trade and foreign exchange markets. In short, it could afford to take the long view.

Despite, for example, the current chaos, the bank had decided to buy into one of the firmer finance companies, Union Asia Finance, because:

1) It was in comparatively good shape, and

2) It could end up, with their help, a contender in a rapidly consolidating industry.

"Of the thirty-three finance companies still operating, some are quite weak," our host explained empathetically, like a distinguished doctor delivering a difficult diagnosis. "We see this company as a vehicle to help us pick up a few of the weaker companies, and possibly put them together."

Bangkok Bank, in other words, was one of the few Thai companies in a position to take advantage of the current situation, and treat it as an opportunity, not a threat. There were many others in that position floating around Thailand—we saw quite a few in our hotel lobby—hoping to pick up distressed and bankrupt properties for a song. Bottom-fishers, vultures, you name it—they were in town. But they were all foreign-based.

According to this source, there were so many vultures flocking around Thailand's troubled real estate sector that he was being forced to talk turkey to his customers.

"I tell them, 'Rethink your strategy—because if you don't want to take a 40 percent hit now, just wait six months and you'll get zero.' "

But, he complained, they wouldn't listen. They were too obsessed with booking a profit.

Follow-up

A few weeks after our visit, Chatri Sophonpanich, the executive chairman of Bangkok Bank, was described in *The Wall Street*

Journal as "scrambling to raise $1 billion in fresh financing" for his beleaguered bank.

And the big news was that certain members of his fabulously wealthy family weren't planning to pitch in. "What about country risk? What about the idea of not putting all your eggs in one basket?" one family member was given to muse, explaining his decision to leave his familial bank high and dry. "It's a question of whether you use your head or your heart."

For the family that controlled more than a sixth of the country's life savings, this was quite a comedown. The problem was, with the family's stake in the bank having dropped in value from an estimated $4 billion in 1996 to $800 million in 1998, could you fault the family members if they decided it was time to diversify? But selling large stakes to nonfamily members raised the dread prospect of diluting clan control.

"A family should stick together at times of crisis," the executive chairman morosely maintained.

They hadn't asked me to become one of their strategic partners, but if they did, I might well have taken them up on it. Curiously, I think I had more faith in the future of Bangkok Bank than the founding family did. Of course, they were a little too caught up in the short-term crisis mode to keep the ballooning balance sheet in proper perspective. To shore up its balance sheet, the bank was going to have to raise at least a billion bucks—not baht—very soon or start seeing red. They were widely rumored to be planning, following the Citibank and ING debacles, to issue some 400 million new shares.

When and if they went to market, we would be more than happy to help out.

Except for one little hitch: that pesky foreign share premium.

Fleecing the Foreigners, Part II

Waltzing out of the bank, I felt buoyed by the big banker's long-term optimism. Certainly, if you look at its awesome preeminence in most of its major markets, and its superb management, and with its stock sunk so low it was grazing 50 percent below peak, Bangkok Bank looked like a no-brainer buy.

Except for one rub: the foreign share premium. The FSP was one of those market anomalies that we desperately hoped the current crisis would sweep away and consign to Trotsky's famous "dustbin of history."

Similar situations dogged other emerging markets—most perniciously, Russia. The FSP was just another one of those perversions that make even savvy investors think twice about global investing, considering it a crap shoot with doctored dice. At its peak, for example, Bangkok Bank shares had been hovering at around 200 baht a share. But with the foreign share premium, the price was 380. The foreign share premium came to a staggering 40 percent.

Now, Bangkok Bank is a first-rate operation, which was why foreign investors had been willing to ramp up the price so high, to reflect its strong long-term growth prospects. But even with its now-depressed price, the FSP still hadn't budged below 40 percent. What gave? Even when foreign investors were fleeing the market in droves, they were still being charged massive premiums over what locals would pay.

Pure Export Plays

Another reason to buy banks when a declining currency is bound to stimulate exports is that it can be devilishly hard in a country like Thailand to make a pure export play.

A prime example was Delta Electronics, a diversified manufacturer of electrical components whose products would at that point in time have been 50 percent cheaper than they'd been six months before, making their prices highly competitive. Delta was an excellent company, very well managed, with a profit growth of 20 percent for the year. But Delta was also one of a handful of Thai companies clearly in a position to benefit from the currency collapse, and had therefore seen its shares soar 150 percent since the devaluation of the baht six months before. By my way of thinking, I'd leave Delta to the smart money.

I was more inclined to buy the banks, because—contrary to popular perception—this would be the most efficient way to make an export play, because the banks were financing the exporters. When an entire country goes bad, sentiment usually quickly sours on the banks. But all the banks, one could safely presume, in a position to do so would be doing what Thai Farmers Bank affirmed as its policy: shifting the bulk of its loans from importers to exporters.

The shares should in time reflect the gathering strength of the export-driven recovery.

But we were also on the lookout for export plays that were not quite so painfully obvious as electronics. And I even had one such outfit in mind. They mainly made—I kid you not—chicken feed. They also happened to be, with $8 billion in annual sales, the largest company in Thailand.

Chicken Feed

Cultured tiger prawns, large shrimp artificially raised in tanks—very good, high-end delicacies in Asia—had long been major contributors to the complex bottom line of the CP Group, run by the fabulously successful Dhanin Chearavanont, the same guy I quoted earlier in this chapter as one of the very few operators willing to stick his neck out and make a pitch for raising foreign ownership in Thailand.

I liked Dhanin's company primarily because it was based in the real wealth of the country: the agricultural sector. The bedrock of the company was—the production of chicken feed. Now, chicken feed may not be sexy, but if you know how to make it and sell it—in pellets and powders—you can rake in the dollars like seaweed.

The company, Charoen Pokphand Feedmill Public Co. Ltd., or CP Group for short, was primarily a producer and distributor of mixed animal feed for pigs, fish, chicken, and ducks. They had also branched out, with excellent results, into swine and chicken breeding, hatching, and farming. The big-ticket items were tiger prawns, although the practice of raising them in artificial pools had recently run up against a host of environmental concerns, mainly prompted by the widespread practice—by some, though not all tiger prawn farmers—of destroying irreplaceable mangrove swamps in order to cultivate these big shrimp in man-made tidal pools.

International protests against the Southeast Asian cultured-shrimp industry, and its deep-sea equivalent, had eventually led to an import ban by the U.S. of all sea-caught shrimp from countries that refused to comply with the ruling that trawlers be equipped with TEDs (turtle excluder devices). Combined with the international outcry over mangrove swamp reduction, this had prompted the CP Group to explore new methods of cultivating shrimp without destroying either turtles or mangroves.

They ended up concocting a method called the "intensive culture system" which relies on raising shrimp in pools inland, away from the sensitive coastal estuaries. As an insert in the front of the company's annual report—complete with a glossy photo of a mangrove swamp—put it:

"The only means of preventing mangroves from being destroyed is the intensive shrimp culture system. This shrimp farming practice has great efficiency and has benefited the mangrove ecosystem by eliminating the need for mangrove regions to culture shrimp."

I also admired Dhanin's long-term thinking when he invested hugely in China, where it controlled some 130 affiliated companies with assets valued at $2 billion.

But now, with banks putting the screws on him to repay about a billion bucks in dollar-denominated bank loans, he was forced to sell off some of CP's key Chinese assets to raise cash—another huge comedown for a once-proud giant company.

The company went to great pains to point out that it was not pulling out of China altogether, just "streamlining" some of its operations. But that involved putting quite a few operations on the blocks, and laying off quite a few workers. It was looking for buyers for its drug, beer, petrochemical, and motorcycle manufacturing operations.

Why?

So it could follow King Bhumibol's prescription and "go back to the land," and set about making more money raising shrimp and tiger prawns back home. Also known as agribusiness.

Charoen Pokphand had benefited from the fact that its chairman was of Chinese heritage in establishing its far-flung links to China. Dhanin had carefully cultivated close links to the Chinese leadership, and had used those ties to set himself up as a middleman to sell Western and Asian high-tech production processes in China.

By the mid-1990s, the Thai "Chicken King," as he is informally known, had a one-fifth market share in the huge Chinese chicken market. CP also manufactured about a tenth of the country's motorcycles, and was operating a large if only marginally profitable brewing business in partnership with Heineken.

But according to widely published press reports, Charoen Pokphand's pull-out from China could not have come at a worse time, because assets there were no longer commanding high prices.

CP Group was caught in a squeeze.

At the same time, given all this bad publicity, the stock in the CP Group had plunged from a recent high of close to 40 cents a share to 14.6 cents.

At that price, I rated it a very strong buy.

Here was a case of a cyclical downturn creating a major-league buying opportunity.

Siam Cement

Businesses Swamped by Oversupply.

Much New Capacity a Big Burden.

Battered by Forex Loss.

Our broker's report was far from optimistic about Siam Cement.

"A major expansion in cement, steel bar, paper, and petrochemicals is exacerbating the oversupply of these commodities, while the slowing economy is curtailing demand. Earnings are also hurt by continued structural decline in profitability, and heavy depreciation plus interest expense on the new capacity."

In other words, new cement plants.

Not only that, but the latest news had grown steadily worse: the company had sustained enormous forex (foreign exchange) losses as a result of the currency crisis. This broker's best estimate of the losses was around 30 billion baht, with more multibillion-baht losses projected in future years, due to the value of future exchange contracts.

All told, not a pretty picture.

Darkening the short-term outlook even further was the stream of gloomy announcements emanating from the company itself. Executive Vice President Tawee Butsuntorn had recently advised the press that "fierce competition in export markets from South Korea and other cement producers with overcapacity" would force SC to scale down its projected earnings in the coming quarter. South Korea alone, Butsuntorn explained, suffered from an oversupply of cement of at least 10 million tons, while the estimated oversupply of the Southeast Asian region was at least 30 million tons. Thailand's own production exceeded domestic demand by 25 million tons, while Indonesia and the Philippines were running 3- and 4-million ton surpluses, respectively.

"The only way for cement producers to survive is to boost their exports," Tawee proclaimed. But practically in the same breath, he freely admitted that "local producers" were concerned "about the possibility of a price war with overseas rivals, especially from South Korea."

Uh-oh. Was there anything left to feel good about? This was hardly a time to expand cement capacity, but that was in fact what the company—in conjunction with other cement companies in Thailand—had been doing right up until the crash. This reflected an intrinsic Asian strategy of gaining market share by cutting prices by keeping costs down. And one of the few positives in the Thai equation was that their basic costs were considerably lower than all of their rivals.

One thing to feel good about was the company's glorious past. It had originally been founded back in 1913 by King Rama VI, a famous royal reformer, to become a linchpin of the industrial revolution in Thailand. The company was still about 35 percent owned by the Royal Property Bureau, the investment arm of the Thai royal family.

But here was another bright spot, which made it an export play for the future: over previous years, it had deliberately diversified into petrochemicals, electrical products, pulp and paper products, and plastics—most notably, polyethylene.

The division manager we met with freely acknowledged the growing glut in cement, and explained how the company was sharply cutting output and capacity in preparation for the growing shake-out. He did say that their costs were low enough, including freight costs, that they expected to be competitive in the Middle East.

"Cement is still our cash cow, but the future of the company, according to our chairman, is going to be plastics."

I didn't think to ask if he'd ever seen *The Graduate*.

"Plastic and steel," he quickly corrected himself.

As the most prestigious, elite industrial concern in the country, one replete with royal and aristocratic connections, Siam Cement had long enjoyed its pick of the best and the brightest Thai students as young corporate recruits.

They were big in paper, reinforced concrete, and petrochemicals. It was getting to the point that in a few years they would not need to be selling cement.

How could I possibly be high on Siam Cement when everyone else was so negative?

You tell me. We were high on Siam Cement, as we were high on Thailand, precisely *because* the prevailing trends were so negative.

And then, just a few weeks after our visit, a few gleams of light began to show through the clouds.

The Bank of Thailand (the Thai central bank) moved to lift most of the currency controls it had imposed during the summer, during the panic phase of the crisis. It allowed local financial institutions to resume trading in baht with nonresidents, an activity banned when the baht hit the skids and the priority was to keep foreigners from transferring baht offshore after selling Thai stocks and bonds.

"Now, Thailand is ready for the judgment of the international money markets," said the central bank's governor, willingly relinquishing the reins of monetary power to global market forces.

Do the Right Thing

Why had the central bank felt that it could relinquish control?

Because the latest trade report showed a monthly surplus of $1 billion, in sharp contrast to the deep deficits of just a few months previous.

Thailand was rebounding to regain its tarnished tiger status.

Why? Because, according to *The Wall Street Journal,* "The new government . . . has won praise from investors for doing and saying the right things."

MOBIUS RULES: THE BUST BOX

56: When you tap into an attitude in any country that says "we're number one, we're the best, no one can beat us" . . . that's the right time and the right country to SELL.

57: When everyone else is dying to get in, get out.

58: When everyone else is screaming to get out, get in.

59: If a broker starts giving you the hard sell, never buy.

60: The best time to buy is when *everyone else* is screaming that there's blood in the streets.

61: In times of crisis, people on the ground start coming to their senses.

62: Easy times make people go soft. Hard times get people going.

63: What goes down usually goes back up, if you're willing to be patient, and don't hit the panic button.

64: Bagging baggage is the first step to freedom.

65: The problem with recoveries is that they don't make good copy.

66: Market meltdowns make headlines. Market recoveries make money.

67: A liquid stock market is one that's easy to get out of, not just easy to get in.

68: After bagging baggage, the most important thing for management is an *ability to listen*—particularly when it comes to analyzing their own mistakes.

69: When your broker says "no-brainer," don't forget you've got a brain.

70: You've sometimes got to do *worse* than the market index in order to *beat* the index in the future.

71: If you watch a bank like a hawk, you'll see in the patterns of their lending practices a blueprint of the macro picture.

72: The first country to get hit, and hit hard, is typically the first one to recover.

73: At times of great stress, rumors are reliable keys to popular sentiment.

PART THREE

◆

Beating the Odds
(Latin America)

LATIN AMERICA

*Boldface capital words are countries Mobius visited   **Boldface lowercase words are cities Mobius visited

Chapter Seven

◆

THE NEXT DOMINO? (BRAZIL)

Flying Down to Rio

If the world needed any greater proof that globalization was 1) here to stay and 2) a force to be reckoned with, the flighty behavior of the Latin American markets in the wake of the Asian crisis supplied it in spades. On a morning in late fall 1997 after we checked into our high-rise hotel on Rio's Copacabana Beach, the high-flying Rio stock market took a stomach-churning 15 percent tumble, prompted by desperate doings in far-off Hong Kong. That same morning, a sickeningly swift 10 percent drop on the São Paulo exchange in the first four minutes of the session forced the governors to halt trading for the first time in the exchange's history.

The steepest declines were racked up by a series of high-flying Brazilian blue chips that had enjoyed an average 93 percent climb in the first nine months of the year. Anchoring the group were the three prime poles of the Brazilian privatization tripod: Telebras, the state-owned telecom company, Eletrobras, the state-owned electrical utility, and Petrobras, the state-owned oil and energy company. With the Bovespa (Brazilian Stock Exchange index) dropping like mercury in an ice storm, it looked as if the second-best-performing stock market in the world (after Russia) was heading full-speed into a brick wall.

Reach Out and Touch Someone

So why were global investors getting so hot and bothered over Latin America, when the currency crisis appeared to be confined to Asia, half a planet away? One easy answer, as well as a true one, was that the whole world was now so intricately interconnected that it was no longer possible to buffer any one market from the behavior of others due to distance alone. Just as chaos theorists had discovered that a butterfly flapping its wings on one side of the earth could cause a hurricane to break out on the other, so the slightest trembles and tremors in one financial market could easily infect and influence the others, even if their commercial connections were rather remote.

Ticket to Ride

Okay, you say, but how does that affect me?

Here's how: these global perturbations present an unprecedented wave of first-class buying opportunities. When markets overshoot and undershoot due to irrational factors, that's when a cool head can win.

And here's how: if market sentiment suddenly sours on an entire country mainly because it's *perceived* to be linked to problems elsewhere, that sentiment may be a function of *irrational panic*, not *cold calculation*.

In the same way, if sentiment sours on a whole country when individual companies inside that country are still doing well, you can find bargains in stocks that are artificially depressed because of no other reason than popular knee-jerk reactions to temporary events.

With most emerging markets overexposed to the ins and outs and ups and downs of flight capital—money that can be moved in and out of a market at a moment's notice—it's critical to figure out whether these sudden panics—as well as flights of "irrational exuberance"—are justified by the fundamentals. Because if they're not, betting against them can be your ticket to ride.

Let's take Brazil, although we could just as easily have taken

Mexico, Argentina, or Venezuela. I'll take Brazil, with 163 million people, because it dwarfs Mexico and Argentina, and because a stable, prosperous Brazil is the key to a stable, prosperous Latin America. Brazil is the world's fifth-largest country, with more people than Russia and an economic output greater than China. The swift transformation from a mixed to a market economy that Brazil has pushed itself through over the past five years had set the pace for a regional record 5 percent growth rate in Latin America in the 1990s, and a record $45 billion in direct foreign investment flowing into the region as a whole.

In Southeast Asia, the forex traders' collective decision to "attack" a currency—otherwise known as short-selling that currency, with many individual players placing the same bet that it will wilt under pressure—sent a signal to less-plugged-in investors that possibly a few things were rotten in the underpinnings of the "Asian miracle." Little things, to be sure, like rampant corruption, insider dealing, and a lack of transparent markets. Now, that behavior sent these markets into a tailspin, but it would have been realistic, not masochistic, for Messrs. Mahathir of Malaysia and Suharto of Indonesia to bless those currency traders, not curse them.

Why? Because by shining their harsh speculative spotlights on the flagrant weaknesses in their economies, the forex folks were expertly diagnosing precisely what ailed them. Those governments didn't need to hire high-priced consultants, because the currency traders were doing the job for free, with the icing on the cake being a quick buck or two if their bets went the right way.

But what about Latin America? The prospect of Asian Contagion infecting Latin America was like a golden door swinging wide open for bargain hunters, because the supposed links between these two vibrant regional economies were not nearly so strong as popular opinion would have it. Yes, these countries did trade together, and did compete as exporters of goods to more mature markets. But just because they shared some superficial similarities didn't make Latin America "just like" Asia. If anything, the two continents were growing less alike than ever before.

When the raft of Brazilian blue chips took their first real nose-

dive in a decade, mainly due to trouble in Asia, I felt in my bones
that we were looking at a phenomenon known as "spooking."

> **Mobius Rule No. 74: When the ordinary run
> of buyers gets spooked, that's the time to
> step up to the plate and start putting your money
> down on the table.**

But for the Grace of God . . .

A major reason that global investors were up in arms over Latin
America, after those same markets had doubled, on average,
over the previous six months, was that some of the same sins—
low account balances, high foreign trade deficits, creeping inflation—that had brought the Asian tigers low were running
rampant in Latin America.

Brazil was more vulnerable to being downgraded in investors'
books than its neighbors, because its currency—the real—was
widely regarded as at least 30 percent overvalued. But it's important to recognize that although the prospect of a currency devaluation—either abrupt or gradual—represents "currency risk"
in action, a devalued currency can be a country's saving grace,
because gradual, panic-free devaluations can kick exports
through the roof.

Some simplistic strategies would have you bail out of a country at the slightest hint of a devaluation coming down the pike,
because the same share of stock will be worth that much less, in
dollar terms, once the currency declines. But I see things differently. If combined with the negative sentiment that such a
prospect represents, I view signs of an impending devaluation as
a signal to buy into a country—because even if the markets do
pull a temporary nosedive, the eventual bounce-back will be all
that much stronger than before.

In Rio, the first casualty of the currency traders' preliminary
skirmishes was the confidence of local stock traders, who found
themselves caught with their pants down by a wave of frantic

short-selling in anticipation of the coming currency crisis. As one young Rio derivatives trader gloomily observed to the *New York Times* on the morning of the crash (perhaps I should say "correction"): "What can I say? Brazil today is no-man's-land. The future is cloudy and stormy, and everyone around here is concerned and desperate. Everything here is so exaggerated. Brazil is a land where death comes suddenly."

Talk about an upbeat assessment!

From my point of view, reading words like these in a daily newspaper was like being handed an engraved invitation to a party. If Sir John Templeton said it once, he's said it a thousand times: the right time to buy is always at the point of maximum despondency. Well, here we were, at rock-bottom, and I was drawing up a shopping list the length of my arm.

Having just left Thailand (which I would have nominated as the global capital of pessimism), it now seemed as if Brazil might be a contender for that dubious distinction.

> Mobius Rule No. 75: Only when everyone else is up on the windowsills preparing to jump do things for me start to get interesting.

Among the many reasons being proffered in the press to back up the purported link between Brazil (and Latin America in general) and the problems besetting Asia was that South Korean banks, when the going was good, had bought scads of high-yield Brazilian Brady Bonds and would now be forced to dump them on the open market, at fire sale prices, in a desperate bid to raise cash.

(Brady Bonds, incidentally, were an innovation devised by U.S. Treasury Secretary Nicholas Brady of the Bush administration, by which the U.S. government backed emerging market debt, permitting such countries to borrow on international markets at lower rates.)

Though the Brazilian-Korea bond fire sounded fine on paper, personally I wasn't buying it. For one thing, the amount of money involved, when compared to the tenth largest economy on earth (Brazil's), was inconsequential. Another supposed connection between Brazil and troubled Korea was that Korean producers were going to start flooding the world with cut-rate cement. Although not entirely off the mark, the adverse effect on a single industry was hardly sufficient to justify the downgrade of a whole country, much less a full-scale market stampede.

It's important to realize that when a panic starts, it only takes the slightest hair-trigger to turn a run into a rout. It can be cement, Brady Bonds, or bubble gum—it doesn't matter. The reason for turning tail could even be a missing millionaire. On our second day in Brazil, a completely unfounded rumor that a major Mexican industrialist had disappeared—presumed kidnapped, or killed—sent shock waves through the region's capital markets. Just as inanely, they promptly bounced back once it was disclosed that the rich gent in question was alive and kicking.

Korean-owned Brazilian bonds, cut-rate Asian cement, allegedly abducted industrialists, all provided jumpy investors with the lazy-headed excuse they were looking for to start dumping Brazil big-time. When things are looking lousy from any number of angles, the collective unconscious always starts snooping around, looking for evidence—no matter how far-fetched—to bolster its depressed emotional state. And that's just the time, as a savvy investor, that you should start taking a serious look at the country.

> **Mobius Rule No. 76:** If the whole world is down on a country for exaggerated, short-term reasons, shift it from a hold to a buy.

Note: You can take advantage of rumors like the missing industrialist by snapping up stock during the moment's downturn, and riding the shares back up north when the smoke clears. But this sort of market timing is a risky, hair-raising strategy—not a move for the novice player or an investor most interested in maintaining a long-term investment horizon.

Sausage Links

Don't get me wrong. There *were* more than a few superficial similarities between Asia and Latin America. Like Korea, and like Thailand, Brazil's once-red-hot export growth had been slowing to a crawl all through the fall, a slowdown that had spread to other Latin American economies. The country's current account balance was starting to look like the credit card bill of a confirmed shopaholic. But in contrast to Thailand, where the government had proved ludicrously ineffective in staving off the forex traders' assaults, Brazil's popular president, Fernando Henrique Cardoso, was determined not to let that shadowy crowd get the best of him. If they wanted to fight, he was more than willing to put up his dukes. In fact, for better or for worse—personally, I felt for worse—he was willing to defend his currency to the political death, if need be.

Unfortunately for his countrymen, who would soon start feeling the heat, President Cardoso had an election coming up. So he had to act, and act fast. The sixty-six-year-old president knew better than anyone that if the Brazilian real—which he had personally created—were to start heading south, he would be hitting the South Polar ice cap right along with it. In short, the man's credibility was on the line. Latin Americans are no more laid-back than Asians when it comes to losing face. Like Spain, this seemed the homeland of *machismo*.

The only problem I had with Cardoso's tough-it-out strategy was that there are times when a devalued currency can kick a failing economy back into high gear, by jump-starting exports. Preventing a currency devaluation can have as much to do with salvaging national pride as with hard-core economic reality. When, in January of 1999—shortly after his reelection—he was forced to let the real float freely, the Brazilian market surprisingly soared. Why? Because the markets were finally forcing the real to face reality.

The Painted Box

From his point of view, Cardoso really didn't have a lot of room to maneuver. Like the Chinese leadership after taking back Hong Kong, Cardoso had deftly painted himself into a corner. Five years before, he'd hitched his political wagon to the star of low inflation and a rock-solid currency. And he'd ridden the resulting deflationary wave straight to the presidential palace in Brasília. Just as the Chinese had realized that they couldn't afford to lose face by letting their peg slip in Hong Kong, so Cardoso knew that if he were to let *his* peg slip, it would look like the currency speculators had gotten the better of him. Permitting the real to be devalued would risk reigniting inflation. And reigniting inflation would cost him the election. And, not at all incidentally, put a screeching halt to his hard-won fiscal reforms. Those reforms, by the way, remained largely unimplemented by early '99, triggering the collapse of the real and, along with it, the real plan.

Debtor's Prison

To get a better handle on where Cardoso was coming from, it's important to recall that just ten years before, during the mid- to late-1980s, an enormous public debt crisis gripped Latin America. Most of the countries in the region owed umpteen billions to American, European, and Asian banks, which found themselves floating in greasy petrodollar deposits from the newly rich oil-producing countries. Prodded and led by Citibank's globe-trotting chairman, Walter Wriston, dozens of the First World's money-center banks had jumped all over themselves pumping the flood of petrodollars they received from the oil-producing countries to the debt-happy governments of the Third World.

Sovereign states don't default on their obligations, Wriston once blithely proclaimed, despite the fact that at many times throughout history quite a few sovereign states had done just that, with impunity. Citibank got hammered some of those times.

But take note: if you'd bought Citibank stock when it was down to $13 because everyone was so edgy about its staggering Third World debt losses, you'd be richer, not poorer, today. One way to take advantage of regional wipeouts is to buy stock in banks exposed to them, and ride the recovery back up to the top.

A few Latin American countries—Mexico, Venezuela, Brazil—were major oil producers themselves during the Roaring Eighties. But their governments went on such a spending spree squandering the proceeds of their country's natural resources that they ended up in a hole just as deep as their oil-dry neighbors.

By the late 1980s, Brazil was running way out in front of the debt pack, owing a whopping $87 billion to foreign banks, making it the world's largest debtor. By that juncture, with government spending turning into a runaway spree, inflation was raging at well over 2,500 percent—which qualifies not just as run-of-the-mill inflation, but that dread phenomenon known as hyperinflation.

If you want to conjure up an image of hyperinflation, think of Germany between the two world wars, when people had to buy a loaf of bread with wheelbarrows filled to the brim with their life savings wrapped up in worthless paper. In Brazil, prices shot up by the hour. The only way that the overheating Brazilian economy was prevented from descending into utter anarchy was a policy, born of sheer desperation, called indexation. With indexation, every price of every good and service was linked to an index of the rate of inflation published in all the daily newspapers, right along with the sports and the market results. Everything from the price of bread to the price of a car was indexed to the going inflation rate—the price of a loaf of bread could literally change—and change dramatically—in the course of an afternoon. Of course, hyperinflation gave consumers every incentive to spend, as opposed to save, because the value of any money that they didn't spend was likely to melt like an ice cream cone on a hot summer's day.

Bank account balances, of course, were also indexed, the real value of money was constantly being eroded—but nobody could ever quite tell by what degree. Even more damaging than this erosion in spending power was that people couldn't really keep track of what the constantly shifting values boiled down to. They couldn't tell, at any given point in time, the true value of what they earned, or what they spent. Not surprisingly, the results could range from mildly disconcerting to utterly disorienting, depending upon your financial sophistication, and your skills with a pocket calculator. It became next to impossible for the middle class, not to mention the lower rungs, to obtain credit for buying even the smallest appliance.

During the darkest days of this off-the-charts monetary whirlpool, a former Marxist radical sociologist by the name of Fernando Henrique Cardoso, who'd written one of the classic texts of *dependencia*—a Third World economic theory that favored cutting "dependent" countries off from the global economy—assumed the post of finance minister in a newly elected Brazilian civilian government. By then, the once-proud author of *Dependency and Underdevelopment in Latin America* (who some years before had been forced into exile by the Brazilian military dictatorship in punishment for his radical leftist views) was calling himself a "Social Democrat." This meant, in practice, that after a prolonged flirtation with left-wing economics, he had at long last seen the light—and the value—of the formidable forces that open societies and liberalized markets can unleash within a once-fettered society.

After being handed the finance minister portfolio in 1992, Cardoso moved forcefully to stabilize the chaotic economy using the only real option open to him: prying a recalcitrant country, long dominated by the public sector, open to the discipline of the global free market. With inflation by then hitting the surreal plateau of 3,000 percent, his prostrate country was ready for anything. In this atmosphere of crisis, Cardoso decided to take a leaf out of Hong Kong's playbook by pegging the jumping bean known as the Brazilian currency to the United States dollar, at a roughly one-to-one ratio.

He called his currency stabilization scheme "The Real Plan," and christened the new Brazilian currency the real. And lo and behold, Cardoso's Real Plan worked like a charm. This came as quite a surprise to some observers, since the political risk involved in hitching the real on a peg to the dollar had been steep. For decades Brazilians—along with most other Latin Americans—had been treated to a steady stream of nationalistic propaganda insisting that the great dictator to the north was hell bent on exploiting the poor Southern Hemisphere economies by taking their resources, and exporting the profits back to San

Francisco and Oshkosh. Under this black-and-white scenario, the dark angels of Satan were the American-based "multinational corporations," while the lily-white defenders of the faith were the "national champions"—the state-owned corporations of the Latin American governments.

The problem with these socialist scenarios was that they were based more on myth than reality. In the real world, the so-called national champions quickly degenerated into national disgraces by becoming political patronage mills, with payrolls so padded they resembled welfare hotels, not companies. As a sideline, they lost buckets of taxpayer money.

By loosely linking the Brazilian currency to the dollar, Cardoso was openly acknowledging that a Latin leftist's worst nightmare had finally come true: in the new, globally integrated economy, the old LDCs (less developed countries)—now optimistically re-named "emerging markets"—had nowhere to run, and nowhere to hide from the new world order. Their economies, for better or for worse, were inextricably linked to the mature markets to the north. The underlying message of Cardoso's pragmatic Real Plan was: "If you can't beat 'em, join 'em."

In Latin America, Cardoso was hardly alone in his newfound devotion to and admiration of the miraculous effects of the free-market mechanism. In just about every other country in the region, from Bolivia to Venezuela to Chile, the wonders of a free market had been gloriously unfolding, as governments frantically back-pedaled from the mixed economy that had been enshrined in their constitutions and collective mind-set for years.

Twenty years before, if you'd happened to ask the Marxist-influenced sociologist Cardoso whether at some future date he would be more influenced by Chicago University's conservative economist Milton Friedman than Karl Marx, he would have laughed in your face. But the irony wasn't lost on most of this new crop of pragmatic Latin American leaders that they were following in the fiscal footsteps of a right-wing dictator, General Augusto Pinochet, who'd grudgingly relied on the advice of Friedman to open up the tightly shut Chilean markets to foreign investment. And then sat back and reaped the remarkable results.

After twisting arms in a reluctant but desperate Congress to approve his Real Plan, the results were indeed phenomenal. Inside a month, after raging in the four-digit range for years, the rate of inflation magically plummeted to 10 percent. Now, with the real pegged to the greenback, lower- and lower-middle-class consumers, who'd been the forgotten victims of the inflationary economy, had at last been handed a tangible stake in the country's economic future. For the first time in their lives, they were able to consider buying appliances, cars, homes, on credit. Nearly 15 million new consumers emerged from poverty.

As an elderly woman who sold vegetables in a Rio street market gratefully told me at the time, "It's so wonderful, because now we can *plan*. Now we can actually think about saving and buying." This may not sound like much, unless for your entire life such mundane realities had been as distant pipe-dreams as a trip to Bali.

Even a foreign stock "manipulator" such as myself—who now could go by the more respectable title of "investor"—could see the difference the moment I hopped off the plane. For the first time in years, I no longer had to change a handful of dollars into stacks of paper bills at the airport bank, hand-stamped with long lines of *red zeroes*. During the surreal era of hyperinflation, the government hadn't been able to print enough money fast enough to keep pace with the skyrocketing cost of living. Now, for the first time in years, the hordes of shady-looking black marketers skulking around the hotel lobbies and taxi stands offering to exchange dollars at "the best rate" had vanished into thin air.

Mobius Rule No. 77: The surest sign of the instability of a currency is the existence of a thriving black market. Only when the street rate and the official rate are one and the same can a country's currency be considered even remotely healthy.

Soccer Star

Cardoso, meanwhile, came out as the hero who'd gamely tamed

the demon inflation and won. On campaign tours during his first presidential run in 1994, he found himself, as one commentator observed at the time, "mobbed like a soccer star."

But after winning the presidency by a landslide, Cardoso was hit with some unexpected hardballs: a major banking crisis, followed by the devastating ripples of the Tequila Effect, which was the Pan-American meltdown stemming from the financial collapse—and subsequent IMF bailout—of Brazil's profligate neighbor to the north, Mexico. But even as his government lurched and ricocheted from crisis to crisis, Cardoso never lost sight of his ultimate goal: the permanent stabilization of the once-rollicking Brazilian economy. To that end, he continued to press, against heavy political pressure from powerfully entrenched vested interests, for deregulation, privatization, and higher interest rates to maximize investment flows into the country.

By 1997, after five years of low inflation and galloping growth, the results of the free-market policies being pursued with zeal up and down Latin America—once the last bastion of statist thinking outside Russia and Eastern Europe—were in: deregulation, privatization, and liberalization had turned Latin American stock funds into bona fide superstars.

Personally, I found these developments extremely exciting, considering that just three years before, in the wake of the Mexican debt crisis, the Latin American markets had been the barking dogs of the global economy. As a longtime fan of the region, and of Brazil in particular, I along with our Templeton Emerging Markets team felt vindicated for our bullish views on Latin America.

Bossa Novas

What a difference a few basis points make! In the first half of 1997, eight of the top-performing stock funds in the world had been pure Latin American plays, with privatizations providing the motive force behind these rich market run-ups. Under the increasingly popular and powerful Cardoso, Brazil rode a tidal wave of privatizations—featuring the ongoing sell-off of the sprawling state-owned telecom company, Telebras, and Eletrobras, the state-owned electrical company—into a giddy cloudburst of financial euphoria. By June 1997, the Bovespa—the Brazilian stock index—had leapt a whopping 75 percent since the first of the year. And the index itself, which had been trading at an aggregate P/E of 13, was hitting 16.

Of course, compared to the U.S. Dow Jones P/E of 23, 16 was scarcely awe-inspiring. And compared to the crazy 100 P/E of the Japanese market at the peak of its bubble, it was practically a downer. Still, for an emerging market, with all of its attendant risks, and in the context of its track record, Brazil's Sweet 16 was starting to look a bit rich for our blood.

As the Brazilian market hit its historic high, we did the same thing we always do when everyone else is going for broke: we quietly, prudently, cautiously began to take stock, switch to cheaper stocks elsewhere, and take profits. Having at one time placed close to 10 percent of our entire global portfolio in Latin American equities, we slowly but surely began to lighten up that percentage, as we awaited the inevitable downturn, which wouldn't be long in coming.

Price Comes Before the Fall

Until the fall of 1997, Latin America had been cruising along like a magic carpet with fuel injection. Until, as always happens eventually, the fur began to fly. We'd been fairly sure that some sort of trouble would start brewing in the region, sooner rather than later. The surprising thing was the quarter from where the crisis originated: Asia. Now, *that* was the bolt from the blue.

As Black October edged into Gray November, things began looking a little hairy in Latin America, as they had back in Asia. And the courageous Cardoso, with his back against a wall, began hauling out the only first-strike weapons in his monetary arsenal:

1) High short-term interest rates, and
2) A hefty pile of hard currency in reserve.

Mumblety-peg

The problem with pegs is that since the country's central bank sets exchange rate and monetary policy, the currency is artificially prevented from seeking its true level in the international currency markets. Once the underlying fundamentals shift, the pegged rate slips out of whack with global reality. This then requires the central bank to spend its hard currency to prop up the pegged rate that would otherwise be allowed to fall—or rise—to its true level.

To keep its peg in position, Hong Kong had stashed away 80 billion bucks in the bank—plus all the money in China. This had proved sufficient to call the currency traders' bluff. Cardoso had 60 billion bucks in his war chest, which wasn't so shabby, as long as he could combine it with sufficient political will to withstand the inevitable domestic backlash that would result from his harsh interest rate hikes.

The first thing that jacked-up interest rates do is tighten the money supply, which makes it next to impossible for people and companies to borrow. This can quickly send a deflating economy into a tailspin. At the same time, high interest rates attract investors to any currency in which borrowers are willing to pay higher than the rates available in less risky hard currencies.

Ironically, while Cardoso was willing to go to just about any length to avoid the humiliation of going to the IMF for a bailout, the harsh fiscal regime his administration felt obliged to impose on his country was not all that different from the IMF "tough love" cure for a pending currency crash. The only difference was that it was imposed from within, not from without, so it didn't threaten Cardoso's macho political posture.

As Brazil's central bank ratcheted up its benchmark interest rate by 50 percent, and the Bovespa index plummeted by 30 percent, Brazilian consumers responded—as predicted—by delaying big-ticket purchases, and refusing to take on any new debt. With cars suddenly costing over 30 percent more a month to finance, the car dealerships we passed on the streets of Rio displayed more clerks than customers. A few weeks before Christmas, the shopping malls of Rio were eerily quiet. But far more important from the macroeconomic perspective, the currency speculators backed off, and the real—for the time being, at any rate—was pronounced safe and sound. Indeed, attracted by the high real interest rates resulting from the central bank's rate hike, first-quarter 1998 financial inflows into Brazil set an all-time record of nearly $18 billion, more than enough for the country to recover all the hard currency reserves it had lost throughout the fall of 1997.

Big Birds of Paradise

On the morning that we flew down from Rio to Brasília, the country's 1930s grandiose modern capital superimposed on the once-empty barren central plain, the federal government announced a widely awaited new fiscal "austerity package." It included some deep spending cuts—of about $18 billion—and a few tax hikes, on drinks, cars, gasoline—amounting to about $6 billion. While helpful, these measures did not, from our point of view, go nearly far enough to allay investors' concerns about the perilous state of the Brazilian economy.

While the global markets reacted positively to these signals that Cardoso was willing to pay the political price to put tough, unpopular measures into action, there were a few things in the package that I'd been hoping to hear, but didn't.

I'd been hoping, first and foremost, to hear more about privatization. As far as we saw it, the main reason to get hot and bothered about investing in Brazil was the scale and scope of privatization, which rivaled only Russia's in the sheer volume of potential riches being offered to the paying public on a platter.

Raising taxes on gasoline, drinks, and cars was great, I'm sure, as a sign of austerity. But I would have been more impressed if I'd seen a firm commitment, in writing, by the government to sell off Petrobras—the state-owned energy company—by the end of 1998. On those key issues, the new package was distressingly silent.

Still, I was impressed by a comment made by central bank

President Gustavo Franco in response to some who questioned the need for even such severe measures: "You don't question the quality of the water when you're in the midst of fighting a fire."

Silence Is Golden

Not so subdued were the group of demonstrators bused into the capital by a powerful left-leaning union, who on the morning of the first fiscal announcement destroyed a bulletproof door leading to the chambers of a congressional committee debating the future of Social Security. The demonstrators raised so much ruckus that the president of the Brazilian Senate was forced to ask the police to use force to subdue them.

"If you have to beat them, beat them!" he shouted. "If you have to shoot them, shoot them!"

Before the police hauled out their water hoses and rubber truncheons, Cardoso, whose progressive credentials were fortunately unimpeachable, signaled from his office directly across the street from Congress that he was resolved to stand firm. "The most important thing," he announced, within earshot of the boisterous demonstration in the Senate, "is to maintain stability. That is the only way to improve the living conditions of the population." Hear! Hear!

The one silver lining that any of us could find in this particular cloud was that there was a chance to provoke the government and Congress into a renewed effort to push through pending constitutional reforms. The fact that the country had come so close to the brink would make politicians more conscious of the vital need to change the status quo.

Four years before, Cardoso had used a different sort of currency crisis—hyperinflation—to ram through his first round of reforms. Now, with a second looming crisis on his hands, he had the chance—certainly his last chance before the upcoming presidential elections—to marshal the political will to adopt the next wave of necessary reform, which would entail a radical restructuring of the relationship between the Brazilian citizen and the state.

Under its old mixed economy, Brazil had adopted a cradle-to-grave social platform that was fast becoming too costly for the government to bear. Radical structural reform meant, first and foremost, slashing government payrolls, and revamping a costly and inefficient Social Security system.

Remarkably, Cardoso was rough enough and tough enough to attempt to push these two key constitutional amendments through Congress, taking on both sacred cows—before the election. He succeeded, in part, by persuading the Congress that any resulting savings would be spent to improve the lot of the poor—improving health care and education and funding pensions for those who needed them most. And when he was ultimately re-elected, he set about trying to push reform even further—with unfortunately mixed results.

Politician's Paradise

We had come to Brasília to get a closer look at what was happening at the highest levels of government as the crisis unfolded. Brazil was still a country where the government called most—although no longer all—of the shots with regard to the direction of the economy. As we flew in over the dry red Central Plateau, I could see out my Plexiglas window that the sparkling, splendid planned city had been laid out in the sign of a cross. Or, as some secular observers would have it, the shape of an airplane poised to take wing into the future.

Brasília, hastily completed in 1960, was the last great concrete-and-steel gasp of a postwar utopian movement that naïvely decreed that newer was better, and social progress meant central planning. After taking office as president in 1955, Juscelino Kubitschek, a self-styled progressive, forcefully enshrined the national government as the savior of the people, and sole ruler of the economy. He poured vast sums into highways, steel mills, hydroelectric plants and dams, and invited foreign carmakers to set up shop in São Paulo, giving birth to the Brazilian car industry. He promised the Brazilian people that he would give them "fifty years of progress in five." And through lavish expenditure of public money, he just about pulled it off, although he also just about bankrupted the state treasury in the process.

I vividly recall a visit Kubitschek made to my high school in Long Island at that time. It was an era of unbridled optimism about Brazil and the socialist path it was taking. We sat in our high school auditorium as Kubitschek entered from the back of the hall to a fair scattering of applause. Then, as this ebullient, dynamically handsome man strode forcefully down the aisle, smiling as he went, he raised both hands with palms upward and waved them to encourage us to clap more and louder. Being impressionable young students, we did. Soon a roar of applause filled the room, as Kubitschek became the hero and savior of our suburban high school, as well as far-off Brazil.

Ironically, although the splendid austere design by the renowned Marxist architect Oscar Niemeyer—a disciple of Le Corbusier—was heaped with praise from art and social critics, nobody wanted to move or live there. In the early years, the sterile, concrete-clad ministry buildings were regularly defaced by shadowy graffiti artists and vandals later identified as disgruntled civil servants pining away for the pleasures of Rio. Even today, as the city has gradually cultivated more amenities, nearly every government pencil-pusher who can afford it maintains a home in Rio to fly back to on weekends.

The multiple ironies of a planned city designed by avowed Marxists replete with hundreds of splendid villas with swimming pools in this dry plain, a distinct "club quarter" and a "hotel sector" and hundreds of gourmet restaurants have, if anything, grown richer with the passage of time. From the plane, we could see the cramped, congested satellite cities on the edge of the dusty plain, out of sight and out of mind of elegant modern Brasília, where the poor worker bees must live on the outskirts— and be bused into the surrealistic city center every morning and out by night—because they could never afford to live within the costly precincts of the "people's capital."

Our first stop was Bloco O—O—on the Esplanade of Ministries, a Lego-block-like row of monotonously symmetrical slab-shaped concrete towers, in which the highest ministries of the central government are efficiently housed. Each ministry's name was emblazoned in gold letters incised into cement facades that were looking a bit the worse for wear after thirty years of weathering the hot dry winds of that flat, barren plain.

I was a bit taken aback to see the Ministry of Social Assistance sharing a concrete box with the Ministry of Work, but that's socialism for you—even in retreat. I was also amused by the detailed map we saw in the elevator attempting to show visitors where everything was. In this relentlessly planned city, with its monotonously similar buildings, it was practically impossible to figure out where you were by visual landmarks. An apt metaphor, I thought, for central planning: lost in the rationalist's maze.

Dismantling the Octopus

I can't imagine what Juscelino Kubitschek or Oscar Niemeyer would have made of our mission to see the young chief of staff of the Ministry of Mines and Energy, whose assigned task under the current administration was the rational management of the process of dismantling the vast bureaucracy that once guided the energy sector with a heavy hand. This man's job, after all these years of heading feet-first in the opposing direction, was to transfer assets and power fairly and efficiently from the public to the private sector in the most strategic arenas of all: mines and energy. My question: once this mission was fully accomplished, would they blow up Brasília? Somehow, I doubted it.

"My brief," volunteered Reginaldo Medeiros, a good-looking, well-spoken young man, "is to promote the privatization of the energy sector."

Though he said this in all seriousness, I'd lived long enough to be amused by the rote way that bureaucrats now spoke of "privatization" in the same glowing terms that they once spoke of "nationalization": as a miraculous panacea for curing everything but the common cold.

But it didn't take long for Medeiros to impress me with his command of the situation. In his own quiet way, he was a revolutionary, although like his boss, Cardoso, he wasn't manning the barricades, but cruising the fluorescent-lit corridors of public power.

My first question was whether, given the current economic pressures, the government was committed to accelerating privatization, or slowing it down. Of course, being a good public servant, he didn't answer my question directly.

"These are really two different issues," he explained, whipping a roller ball pen out of his pocket and leaning forward to draw diagrams on a sheet of paper for our benefit. "The first issue is the restructuring of the energy sector, which must be accomplished before we sell it to the public. The second stage is the privatization process itself."

He explained that the government, in its wisdom, had decided that the entire energy sector needed to be reorganized and split up into its component parts, so that the various pieces could be spiffed up, shined up, and their loose ends tied up to enhance their appeal to private investors.

A second critical decision taken recently by the government was that, for the present, the government had decided to retain control of Petrobras, the state-owned oil company. This bloated behemoth was widely regarded as the last crown jewel among the few remaining public assets in state hands.

Founded in 1953, Petrobras was the quintessential strategic asset, controlling, among other invaluable resources, Brazil's entire oil and natural gas reserves. To some sectors of society to whom privatization was the devil incarnate, the act of turning control of the nation's oil and gas over to "foreign interests" would have been *the* unforgivable sin. The small carrot that the government was willing to dangle, for the time being, was the prospect that foreign companies might be permitted to enter into "public-private partnerships" with Petrobras.

"There will be ample opportunities for joint ventures with foreign companies for specific projects," Medeiros cordially explained. That was just fine by me, but hardly the kick in the pants amphetamine rush to the laggard economy that privatizing Petrobras would have been.

On the other hand, the joint ventures under discussion—grouped under the generic rubric "Partnership Program"—were nothing to be sneezed at. Negotiations were currently under way on some fifty projects of varying size, many at an advanced stage of deal-making. In a transparent bid to show the world that even a public company could keep up with the times, Petrobras had produced a handsome CD-ROM detailing these potential joint venture projects, which had attracted the attention of such international players as Amoco, Chevron, Conoco, Elf Aquitane, Mobil, and Texaco. All the legal ramifications of these pending deals were still being hammered out by Brazil's newly established National Petroleum Agency (ANP).

A critical first step in the privatization of Petrobras had been taken, Medeiros pointed out, with the recent introduction of a bill in the Brazilian Senate providing for the gradual phase-out of a complex web of subsidies and incentives—and disincentives—under which the giant company had operated as a monopoly for the past several decades.

Up until 1995, Petrobras had enjoyed complete control over exploration, production, importation, and transportation of crude oil and oil derivatives inside Brazil. But with the passage of the latest energy sector privatization law, the days of Petrobras's monopoly were clearly numbered. The bill provided for a complete phase-out of subsidies and controls in five years. From reliable sources, we were told that the reality might be even quicker than that: a complete phase-out by the end of the coming year.

Although Petrobras had not yet been fully privatized, shares in the company were being sold on the open market, although not yet in ADR form. While officially determined to maintain a controlling 50 percent-plus-one share in the company, the government continued to cling to about 80 percent of the group's outstanding common shares.

Plans had lately been announced to eventually sell off the roughly 30 percent of the company that would still leave the government in control of its 50 percent plus one. But the details and a precise timetable had not yet been revealed, primarily for political reasons. With an election in the works, privatizing Petrobras was a political lightning rod. Once Cardoso was safely back in office, we could assume that Petrobras's privatization would be one of the first items to be tackled.

Still, rumors were running rampant around the capital that the government was planning to go further, possibly even before the election, if the political coast was deemed clear. The ultimate goal of fully turning control of Petroleo Brasiliero (Petrobras) over to the private sector was said (by some) to be near at hand.

Brazil Denies Plan to Sell Off Oil Giant

Brazil says that it has no intention of privatizing oil giant Petrobras SA or dismissing members of the company's board. The government was reacting to widespread reports in the Brazilian news media last week suggesting that the government was preparing to sell off Petrobras, and that a presidential decree to that effect was in the making. Petrobras lost its monopoly in the oil sector last year, and now has to compete with private enterprise on an equal footing.

—*The Wall Street Journal*

Were these denials true, or merely for the record? We honestly couldn't say. What we did know was that any loosening of the law compelling the government to hold on to that controlling share of the Petrobras pie would unleash a land-office rush in its shares.

As recently as six months before, Petrobras shares had been selling at $280 a share, and were now down to the mid-$200s. Along with nearly every other Brazilian stock, Petrobras was— along with the rest of Brazil—suffering from a bad case of the global spread of the Asian Flu virus.

The question was: Should we buy more Petrobras stock in anticipation of further privatization? Or should we buy more Petrobras stock in anticipation of an overall market recovery? As you can tell from the above questions, I felt in my bones that at current discount prices, buying Petrobras (as opposed to holding or selling it) was a pretty good bet.

Not So Fast, Bub

Still, there were a few potential pitfalls.

Viral issues aside, the brightest red flag with regard to Petrobras was growing concern about the state-appointed management's capacity to function effectively in a competitive environment.

As one of our broker's reports cautiously commented: "While the technical capacity of the company is unquestioned, its corporate culture seems unsuited to the competitive environment of the private sector."

True or false?

Truth or Consequences

Determined to get an answer to this question straight from the horse's mouth, we met with one of the top dogs at Petrobras over an elegant lunch of tasty Amazon River flying fish served by white-coated waiters bowing and scraping at a restaurant so chic and sleek it would have put New York's SoHo to shame.

"How's the oil business?" I asked.

"Oh, very good," he replied, chuckling amiably.

But then—after reading from my pensive expression that this was a serious question, demanding a serious answer—he carefully qualified his response.

"If we're speaking about collecting economic rent, in the Ricardian sense of the term, we're doing exceptionally well," he elaborated, without seeming to boast. "But if you're talking about our possible restructuring . . ." He shrugged philosophically, as if to say, "Who knows what the future will bring?"

The "Ricardo" to whom he was referring was not Lucille Ball's husband, Ricky, but the nineteenth-century British free-market philosopher David Ricardo, a successor of Adam Smith. In plain English, this guy—who as you no doubt can tell, was a well-educated fellow—was telling me that, as a de facto monopoly, the company was raking it in hand over fist. As the monopoly player in the highly lucrative oil and gas sector, that practically went without saying. But from a potential Petrobras investor's point of view, the looming question was: how long would the good times roll?

The real 64-billion-dollar question for potential Petrobras investors was whether the good times would get better as the monopoly broke up, or whether a no-longer-coddled company, suddenly befuddled by competition, would find itself floundering in a wide open sea.

"If you look at the situation in terms of the shifting regulatory environment," our man went on, sipping casually on a chilled glass of white wine, cleverly anticipating my next question, "I would honestly say that if the government is planning to turn us into a full-blooded oil company anytime soon, we're in pretty good shape."

That was awfully nice to hear, although some well-informed analysts would have begged, respectfully of course, to disagree.

One widely voiced fear was that four decades of unchallenged control over Brazil's oil and gas industry would leave Petrobras in a position to retain a de facto monopoly over petroleum energy production and distribution even after its monopoly days were officially over.

The Privatization Tango

The richest irony of publicly owned corporations is that because they were never permitted to fail, they were never able to honestly prosper. By "honestly," I mean that if they were not coddled by government in a vast web of regulatory caresses, the vast majority of these bloated dinosaurs would have been blown off the map decades ago.

But Petrobras was, is, and was likely to remain a special case: in some aspects of its operations—deep-sea oil exploration and drilling, for example—it was a top-notch, global player. But just like some of its Russian rivals (whose strictly *technical* skills have never been in doubt), where Petrobras tended to fall short was in the marketing and management areas, where it still remained mired—at least in some critics' view—in the dark ages of a sleepy socialism.

Untangling the Maze

The process of dismantling regulatory mazes can be a complex and arduous one, fraught with political peril, whether it's being done in the U.S., Great Britain, Italy, France, or Brazil. But the real reason that the stocks in most public companies around the world, in Western as well as Eastern Europe, Latin America, and Africa, tend to shoot for the roof after privatization (and continue to command premium prices thereafter) is this:

Most investors are willing to bet that free-market forces will pressure the company to improve its performance, even if the old management is still groping around in the dark.

Why? Because if a state-owned company is finally allowed to fail, its long-term survival prospects are not diminished, but actually enhanced.

To paraphrase what Dr. Johnson once said about the prospect of being hanged in the morning, nothing focuses an organization's mind on success more than the prospect of failure.

If Petrobras's present management refused to learn how to play on the new faster, broad, global playing field, then Petrobras shareholders would just have to get their acts together and force the deadwood out and find new blood—usually younger blood—who knew how to rumble on world turf.

The Rumor Mill

It pays to pay attention to rumors. In this case, the rumors—as reprinted in *The Wall Street Journal*—concerning the pending replacement of the Petrobras board. I've found that it often makes sense to move quickly to determine if the rumor is true and if there seems to be some truth in the rumor, to act quickly.

Mobius Rule No. 78: Even if the *denials* to a rumor are true, they're often only temporary. If you buy or sell on the basis of *confirmed and investigated* rumor, sooner or later the price will often reflect the reality.

Size Matters

With an annual turnover of $26 billion, ranked strictly by sales, Petrobras was the fifteenth largest oil company in the world—according to a recent ranking by *Petroleum Intelligence Weekly*—just behind Atlantic Richfield. Exxon, Royal Dutch/Shell, and Mobil held up the number one, two, and three positions respectively; of course, the recently announced merger of Mobil and Exxon would soon push that combo to the top of the barrel. Petrobras now produced in excess of 1 billion barrels of oil every day, and was widely regarded as a technological leader, particularly in the more advanced and arcane realms of deepwater drilling and production.

But Brazil's galloping oil consumption, based on high growth rates, meant that even though it was Latin America's third largest producer, the country still had to import 40 percent of its annual energy needs. On the face of it, this made absolutely no sense. Why should a country sitting on 8 billion barrels of known reserves need to import nearly half of its domestic energy needs? The reason had everything to do with the complex economics of resource extraction, and the sort of market distortions that a monopoly can be forced to navigate in a mixed economy.

As our source freely explained: "As we get rid of the monopoly, we have to start thinking about how much of Brazil's annual consumption should Petrobras supply, and how much of Petrobras's capacity should be sold in Brazil."

Under the old subsidized system, he explained, Petrobras never had to think about how much oil to sell inside the country, and how much to export, because all of its oil had been targeted for domestic consumption, as part of its mandate to supply local industry with as much fuel as it could—at subsidized prices.

As a "national champion," Petrobras's primary reason for being had not been to make money as an oil producer, but to act as a source of boundless energy for Brazil's industrial expansion. The greatest distortion affecting—perhaps I should say afflicting—Petrobras's prior behavior had been that over the years successive governments had forced the company to charge the same price for its oil at every location in the country, regardless of the costs associated with pumping it by pipeline or shipping it by tanker to remote regions.

"Under the military government," my friend observed, "the cost of fuel had to be the same at the refinery as in the middle of the Amazon. So in order to keep our costs down, we said to ourselves, 'Why bother to build pipelines to the Amazon?' "

Under the new, deregulated environment, it probably wouldn't pay for Petrobras to build pipelines to the Amazon either. Instead, the most cost-effective supply route for that region would probably run from Peru. But being freed of the obligation to sell oil in the Amazon at the same price that it charged in Rio or São Paulo would be an enormous boon to the company—and to its future shareholders.

Where the most glaring faults of Petrobras's current management really showed up were in its pathetic price-to-earnings ratio. At the time 85 as compared to 20 for Exxon and 18.7 for Mobil, it remained one of the highest on earth. The company's sales per employee were equally dismal: $387 as compared to $1,654 for Mobil and $1,478 for Exxon.

These lousy numbers told a story familiar to anyone who has ever taken a gander at the books of a publicly owned corporation. Over the years, Petrobras had become a holding pen for political appointees, as well as a convenient vehicle with which to pursue a wide range of social and political agendas. In order for the stock to reflect the level of valuations that investors routinely place on similarly sized private corporations, the company would have to start trimming fat, ramping up investment to exploit its own reserves, and begin seriously exploiting its ample natural gas resources, valuable commodities being currently squandered.

To this end, the company had lately released plans to aggressively invest—to the tune of some $6 billion—in developing its own known reserves, a plan that one oil industry analyst we spoke with characterized as containing "one of the highest growth rates of any global oil or gas company in the world."

On the downside, at least a third of that investment pool would have to be borrowed on international markets, thereby increasing the company's debt load.

On the upside, Petrobras enjoys a fine reputation with international lenders and investors, so that we could safely reckon that high level of investment would enjoy a healthy rate of return.

And now for the good news. We reckoned, on balance, that the eventual lifting of price controls and subsidies on crude oil and gas would positively impact Petrobras's bottom line to the tune of at least $2 billion in additional cash per year.

That was more than enough, we figured, to allow the company to comfortably meet its targets for investing in developing its own untapped resources.

As we saw it, the key consideration for any potential investor in Petrobras was this:

How much of the income anticipated to flow in as a result of the withering away of subsidies would be productively invested in expanding its production and distribution capacity?

In response to that question, our man spoke with scarcely concealed excitement about the greatest oil strike in Petrobras's history: the discovery of the Rocodor oil field. This vast field not only added several billion barrels to the country's known reserves, but dramatically improved Petrobras's competitive position, because its light oil mixed easily with heavy oil from other local fields. This permitted the company to export the mixed product at premium prices, and to import less mixed oil itself.

The company was now planning to rapidly expand the domestic market for natural gas, after neglecting that potentially profitable market for decades, in anticipation of a lifting of price controls and subsidies in that fledgling market. As the chief of staff of the Ministry of Mines and Energy had observed at our morning meeting: "Petrobras was always sitting on so much oil that they never bothered about the gas. Now, with Petrobras competing with other companies, I'm sure they'll start finding lots of gas."

In the early stages of the Rocodor project, the natural gas would be flared—burned off. But at a later stage of development, the gas would be piped out and sold. That in and of itself was a revolution for Petrobras. In addition to Rocodor, Petrobras was engaged in two other big natural gas projects—a Bolivia–Brazil pipeline, and a project called Urucu in Amazonia. In preparation for the eventual deregulation of the domestic natural gas market, Petrobras was determined to become a major natural gas player.

This was a perfect example of:

Mobius Rule No. 79: The mere prospect of competition down the road will force a slumbering company to wake up and smell the coffee.

Petrobras had been sitting on an invaluable resource, and literally burning it, like leaves in a garden. Why? Because it had been under no great pressure to do anything else with it.

A second major plus for the company going forward was a plan to leverage the wealth of technical know-how the company had acquired over the years in the rarefied arena of deep-water drilling. One of the company's most ambitious projects to date—the $1.5 billion development of the deep-water Albacora Leste field, required forty-four wells to be drilled in waters up to 2,000 meters deep—this was Petrobras's viscous cup of tea.

Once again, forced to think about competition and leveraging underutilized assets, Petrobras had belatedly realized that their $200 million-plus annual investment in deep-water exploration R&D could be turned into a profit center if the company rented itself out as a high-paid consultant to other companies lacking their deep technical base.

In conclusion, at least they were walking the free-market walk and talking the talk. If you believed their public posture, Petrobras's senior management was positively salivating at the prospect of being privatized. Why? Because, as our man said, "We at long last realized that under the old system, *our people had lost their appreciation of risk.*"

Those people would, soon enough, be placed squarely on the front line and would regain their appreciation of risk, or else.

Because to compete effectively with its private sector rivals, at least 7,000 of the company's 44,000 employees would have to be handed pink slips. This was, of course, political dynamite. The long-term deal between the state-owned companies and the labor unions was to keep padding payrolls. After all, the only loser was the anonymous taxpayer. The company was seeking permission to slash staff, but the labor unions, which still exerted considerable political muscle in Congress, were predictably resisting tooth-and-nail.

A failure to quickly reduce this tremendous drag on the bottom line—a top-heavy, out-of-whack padded payroll—could seriously threaten everything that the company hoped to achieve in the near future. And this was the primary reason that global investors, when pricing the value of the company, discounted the company's known oil reserves by 40 percent in comparison to its private sector competitors. The "enterprise value"—the value placed on the entire enterprise—for Petrobras was $4.6 per barrel, as compared to $8 for the big boys.

But what potential Petrobras investors should have taken note of was this: if the company were to be successful in implementing its plans to more efficiently exploit its resources, the stock at its present price would have been woefully undervalued.

In conclusion, I had to determine whether some remarks made by the Petrobras CFO, Orlando Galvao Filho, during our visit were sincere and accurate, or merely window dressing.

"There is a general consensus," he said—he didn't specify among *whom*—"that the company will dramatically improve after the change in regulation. Although Petrobras is a state company, it is run more like a private company," he insisted.

Personally, I wasn't so sure about that, but why quibble over details?

"We have over 200,000 shareholders," he pointed out proudly, "all of whom continually demand more efficiency and more dividends."

He was right on the money about that—we proudly counted ourselves among them.

"Under a deregulated market," he continued, "we will be given the freedom to develop partnerships and the chance to explore areas which we have not been able to develop now because of the lack of funds due to price controls and limitations on investment. We will also be allowed to sell, close, or transfer operations that are not profitable but that we've been obliged to maintain."

This was, of course, an optimistic official projection, not to mention a party line targeted at foreign investors.

But, according to our best estimates and projections, he was basically telling it like it was.

We assessed the overall impact of the reformed structural environment on the company's bottom line as follows: at the end of the day, cash generation by Petrobras for 1998 would be 120 percent higher than in 1996.

So if that positive trend continued over the next five years or so, Petrobras stock—particularly if you threw in the Asian Flu discount—was still a steal.

Eletrobras

I wish I could have said the same thing about Eletrobras, the state-owned electrical company. Not that it wasn't a buy, because we'd made a king's ransom on it over the years. It was just that as a company it was so much more complicated to evaluate than Petrobras. About the only thing it had in common with Petrobras was that it also was one of our top ten performers to date: a major member of our 200 percent-plus club.

We'd started snapping up Eletrobras stock back in 1991, when hyperinflation was raging out of control, and the economic situation was, to say the least, chaotic. Our main reason for buying the stock at that time was that, by applying a number of different benchmarks, we estimated that the company's NAV (net asset value) was more than 10 times its market cap.

Note that the best way to evaluate a company's right or strike price is to compare NAV with market cap: if the NAV is much higher than the market cap, it's by definition undervalued.

With a ratio of market cap to NAV at more than one to ten, Eletrobras was *one of the cheapest electrical utilities on earth*. This despite the ups and downs of the Brazilian currency.

In the years since, Eletrobras stock had risen 211 percent measured from trough to peak. The peak had come the previous July, just as the Bovespa went stratospheric. And now, although it had hit another trough induced mainly by the Asian Flu factor, at around $500 per 1,000 preferred shares, it wasn't at all clear that at that price it was anybody's idea of a bargain.

After Telebras and Petrobras, Eletrobras was the third-largest company in Latin America. Its market value—as measured by the aggregate worth of its stock—hovered at the time around $30 billion. This sprawling holding company controlled the four state-owned electrical generating companies in Brazil: Furnas, Chesf, Eletrosul—the energy companies of the south—and Eletronorte—the energy company of the north. It also owned half of Itaipu, a 50-50 Brazilian-Paraguayan joint venture project that is the largest hydroelectric plant in the world.

It also controlled Light—the electric utility supplying Rio de Janeiro state, which had recently been privatized. Oh, and it also had Nuclen, a consortium of nuclear power plants.

Eletrobras, in other words, still controlled the lion's share of Brazil's electric power generating, distribution, and transmission facilities. But it also operated as the financing arm for the entire national electrical utility sector.

Which meant, in practice, that it packed the financial muscle to borrow huge sums of money on the international markets, and that it lent that money out to its maze of dependencies and subsidiaries—to the tune of some 25 billion bucks.

On the afternoon that we stopped by the company headquarters in Rio, an inner circle of senior directors was huddled behind closed doors, pondering in a hush-hush meeting the latest phase of the company's ongoing privatization.

Among the many proposals contained in the latest government austerity package had been a scheme to sell off the company's $25 billion loan portfolio to the private sector. This was to be accomplished by "securitizing" these assets—taking the assets and bundling them as securities—and converting them into high-yielding bonds. The plan was to take the proceeds and use them to reduce Eletrobras's staggering debt load, thus making it more attractive to wary investors.

Now what was an electrical utility doing behaving like a bank?

The basic answer to that was: when a federal government is calling the shots, a gorilla can turn into an orangutan, but still be called a gorilla, if the government wants it to be. Over the years, without anyone much paying attention, "Banco Eletrobras" had monstrously swollen into the second largest bank in Brazil, eclipsed only by the state-owned Bank of Brazil, itself hardly a paragon of air-tight fiscal management.

Only in a mixed economy can a state-owned electrical company morph into a bank!

And only in an economy in the process of *de-mixing* could that bank be turned back over to the private sector. Around the world, securitizing bank debt was *the* happening thing.

NAV

We calculated the bank part of Eletrobras—"Banco Eletrobras"—as worth a bit over $4 billion. This figure included some $8.4 billion in its asset portfolio minus $4.3 billion in liabilities. Going right down the line, we figured that the installed generating capacity of the company—which accounted for roughly 60 percent of the country's annual electrical power consumption—was worth around $20 billion. And we valued the company's far-flung transmission grid—which had been constructed at a daunting cost of more than $17 billion, at 0. That's right: zero. Nada.

Now, let's take a look at that number, because it was a key to the entire equation. How could we have assigned a value to an asset that the company carried on its books at a whopping $17.2 billion of ZERO?

Because the consumption of electricity in Brazil was rising so rapidly—at over 5 percent per year—that whether it was Eletrobras or some private successor who had to do it, the amount of money that would have to be invested to expand that grid far enough and fast enough to meet demand was more than the grid could now generate in income.

With Eletrobras stock—which had as recently as two months before been trading at $50-plus per thousand shares—now selling for $450, we set the NAV at around $34 billion. So with a market cap of around $25 billion—at present prices—the $10 billion difference between the NAV and the market cap repre-

sented the value to the shareholder of buying shares in an undervalued company.

There were, of course, other questions to be answered than
ratio of NAV to market cap.

As potential Eletrobras investors, we needed to get a sense of
what prices the companies to be spun off from Eletrobras would
be sold at. We knew that the government had decided to break
up the holding company into three parts: transmission, distribution, and generation. But the challenge that the government
faced was to reconcile two conflicting objectives:

1) To foster competition in the energy sector, and
2) To maximize the proceeds of privatization.

If the government chose to maximize competition, it would
get less money for selling the assets, because the spun-off companies would face competition, which might—at least in the
short run—cut into their profits.

But if it chose simply to maximize the proceeds of privatization, the prices being asked for the stock in the spin-offs might
well be too high for bargain hunters.

So why was the government going to all this trouble to hive
off these assets to the public?

The answer was simple: they could make one heck of a lot of
money.

Telebras

A few key things to know about Telebras, the state-owned
Brazilian telephone company:

With a market cap of $40 billion, it is the largest company in
Latin America. It is also the most liquid stock in Latin America.
Its price reflects the sentiment that investors as a whole have
about Brazil. As Brazil goes, so goes Telebras.

We started buying stock in the company in January 1992,
when it was in the first stages of privatization. At the time,
judged on the basis of market cap per line—perhaps the best
benchmark for judging any telecom company—it was just about
the cheapest phone company in the world, bar none.

By the time we visited Telebras's high-rise Brasília headquarters at the end of a long day nearly six years later, the share price
had risen 325 percent in U.S. dollar terms.

Need I say more?

I think so.

Looking Backward

This gargantuan holding company had been cobbled together in
1972, when the government decided to integrate some 1,000 existing phone companies scattered across the country into one
vast national network. The big buzzwords back then were "integration" and "consolidation." The idea being that it made
more sense to combine all these disparate companies into one
big fat monster. Bigger, in short, was better.

There were twenty-six different states in Brazil. So the government, in its wisdom, at the stroke of a pen created twenty-six
separate phone companies, all answerable to Telebras management in Brasília. A separate long-distance company was formed,
called Embratel.

Of course, Telebras also owned nearly all of that too—97 percent of it, to be precise. That went without saying too. That was
known as central control.

A few other key facts:

In 1972, there were 1.5 million main lines in Brazil.

By 1980, there were 6 million main lines.

By 1992, after twenty years in operation, there were 10 million main lines—about 7 million residential subscribers, and 3
million business subscribers. In a country with a population topping 160 million, the penetration rate was woefully low: under
10 percent.

This wasn't so surprising, when you stopped to think about it.
Because every subscriber, before being granted the privilege of a
phone line, was forced to fork over the equivalent of several
thousand dollars to enjoy the ultimate luxury of placing phone
calls from home or office. Owning a telephone—much less ob-

taining one—was pretty much a rich man's, or rich woman's, pastime.

Even by 1998, the waiting list for telephone lines numbered in the millions of names, not in the thousands. Needless to say, this sorry state of affairs stifled economic growth in the country, because it kept communications in the dark ages, and made high-speed data transmission and networking and all those wonderful things virtually impossible.

We knew that game well. In 1996, we opened an office in Rio. A year later, we still hadn't been able to wangle enough phone lines to run our faxes and computers at the same time. It didn't matter that we were paying sky-high rents in one of the few really modern towers in Rio, perched above the first-class Rio Sul shopping center, with a fabulous view of Copacabana and Ipanema.

So how do you get a phone line in Brazil?

Step One: You put an ad in the paper.

Step Two: You sit back and wait, sometimes for weeks, sometimes for months, hoping that someone calls you—on their own phone—and offers to sell you one. (Of course, since you still don't have a phone, they have to call you on someone else's line and leave a message.) The price? The sky's the limit.

Step Three: While waiting for Steps One and Two to take fruit, you tell everyone to call you on your cell phone, and you pay through the nose for every call you make, and every call you take.

Clearly, telephone service in Brazil had a long way to go before it reached anything remotely approaching world standards.

So how was the company planning to go about doing that?

By going backward and undoing everything that had been done since 1972. In other words, by breaking itself up into tiny little pieces.

Breaking Up Is Hard to Do

"Chop, chop, chop," Telebras's director of finance, Sergio Luiz Goncalves Pereira, said with a smile; and with a sharp karate motion with his hand over the polished top of the vast conference table, he illustrated the pending fate of one of the greatest telephone monopolies on earth.

"Chop chop chop—into little pieces. That's how the Chinese like to cook their food."

And how the Brazilians had decided to deal with their phone company.

The reason? The theoretical basis for both deregulation and privatization is that the free market will do a better job of ensuring the largest number of people the best service than a highly regulated monopoly will do—government owned or not. In the case of AT&T in the U.S., it wasn't government owned, but it was a monopoly, in the then tightly regulated field of long-distance service. After it was forced to break up into Baby Bells, all free to compete—with some limitations—against each other and against new entrants like Sprint and MCI, it turned out that all the companies flourished, service improved, and overall prices dropped. Where you saw price increases was in local markets, where long-distance service no longer subsidized local calling.

The AT&T breakup was clearly a model for the impending breakup of Telebras into a dozen or so so-called Baby Brases. Like Humpty Dumpty, come July 1998, neither all the king's horses nor all the king's men—or their designated agents—were supposed to be able to put Telebras back together again.

All the details had not yet been worked out. But the basic idea was to carve the monopoly into twelve or thirteen companies, the exact number as yet to be determined. The point was that each would be granted licenses to cover specific geographic areas—not monopolies, but competitors with rival entities that might apply for and be awarded licenses to serve the same areas.

For each share in Telebras a shareholder currently held, that shareholder would be given twelve or thirteen proportionate shares in the dozen-odd new companies. Sounds simple, right?

At the time of our visit, the Brazilian government had just appointed a consortium led by Salomon Smith Barney to handle (the technical term would be "underwrite") the sale of the government's remaining stake in the company, which at the time comprised 21 percent of the outstanding common shares in Telebras, and just over half of the voting shares to a series of strategic partners. This sale was intended to roughly coincide with the breakup of existing Telebras ADRs into ADRs for the new spin-offs.

We understood that nearly all of the major telecom players in the world—AT&T, MCI, GTE, Bell Atlantic, Bell Canada, Telecom Italia, and France Telecom—were salivating over getting their hands on various pieces of this puzzle. As one of the heads of Latin American equity research at Merrill Lynch said, "There are not too many opportunities like this left in the world—huge telephone service markets with pent-up demand." The hunger out there for Telebras shares was positively ferocious.

Though valuations on the spin-offs vary wildly, most stock pickers agreed the parts would be worth considerably more than the whole—in time. Merrill Lynch, for example, valued the sum of the parts anywhere from $113.61 on a pessimistic basis to $195.72 on a more optimistic analysis—that would be for the group of twelve or thirteen ADRs that investors would receive for their single Telebras ADRs.

The Telebras spin-offs were going to range from a wire-line company serving bustling São Paulo to a cellular firm in the sprawling Amazon. There was going to be a single phone company covering the central and southern states that was widely rumored to make a likely takeover target. There would be three fixed-line companies and eight cellular companies, and a long-distance provider, Embratel.

The most hotly sought-after companies, post-breakup, were bound to be the cellular and fixed-line companies serving the most prosperous major metropolitan areas, namely Rio de Janeiro and São Paulo. Given Brazilians' love affair with cellular telephony, the cellular stocks were expected to soar, thanks to pent-up demand and the fact that Brazilians spend roughly double per month what U.S. customers do, a function of the poor quality of land lines and a lack of competition. One analyst was quoted in an article in *The Wall Street Journal* about the impending breakup as follows: "Cellular stocks are bursting with value whereas wire line will, by comparison, perform poorly."

But my own innate caution about cellular stocks made me skeptical. In my view, they were being highly oversold by brokers and investors with an overly short time horizon. It's much easier for new companies to enter a new market for cellular services, because the barriers to entry aren't nearly so high. By contrast, fixed-line phone companies, with their huge installed base and admittedly antiquated networks, still had the jump on the competition in many regions, and were—from my point of view—potential sleepers.

One of the greatest question marks of the Telebras breakup was Embratel, the long-distance company, which would face limited competition for the first three years after privatization, and an entirely free market after 2002. Its market would be the easiest to penetrate by the international players dying to break into the high-growth Brazilian market.

If the most frequently invoked analogy to the AT&T breakup held true, than it made sense to buy as many Telebras ADRs as you could before the breakup. If I were a betting man, I'd have to say—hand me the brown paper envelope please—yes, this was the Brazilian AT&T.

And I do mean yes. Don't quote me on it, but yes, I said yes.

One yardstick to determine the value of what Telebras might be worth post-breakup was the whopping $2.45 billion forked over to the Brazilian government by a consortium led by BellSouth (one of the aforementioned Baby Bells) for the cellular rights to the São Paulo area.

Another benchmark was the 1991 privatization of the Venezuelan telephone network, after which management was farmed out to GTE, which cut the number of employees by 28 percent and increased the number of phone lines by 63 percent.

That company's stock, first listed as an ADR on the New York Stock Exchange in November 1996 at $18, now stood at $35.

The key question in determining the once and future value of Telebras shares—and their subsequent spin-offs—was: how was competition going to affect the performance of the domestic companies?

At some point in the not too distant future, all of the major international players—AT&T, Britain's Cable & Wireless, MCI, and Sprint—would all be breaking down the doors to enter the hot Brazilian market, in competition with the spun-off heirs to the Telebras monopoly. These, in homage to the Baby Bells, were popularly known as Baby Brases.

Now, the long-term question for holders of Telebras stock was this: would some Baby Brases wither on the vine and get killed by competition, while others flourished in a new more competitive environment?

The way I saw it, even if one of the Baby Brases grew weak, that would make it ripe for the picking by an outside interest, which would make it a takeover target, and therefore a good buy.

> **Mobius Rule No 80: It nearly always pays
> to go with the locals.**

So practically any way we sliced and diced the equations, Telebras shares came up a winner.

As one of our broker's reports put it: "There is no doubt that as new rivals start to enter the sector, the environment will become more competitive. A fall in prices will probably affect the profitability of certain services. On the other hand, new services will undoubtedly produce extra revenue. There is no reason why local companies should be immune from the trend toward greater efficiency. We must not forget that there is enormous scope in Brazil not only for boosting efficiency, but also for cutting costs."

Cheaper by the Dozen?

The question of how to play this particular privatization revolved around four basic unresolved issues:

1) Would Telebras shares peak just before the privatization, due to investors' possibly well-founded fears that keeping track of a dozen different companies would be too confusing? Particularly if the different companies were operating in dramatically different environments?

2) Would some of these companies be such small fry that they would be eaten alive by the majors?

3) Did it make sense to dump the small fry before they took a tumble?

4) Did it make the most sense to hold on to all twelve companies for the long haul, and ride out the turbulence in the short term?

The answers to those questions largely depended upon whether you adopted the short-term or long-term view of the issue. By our long-term lights, and sights, we were chiefly interested in projecting the performance of the Telebras spin-offs out to a five-year time horizon.

So if a few of the small fry were dumped due to investor fears, as opposed to fundamental weakness, then it made sense to hold on to them—or buy them. Because that was just pure emotion, stuff you can make money on, if you know how to ignore it.

Our philosophy dictated faith in the Baby Brases. Investors in AT&T who had faith in the Baby Bells had done just fine by them, thank you.

Sweet River Valley, Valley So Low

Companhia Vale de Rio Doce (CVRD) was the largest iron ore producer in the world, as well as the largest—and most alluring—property still in state hands. Privatizing CVRD was a high priority for the present government, because they figured that the mega-billions its sell-off could yield could be put to better use than trying to make iron and steel and manganese.

But the Great Sell-off was in dire danger of being stymied by the usual round of suspects: labor unions and leftist lawyers, whose typical obstructionist tactics were to file a blizzard of injunctions against the sale, usually in the most remote areas of the country, and the most ill-equipped to adjudicate such complex cases, and with the judges that were easiest to cajole.

It took the government two turbulent years to privatize Light, the company that distributes Rio's electricity, as a flurry of technical arguments and last-minute appeals wended their way through the courts. From the intensity of the legal skirmishing involved, it was reminiscent of the way anti-death-penalty lawyers seek to file injunctions against every execution anywhere. And in a way, the analogy is not all that far-fetched, because privatization—if it were allowed to proceed unchecked in the country—represented the death of a hard-fought ideal: socialism. Power to the People. Property Is Theft. And all that.

But this time around, an experienced BNDES—Brazil's National Development Bank—got its ducks all in a row before spending even one day in court.

"We hired fifteen mining and financial consulting firms to evaluate the worth of CVRD's assets over a six-month period," one BNDES higher-up would later recall. "We made the evaluation of assets and pricing highly transparent. And we marshaled more than 200 lawyers to fight any legal battles that might come up."

It was a picture-perfect privatization. One for the history books.

All relevant data were made available to bidders and the financial press in preparation for the Great Sell-off well before the Big Day. The idea was to sell 42 percent of the company's voting shares to a grateful public, which would still leave the government a controlling stake. But if the sale netted, as was expected, over $3 billion, that placed the market cap of the company at over $11 billion.

Not too shabby a pot for the feds to take in, or rather, rake in, for a company getting a little too big to manage effectively anyway.

BNDES, to avoid any hint of operating behind closed doors, rented out the trading floor of the Rio Stock Exchange for the Big Day, and cleverly arranged to have the auction nationally televised.

A day before the Big Day, a security fence was erected around the Rio exchange, while trained riot troops armed with water cannon, truncheons, and shields mobilized to contain and control any street protests.

This was still rough-and-tumble Latin America, after all, and both sides of this battle were playing for keeps.

Members of the two consortia competing to buy the chunk

of shares stood by in rented offices near the exchange, waiting for the signal to begin bidding. Bidding was scheduled to kick off the moment the last injunction blocking the sale was cleared by the courts.

"We knew that the window of opportunity might last only a few minutes before a new injunction was filed," explained one BNDES lawyer, one of a few dozen BNDES lawyers placed on red alert, prepared to take off in a fleet of private planes to any courtroom in the land where an injunction might be filed, prepared to quash the killjoys at a moment's notice.

The last remaining injunction blocking the sale was cleared on a Tuesday morning. This just happened to follow a long holiday weekend. Within minutes, the judge conducting the auction had picked up his gavel and advised the two main bidders that they had three minutes in which to top a previous bid. In tommy-gun spurts, thirty-seven rounds of bidding were completed in under ten minutes.

As the judge's gavel was poised to fall for the last time, knocking down the CVRD shares for good, a crowd of shouting protesters broke through the line of linebacker brokers to present the judge with a fresh injunction.

It took BNDES six hours to quash that one. And then, the bidding geared up again.

And the winner was . . . a forty-four-year-old head of Brazil's largest steel maker (CSN), as well as the scion of the family that owned the Vicunha Group, Brazil's largest textile manufacturer. A partner in the deal, a company appropriately called Sweet River, had been hammered together by NationsBank, the fast-growing U.S. bank with an abiding eagerness to get into Brazilian mining.

Sweet River Shares

For starters, CVRD is the world's largest iron ore producer. But it's also a major exporter of forest products, gold, manganese, and a transportation giant to boot. Its more than fifty subsidiaries are scattered across ten Brazilian states and six foreign countries, including Argentina, France, Belgium, the U.S., China, and Japan. Last year its gross revenues were $5 billion.

So we knew that we wanted to participate. But at what price?

Iron ore and steel were both down, for example. But manganese was on its way up. One CVRD subsidiary the year before had picked up a railroad—a major railway network formerly owned by a state government at—you guessed it—a privatization auction.

So what was that subsidiary worth?

Who knew?

We weren't even sure anyone at the company knew, at least not for sure. That was the main reason, we figured, that it was being broken up.

On our last day in Rio, we stopped by CVRD's offices to find out about picking up a few bits and pieces of the next group of shares to be sold. Despite the heat surrounding the recent auction, it was still a devilishly hard company to read, and a tough nut to crack, because it's so deeply diversified.

We were informed at this meeting that the "international market for maritime transportation was not favorable for ship owners and operators."

Gold prices, for their part, were deeply depressed.

The company spokeswoman that we sat down with was openly ignorant—not because she wasn't very smart, but because the details had yet to be worked out—of the privatization plans for these various component parts.

Who would end up owning what, and when?

Would pulp and paper be spun off?

"They will be restructured as a function of market conditions," we were informed.

The company was so huge, so complex, so intricately interconnected that we left their elegant offices scratching our heads, with more questions going out than we had had going in. The one conclusion that it was probably safe to draw, because it's more often true than not, was that the company would doubtless be worth more broken up into parts than it was all stuck together.

But this was so far from a no-brainer, it was a brain drainer.

Our heads spun from the spin-offs.

We'd heard that the market—for what that was worth—expected all the noncore businesses to be spun off eventually, and that the company was sitting on $2 billion in cash.

But—never one to buy on gut instinct, we hustled over to BNDES to get an overview of what was going on not only with CVRD, but with the country's privatization program as a whole. We ended up learning next to nothing more about the future of CVRD—mum was the word—but we got quite a bead on the privatization process, which had the potential to pull the entire Brazilian economy out of its current quagmire.

Oh Cicero!

We hunkered down in a small, modest office with Irima da Silveira, a courtly gentleman of the old school, soft-spoken and worldly-wise, with the rarefied air of a Portuguese diplomat.

This guy was a class act, but his organization retained a few public sector quirks. The secretary sitting directly outside his office was playing digital mah-jongg on her desktop PC.

BNDES, the banker said, had hauled $4 billion into the government coffers in that year alone, primarily from privatizing one state-owned petrochemical company: Petroquisa.

They were also moving full speed ahead on the privatization of Light, the power company in Rio, which, incidentally, had originally been owned by a Canadian company before it was nationalized, back in the dark ages, when governments were believed to have all the answers.

Privatization was going to bring the Brazilian government over $60 billion over the upcoming five years. Money which, the government now figured, would be much better spent doing what governments do best: paving the roads, providing health care and education, underwriting high-tech R&D.

Let business do its business, was the new prevailing philosophy, and let the government be the government. That was the general principle outlined by Adam Smith in *The Wealth of Nations*, first published a little over two centuries ago.

Sounds simple, right?

Well, if it was so simple, why had it taken such a heck of a long time to get back to square one? Quite a few very smart and well-meaning people had had to change their minds about the benefits of letting Adam Smith's invisible hand guide them before free-market thinking could once become the conventional wisdom.

I couldn't help noting, with approval, a poem that Irima da Silveira had nicely framed on the wall above his spare, monkish desk:

The national budget should be in balance.
The public debt should be reduced.
And the arrogance of the authorities should be moderated and controlled.
Any debt to foreign governments should be reduced in order to avoid bankruptcy of the government.
The people should learn to work instead of living off the public dole.

We smiled together as, together, we haltingly translated the poem from Portuguese into English, for the benefit of the assembled group.

I was tickled by the fact that times had changed so little since those worthwhile sentiments had first been penned, in ancient Rome, by the famous orator and statesman Marcus Tullius Cicero, circa 55 B.C.

MOBIUS RULES: THE BRAZIL BOX

74: When the ordinary run of buyers gets spooked, that's the time to step up to the plate and start putting your money down on the table.

75: Only when everyone else is up on the windowsills preparing to jump do things for me start to get interesting.

76: If the whole world is down on a country for exaggerated, short-term reasons, shift it from a hold to a buy.

77: The surest sign of the instability of a currency is the existence of a thriving black market. Only when the street rate and the official rate are one and the same can a country's currency be considered even remotely healthy.

78: Even if the *denials* to a rumor are true, they're often only temporary. If you buy or sell on the basis of *confirmed and investigated* rumor, sooner or later the price will often reflect the reality.

79: The mere prospect of competition down the road will force a slumbering company to wake up and smell the coffee.

80: It nearly always pays to go with the locals.

◆

PART FOUR

The Final Frontier
(Africa)

AFRICA

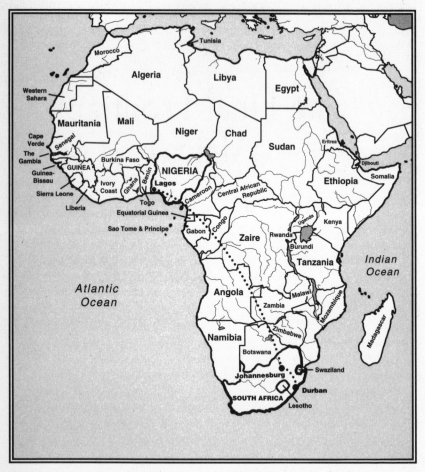

Tunisia
Morocco
Algeria
Libya
Egypt
Western Sahara
Mauritania
Mali
Niger
Chad
Sudan
Eritrea
Cape Verde
Senegal
Djibouti
The Gambia
Burkina Faso
GUINEA
NIGERIA
Ethiopia
Somalia
Guinea-Bissau
Ivory Coast
Ghana
Benin
Lagos
Central African Republic
Sierra Leone
Togo
Cameroon
Liberia
Equatorial Guinea
Gabon
Congo
Uganda
Kenya
Sao Tome & Principe
Zaire
Rwanda
Burundi
Tanzania
Angola
Malawi
Atlantic Ocean
Zambia
Mozambique
Indian Ocean
Madagascar
Zimbabwe
Namibia
Botswana
Johannesburg
Swaziland
Durban
SOUTH AFRICA
Lesotho

*Boldface capital words are countries Mobius visited   **Boldface lowercase words are cities Mobius visited

Chapter Eight

◆

NIGERIA

After landing at Lagos airport after midnight, we couldn't see much from the plane. As we taxied to a full stop, the ground crew directed us to a finger-shaped landing pier, where a neatly dressed woman was waiting to greet us, her hair and skirt blown around by the downdraft from our slowing turbines. As we disembarked, she introduced herself as our "protocol person," whose services had been arranged by our local broker to facilitate our entry into Nigeria. Without any further pleasantries, she briskly ushered us toward the passenger terminal, where I hoped we wouldn't be detained for long. This was one border I was eager to cross quickly.

As she escorted us firmly toward the gate, she filled us in on her depressing raison d'être: given the state of affairs at Lagos's Mohammed Murtala International Airport—one of a handful in the world formerly classified as "insecure" by the U.S. Department of State—foreigners are strongly advised not to even attempt entry without engaging the services of a reliable, reputable protocol person first. Without someone like her in our court, she explained, we stood a pretty good chance of becoming victims of "criminal activity."

Among the many illicit pursuits commonly practiced in and around this den of iniquity, extortion by corrupt immigration and customs officials ranked high on the list, followed by loss of travel documents to con artists, and last but not least, hijacking and robbery by crooked cab drivers.

As we waited inside the terminal for a customs official to interrogate us, I found myself staring vacantly at a half dozen empty fluorescent tube sockets that once illuminated this seedy stretch of linoleum-lined corridor. Now they were as bare as the government coffers that had been so skillfully stripped clean by the country's rapacious rulers. No wonder the National Electric Power Authority, or NEPA, is popularly known as "Never Expect Power Again." Those long-missing fluorescent tubes, lifted eons ago by some anonymous sticky fingers, struck me as symbols of everything that had gone wrong in this country, the most populous in Africa, in the nearly forty years since the British reluctantly relinquished it in 1960. At independence, Nigeria had been widely considered "The Hope of Africa." Now, it stood out as a "worst case scenario."

Jewel in the Crown

Forty years ago, Nigeria was assumed to have everything going for it. The country was richly endowed with natural resources—including major-league oil and other mineral reserves. The British left behind a fine infrastructure, a well-developed agricultural base, and a disciplined civil service heavily dominated by members of the educated Ibo tribe—Southern Christians who had long played second fiddle to the tall, haughty Muslim Hausa of the North. The Ibo were not only great civil servants but hardworking merchants, traders, and shopkeepers, who kept the economy humming along and the trains running on time. The politically dominant Hausa, horse-loving ranchers and cattle-keepers and soldiers, had been heavily favored by the British, who left them in control of the Nigerian Army, and the upper echelons of government.

With independence, the traditional tribal tensions between these two vying factions soon erupted into a bloody civil war. The Ibo—fearful of being violently oppressed by the Hausa now that the British weren't around to keep them in check—sought to secede from the Nigerian union and form their own country in their traditional stronghold, the then-renegade province of Biafra. The gruesome Biafran war of the late 1960s split the young country apart, and though the central government won in the end, the tangible and intangible costs were staggering. Some say that those costs are still being repaid in the form of a crippled economy and political system.

As is true elsewhere in Africa, Nigeria's economic problems are mainly political, social, and ethnic in origin. Colonial rulers who ruthlessly exploited their colonies as sources of cheap labor and cheap raw materials for their home industries were replaced by an indigenous elite who used a veil of populist rhetoric to disguise the wholesale diversion of their nations' remaining resources into their own and their cronies' Swiss bank accounts.

But while the colonial rulers kept ethnic and tribal tensions in check—usually by pursuing a policy of divide and conquer—local leaders had a harder time avoiding the traditional traps of favoritism, nepotism, and civil and social unrest. The result, in Nigeria and in most other post-independent African countries, was a swindle of unprecedented proportions. Take just one revealing, depressing, and unofficial statistic: of the roughly $270 billion the country is believed to have generated in oil revenues since 1970, only about $150 billion has been accounted for, by published accounts. Where did the other $120 billion go? Lord only knows, but many informed sources believe that the country's prior crop of leaders controlled some $50 billion in secret bank accounts. Which leaves a remaining $70 billion still unaccounted for, which we assume found its way into the pockets and savings deposits of earlier despots.

Independent Nigeria has had nine presidents in those forty years, which in practice means nine governments, because each time a new president is "elected" (or selected) he enjoys absolute power, featuring the absolute right to select "suitable people" to serve in his administration. Of the nine Nigerian presidents to date, just three have been civilians, and all were deposed by military dictators who claimed to be replacing corrupt, inefficient regimes. Of course, those regimes were corrupt and inefficient. But the military rulers who replaced them, promising to clean house, combined corruption and inefficiency with heavy-handed repression and crude economic control. The one bright spot in an otherwise dismal scenario was the sudden and unexpected death, in June 1998, of General Sani Albacha and his replacement by the ostensibly more reform-minded (and honest) General Abdul Salami Abubakar.

Hey Guys! Business or Pleasure?

In contrast to the stern portraits of generals posted in their offices, the immigration and customs officials we met at the airport couldn't have been friendlier. But I wouldn't have concluded from that that they were honest—only that they'd been well taken care of by our protocol person. As we stood outside the shabby terminal waiting for a cab driver who wouldn't be packing a rod, I couldn't help but overhear a visiting British businessman's heated discussion with a group of locals, who'd apparently passed themselves off as his protocol people and had absconded with his passport. He'd made the mistake of not checking their bona fides, and was paying a price for his misplaced trust: he now found himself in the awkward position of demanding, at the top of his lungs, to have his passport returned to him—at once. Or else . . .

Con Artistry

That "or else" rang as an empty threat in my ears. Or else what? Maybe he felt like screaming some more, or possibly waving his hands around a little more frantically. From my protected vantage point, it was easy to see that the locals were holding all the cards in this game. To her eternal credit, our protocol person bravely waded into the fray, assuring the businessman that he'd get his passport back, and with a few whispered words dispatched one of the suddenly cowed con artists to return this man's passport to him, at once—or else.

This time, the "or else" seemed to have teeth to it, because the guy took off like a shot. I admired her grit, and was impressed by her clout—it occurred to me that in her line of work, permitting freelancers, particularly crooked ones, to cut into her territory could not have been good for repeat business. As we pulled away from the curb I had a sneaking feeling that the victim of this little scam wouldn't be seeing his passport anytime soon without some serious change changing hands. Badly as I felt for him, we'd done what we could—in the jungle, it's every man for himself.

We Flew by Night

Compared to some of the run-down dumps I've stayed in, the Lagos Sheraton wasn't bad: pretty clean, pretty well furnished, and pretty well maintained. My room even had working air-conditioning. To add to our good fortune, the driver we'd hired to chauffeur us around town turned out to be a godsend. After he showed up, promptly the next morning, I quickly appointed Olatunde—who like many of his countrymen used the diminutive of his name—the antidote to all the corrupt businessmen and government officials and movers and shakers on top of the heap who were so busy looking out for number one that they ended up making everyone else's lives miserable.

Tunde, as he called himself, had earned an engineering degree from one of the local colleges. But he considered himself lucky to be driving a cab. His thwarted career spoke volumes about the desolate state of the Nigerian economy, which despite its vast potential continued to fail to fulfill the ambitions of 120 million people, an overwhelmingly high percentage of whom were under twenty. Most of these young people were unemployed and, in many cases, unemployable.

So what, you may ask, on earth was I doing in the pariah of Africa, on the lookout for long-term investments?

Was I insane?

Possibly.

Was I in the wrong?

I don't think so.

Moral and or Ethical Investing

Would you believe that despite the turmoil and turbulence, the Nigerian Stock Exchange—heavily influenced by the boom and bust cycle of the oil industry—had at the time of our visit in early 1998 over 180 listed companies and a market capitalization of $3.2 billion? Would you believe that despite the political turmoil and unrest, its market cap has close to doubled in the past two years? Despite the dismal state of the domestic economy, the Nigerian capital markets had been growing by leaps and bounds.

And what do I make of that? I think that if the place was not being skimmed clean by the local fat cats, it could soon be vying with South Africa as an engine of growth for the entire continent. Judged strictly by potential, after South Africa, Nigeria still could be the hope of Africa.

Even more to the point, I think that some day sooner rather than later, Nigeria may start hitting its stride. And when that day comes, we want to be there. What is more, we want to have already been there for a while. While many African countries have yet to emerge from their dark, red socialist periods—due to political oppression or economic bungling—it pays to keep tabs on these basket cases, because they may one day emerge, when everyone's looking the other way, as regional powerhouses. In fact, under General Abubakar, the long, slow process of economic and political reform was shortly to be initiated.

This could be interesting.

Idi Amin No More

Let's take Uganda. After independence, the crackpots and thieves who ran the country with a heavy hand—Idi Amin being only the most notorious—used Marxist rhetoric as a veil to justify strict control over the economy. In practical terms, they kept all the money in the country to themselves. One of the richest coffee regions in the world was forced to submit to a Coffee Board charged with "supporting" coffee prices. The Coffee Board paid farmers 20 percent of the going world price, and the government pocketed the rest. Once-wealthy coffee planters went bankrupt in no time.

In 1991, after decades of such racketeering, the newly elected Ugandan president, Yoweri Museveni, deregulated coffee prices and unceremoniously canned the Coffee Board. Lo and behold, all of a sudden the few coffee farmers who'd managed to survive the interlude were keeping 80 percent of the going price, and the middlemen a more reasonable 20 percent. In the years since commodity price deregulation, coffee production in Uganda has more than doubled. Economic growth has averaged 7 percent. By the end of 1998, 85 percent of state-owned companies were slated to be privatized. And the country, particularly in comparison to early decades of disaster, was on a roll.

Of African countries considered to be "groping toward democracy and free markets," a leading U.S. business magazine recently included: Botswana, Mauritius, Cameroon, Gabon, Ivory Coast, Ghana, Malawi, Mozambique, Tanzania, Zambia, and Zimbabwe. And by mid-1998, we could cautiously include Nigeria.

None of these places are economic powerhouses just yet. But with the exception of Zimbabwe, all are on the upswing, which is a pretty far cry from where they were languishing just a few years back. The problem, unfortunately, with most of these countries is that, even if their policies are in the right place, their capital markets tend to be small, and the listed companies tend to be small, and not very liquid. Excluding South Africa, there were seventeen stock exchanges in Africa in 1998, with a total market cap of about $55 billion. Of even greater concern to long-term, high-volume buyers like us is that a severe shortage of liquid, tradable stocks has led to a perilously low market turnover: less than $9 billion in stocks changed hands in those exchanges throughout 1997. That's the equivalent of about five minutes of trading on the New York Stock Exchange.

But Uganda's stock exchange, primed by rising commodity prices, was due shortly to take off—and was widely regarded as likely to soar. Tanzania, Cameroon, and Madagascar were all in the process of setting up their own stock exchanges. Even more important, African governments were coming around to the once-shunned idea of privatization: one 1997 estimate of all state assets sold throughout the region was $3.7 billion, while the 1998 figure was put at close to $5 billion.

Still, with a market cap of $3.2 billion, despite its troubles, Nigeria's capital market continues to dwarf the little guys. Although for foreign investors, we consider it at best a pure-risk play on a five-to-ten-year time horizon.

But a day will come, I can assure you, when it's the right time to invest in Nigeria. And when that day dawns, I can also assure you of the validity of:

Mobius Rule No. 81: By the time everyone and his brother believes that it's the right time to invest, the right time will have long since come and gone.

Moral and Ethical Quandaries

So what do I say to high-minded people who argue that plunking even a plug nickel into a pariah regime like Nigeria is . . .

1) Throwing good money after bad, and
2) Lending support to an immoral government?

I say, quite frankly, that that's hogwash.

Don't get me wrong. I would never (and could never) invest in a country without a viable capital market, or buy stock in a country where the local government is openly hostile to the formation of capital markets, or to foreign investors. I believe strongly in fair, equal, and liquid markets.

But investing in honest companies in a corrupt country is supporting honesty, not corruption. I would be the first to admit that investing in markets like Nigeria in 1998—or Russia in 1994—which lack a firm foundation in the rule of law can make for some sleepless nights. But it's also important to realize that since there's such a close correlation between risk and reward, sometimes you need to tolerate a certain degree of uncertainty in order to benefit from the premium placed on high-risk returns.

As of early 1998, we judged the situation in Nigeria to be too chaotic to make even long-term investment practical, for the most part. But that didn't stop us from checking the place out, and if we saw something we liked, to at least keep an open mind. And as of late 1998, although we judged the situation to be on the upswing, we still felt that the economy was too unstable and immature.

Continental Drift

The entire continent of Africa tends to get a bad rap in the West. But that in and of itself is finally changing. Markets throughout the region are becoming less volatile as governments become more sophisticated.

As of mid-1998, we had a weighting of about 2 percent in Africa—including South Africa. And we firmly believed that Africa could be just the place for the serious bargain hunter willing to play with a long-term time horizon. Since negative sentiment tends to exaggerate as much as positive sentiment, it's advisable to keep tabs on markets that everyone else thinks it's crazy to bet on. Chances are that sooner or later, even the losingest places on earth will find some way to redeem themselves.

There are places for which the only way to go is up.

Unfortunately, Nigeria circa 1998 was not yet one of them.

Highway from Hell

As we jostled and jounced across one of three bridges linking the business district on Lagos Island to Ikeja on the mainland, site of the Sheraton, to the rest of this chaotic, sprawling city, we crawled along what once must have been a spectacular highway when it was built in the 1960s—no doubt with pots of Western aid money. As we whizzed and whammed along a section of road overlooking the Gulf of Guinea, I could see the ocean through the gaping holes in the expansion joints separating the concrete slabs of the highway. The rubberized asphalt fillers that had once joined the slabs had long since turned brittle and fallen into the sea. It wouldn't be long before the rest of the road joined them in the drink. But before the highway collapsed, Lagos's fearless drivers were determined to get every last bit of mileage out of it. We could see them—you could hardly miss them—blithely gunning their sagging, dented, worn-out jalopies like hot-rod drivers in a demolition derby. Nearly every car that we passed (or that passed us in a cloud of soot you could cut with a knife) was so badly battered that it wouldn't have been considered worth stealing by most car thieves elsewhere in the world. Dents due, Tunde cheerfully explained, to the philosophy of the local drivers, which was to ram your car into any available space on the road, even if a rival car was heading there too, at top speed.

We couldn't help but notice the large number of motor scooters threading in and out between the cars, like insects around a hive. These were taxis, and the transport of choice for anyone hoping to get anywhere through Lagos's legendary gridlock in a hurry, which rivals Bangkok's in its resemblance to a painter's still life.

The perpetual gridlock is a mixed blessing for the thousands of hawkers and beggars who dive in and out between the cars, playing chicken with drivers who think nothing of leaning out their windows and negotiating for a few sealed plastic bags of water or bread or a toothbrush while stalled in traffic, or even while in gradual forward motion. Some of the better-off hawkers occupy curbside stands from which they sell smoked snake and beef, and on at least one occasion—which we actually witnessed—smoked rat.

Lagos is still mostly a city of ramshackle one-story concrete shacks topped by rusty corrugated iron sheet roofs. The few "skyscrapers" in town mostly date back twenty years to the peak of the mid-1970s oil boom, when Lagos briefly became a global real estate investors' dream. Lately, it has degenerated into a nightmare, where one wonders how anything gets done. It's a testament to the resilience of the entrepreneurial spirit hereabouts that so much commerce is even transacted at all.

Multinational Inc.

We'd been scheduled to meet with the managing director of a major multinational corporation—you have brands of theirs in your house at this very moment—at their downtown headquarters. But just a few minutes before we were due to arrive there, we received an urgent call on our portable phone redirecting us to the managing director's home in an affluent Lagos suburb.

The luxurious houses were all surrounded by high walls and concertina-wire-topped gates manned by stern-looking security guards in dark glasses and combat fatigues. When we arrived at the man's door, the distraught owner let us in, but not without sneaking a furtive look up and down the street, to make sure that the coast was clear. Jeremy Taylor (note: not his real name) explained in great agitation that he'd been forced to relocate our meeting because his company's offices had been closed down on the Friday last by a so-called tax task force.

The Tax Man Cometh

We were hardly surprised, under the strained circumstances, that he launched into a tortured discussion of Nigeria's problems, which quickly overwhelmed any detailed accounting of his company's welfare. Although, to hear him tell it, the two were pretty much one and the same.

"Local government in Nigeria," he bitterly complained, "has no legal power to raise taxes. So what they do is bust down your door and start making outrageous demands."

In today's Nigeria, they've refined the fine art of tax collection into a form of torture worthy of a Chinese warlord. Since the national leadership does precious little leading, it makes up for its shortcomings by refusing to raise taxes, since that would push an already outraged electorate over the edge. Since so many people don't pay any taxes, the central government had coped with this problem by simply refusing to distribute money from the national treasury to the local governments. Since these were still under some obligation to provide whatever minimal services were being offered, the local governments very quickly ran out of cash.

At the time of our visit, the central bank had not disbursed any funds to the local governments for six months. The state government of Lagos province, in desperation, had begun targeting local subsidiaries of large multinationals for random tax "audits," which were more like armed assaults. They'd formed what they grandly termed a "tax task force," and bestowed upon the civilian in charge the promise of a sizable commission on any tax he collected, using whatever means necessary.

This tax task force, to show that it really meant business—or you could say, the end of business as we know it—had been provided with a heavily armed police contingent authorized to enforce its sweeping powers by whatever means necessary. Remarkably, even if the official tax authorities had declared the company current in its payments, this freelance official was empowered to use his "best judgment" in assessing the company right then and there for whatever payment he deemed appropriate. If the company refused to comply, the police shut down the operation.

On the previous Wednesday, the tax task force had turned up, unannounced, on the company's doorstep, and would have burst down the door in a show of strength if the receptionist hadn't politely opened it for them. After a cursory inspection of the company's books, the civilian in charge had levied an outrageous bill, and informed the managing director that it had to be paid by that Friday—or else.

When the bill hadn't been settled by Friday—because the company had in the meantime lodged a formal protest with the military governor of Lagos province and appealed to the Nigerian ambassador in its home country—the police detachment padlocked the offices, left an armed guard behind to secure the premises, and vanished into thin air. Now it was Monday morning, and some of the company's staff had been locked inside their offices all weekend. The tax task force, meanwhile, was nowhere to be found. Talk about turning the screws!

"In Russia," I said sympathetically, "they call this sort of thing 'fleecing the foreigners.' "

I think that he made a mental note to turn down any future assignments in Moscow.

I commented that I couldn't see any difference between the behavior of the government and that of the crooked cabbies who stuck you up at the airport. Taylor remarked that the crooked cabbies were probably all working for the government anyway, or would be soon.

A major multinational corporation like his, Taylor pointed out, was at a distinct disadvantage in dealing with rogue tax collectors, because they were bound by their own ethical guidelines not to bribe public officials. What made the situation even more outrageous is that the tax task force, well aware of this fact, took unfair advantage of their stated commitment to abide by international standards of conduct. This obviously made them easy prey for the tax task force. Other, locally based rivals, not bound by the same standards of conduct, made a practice of bribing the head of the tax task force to leave them alone. Which simply put additional pressure on the tax task force to collect what it could from the only sources likely to pay up: law-abiding foreigners.

The ashen-faced Taylor was a middle-aged white South African who'd obviously developed, and for good reason, a deeply pessimistic attitude about the prospects of his adopted country to change for the better anytime soon. He'd had it and, like the hero of the movie *Network,* was mad as hell and not going to take it anymore.

But what, precisely, was he going to do? The first thing he was going to do was vent to us, which I think at least had the benefit of being therapeutic. This sad situation might have been simply absurd, if it hadn't been so tragic.

He did mention a recent run-in with the local tax goons which did qualify as simply absurd. A few months before, another tax official—the country was apparently crawling with them—had paid an unannounced visit to their offices. Within minutes the man pronounced *a ten-year-old broadcast antenna* he stumbled across "higher than the legal limit." On the spot, he levied a tax on the number of feet this antenna exceeded its "legal limit." But when asked what the legal limit was, he wasn't free to say. It was pretty clear that he'd made the whole thing up. After negotiating to pay a somewhat lesser amount, the company ended up forking over the antenna tax. They didn't want to face being closed down over such petty harassment. But now Taylor deeply regretted this course of action, because it made the company look like a soft touch—and probably made them an even more attractive target to the armed thugs on the tax task force.

"Do you think that the government is discriminating against

foreigners as a way of driving them out of the local market?" I wondered out loud.

The possibility had certainly occurred to him, many times, and he wasn't prepared to entirely discount it. But after bitter personal experience he'd pretty well decided that it was probably not so much an organized conspiracy against foreign interests as an expedient like that practiced by the bank robber Willie Sutton, who when asked why he robbed banks, proudly replied: "Because that's where the money is."

But this latest episode was forcing their proud giant company, which had maintained a prominent presence in Nigeria since well before independence, to seriously consider whether it was worth sticking it out for the long haul. Back at headquarters in Europe, some people were beginning to wonder out loud if the Nigerian operation was waiting for a recovery that might never take place in their lifetimes.

"Back in the 1970s, at the height of the oil boom," Taylor sighed wearily, "this company had *huge* plans for Nigeria. The country was going to be the showplace of Africa, and our headquarters here was slated to be our regional hub. But now, we're finding it harder and harder to justify doing business here, except to protect the investments we've already made."

As recently as three or four years ago, they had drawn up plans to build three new factories and a new headquarters office building in downtown Lagos. But now, all such expansion plans had been put on hold, until the political situation either sorted itself out, or didn't. In the meantime, the choice plot of land they'd earmarked for the new headquarters had been sold off, at a loss. The only consolation for Taylor was that the new headquarters was "probably just an ego trip anyway."

Bad as I felt for the company, I felt even worse for the country. Take this one company's plight and multiply it by all the other companies suffering under the same strains, and you had a nation being denied desperately needed foreign investment because of the sheer shortsighted selfishness of the people in power.

Warming to his theme of widening anarchy, Taylor told us that the only denominations in which the Nigerian currency, the naira, came in were 5, 10, and 50. This not only irritated local people who had to run around the crime-ridden streets conspicuously carrying wads of money, it also exposed the fact that the currency was so debased that it cost 8 naira to make a 5 naira note.

"How could that be?" I wondered, barely trying to conceal my astonishment.

"The high cost of the imported paper and ink," Taylor explained, almost gleefully. "And the reason for *that* is that the company who bribed the government to grant them a monopoly on importing the paper on which the money is printed want *more* paper to be imported, so that they can make even more money making more money!"

Okay, I thought to myself: it actually cost the government more in raw materials to print the paper currency than the currency was worth on international markets, or for that matter, in local purchasing power. I was starting to think that we were all trapped inside a Gilbert & Sullivan operetta.

The most irritating thing about Nigeria, Taylor continued, suddenly turning morose, "is that it still has so much unexploited resources. There's more than enough sugar, palm oil, and rubber to go around. There's more than enough to make everyone comfortable, if not rich."

What had killed the country, he contended, was oil. It had driven the rapacious rulers crazy with greed, and given everyone else an excuse to kick back and settle into complacency.

"Did you know," Taylor asked, "that back in the 1970s, Nigeria *exported* palm oil?"

As a matter of fact, I did.

"But now they have to import it, because once they started pumping fuel oil, no one thought it worthwhile to trouble with little old palm oil.

"And the *worst* thing," Taylor bitterly concluded his list of bad things about Nigeria, "is that the people here seem to have given up hope of *ever changing things for the better*. They've been so beaten down by the system, they're just so damned tired out by just trying to make ends meet, that they just don't have any energy left to mount a popular protest."

The last man to try, he pointed out, had been an internationally known writer and human rights activist who'd sought to call the world's attention to the fact that none of the oil extracted from his native province went to the local people at all. For his trouble, Nigeria's ruling military, ignoring widespread international protests, had hanged him. But would such strong-arm tactics work in the long term? Personally, I thought not.

The International Packaged Goods Company

We met with Mr. Benoj (not his real name), who appeared to hail from the Middle East, in his modern, well-appointed office overlooking the harbor. I remarked on the pleasant view. He replied with a sad sigh that neither his office nor the view were anywhere near as good as he'd enjoyed at his previous post: Abu Dhabi.

"This is my second term of duty here," he said, using the old soldier's phrase, "and I can't wait to move on."

Things had deteriorated dramatically since he had last been in residence, in 1983, he said. "Last month, my house was burgled by *fifteen armed robbers*. Now I keep six security guards on duty at my house every night, and I have to pay an off-duty policeman to keep an eye on them."

Who, I wondered, would he need to pay to keep an eye on the moonlighting policeman?

The corporation of which this local company was a subsidiary was one of the largest soap manufacturers in the world. They didn't need to stay in Nigeria to make their balance sheets look good. They were in Nigeria for the same reason that we were visiting the place: out of respect for its enormous potential.

"This is the largest country in Africa," Benoj explained with a resigned shrug. "We can't afford *not* to be here."

But they too were pulling in their limbs, and hunkering down in their shell. In response to current conditions, they'd sold off stakes in a local brewery, a plastics company, and a tractor manufacturing company, in order to concentrate on their core business: soap.

Soap Opera

"When the economy turns around," Benoj gamely contended, although without much conviction, "we will be strong again in a surging market!"

I wondered whether this was genuine optimism, or mere self-delusion.

"Despite all of the problems," he hastily reassured us, "we actually do pretty well here."

Since they'd been reluctant to break out the numbers, we had to take this one on faith. Their largest lines were laundry detergents. He named a rival local company that, despite the poor quality of its products, enjoyed a share of the soap market easily twice theirs. They had a 50 percent share. He had just 25 percent.

"Ours is the better detergent," he pointed out, helplessly. "But due to low consumer spending power, people buy detergent from vendors by the cupful. That's the only way they can afford to buy it. It really is such poor detergent, but that's all they can afford."

As a high-quality, high-cost manufacturer, his organization had seriously misread the market. But—if? when?—the economy picked up, he hoped to gain a larger market share.

"With our superior technology and support from our international operations," he defiantly insisted, "we could afford to corner the detergent market in all of Nigeria!"

He sounded like a would-be Soap Napoleon. He claimed to have a master plan all mapped out, and tentatively approved by his central headquarters, to do just that: lower their prices below costs, to blow the local companies out of the water.

And what was stopping them from implementing this plan now?

"We're in no hurry," he replied defensively, "with the economy in such terrible shape."

But if they waited for the economy to improve, his stealth plan to capture the market wouldn't be necessary. I had a feeling that this guy was just spinning his wheels, fantasizing out of mounting frustration with the situation. Spending time in Nigeria did weird things to people. He would be much better off, I decided, trying to become the Soap King of Abu Dhabi.

Do Your Duty

One of the worst problems that his company faced in competing under these terrible conditions, he bitterly pointed out, was the presence of well-organized, well-connected, well-protected criminal gangs. They boldly, brazenly smuggled his very own Famous Brand Name products into the country, without paying import duties on them! This illicit activity, he whispered conspiratorially, took place with the connivance of higher-ups in the government.

While he waxed increasingly indignant over what could be considered routine corruption, I wondered if it had occurred to him that there was such a thing as crying over spilled soap.

"I've seen with my own eyes our own brands on the shelves of supermarkets that were not put there by us, but by our competitors, who make counterfeit soap!" he positively shouted. I recognized that manic, homicidal gleam in his eye from Taylor—they all had the look, as if they'd like to go out and kill someone.

Unfortunately, President General Sani Abacha, the most obvious target of such an attack, was not only extremely well defended but, according to his own press reports, was a peerless promoter of private enterprise. A local company run by a claque of his cronies had recently introduced a TV set into the local market under the brand name Abacha, in honor of the much-maligned, soon-to-be deceased President for Life. With a name like that, they could be pretty well assured to have a winner, even if the sets didn't pull in a single channel. Of course, after General Abacha's death, the toadying manufacturers would no doubt be hard pressed to rebrand their politically correct TVs Abubakars.

One of our analysts concisely summed up the soap company's prospects as follows: "Management will be unable to grow the business without involving themselves in the same unscrupulous and illegal activities that some of their competitors are involved in."

Since that—this company's alignment with local criminal interests—was extremely unlikely to take place anytime soon, we had to rate this one a sell.

Fortunately, we didn't own any shares, so we wouldn't have to sell it.

The Multinational Packaged Goods Company

After our first two downbeat meetings, we were beginning to think that everyone doing business in the country was at the maximum level of despondency. And in this case, we couldn't even be consoled by Sir John Templeton's rule that the best time to buy is when people reach their maximum despondency quotient.

But the broad picture we received from the handsome, articulate corporate representative in an appropriately handsome boardroom was much less pessimistic than the dark landscapes we'd been viewing all morning. The reason for this difference in perspective was obvious once we met him. The guy was Nigerian, and was—for better or for worse—more plugged into the local power structure than the deeply depressed expatriates we'd been seeing all morning.

Not that Mr. Masafungi (not his real name) didn't concede that, as he delicately put it, "government policy is inconsistent. We have a poor infrastructure and inefficient public utilities." But where he differed radically from his foreign-born competitors was that he saw a few streaks of light at the end of that very dark tunnel.

"I think that change for the better is under way," he ventured cautiously, although in practically the same breath, he admitted that the process of change was "slow." He and some other "senior businessmen," he said, had been "actively involved in dialogue and lobbying of the government to effect change." As a realist, he soberly noted that "it is the tendency of soldiers and military men to bark orders, and expect others to follow and to listen." He was, in short, awaiting the window of opportunity shortly to open with the death of General Abacha.

But the mere fact that he and his fellow "senior businessmen" were 1) native Nigerians and 2) successful native Nigerians (thus honorary members of the ruling elite) meant that the people in power had a harder time simply ignoring what they were saying. Much as they hated to be seen as "taking direction" from the civilian sector, they at least paid lip service to their complaints.

First on their list of demands, which were presented with the requisite finesse, was that "privatization must keep going forward if we are to make any progress as a nation," he said.

I certainly liked the sound of that.

"Red tape will have to be cut."

Okay by me.

"Corruption curtailed."

This certainly sounded like a moral lecture, which could be safely assumed to have fallen on deaf ears. But there were, he insisted, some signs afoot that they had been listened to.

"We are finding less red tape in general, and the bureaucracy is gradually reducing the cost of doing business," he contended.

When, in our skepticism, we pressed for details, he impressed us by providing at least one: "Imports are coming through the docks quicker, so less stock has to be held in our warehouses. That is reducing the cost of doing business."

He deftly shifted the subject to the more savory one of the strategies they had evolved "in order to stay in business in this highly competitive environment."

They'd learned, for example, to package their products in smaller packages and create new cheaper brands and products so the common people could afford to buy them. One example he gave of this strategy was a chocolate drink mix with a formula altered from their premium brand, containing less cocoa so it was cheaper.

This stood in stark contrast to the blatantly misguided strategy being pursued by the poor chap we'd just met, who'd wrung his hands and shrugged and cried about his rivals selling their soap in cheap plastic cups. They'd gone so far as to hatch a desperate plan—not yet finalized—to undercut their competitors on price, but they had apparently never even considered reformulating their world-famous brands to conform to the local market.

But this locally born and bred guy had a different idea: "Beat the bums at their own game."

As a native Nigerian, he was less likely to wring his hands, diss the damned country, and go on to his chums at the club over whiskey and soda about the country going to hell in a handbasket. Not that it wasn't, but this guy didn't have the luxury of counting the days until he could be posted someplace else. He had been forced to figure out how to survive and thrive where he was. This gave him a different form of pragmatism, and a determination to win, even under adversity. I wish we could have bought more of his stock, but we had all we could handle of Nigeria.

> **Mobius Rule No. 82: When looking at managements of companies in countries where the business climate is complex and difficult, locally trained managers tend to make a better fit with the local environment.**

You can usually tell if the senior managers of a company are local (or locally trained) by carefully reading the company's latest annual report.

Country Assessment

At this point in time, Nigeria wasn't for us—and probably not for you either.

It was like an unripe fruit—possibly even a rotten one. At this stage of the game, the situation was just too chaotic and uncertain even for us—connoisseurs of chaos.

I've included this dismaying trip to Nigeria in our around-the-world tour not because it's in any way symbolic of the direction Africa is headed in today, but for the opposite reason: it stands out like a sore thumb in Africa today. It is an outstanding symbol of the supreme danger posed by political risk, which brought with it market risk, currency risk, transaction risk, and just about every other form of risk imaginable.

Fortunately for us, and fortunately for Africa, Nigeria at present is more of a symbol of Africa's wrongheaded past than any taste of its probable future. There's nothing whatever wrong with Nigeria that political evolution—perhaps even a revolution—wouldn't fix. And fortunately for Nigeria, just a few months after our visit, the macro picture had begun to improve more than marginally.

Chapter Nine

◆

SOUTH AFRICA

So what's the biggest question looming over South Africa today?
Here goes:
Under its new majority leadership, will South Africa:
1) Successfully compete in the global marketplace by opening up and liberalizing its economy?
Or:
2) Will it bow to short-term political pressure and seek to solve its social problems by embracing one-party rule and a rigidly planned economy?
Most observers, after close and often anxious observation of the behavior and rhetoric of Nelson Mandela and his African National Congress (ANC) colleagues, are leaning toward a qualified optimism that the country will—probably in fits and starts—adopt the former (and we believe better) path.

Political Football

As is true just about everywhere else, the economic issues and challenges faced by South Africa are heavily colored by political realities, which in this country basically means racial and ethnic divisions. For the long-disenfranchised young urban blacks of the townships, radical rhetoric and radical policies appear to point the way to a better South Africa: an egalitarian, socialist utopia.

Fortunately for those who profoundly disagree with this approach, one of the only upper-level ANC figures publicly proclaiming such radical methods and solutions is Winnie Mandela, the president's controversial ex-wife, who enjoys great popular support among the angry Young Turks but gratifyingly grudging respect, if any, from most other sectors of society.

Despite a history of espousing Marxist doctrine and occasional bursts of virulently populist rhetoric, the responsible leadership of the new South Africa seems reluctantly reconciled to renouncing its old dream of building a socialist workers' paradise on the wreckage of the apartheid system.

The Strong Man of Africa

In neighboring Zimbabwe, which two years before had been stricken by a severe drought, an embattled President Robert Mugabe had resorted to scapegoating the white minority—which still controlled more than its fair share of the economic pie—as the source of most if not all the country's woes. Mugabe had sternly suppressed nearly all dissent to his one-party rule, and had frequently announced plans—fortunately not always implemented—to forcibly seize white-owned land for supposed distribution to the poor. In November 1998 "attachment orders" were served on farmers in Zimbabwe effectively seizing those farms. He'd shown the world every sign of seeking to construct a cult of personality reminiscent of the now-discredited strongmen of post-independence Africa. The results of these policies and pronouncements—which to Mugabe's slim credit have often amounted to more smoke than fire—had been a sharp decline in the local stock market, and a steep loss of confidence on the part of global investors in Zimbabwe's future as a secure place for their investments.

Reality Check

The reality facing most emerging markets today is that:

1) They desperately need outside investment to grow their economies.

2) If they want to gain outside investment, they have to actively create a safe haven for foreign investors, or lose their risk capital to countries who will.

As he consolidated power in South Africa, the question facing Thabo Mbeki—Nelson Mandela's hand-picked successor—was this:

How to balance a crying need to redress decades of discrimination and oppression with an equally crying need to retain skilled managers, entrepreneurs, and capital.

Even the moderate degree of uncertainty surrounding the probable policies of an Mbeki administration toward business (and toward white-owned business specifically) had had negative consequences for the South African market as a whole. In recent years, the largest, most dynamic market in Africa had been like a crab: moving slowly sideways.

In two years, between January 1996 and January 1998, the South African market cap had declined from $250 billion to under $240 billion. This drop could be mainly attributed to a steep loss in value of the South African rand against the U.S. dollar. But the currency collapse was itself a sign of caution on the part of forex traders—whose business it is to sniff the winds of the future—as to the future South Africa's economic direction. Even when ranked by market cap, the South African stock market has gone from tenth largest to nineteenth largest in the world in two years.

It was obviously to South Africa's advantage that Nigeria, with its wealth of resources, was such a godawful quagmire, because it otherwise might have been a fierce competitor. But South Africa could no longer count on chaos elsewhere on the continent to save its own skin. If it wanted to succeed over the long haul, South Africa was going to have to get its economic house in order, or face the consequences: a sharp fall-off in critical capital investment.

Risk Premium

But you must remember this:

Mobius Rule No. 83: Political uncertainty—like any other form of uncertainty—can be your green light to move into a market. Uncertainty depresses stock prices. If you have faith in your own crystal ball—or, better yet, your own independent analysis—an uncertain atmosphere can be just the break that you've been looking for to pick up large-cap, blue chip stocks that otherwise would be too expensive to even consider.

And you also must remember this:

Mobius Rule No. 84: Once uncertainty becomes certainty, and anyone with two nickels to rub together can with some degree of accuracy predict the likely outcome of events, that beautiful risk premium will have evaporated in a puff of smoke.

Risk Pool

With uncertainty prevailing on so many fronts, some savvy investors were taking advantage of the resulting market doldrums to take the plunge into Africa—a region still widely considered the "Final Frontier" of international investing. In early 1998, while direct investment in Africa represented just 5 percent of investment in all emerging markets, foreign investment in South Africa had more than tripled over the previous year's level. Still, to keep matters in perspective, the entire continent of Africa (excluding South Africa) still had a GDP (gross domestic product) smaller than that of Belgium.

From our point of view, the outstanding opportunities available in South Africa were the hundreds of world-class companies run by top-flight managements with global experience. We've also discovered, to our delight, that with South African companies now being welcomed with open arms elsewhere on the continent, we (and now you) are able to gain critical exposure to the whole of Africa by investing in large, well-capitalized, highly skilled South African companies.

But, like most other outside investors, we are going forward with one major caveat:

Given the current political and social climate, the greatest challenge facing Africa's world-class companies is to persuade the new leadership that they have the good of the country at heart, not merely the good of a once-dominant white minority. Companies perceived as dedicating themselves to shoring up white privilege are likely to get hammered, and hammered hard.

Diamonds Are Forever?

"The aims of this group have been—and will remain—to earn profits, but to earn them in such a way as to make a real and permanent contribution to the well-being of the people and to the development of Southern Africa."
　　　—Sir Ernest Oppenheimer,
　　　　Chairman, Anglo American Corporation,
　　　　1917–1957

Far and away the largest corporation in Africa, with a market cap of nearly 15 billion, is the far-flung Anglo American Corporation. Founded by Sir Ernest Oppenheimer in 1917 with 1 million pounds (sterling) in capital provided by a consortium of British and American investors—hence the name "Anglo American"—this octopus-like web of holding companies and related subsidiaries bestrides the South African economy like a mighty colossus. Anglo American is not only the preeminent metal, minerals, and mining organization in the world. Much like Telebras in Brazil, Anglo American is the bellwether stock of the entire South African market.

It's also a bellwether for the political games being played out across corporate South Africa. Anglo American, although never a backer of the apartheid system or of the now-waning National Party—the party of the once-all-powerful Afrikaner elite—has been a redoubt of white privilege and a pillar of the country's vested business establishment. As South Africa emerges from an era of sanctions and international isolation, companies like Anglo American are being forced to modernize. During the decades that the country sat outside the global swim, the world evolved and changed while South Africa stubbornly stood its ground.

If I can, I always try to kick off a corporate tour of South Africa at the elegant offices of Anglo American at 44 Main Street in downtown Johannesburg—a troubled city that grew up around the hugely profitable South African mining industry and which, unfortunately, is now suffering from a terrible crime wave.

Even the five-star Carlton Hotel (in part owned by Anglo American) downtown, which once sheltered the cream of Johannesburg society, has shrunk to a dim shadow of its former self. If it isn't granted a casino license soon, all bets are off as to whether the grand old pile will survive. When I dropped by on our last visit, all that remained of a once-glittering social focal point was a dwindling annex. All the high life in Joberg had long since moved out to the safer, more secure suburbs.

When, on a previous trip, I stayed at the Carlton, I checked into the hotel in early afternoon and was ushered to an elegant room in the new annex. I quickly donned my jogging shoes, shorts, and T-shirt and headed for the street, to lose my jet lag by running around the once-prosperous downtown. As I loped out the front door, the receptionist politely inquired where I was headed.

"To take a jog," I replied.

"Oh no you're not!" she reprimanded me sternly. "This is a *very dangerous city* and you can get mugged even in broad daylight. We strongly suggest you don't do that."

I retreated to my room for a stationary jog.

As AA goes, so goes South Africa. At least that's been the conventional wisdom for most of the eight decades since Anglo American took control of De Beers—the largest diamond company in the world—as well as the lion's share of the country's gold industry, and other, lesser metals as well.

For much of its history, South African wealth and prosperity has been closely tied to the extraction and marketing of two precious commodities: gold and diamonds. This means in practice that South Africa has seen its fortune tied to two precious materials that have next to no intrinsic value. They are only valuable, and only stay valuable, because we arbitrarily assign value to them.

This situation places pressure on a company like Anglo American to:

1) Diversify away from the highly cyclical commodities business, and

2) Behave as much like a monopolist as is practically possible, in order to maintain and support the prices of two commodities highly vulnerable to the fluctuations of market forces.

Today, Anglo American is as much a financial behemoth as a metal and minerals producer, and more of a metals and minerals marketing and distributing powerhouse than an ore-crushing commodities firm. Its ownership structure is, to put it mildly, complex, with an interlocking series of cross-holdings that not only reflects the diversification strategy pursued by the company but tends to minimize any appearance of total control of whole sectors of the South African mining and metals industries.

Political Risk Personified

Fortunately for its thousands of shareholders, Anglo American was no Johnny-come-lately to the idea of a fairer, desegregated South Africa. Its founding Oppenheimer family, British by descent, kept aloof from the machinations of the old National Party, which ruled over South Africa as the political vehicle of the Afrikaners, the so-called white tribe of Africa.

Sir Harry Oppenheimer, Sir Ernest's successor as Anglo American chairman, was a longtime champion of social justice in South Africa. Today, as a sign of the regard in which the company is held by the present leadership, M. Cyril Ramaphosa, one of the leading lights of the ANC power struggle, sits on Anglo American's star-studded board of directors.

Since its inception, the company has held itself up as a model of a progressive South African company, with the well-being of the majority of South Africans at heart.

"Anglo American's guiding purpose is to earn profits for its shareholders," proclaims one company statement of principles. "But with the uncompromising commitment that these profits will only be earned in a way which contributes meaningfully to social and environmental well-being."

But how do you square such high-minded goals with the fact that Anglo American has long operated in at least one of its operations as a real or a virtual monopoly? And how long, in a global marketplace, can such a quasi-monopoly maintain its privileged position? The big question hanging over Anglo American now: how will it adapt to the new political and social realities, in its own country, and in the world?

One answer to that question was provided by Anglo American itself when, in mid-1998, it officially relocated its global headquarters—and primary stock exchange listing—to London.

De Beers Consolidated Mines Ltd.

We met with the communications manager for De Beers in an old colonial building in downtown Johannesburg that houses Anglo American's major subsidiaries. The boardroom was furnished with an enormous round table, highly polished, which reflected the large number of members that Anglo and De Beers boards typically recruit.

The CM opened the meeting by philosophically observing that: "The diamond industry is largely based on confidence and faith."

I saw his point. The whole thing was, in large part, a business of image, and smoke and mirrors. *The Economist* magazine, I recalled, once called diamonds "glass with attitude." The responsibility for maintaining the world's "confidence and faith" in the bright, shiny future of diamonds falls squarely, as our source explained, on the London-based Central Selling Organisation (CSO). This entity, which at first he claimed—with a straight face—was only an ordinary "trade organization," is in fact comprised of De Beers along with a handful of other Anglo American subsidiaries.

"There are so many myths surrounding the dealings of the CSO," our source sighed, "it's often hard to distinguish fiction from reality. But," he solemnly assured us, "it's really a perfectly straightforward operation."

I was all ears.

"The sole object of the CSO," he insisted, "is to form a control structure for managing the flow of product into the market."

I couldn't argue with that. But I should probably point out that the OPEC oil cartel's charter members would have said the same thing.

The Diamond Club

The CSO had been cobbled together in 1934 by Anglo American founder Sir Ernest Oppenheimer, during the depths of the Great Depression, at a time of serious distress for a depressed diamond industry. The Roaring Twenties had been a high-water mark for diamond-buying, second only to the Gay Nineties, when newly rich vulgarians like Diamond Jim Brady—an obese American gangster—could afford to literally drape themselves in high-carat rocks and think of themselves as real swells. The 1920s should have been a golden jubilee era for diamonds. But after a dynamite decade, the boom concluded with a bang on Black Friday, October 1929.

With the collapse of global prosperity, desperate diamond producers outdid each other to extract more and more diamonds, and undercut one another in a fierce, ultimately self-defeating price war. The result was great news for consumers, but a disaster for producers.

The industry leader had been forced to pitch in, mounting a last-ditch effort to save a fast-failing industry from near-certain disaster—that's at least how the folks at Anglo American like to portray it. Sir Ernest Oppenheimer persuaded his fellow producers to band together to found the CSO as a way to put an end to their suicidal price war.

For public consumption, Anglo American maintains that the sole purpose of this cozy arrangement has always been simply to "flatten out short-term fluctuations in the supply/demand equation." And it likewise insists that "there is *no one* concerned with diamonds, whether a producer, dealer, cutter, jeweler, or consumer, who does not benefit from this policy in some way."

Trust Busters

An American antitrust expert might beg to differ with that statement, particularly with the consumer part. Trust busters maintain that any cartel—whether it be one that controls cloves in Indonesia and is run by members of the Suharto family or a diamond cartel in South Africa controlled by members of the Oppenheimer family—damages consumer interests by keeping prices artificially high.

It's ironic to think that if South Africa ever had to head hat in hand to the IMF for a bailout, the IMF would probably insist (in the interests of fairness) on the dismantling of the De Beers cartel as the price of South Africa's admission to the new global economic order.

If it is true that the story of the end of the twentieth century is the story of the triumph of American-style free-market capitalism, then the days of global cartels and monopolies are surely numbered. But I would never want to bet against Anglo American, or any of its subsidiaries. Because: 1) they know what they're doing, 2) they've been doing it a long time, and 3) in their quiet way, they know how to dominate a market like nobody's business. And, frankly, since they are dealing primarily with a product that no one needs to keep alive (even though "diamonds are a girl's best friend"), I see nothing wrong with it.

Playing Monopoly

As our source readily explained, De Beers produces about 50 percent of the world's diamonds from its own mines. But it controls the distribution and marketing of nearly all of the rest through the CSO, which has contracted to market diamonds produced by all the other major mining companies as a means of "ensuring stability for producers and consumers alike." They've put up a dike around the diamonds of the world, and are free to pretty much charge what the market will bear. Just as long, that is, as the dike holds.

Anglo American renders the question of its dominance over the world diamond industry even more complicated by pursuing a practice of shareholder cross-holding. This means that shareholders in one corporation hold shares in another, related second corporation, while the shareholders in the second corporation hold shares in the first corporation.

For example: Anglo American holds a 50 percent-plus controlling stake in a holding company called Anamint, while Anamint and Anglo American *together* hold a 50 percent-plus stake in De Beers. De Beers, for its part, happens to be the largest single shareholder in Anglo American!

Got that?

It's complicated.

What's more, it's meant to be.

Among other goals, this pattern preserves, through a complex network of holding companies, ownership and control by members of the founding Oppenheimer family. It also makes investing in the company a trifle tricky, while providing the benefit to investors of letting them choose whether they'd like to get into the diamond business, the gold business, the minerals business, or the financial services business.

A Complex Consortium

In early 1998, the Anglo American Corporation was listed on the following exchanges:

1) Johannesburg
2) London
3) Paris
4) Brussels
5) Antwerp
6) Frankfurt
7) Geneva
8) Basel

It was not, at least not yet, listed on any American exchanges. Under the Anglo American umbrella the company had a number of large listed subsidiaries:

1) De Beers
2) Anglo American Properties
3) Anglo American Investment Trust
4) Anglo American Coal Corporation
5) New Central Witwatersrand Area
6) Anglo American Gold Investment Company
7) Anglo American Industrial Corporation
8) Eastvaal Gold Holdings
9) Minorco Société Anomyne
10) The Southern Life Association
11) Anglo American Platinum

In addition, the company held sizable stakes in thirty-seven other listed companies, as well as a number of unlisted holdings, the largest being Mondi, a paper and pulp company.

As of early 1998, Anglo had no sponsored ADR or GDR program, but it had announced plans to apply for a sponsored ADR for AngloGold Limited—its new gold subsidiary.

One example of Anglo American's recent attempts to present a more coherent image to global investors is that it has recently restructured its far-flung gold holdings and put them under a single corporate umbrella: AngloGold, a company for which Anglo American plans to apply for a sponsored ADR. Still, for most investors, Anglo American is a lot like a Chinese menu: "One from column A, one from column B."

By mid-1999 there will be only one Anglo, with its primary listing in London.

Diamonds Are a Girl's Best Friend

Like Gaul in Julius Caesar's time, the diamond business can be divided into three parts.

1) The largest segment of the industry is comprised of producers.

These are the mining companies, of which De Beers is one of several. The largest producers of diamonds are Botswana, the Democratic Republic of the Congo (formerly Zaire), and Angola. Through a network of subsidiaries, De Beers operates mines in nearly all of the above countries, including Namibia, where in addition to diamond mines, it's actively exploring for diamonds offshore.

Breaking Away

Outside Africa, the major diamond producers are Russia, Australia, Canada, and a handful of Latin American companies. But because Australia mainly mines low-quality, colored stones, the fact that they have been selling diamonds not through the CSO cartel isn't filling the folks at De Beers with any great dread. A potentially greater threat to De Beers's lock on the market lies with a group of Canadian producers, who would very much like to tap into the lucrative American market—still far and away the largest diamond market in the world. But there is a problem. Some of these companies "may not want," as our source diplomatically put it, "to be tainted by De Beers antitrust exposure." As a result, for the Canadians to sell through the CSO posed for them a real dilemma: on the upside, the CSO guarantees quality and quantity for its members, and keeps prices stable. But on the downside, as full-fledged CSO members, they would have problems complying with U.S. antitrust laws.

Russian Roulette

Yet a third threat to CSO/De Beers diamond dominance lies in the possibility of rogue Russian producers doing an end run around the CSO to gain market share. But the CSO has recently concluded an agreement with the Russians to prevent such a catastrophe for the cartel. Still, our source candidly conceded that, like everything else in Russia, the contracts between the CSO and the Russian producers were "not exactly concrete."

A major leak right in De Beers's backyard was the $200 million worth of diamonds sold into the market (though not through the CSO) every year by the UNITA rebel organization operating in Angola. The UNITA leader, Jonas Savimbi, has been able to keep up his fight with the nominally Marxist regime in Luanda indefinitely because he can count on revenues from diamonds mined in territory under his control. None of those diamonds are sold to the CSO. De Beers will not deal with UNITA. But a new diamond mine operating under the control of the official Angolan government will soon improve De Beers's position there. And as of our last visit, UNITA had come to terms with the government in Luanda and had joined a loose-knit coalition with them, but that tenuous truce would in due course break down.

The Glittering Pipeline

2) Curious to learn just how the CSO maintains such close control over the second segment of the market, the brokers and middlemen who turn around and sell their rocks to retailers, I asked the straightforward question: how do you do it?

By inviting some 160 "sight-holders," he said—that's what De Beers calls their authorized diamond brokers and middlemen from all over the world—to attend a series of so-called diamond sights about ten times a year in London.

Before every sight, De Beers analyzes brokers' requests from around the world to determine what mix of diamonds best suits market conditions, and "to establish the supply and demand balance." At these carefully choreographed events, the sight-holders are ushered into a room and handed a box of diamonds to evaluate. If the brokers decide that the pricing and product mix meet their specifications, they buy the box. And that's it. That's a diamond sight.

Sounds simple, right? In its own way, our source was right: the CSO really was "a perfectly straightforward operation." But of course nearly all monopolies are simple and straightforward.

The next link down the chain, comprising the third segment of the industry, are the:

3) Cutters, polishers, and retailers. De Beers and the CSO strongly support this end of the market by paying for costly promotional campaigns all over the world. You know the slogan "Diamonds Are Forever"? That's the CSO's motto. In Japan, as recently as the 1960s, diamonds only made up 6 percent of the total jewelry purchases. Now, with saturation advertising creating demand, diamonds make up nearly 70 percent of the Japanese jewelry market.

Turning Off the Tap

The CSO keeps the supply of diamonds in balance by carefully regulating the flow and volume of product moving to market, like turning a valve with a monkey wrench. The goal of this game? Glut-busting.

Glut-busting requires careful monitoring of the market to keep demand tight, and prices high. In 1998, for example, the CSO planned to reduce the number of sights, to insure that retailers didn't suffer "liquidity problems." And, just as important, prevent dealers from cutting prices to move inventory.

How long can this cozy cartel stick together?

As long as Anglo American and De Beers continue to cut deals with potential renegades, and to offer better prices than distributors who operate outside their jurisdiction.

And: as long as the South African government makes no moves to challenge the validity of the cartel.

And: as long as no global antitrust organization emerges and becomes strong enough to crack it open.

Philosophically opposed as you may be to monopolies, the fact is that some of the best investments—particularly telecom companies—are monopolies of one form or another. Would De Beers benefit from increased competition in the diamond market? Probably not. Is that likely to happen anytime soon? Probably not. Is that a good thing? Probably for consumers, since the value of their purchases is maintained.

For investors? I'd also have to say yes.

Black Chips

"Black Chip Stocks Take Center Stage in South Africa."
—THE WALL STREET JOURNAL

"Since the fall of apartheid [black chips] have turned red-hot," the *WSJ* writer reported. "Like the 'red chips' in Hong Kong, the stocks of South Africa's emerging black businesses are the hottest sector of the Johannesburg market."

Now I would be the first to admit that the fact that fifty-three black-controlled companies with a total market capitalization of $22 billion now make up about 10 percent of the Johannesburg exchange's total market value is a positive development for the new South Africa.

Nearly all of these companies—the so-called black chips, also called black empowerment companies—were founded since the African National Congress came to power in 1994. Black chips are companies in which black investors and managers control a majority of shares. Most were launched in advance of the 1994 elections by black labor unions—often in concert with white-controlled banks and businesses—as a way of forestalling the threat of nationalization or, even worse, forced distribution of assets by an ANC government.

In the end, the ANC didn't nationalize private business, or redistribute wealth in any significant way—although land reform remains high on its agenda. What it has done is funnel and channel an increasingly large share of the approximately $10 billion it spends every year on goods and services toward black-owned and controlled businesses.

Which is, after all, only fair: for decades, the government run by the white-ruled National Party did precisely the same thing for themselves and their friends.

And which is all well and good, as a beacon of social progress. But like red chips in Hong Kong, South African black chips are something of a fad. They represent investors' attempt to play the political card. Like most investment fads, once they catch on with a crowd, they quickly lose their luster.

So while black chips outpaced the rest of the Johannesburg market by 16 percent in 1998—due to intense demand by local institutions and individuals—some prices became so inflated that when the market ultimately got hit by fallout from the Asian crisis, they fell much further than the index.

But the real reason that the black chip index continued to outperform the rest of the market by 16 percent is that the market simply reevaluated many of the so-called black empowerment companies to factor in their potential for racial or ethnic leverage. This means that once *we* (or you) take the "black empowerment quotient" into account in evaluating a company, the market itself has probably already done the job for you, and us.

Poof! There goes your leverage.

Don't get me wrong. I am not against buying stock in mainland Chinese companies listed on the Hong Kong exchange—we've bought literally thousands of such shares. Nor am I, as a matter of principle, opposed to buying stock in South African companies run by black entrepreneurs.

But I am against buying shares in companies based strictly on political influence. Or, even worse, visions of political influence in the future.

Invest in companies with good financials, fundamentals, management, a good product or services offered, and a well-thought-out strategy for succeeding in the future.

Like any savvy investor, we pay close attention to the operating environment. And it's in this hard-to-evaluate, often intangible area—often plunked down under the category "goodwill" on a balance sheet—where certain black empowerment companies *may* stand to gain from a higher chance of being awarded government contracts, and orders from black entrepreneurs.

We did find one black chip that we liked very much. But that

was because it had all the above, in addition to a black empowerment factor that was hard to ignore.

Black Chip, Blue Chip, Red Chip, New Chip

Don Ncube, the executive chairman of Real Africa Holdings
(RAH), worked as an executive at Anglo American for twenty-
two years before launching RAH just before the elections of
1994. As an Anglo-American veteran, Ncube had a head start as
a qualified black entrepreneur with a strong managerial track
record. And he knew how to use that to his and his company's
advantage.

As one stockbroker wrote in an upbeat report on the company: "Don Ncube built healthy relationships with key stakeholders in the S.A. economy during his twenty-two years at
Anglo American."

When we met with him at his surprisingly spartan offices in
the Johannesburg suburb of Houghton, Don Ncube explained
that his original goal when seeking backers had been to broaden
his investment pool to include people drawn from "all from the
previously disadvantaged black, colored, and Indian communi-
ties."

It was a concept, Ncube explained, which had first occurred
to him while at Anglo American, during a period in the early
1980s when the company had decided to outsource a number of
its noncore businesses, and in so doing, had encouraged the development of small business units.

"I'm talking about catering, cleaning services, gardening,
liquor, and other outlets in the mines," he explained.

Anglo American was showing its smarts by looking ahead to
a post-apartheid South Africa, and as Ncube explained it, "the
rationale was to introduce to the disenfranchised members of the
South African society the concept of participating in the ownership of equity and productive assets."

The first germ of the idea had been to launch an all-black mining operation, with Anglo American's backing. Interestingly, even
before the fall of apartheid, Anglo American had been receptive

to this idea. But Ncube himself had finally scotched the notion, out of a fear—well founded, as it turned out, by future events—that if the operation failed, it would set back the cause of black entrepreneurship in South Africa by years, if not decades.

But with the seed sown, Ncube began to think about areas of the economy in which blacks could and did play a significant role. Life insurance seemed like a prime candidate, since some of the smaller life insurance companies already employed well-trained black managers and sales staffs to cater to a black clientele.

Africa Life was the first major investment made by RAH in 1994, before the general elections. At the time, Don Ncube was a member of Anglo American's board of directors, and he decided to form Real Africa Holdings as a vehicle to purchase Africa Life. The cost to buy it from Southern Life, a subsidiary of Anglo American Corporation: 200 million South African rand.

In the light of later "black empowerment deals," this amount may seem like small change, but at the time it was monumental. When Ncube began to ponder the "centers of power and influence" within black society, he immediately thought of the labor unions. It dawned on him that although few blacks personally had much disposable income, "as a collective they controlled vast sums of money through pension funds." There were also black church groups, and other nongovernmental organizations.

These were the people, formerly ignored by South African big business, to whom Ncube would turn to build his shareholder base. To his delight, he was remarkably successful in selling shares to these individuals, some of whom have since gone on to form their own companies with money they made on selling their stakes in Real Africa. Along with all the other black chips, RAH has seen its shares soar on the Joberg exchange even as the rest of the market sat, flat as a soda with its cap off.

"I think that I'm most proud," Ncube mused, "of my competitors."

That was a new one on me. I wondered why.

"Because so many of them," he replied, "were originally our shareholders, and we gave them their first taste of capitalism."

What truly irked Ncube about the way black chips were perceived by the white business community was that some whites felt compelled to patronize RAH as "more of a charity case than a business." Like successful black entrepreneurs all over the world, he wanted most of all to be judged on his merits, and by his own bottom line, not some fuzzy-minded notion of social empowerment. He didn't want charity, he wanted dignity, and a chance to succeed in competition with the best on the block.

He was no great fan, he didn't mind telling us, of the buzz-words "black empowerment." As a matter of principle, he felt that it was up to people to empower themselves. Personally, he preferred the term "black enablement." I made a note of that, for future reference.

"Africa Life's growth has been substantial," he said quietly. "By accessing union membership bases and producing the right type of product, we project per annum growth at in excess of 30 percent."

Not too shabby, for a new kid on the block.

Africa Lifecare, RAH's subsidiary that managed government hospitals, was the beneficiary of creeping privatization. As a private company, they could operate a government hospital with far less padding and waste than the government itself could. As a result, their profits on their management contracts were so high that they were frantically taking those profits and using them to expand into other areas of health care management. Ncube freely admitted to being concerned that once the government managers got a load of their numbers, they'd be tempted to revise the contracts to reduce RAH's juicy margins.

Real Africa Asset Management (RAAM), an entity designed to manage money for South Africans of all income groups, now had a billion rand in funds under management. It was actively constructing its data and management systems and was also expected to see strong future growth. It had made a major commitment to training black professionals as fund managers, dealers, and researchers—areas in which, up until now, few qualified black managers could be found.

Here again, RAH was targeting a group that had been ignored by mainline asset-management companies: blacks who had amassed ample assets, and were interested in purchasing bonds and equities and mutual funds of all sizes and stripes.

One nuisance that Ncube and his senior managers hadn't anticipated was that the company had suffered some criticism for employing "too many white managers."

"I would like more black managers," Ncube observed, a little defensively. "But at the moment there are simply not enough skilled black managers to go around, and we believe, as a matter of principle, that we have to have the best man or woman for the job."

He despised the notion of affirmative action as practiced in the U.S. As far as he was concerned, all it achieved was the erosion of confidence by contributing to a popular perception that blacks don't deserve the jobs they do get, but only get them because they are black.

Down the road, he foresaw great opportunities for his companies in infrastructure development and in participating in the government's privatization program, which had gotten off to a slow start.

Contrary to conventional wisdom, he expected privatization to gain momentum after the 1999 election.

"After the election," he predicted, "I think that the government's current preoccupation with giving blacks a leg-up, whatever the cost, will be replaced by a more pragmatic policy based on performance in whatever area is important."

As a holding company, RAH was basically a vehicle for making investments in ongoing businesses that had established a niche in the market. One such operation was a deep-sea fishing business, which was doing exceptionally well.

I asked him about his investment philosophy.

"We stay away from risky deals," he concluded, "because we value the trust and respect of the business community, which has been so hard to build up. One bad deal could destroy us. I will only invest in a black empowerment project if the empowerment adds actual value."

A Black-and-Blue Chip

"One bad deal" that could have destroyed him, but from which he'd prudently stayed away, had utterly destroyed the largest black empowerment company established to date.

The recent calamities affecting the century-old mining firm

JCI had profound implications for the future of black chips and black empowerment companies all over South Africa.

"I call the JCI fiasco a black *disempowerment* deal," Don Ncube said, shaking his head in bewilderment. "They offered me a piece of that pie, and fortunately, we didn't take it."

Ironically, it was the germ of a notion—a black-owned and -operated mining firm—that had first sent him on the road to founding RAH. But Ncube, concerned about the lack of skilled and trained black professionals in the mining industry, had shunned that deal. A good bet.

A Hero's Welcome

In the fall of 1996, when Anglo American Corporation announced that Mzi Khumalo, a former political prisoner who had spent twelve years locked up on Robben Island with Nelson Mandela, had placed the winning bid for a 34.9 percent stake in JCI, cheers went up all over South Africa. Here was the ultimate black empowerment deal! It seemed to many well-wishers that it heralded the dawn of a new, fairer era in South African business.

Anglo American certainly garnered enormous credit for its part in nurturing the largest black empowerment deal in South African history. The forty-two-year-old Khumalo, a former partisan turned gold magnate, was aided in his quest for corporate power by thirty-three-year-old Brett Kebble, the brash, boyish gold bug and chairman of rival Randgold, the most prominent and enthusiastic backer of Khumalo's African Mining Group's winning bid.

But when all the smoke had cleared, it emerged that Anglo American—and its investment advisors, SBC Warburg—had gotten a very rich price for the company. Even with gold prices buoyant—as they were when the deal was first proposed—its terms were widely believed to give Anglo American a premium of at least 10 percent over what many people considered a fair-market price.

Before JCI, although they were certainly not charity cases, the terms under which most black empowerment companies had been put together were highly favorable to the black chips. But with JCI, Anglo American drove a hard bargain; the price asked—and paid—was predicated on optimistic forecasts of future gold prices.

When the deal was first struck, gold prices were just hitting a five-year high.

Realizing that what goes up can also go down, wary institutional investors stayed away from the JCI IPO (initial public offering) in droves. This forced the deal's underwriters, SBC Warburg—with its reputation on the line—to contribute the lion's share of Khumalo's financing from its own funds, or see the public relations coup of the century blow up in its face.

Bad judgment was soon joined by bad luck. Within weeks of the JCI buyout, the price of gold started to sag. This left the elaborate corporate structure JCI had been saddled with by Anglo American appearing unwieldy, clumsy and complex to potential investors. Within a year, with gold prices hitting the skids, and with their backs up against the wall, rival gold companies began frantically streamlining and structurally simplifying to give their sinking share prices a boost.

Consolidations, mergers, and acquisitions were the name of the game, as small gold companies sought to seek refuge in size. But poor JCI, with its huge burden of debt, found itself like the wallflower at the party, without any names on its merger dance card. It was an ugly duckling.

Even the venerable Anglo American, whose various gold subsidiaries were long overdue for a similar makeover, hastily announced plans to revamp its far-flung gold operations and put a web of competing subsidiaries under the same roof under a new name, AngloGold.

JCI, for its part, was left out in the cold.

After a torturous year of operations, the company's board, lacking all other options, asked its shareholders to approve the sale of JCI's two richest assets—its largest gold mines—back to . . . Anglo American Corporation!

In an even more desperate move, the board announced an agreement to dismantle and sell most of the remaining assets to the U.K.-based Lonrho commodities group, in exchange for Anglo American's 26 percent stake in Lonrho. Lonrho ended up acquiring the shares that Anglo American owned, and all of JCI's once-profitable coal business.

The notion that one of South Africa's largest and potentially richest gold companies would end up being carved up and hived off to foreigners didn't sit well with South Africans on both sides of the color divide. In the ultimate humiliation, and sign of his transformation from hero to villain, Khumalo failed to show up at a shareholder meeting where the proposal to break up the company was to be voted upon, and where he was expected to get a grilling from irate shareholders.

The deal turned out a disaster for advocates of black empowerment, who'd naïvely believed that permitting black managers to "control their own destinies" would somehow absolve them from the need to compete in the market.

Of course, there would always be cynics who would say that it was all a setup. That the whites who put the deal together had somehow choreographed it to fail. But conspiracy theories didn't even wash with most people, who blamed faulty management for the catastrophe.

"Managerial incompetence or ineptitude can cause far more damage than anything the markets throw at a company," thundered an irate editorial in the Johannesburg periodical *Business Day.* "Khumalo has had his chance to prove that his management skills could create wealth." Instead, their absolute lack led to the destruction of a once-proud company.

Whatever the long-term implications for South African society, JCI's downfall at least briefly sent the black chips spiraling southward.

Which, to my mind, was not necessarily a bad thing, since so many of those companies were being unrealistically bloated in their evaluations by mushy, rosy social scenarios, instead of hard-core profits and long-term growth.

Water into Wine

Contrary to the perception of some, the synthetic fuel company Sasol was not founded as a sanctions-busting company. It was set up in 1950, after World War II, as a state-owned strategic asset. Sasol's strategic value lay in its development of a process to convert coal, which South Africa has a lot of, to oil, which it hasn't much of at all.

Sasol's place in the general scheme of things was certainly enhanced during the 1970s and 1980s, when the U.N. imposed sanctions against South Africa as a means of pressuring the country to dismantle its apartheid system. No matter how high-minded in purpose, sanctions can have a perverse boomerang effect on a target economy. Under sanctions, some companies flourish when cut off from foreign competition, while others wither on the vine. During the sanctions era, the strategic importance of Sasol's coal-to-oil conversion technology was essentially priceless, since if the world had chosen to cut off the country's oil imports, it could have survived on its coal. In short, as much as a result of sanctions as anything else, Sasol flourished.

In 1979, the company was privatized and listed on the Johannesburg Stock Exchange, and has been steadily rising ever since. Today, Sasol supplies post-apartheid South Africa with 41 percent of its liquid fuel and the lion's share of its petrochemical feed stocks. In 1997, it had foreign sales of $840 million, representing 20 percent of total turnover.

Of course, with sanctions no longer a factor, Sasol's unique Fischer-Tropsch process has had to struggle to find a niche in a world currently awash in oil. While the core technology is under study by other international energy players, they are mainly experimenting with it. Sasol has been doing it—converting coal into oil—for years.

Eco-Okay

Perhaps the greatest advantage of the synfuels process in today's market is that it's unusually environmentally friendly.

Fischer-Tropsch produces lower emissions than the EU (European Union) standard, currently the strictest pollution protocol in the world.

As environmental controls go increasingly global, this single factor is expected to propel this once-arcane process to a higher public profile, as it's licensed to international competitors.

The process is also dirt—or "coal"—cheap. A wide range of petrochemicals, from plastics to other chemical feed stocks—can be produced by it without a costly "petroleum cracker"—that's a chemical reactor that breaks oil and gas down into their component chemical parts. And it is made even more cost-effective by the fact that Sasol's Chemicals Division recovers valuable petrochemicals from it, apart from its by-products natural gas and oil.

Sasol can cheaply and easily convert gas—which in the oil field is usually either flared off or transported by expensive gas carrier ships—into liquid fuel that can be transported more cheaply than natural gas.

And the diesel fuel produced by this process is of such high quality that it is used by foreign suppliers to blend with their own lower-quality diesel, to create a higher-quality product.

Sasol is one of a very few energy stocks we like that isn't cheap by world standards. When benchmarked against other, comparable energy companies, Sasol is certainly no bargain. But this is a case in which the exception proves the rule, because there really are no energy companies out there which can legitimately be compared to Sasol. It's an entirely different breed of cat.

And it's a prime example of a South African company that's succeeded in a global industry against major players by developing its own strengths, and sticking to its last.

Polifin

A partner with Sasol in converting synthetic fuel into petrochemicals, Polifin takes gases produced by Sasol's synfuels program and turns them into polymers. That, as you may know, is a fancy name for plastics and other synthetic materials.

But how would "I have one word for you—polymers!" sound? Precisely my point. That's why most people prefer the term "plastic."

At one time, not so long ago, all of the world's plastics and other synthetics were made from coal. But in recent years, oil and natural gas have provided the bulk of the world's petrochemical feed stocks. Polifin, in effect, turns back the plastic clock by "cracking" Sasol's oil and natural gas into their chemical component parts, thereby producing everything from polyethylene (PE), to polypropylene (PP), to polyvinyl chloride (PVC)—as well as a wide range of plastic products.

The company exports nearly 10 percent of its turnover. Half goes to Africa, while the balance goes to Hong Kong and China. Remarkably, due to low labor costs, technological efficiency, and the low cost of their materials, Polifin can still compete with low-cost Asian plastics producers in their home markets. That's just about unique in the world.

What I like most about Polifin is their practically unchallenged dominance of the plastics and synthetics market in South Africa. In polyethylene their domestic market share was 45 percent. In most other synthetic and plastic products—with the exception of a few specialty imports—they were the sole suppliers in the country.

Any long-term negatives on the horizon?

Our source thought long and hard to come up with a few.

"Traditional products," he conceded, "like wood and glass, do have potential to slow plastics growth." But even then he couldn't entirely follow through on the negative. "In this country," he insisted, "plastic is too entrenched to ever be ousted, as long as prices are kept reasonable."

Polifin had recently opened up a brand-new high-tech R&D Center, staffed with sixty researchers and scientists. But this was far from primary R&D—which they felt was better off left to the majors—but was rather a center uniquely devoted to adapting existing plastics and synthetics to the African environment.

Oh, and before we left, our source wanted to mention: Polifin had an "excellent relationship with its unions, and almost no debt."

At its current low price, as benchmarked against comparable plastics companies around the world, we classified this one as "a world-class company that is remarkably cheap."

We rated it, at the time, a clear buy.

Engen

I was almost hoping to find some major fault with Engen, one of the only remaining independent energy companies left in South Africa. Partly owned by the Malaysian state oil company, Petronas—whose twin office towers in downtown Kuala Lumpur are the tallest buildings in the world—Engen had originally been the South African subsidiary of Mobil Oil, before sanctions and public disapproval prompted Mobil to divest itself of its South African holdings.

When Petronas bought into Engen, it had been the largest single foreign investment in post-apartheid South Africa. Now, rumors abounded that Mobil, eager to get back into the South African game, was interested in picking up the part of Engen that Petronas didn't already own—or perhaps even the part that it did—at practically any price. Of course, the irony was lost on practically no one that Mobil had sold the company for a song back in the dark days of sanctions, and would have to pay through the nose now to get it back.

Of course, if Mobil were to buy it, or even by showing strong interest touched off a bidding war for Engen, that would be a boon to Engen shareholders. But much as we like takeover targets, we don't invest in companies because of rumors.

What we liked about Engen was probably the same thing that attracted Mobil and Petronas to it: it was doing everything in its power to play catch-up with the twenty-first century. The company had recently formed a strategic joint venture with the American energy organization Brown & Root, under whose guidance they had developed a top-of-the-line training program, a virtual necessity in South Africa, where the public educational system leaves something to be desired.

The big question hanging over the South African energy industry at the moment was the likely direction of government policy following the 1999 election: to reregulate, or deregulate?

The Engen man outlined the government's core dilemma: while deregulation was good for business, and in that sense good for the economy, regulation was good for keeping employment up. It was therefore popular politically.

Under the present climate, Engen was doing just fine. It was, in fact, raking in over 37 percent of oil industry profits nationwide, based on just 24 percent of total fuel sales.

Did you catch that?

Thirty-seven percent of oil industry profits nationwide, based on 24 percent of sales.

That was enough for us. Everything else—takeovers, bidding wars—all that was just icing on the cake.

At the close of the meeting, one of our local analysts discreetly passed me a note: "We should buy more."

I nodded, just as discreetly.

And so, we did.

But it was not too long afterward that Petronas decided to purchase the entire company at a premium to the market price. Unfortunately, that price was less than what we calculated the company was really worth. But with the prospect of holding a stock that could be delisted after Petronas obtained majority control from South African investors eager to sell at a premium to the market price, we decided to sell.

Tongaat–Hulett Group

One of the most interesting companies we visited in all of South Africa was a forty-five-minute drive north of Durban, a coastal city popular with surfers, and the business center of strife-torn KwaZulu/Natal province.

KwaZulu/Natal (formerly Natal province) is the homeland of the huge, powerful Zulu tribe, as well as one of the last redoubts of the British in South Africa. Many of the British Natalians are wealthy sugarcane farmers. As we drove though green, lush fields of sugarcane on our way up the coast to the offices of the Tongaat-Hulett Group, we were pleasantly surprised by its beauty.

The office, in keeping with the landscape, was stunningly furnished with original artworks.

We met with a senior official of the group, a Mr. Naidoo, who launched his presentation with a general discussion of the overall economic picture. According to this distinguished gentleman, who was of Indian descent and distantly related to Gandhi, the GDFI (gross domestic fixed investment) in a region is a very fair measure of growth in the local economy. By that yardstick, KawaZulu/Natal province was getting the short end of the stick.

Though he didn't come right out and say it, there was a political element to all of this. As the bastion of the Zulu, who under their chief Mangosuthu Buthelezi had long fought the ANC for dominance of the future South Africa, the current leadership would hardly have been predisposed to lavish its beneficence on the homeland of its former enemies.

What he did say was that while the government had promised to improve three areas when it came to power—education, housing, and electrification—they had failed to deliver on their promises. After three years of ANC rule, there were no new schools, no new hospitals, no construction of roads, and no new jails in KwaZulu/Natal. And as far as local business went, there had been little to no government spending in the vicinity and, he felt, precious little elsewhere in the country.

"The South African consumer is starting to feel the pinch," he warned, adopting an ominous tone. But when he turned to the specifics of his company, the group was doing awfully well in all of its core areas. That was seven—that's right, seven—separate and distinct businesses.

Talk about deep diversification!

The Magnificent Seven

The largest division in the group, contributing 40 percent to group profits, was sugar.

Along with gold, diamonds, and coal, sugar was a key commodity and a pillar of the South African economy.

While there had been "some speculation regarding the potential for an El Niño drought effect," so far at least, El Niño had been more of a scare than a fact. At any rate, they routinely made provisions for at least one drought year out of every five, so even if El Niño did catch them by surprise at some point, they had more than enough storage capacity to tide them over. The same thing was true of their land in Zimbabwe, where even during a long drought, Tongaat-Hulett's sugar plantations enjoyed ample irrigation and water.

TH's Consumer Food Division, a joint venture with CPC International (one of the top five consumer food companies globally), had acquired the right to manufacture and export CPC brands to the rest of Africa. Another company had the rights to sell CPC stuff in South Africa. Skippy Peanut Butter was one CPC product that was going gangbusters all over southern Africa.

Building materials might have seemed like a ho-hum arena, but TH's operation was the main player in the South African market for bricks and paving blocks.

Hulett Aluminum (HA) had a 50 percent share of the aluminum market in South Africa.

TH's property subsidiary, Moreland Estates, was one of the largest landowners in the KwaZulu/Natal region, with a holding of 50,000 hectares. The land was largely undeveloped, but the company had plans to develop it over three phases, into industrial, commercial, residential, and resort properties. Some of the land adjacent to the head office, where we were visiting, was slated to be sold to the government for the development of the new Durban International Airport. Moreland Estates was also developing a casino, on a mega scale, as well as a huge shopping center.

With its fingers in every pie you could find in its region, Tongaat-Hulett was pursuing diversification on a grand scale. What impressed me most about it—apart from the obviously high quality of the artworks on its headquarters walls—was its capable management, as well as the smart way that they were using an agricultural base product—sugar—as a cash cow to invest in a number of future-oriented, high-growth industries.

So even if sugar was down one year—let's say El Niño did it—they always had aluminum, building materials, property, food, you name it.

That was called playing it smart.

Africa the Beautiful

I think that the most important lesson that we learned on our African trip was that no place is unworthy of investment because of its supposedly low level of development. Ever since the darkest days of the colonial era, when phrases like "white man's burden" could be used without irony, the Western European and North American take on Africa was that it was populated by lazy, ignorant savages who, if left to their own devices, would quickly let their countries slide into decay.

The post–World War II era of the great strongmen of Africa, from Nkrumah in Ghana to Kaunda in Zambia, to Mobutu in the Republic of the Congo (the former Zaire), was one in which, due to massive failures of leadership, those irrational prejudices were, if anything, reinforced.

As the notion of basket case Africa took hold, a place of crying, ineradicable poverty that needed buckets of foreign aid to survive, the natural market economies of these countries—free-market trade links and routes that had existed for thousands of years before the arrival of the white man—were allowed to wither away and die from sheer neglect and disuse.

Now, for the first time in hundreds of years, since the dawn of the colonial era, natural market economies in Africa are being permitted to flourish and take root, and evolve into forces of unprecedented sophistication, with the prospect of succeeding on a grand scale in the global economy.

No longer will Africa be relegated to supplier of raw materials and commodities for European industry.

No longer will Africa be simply a net beneficiary of the charity from the West, of foreign aid, which if you want my opinion has had nearly as much of an adverse effect as its guns and slave drivers. Africa, at long last, has arrived at a place where it can stand on its own on the global scene. It has finally and proudly shown the rest of us that success in this life is largely a matter of permitting natural incentives and disincentives to work their magic, without undue interference from patronizing, meddling experts in Third World Development, or from the autocratic dictates of some haughty indigenous elite.

We see Africa as one of the greatest untapped pockets of potential on earth.

Take my advice and go see for yourself.

I can promise you one thing: you'll be surprised.

We were.

MOBIUS RULES: THE FINAL FRONTIER BOX

81: By the time everyone and his brother believes that it's the right time to invest, the right time will have long since come and gone.

82: When looking at managements of companies in countries where the business climate is complex and difficult, locally trained managers tend to make a better fit with the local environment.

83: Political uncertainty—like any other form of uncertainty—can be your green light to move into a market. Uncertainty depresses stock prices. If you have faith in your own crystal ball—or, better yet, your own independent analysis—an uncertain atmosphere can be just the break that you've been looking for to pick up large-cap, blue chip stocks that otherwise would be too expensive to even consider.

84: Once uncertainty becomes certainty, and anyone with two nickels to rub together can with some degree of accuracy predict the likely outcome of events, that beautiful risk premium will have evaporated in a puff of smoke.

Conclusion

◆

WINNERS AND LOSERS

Okay, you win some, you lose some—you can't avoid it. It's not only the name of the game, but the only game in town for emerging markets investors. But some losses are not only avoidable, but meaningful, because you learn lessons from them.

With just about every major loss we've incurred, we've picked up a few pointers. I try to avoid repeating the same mistakes again and again. Because, like most people, I hate being wrong too often, and I know that fund managers are only as good as their last performance.

On the theory that we learn more from our mistakes than our successes, I'll start out with the losers. We've had our fair share, believe me. But at the end of the day, we must be ready to make mistakes, otherwise we would never learn. You might even say that hitting a few foul balls goes with the territory.

No Exit

Always have an exit strategy. Always—repeat *always*—maintain a way to GET OUT.

The most discouraging thing that can happen to a fledgling—or even veteran—emerging markets investor is getting stuck holding a bagful of illiquid stock. That's not a soup recipe, but a stock you can't sell, come hell or high water. Holding a batch of illiquid stocks for any length of time is like clutching a container of nitro: you're dying to get rid of it, but no one in their right mind will take it off your hands. Getting stuck with a seriously sick stock is like wearing a hundred-pound ball and chain while whitewater-rafting. It'll drag you down into the depths with it, with you kicking and screaming all the way, ruing the day you ever heard of . . .

(In our case:)

1) Mesbla (a Brazilian department store chain).

2) Cukurova (a Turkish utility).

3) Yaohan (a Japanese department store chain with a shaky presence in China and Hong Kong).

The list goes on. But fortunately, not on and on.

Even today, when the worst wounds have healed, the mere mention of those names—along with a handful of other losers—fills me with dread and regret. But, curiously, not anger—because any hard feelings are softened by the fact that we invariably learn from the experience.

As someone who's been burned more than once, I have some advice for you:

Roll with the punches.

If you're going to take real risks, you can't always count on rewards.

Fighting Back

Of course, a possible alternative to passive acceptance is fighting back.

Personally, I don't recommend it. Not unless:

1) You're in it for the long haul, and

2) You've got unusually deep pockets.

In our position, things are a little different. As a major player, sometimes we've got to put up our dukes, or pushy owners or managers will decide they can take advantage of us minority investors with impunity. As passive or portfolio investors—as opposed to strategic ones—we don't want to become involved in actually managing a company or interfering with the management of a company. If we do, we only do so with utmost reluctance, and only after all other options have been ruled out. If we don't like what we see going on at the top, we'll kick up one heck of a fuss. Because if we don't, we're not protecting our interests, those of our shareholders, or those of minority shareholders in general.

SOS

If you follow the contrarian path, you're going to find yourself buying stock in distressed companies. You can't avoid it, because the vast majority of the bargains out there are in shares of organizations that have made a few mistakes along the way. That's why these stocks are so cheap. That's why a whole lot of smart people think they're headed nowhere in a hurry.

Your job, and ours, is to prove them wrong. So how can we be so arrogant?

Because we have the luxury, and the opportunity, of shifting our focus to a five-year time horizon. We can look ahead to a point out there in the distance where the long-term outlook may be more positive than the short-term. We also have the advantage of stacking the company up against other, similar companies elsewhere, often faced with similar challenges. Sometimes, we can see a light at the end of a tunnel where others see only darkness. And of course, sometimes, we're wrong.

We like finding good companies, and good countries, that have fallen on hard times, but only—we hope—temporarily. Companies, and countries, poised to stage an unlikely comeback. Companies, and countries, fighting an uphill battle to thrive, even to survive.

Because only when the odds are against you are you going to find any real bargains.

Belly-up

Given such high risk factors, a few of those companies are obviously not going to make it. But if you do find some company poised on the edge of oblivion, and it does defy logic and stage an unlikely comeback, you're way ahead of the game.

Those are your big winners, your 200 percent-plus club. More often than not, the line separating the winners from the losers can be embarrassingly thin.

Bad Company

Not surprisingly, some floundering companies have taken a tumble because their managements are incapable, disinterested, or involved in fraud. Sometimes they're just incompetent. Sometimes, they're crooked. The real hardball players are the unscrupulous ones who plan on profiting from innocent minority (often foreign) investors. Again, the management may be out-and-out con artists. But more often than not, they're ordinary Joes with their backs against the wall, who see no other choice than to cut corners, or fudge a few numbers, just to keep their leaky boat afloat a while longer.

Lock, Stock, and Barrel

When counseling would-be global investors, I always stress:
    The law matters.
    The other side of the same coin: the lack of law matters.
    Remember the FELT doctrine?
    Fair, efficient, liquid, and transparent markets.
    The greatest problem facing emerging markets today is the lack of FELT in markets lacking the legal structure and enforcement methods required to protect foreign and minority shareholders against abuse. Such abuse can range from the fairly harmless—being saddled with a foreign share premium or being excluded, as a foreigner, from owning voting shares—to sophisticated white-collar crimes and elaborate schemes to separate shareholders from their money. In short, out-and-out fraud.
    Prosecuting white-collar crimes, even in mature markets, can be frustratingly difficult. That's because the activities involved

tend to be so arcane—difficult for judges, let alone jurors, to follow. Most of these schemes involve diverting or siphoning off shareholder funds to entities controlled by management interests.

And even some legal experts are often not entirely sure that a management fooling around with money entrusted to them is really no different from out-and-out theft. And in the absence of criminal prosecution, obtaining satisfaction through civil action can be costly, tedious, and futile.

In a country like Nigeria, you'd be crazy to invest under the current climate, because most custodians won't touch Nigerian stocks—for the most part because the chances that the bank to which your funds are entrusted may be corrupt are just too high.

Likewise in Russia, although the authorities have made progress in solving the problem, the lack of a comprehensive central share registry, a transparent, fair, and understandable tax system, and of a reliable system of securities laws and enforcement is keeping the country at a scandalously low level of capital formation.

No one likes putting money where it isn't going to be safe, unless they're getting handsomely paid for their trouble.

In too many countries, it's still too easy for controlling or majority shareholders to ride roughshod over us little guys. You might be surprised to find mutual fund managers in the same club as the small investor. But as a minority shareholder going up against management, the forces ranged against you are large, while those behind you are small. In most cases, you can't fight your battles by conventional means. You have to resort to the methods of the guerrilla warrior: hide, feint, dodge, and hit 'em when they've stopped looking for you.

In many emerging markets:

1) There are no laws on the books designed to protect you, and/or

2) The local powers-that-be don't want you to win your case. Often because they have a vested interest in your losing . . .

Let's take, for example, Cukurova.

Yes, take it please.

Clan Warfare

In 1952, the Turkish government established the Seyhan hydro-electric/irrigation project as a means of delivering irrigation and electrical power to an underdeveloped region on the southern Mediterranean coast. They applied to the World Bank for funding, but were turned down on the grounds that a private company would do a better job of financing the project, and of ultimately reaping the rewards.

So the government decided to form a new private company to generate electricity, and a new public entity to handle the irrigation. They called the private power company Cukurova Electric AS (CEAS), and over the years, it became successful not only in obtaining generous World Bank funding, but in generating power for the entire region.

So successful were they, in fact, that by 1993 (close to four decades after its founding) CEAS's sales and customer base had grown by leaps and bounds, in pace with the rip-roaring Turkish economy. With the Istanbul stock market bobbing up and down like a life raft, the Turkish government decided to cash in on the good times by launching a long-delayed privatization drive.

Cukurova, meanwhile, was preparing to embark on its most massive project to date: a massive dam and hydroelectric generator to be contracted at a cost of $670 million (of which the World Bank had agreed to provide more than half). When the project was complete, and with six other major hydroelectric power plants under its control, Cukurova Electric would no longer be some sleepy little regional utility. It was about to become, literally, a regional powerhouse.

That was when the Uzans decided to get into the act.

The Uzans are a locally powerful family who owned banks and other businesses all over Turkey, but were heavily based in the southern region—Cukurova's home base. They prevailed upon the government to include Cukurova in its new privatization program. As it turned out, they had had their eye on this potential plum, ripe for the picking, for some time.

In 1993, the Uzans snagged an 18 percent stake in the company from the government, at around $1.25 per share. With that chunk in hand, various members of the family began gradually accumulating more shares, until they ultimately controlled 67 percent of the company.

At which point, the stock took a sudden nosedive. Why? Because rumors had begun circulating through the Istanbul Stock Exchange (a notoriously volatile market) that the Uzans were out to squeeze the company dry. The word on the street was that they planned to use Cukurova as a cash cow to generate funds to invest—some would have said bail out—a number of far-flung family enterprises.

Now the overriding question for us, as major stockholders, became: Should we pay attention to these rumors? Or should we ignore them, and follow the fundamentals?

Curious as to how the new management was planning to face the future, we took a seven-hour bone-jarring ride in an open-backed truck to check out the new team, at CEAS headquarters about half an hour south of the coastal city of Adana, overlooking one of the company's dams and reservoirs.

Despite the fact that the Uzans were in complete control of operations, the profit potential of the company's new transmission lines still looked promising. The balance sheet seemed sound. When we compared Cukurova's profit margins and rate structures with other, similar power projects elsewhere, we found its P/E of 6 more than acceptable, and its price-to-book-value ratio of 60 percent appealing. Comparable electric utilities, operating in comparable environments, were selling at P/Es of 12 to 15, and at steep premiums to book value.

On paper, in short, the stock was a steal.

There were just two things wrong with this picture.

1) Those nasty rumors, which just wouldn't go away . . . and

2) The new management wasn't exactly eager to meet us.

In retrospect, we should have paid more attention to these intangibles, instead of getting caught up in our analysis of the audited financial statements. That was our big mistake, and it just underscores how important in our business it can be to suss out the management, with a face-to-face meeting, if possible. In this case, face-to-face contact couldn't save the day. But at least we made the attempt.

The first hint of trouble emerged when irregularities were un-covered in an audit conducted by Turkey's Capital Markets Board (CMB), based in Ankara, of a Cukurova subsidiary called Kepez Electric. The auditors determined that funds raised from a new rights issue—a sale of new shares—had been used by the Uzans to speculate in foreign exchange markets, instead of being invested in the capital expenditures for which the funds had been raised.

For good measure, the Uzans had also pulled a few other questionable stunts. According to a report by the Turkey Capital Markets Board, they'd failed to make adequate provisions in the balance sheet for certain disputed receivables (money owed them but possibly not collectable). Plus they were caught holding large sums of company money in non-interest-bearing cash deposits in a bank affiliated with the family. In a Western publicly owned corporation, that's a no-no, because it's like handing yourself an interest-free loan.

Concerned by these findings, we conducted our own personal audit of Cukurova's financial position. A few things we found hardly bolstered our confidence.

1) Debt levels shooting up.
2) Share prices shooting down.

With CEAS stock hitting a new low of $.018 (down, down from the $1.25 the Uzans had paid to acquire the company only a year earlier), profits had dropped more than 30 percent, from $59 million to $41 million. After a year of Uzan mismanage-ment, CEAS posted a $18 million loss for the first nine months of the year. This was the first loss in the company's history.

Clearly, something was seriously amiss with this company. To make matters worse, the Uzans, in a desperate attempt to bolster their authority, embarked on an ill-fated slash-and-burn cost-cutting campaign, featuring massive layoffs. The result was a slew of strikes, labor unrest, frequent slowdowns and show-downs, and at one melodramatic point, a lockout of local man-agers, who ended up picketing the premises. The family hired their own security guards to blockade their headquarters from protesters.

We knew now that the company was being run into the ground. We didn't precisely know why, except that our stock was headed straight down the drain. Our only recourse, as we saw it, was to attend the upcoming annual shareholder meeting and go public with charges that the family was corrupt. Our game plan was to delay, if we could, rumored attempts on the part of the family to revise the company's articles of association to tighten their grip on the company.

There was just one hitch. If we wanted to attend this meeting, we were going to have obtain an entry card, which were only provided to holders of "registered" shares. Astonishingly, although we owned nearly a million shares in the company, the process of registering them was still excruciatingly slow. Once again, as would occur later in India, Russia, and elsewhere, we found ourselves locked in a pitched battle over the registration of shares—a matter so routine in most nonemerging markets that brokers take care of it as a matter of course.

In all too many emerging markets, however, share registration can be an area rife with corruption and abuse. After being asked to register our shares formally in our name, Citibank Istanbul wrote to our custodians, Morgan Stanley, in Luxembourg:

"Share registration is not a requirement for custody [in Turkey] and is not a market practice. If a foreign investor wishes to attend a meeting or vote by proxy, the investor should assign a power of attorney to its custodian to register the securities with the undersecretary of treasury and foreign trade as direct investors, as opposed to portfolio investors. Direct investors are subject to Turkish capital gains tax."

Which stood, we were astonished to learn, at 48.3 percent for nonresident investors in equities! That meant that we would have to pay nearly half of our profits in taxes, if we wanted to vote the shares, and then sell the stock. No way. The letter continued:

"In most cases, share registration allows shareholders to attend the meeting or authorize its subcustodian to vote via proxy. If you do commence registration, you will not be able to sell the shares until the process in finalized, and the shares will no longer be under our custody."

The local laws had slammed us between a rock and hard place. If we registered our shares to vote them at a shareholder meeting, not only would be stand to get hit with a nearly 50 percent capital gains tax, we'd effectively lose control over them. This prospect, not surprisingly, stuck in our craw. Particularly since the party to which we were being asked to tender control was the *same* party we were aiming to unseat.

As a matter of principle, and in an attempt to establish a precedent to protect minority shareholder rights in Turkey, we formally applied to the Turkish FID (Foreign Investment Directorate) to register our CEAS shares. Approval was slow in coming, because no foreigners had ever attempted to register their shares with the bureau before. Like all bureaucracies, any new form of rubber-stamping was approached with extreme caution.

The FID ultimately denied our request, insisting that our shares could not be registered unless they were handed over to the company itself for "safekeeping." Outraged by this ruling, we wrote directly to the prime minister of Turkey, Tansu Ciller, to request an unprecedented intervention with the FID.

A bit like a genie in an old Turkish tale, the prime minister's office granted our wish. They pressured the company into recognizing our right to have our shares properly registered. In due course, an entry card to the meeting came in the mail. Round one to Templeton.

As we expected, at the annual meeting management proposed a number of changes to the company by-laws which would have made it a lot easier for them to advance their own interests at the expense of minority shareholders. Although we voted against these proposals, we lost on the first ballot. This was scarcely surprising—we were, after all, minority shareholders.

But as a result of our aggressive action, the Capital Markets Board (CMB) in Ankara took up our cause. They took the Uzans to court, accusing them of violating Turkish commercial—as well as criminal—law with regard to an alleged siphoning of funds from a publicly listed company. The suit specifically stipulated that the company had received funds from the World Bank which were to have been invested in the upcoming power project, but had instead been diverted to a number of related companies and entities, and into—once again—non-interest-bearing accounts at Uzan-controlled banks. And, as at Kepez Electric, management reportedly was rashly speculating in high-risk foreign exchange transactions, exposing shareholders to fresh liabilities if these "investments" were ever to go sour.

With the release of this devastating—to the Uzans—report by the Audit Department of the Capital Markets Board, a curious development occurred: the General Directorate of Foreign Investment began to conduct its own investigation of the case. In response to the CMB's scathing report, the Ministry of Energy shut down CEAS, and replaced its Uzan-dominated board of directors with one selected by the Capital Markets Board.

The Uzans had further shot themselves in the foot by failing to make tax payments to the Turkish Electricity Authority (TEA). To add insult to injury, they'd allegedly cheated on the purchase of a license to enter the cellular phone business—an error of judgment which ultimately caused their cellular license to be revoked by Turkish Telecom.

With the Uzans reeling from these multiple blows, the Capital Markets Board then waded back in for the kill. They suspended the right of a few Uzan-controlled companies to trade in securities—preventing them from squandering shareholder money on foreign exchange transactions—pending resolution of their inquiry. In what looked for a while like a final nail in their coffin, they shut down a Uzan-controlled bank for alleged irregularities in trading on shares in Kepez Electric.

For a brief period, it looked as if we were going to win our battle. Perhaps more importantly, we'd struck (apparently) a strong blow for truth, justice, and the new global order in Turkey. But then, the Uzans struck back, and hit hard. They used a family-owned TV station to cast aspersions on the prime minister's family; they lobbied political supporters in the opposition parties; they rallied domestic interests against the alleged machinations of the "evil foreigners." They moved quickly to settle all outstanding disagreements with the public sector groups they had offended. They patched up differences with the Ministry of Energy and paid the back debt they owed the TEA.

Now only the Capital Markets Board stood in the way of the Uzans getting back in the saddle. But the Uzans rallied the Ministry of Industry and Commerce to appoint a special auditor, who called a meeting, at which—surprise, surprise!—the Uzans were voted back into power.

We ended up losing the battle for Cukurova, although I console myself with the knowledge that we had called media and public attention to the neglected plight of minority shareholders in Turkey. We also, along the way, established a few precedents that may help our cause in the future. But one must never underestimate the ability of politically powerful interests to maintain their own privileges, regardless of paper legality, in countries where the rule of law is weak.

The number one lesson to be derived from the Cukurova catastrophe:

The people *behind* the company are just as important as the *numbers*.

Here you had a terrific company on paper—great assets, great contracts, great future. But if the people are bad news, none of that matters. Which is why, I believe, it's so important to meet with managements and understand their background before buying stock, if you can.

A second lesson:

Never assume that the law is on your side.

While it may be in most mature markets, the law in most emerging markets isn't going to protect you. It may, in fact, work against you. Particularly if you're a foreigner, and particularly if you're a minority investor.

Lesson No. 3:

If things turn sour for a company and it begins to lose money, the loss may be an opportunity for you to get in, but you must investigate very, very carefully:

1) To determine where those losses come from, and

2) Whether these management problems are being addressed.

Lesson No. 4: Always look a bargain, not to mention a gift horse, in the mouth.

Oh, and one final heads-up (Lesson No. 5) . . .

If the management or majority owner doesn't want to meet with you, watch out.

They've probably got something to hide.

Mesbla

Once upon a time, there was a highly successful mass-market department store in Brazil. It was named Mesbla. It was never the Brazilian Bloomingdales. In U.S. terms, it was more like the Macy's, or perhaps even the JC Penney, of Brazil.

The company had been on the scene since 1912, and was owned and operated by an old, reputable, and fashionable Rio family, widely regarded as pinnacles of Rio society. By the time we first bought Mesbla shares for our Emerging Markets Funds in August 1989, the company had expanded to include a profitable chain of auto dealerships, and was going great guns in a hyperinflationary monetary environment.

Over the years, we visited the company—and the family—regularly. I can recall one particularly gracious dinner at the family patriarch's historic mansion in Rio, home to a nationally known Brazilian folk art collection. I came away deeply impressed with the probity and dignity of this wonderful, charming, and traditional family.

During these visits, which were invariably pleasant, the family and its management representatives consistently assured us that things were going well for them. And we had no reason to doubt these rosy projections as the company consistently racked up steady profits. In 1991, however, the once-steady stock began its long slide down a slippery slope.

Mesbla's problems began with the introduction of President Fernando Collor de Mello's "Novo Brasil" plan, which in a radical attempt to bring hyperinflation under control, froze all the financial assets in the company and virtually crippled the economy overnight. Mesbla's sales ground to a halt, and to keep the chain in operation, management had to resort to asset disposals to finance their contracting business.

Even as management persistently assured us that things were well under control, the company was slipping swiftly toward bankruptcy. In late 1994, it was forced to disclose liabilities far exceeding its assets. That might not have been so bad, except that even those assets ($900 million) were suspect with regard to valuation, because they were almost entirely composed of debt, of both the short- and long-term variety.

Staggering under the weight of this mounting debt, and faced with a severe liquidity crisis, the company filed for bankruptcy—in Brazil they call it the *concordata*—in August 1995.

Mesbla, along with a number of other companies, particularly in the retail sector, had during the era of hyperinflation been making at least as much money "on the margin" as from the outright sale of goods. This means that they were making money off money, not furniture, automobiles, lamp shades, or what have you. Like a lot of other companies throughout Latin America during the hyperinflationary spiral, they'd been taking deliveries of goods, and then taking advantage of the month or so grace period they had been given by their suppliers to pay for the goods.

During that grace period, they had full possession of the goods free and clear. So they'd take whatever money they derived from the sale of those goods and deposit it in a local bank. There, high-yielding certificates of deposit paid marginally higher interest rates than the prevailing rate of inflation. So the spread between the money they made on bank interest, and the value of the money they had to shell out a month later to pay for the goods, amounted to a tidy little profit.

There was nothing whatsoever wrong with this. It was perfectly aboveboard, legal, and under the prevailing circumstances the sound and sensible thing to do with the money. But what happens when you start making money from money, and not from sales, is that if you are in the sales business, and the fiscal wind suddenly shifts, you can get caught with your pants down.

In Mesbla's case, the family management, lulled into complacency by the super-high interest rates, fell asleep at the wheel. They lost track of how to make profits from stuff.

Unfortunately, that was only the start of their problems. Unable to finesse the shift to a more normal inflationary environment, Mesbla began cutting a few corners—to put it mildly. Filing for bankruptcy protection was one thing, but at least that was supposed to give them a little breathing room by letting them pay off their $280 million debt over two years, at favorable terms.

We looked at the assets during this interim period, and attended a series of meetings with management, at which we were repeatedly assured that they had the situation well in hand. Then, in June 1996, the company shocked us by announcing year-end 1995 results reporting a net loss of $262 million.

That was not even the half of it. Upon closer scrutiny, their P&L statement revealed a few unsettling items, tucked away here and there, in the fine print.

1) A significant portion of that whopping loss was due to non-operating items.

2) A $90 million loss was attributed to "property revaluation." Now what was that?

Under Brazilian law, the company had six months in which to call a shareholder meeting to approve these financial statements. No such meeting was called. The company's net worth, meanwhile, dropped from $262 million to $11 million. This was a full-scale collapse.

After a few irate suppliers sued, all trading in Mesbla shares was suspended on the Rio exchange, pending the resolution of these suits. Snooping around, we learned that the suspect $90 million in real estate "revaluation" losses was due to a series of sales-and-leaseback transactions carried out by the company to raise ready cash, in which the properties were sold to a series of undisclosed buyers, at a steep discount, and then leased back to the company, permitting management to book these "sales" as "losses" on the books.

This financial legerdemain in part accounted for one of the more disturbing aspects of the latest revelations: that even after these so-called sales, the company's debt ballooned during the period. The sales, in other words, far from alleviating the company's woes, had added to them.

We sought an explanation from the company for three outstanding items:

1) The reason for these sales.

2) The identities of the mystery buyers.

3) The reason these assets were sold so cheaply.

Our requests for information were repeatedly and summarily rebuffed by the company. No explanations were forthcoming. Our old pals the family, meanwhile, had managed to quietly transfer their 17 percent stake in Mesbla (comprising 51 percent of the voting shares) to a company we understood to be controlled by Banco Pactual, a Rio-based investment bank advising Mesbla's major creditors.

What really burned me up was that the majority-shareholder family had gotten their money out of the company at around $14 for a thousand shares—a price provided by an "independent consultant" hired strictly for that one transaction. But on the open market, the price before trading was suspended had sunk to under $5.00.

Oh boy, we should have sold out at that price! But by the time we got full wind of the depths to which the management had sunk, it was too late: trading in the stock had already been suspended. The fact that the family had been paid close to three times the price of the going rate caused us heartburn. And it caused us to start agitating for some fairer treatment for the rest of us.

Inadvertently but still stupidly, we'd broken a cardinal Mobius Rule:

Always maintain an exit strategy. Always maintain a way to get out.

Now, we had no way out.

Our only recourse was to fight.

Guerrilla War

We would never have taken the time and the trouble to embark on our quixotic pursuit of justice in "L'Affaire Mesbla" if we hadn't felt just so burned and betrayed by it all. And if we hadn't felt it worthwhile spending money to establish some rudimentary rules of minority shareholder protection in Brazil.

With the family conveniently out of the picture, Mesbla's three largest creditors—a trio of big Brazilian banks—set about restructuring the firm strictly in their own interests, which disadvantaged the minority shareholders.

Under their so-called restructuring plan, the banks converted the company's $850 million debt into equity. If carried out, the plan would have resulted in the dilution of the share of the company held by existing shareholders from 100 percent to less than 3 percent.

That's right: from 100 percent down to 3 percent.

In June 1997, Mesbla published their newest set of dismal results for 1996. They had racked up a stupefying loss of $586.6 million. Once again, a significant portion of that loss was due to nonoperating items not specifically explained to shareholders. Following the announcement of these appalling results, the company called a general shareholder meeting, to seek approval for the previous two years' pathetic financial statements.

According to Brazilian law, if a company does not pay a dividend for three consecutive years, owners of preference shares—the kind we had been sold—are granted voting rights. But at the shareholder meeting, over our strenuous protests, we were not permitted to vote our shares. Our vote against the motion to reorganize the company according to the major creditors' plan could have stopped the restructuring from going forward. But when the conversion of $500 million of Mesbla debt into equity was put to a vote, we were denied the right to vote. Consequently, the conversion was approved by a majority of common shareholders.

Suffice it to say, we were fit to be tied.

Convinced that the company had grossly understated the value of our shares, and that our funds' holdings were about to be diluted into insignificance, we took Mesbla to court, seeking an injunction to block the debt conversion. The injunction was promptly granted, but just as promptly lifted by the *concordata* (bankruptcy) judge, who bowed to the company's desperate appeal that if the restructuring were in any way obstructed, management would have no other choice but to close the doors, resulting in the loss of thousands of Brazilian jobs.

As the judge intimated, our position might well have had merit, but he was loath to make the company's employees jobless.

In most emerging markets, if your interests don't jibe with those of the employees, your interests as a minority shareholder are likely to be ignored. In countries where keeping people employed is the number one social goal, shareholder interests are too often likely to take a back seat.

Errors and Omissions

Let's take a brief break in the relating of this sordid South American saga to review the mistakes we'd made up to that time. When the macroeconomic picture shifted dramatically, we should have taken a closer look at Mesbla. We should have asked ourselves (and management) a couple of key questions:

1) Just precisely how are you guys making your money?

2) If you're making money off OPM (other people's money), what contingency plans do you have to start making money off your core business, namely selling goods to the public, if the inflationary spiral were ever broken?

Depending upon our level of satisfaction with their answers to these questions, we should have:

1) Demanded to review the company's books, and

2) Sold all our stock in a flash if they refused.

Runaround Sue

Instead, we were forced to play catch-up, and pay costly corporate lawyers through the nose, to basically get the same runaround. So there we were, caught up to our necks in the labyrinthine, Byzantine Brazilian court system, wandering blindfolded, as if in a maze, forced to shell out major reals for, basically, the privilege of getting the dope on how we'd been totally tubed.

The goal of the "restructuring" soon became clear, when the "reorganized" company announced its plans to be sold to one Ricardo Mansur, the majority shareholder in a rival retail chain called Mappin. Banco Pactual, the bank selected by the creditor banks to undertake the restructuring, had installed as Mesbla's new CEO a handpicked recruit, the former head of an outfit called Lojas Americanas.

If successful, the bank and its handpicked CEO were to profit handsomely from their efforts: Banco Pactual and the new CEO were to receive a staggering fee of approximately $10 million. In addition, they were to receive 8 percent of the restructured company's net worth, which at around $900 million came to a total take of $72 million.

As we later asserted in court documents, we considered this fee of $82 million excessive, given that the current market cap of Mesbla was $14 million, and its net worth less than zero.

What really surprised me was when, after we threatened to sue to block the debt conversion, a senior officer of Mesbla was quoted in the *Journal Do Brasil* asserting that I was a "pirate" and a "thief." He also accused me of a form of commercial extortion, claiming that I had offered to give the restructuring a green light as long as we got paid in full. This was fanciful hogwash, and was fabricated to make it look as if we were only out for ourselves. In fact, we *were* fighting for ourselves, but also for the rights of minority shareholders in Brazil.

We decided to:

1) Proceed with legal action against the company to try to overturn the results of the shareholder meeting of June 1997.

2) Explore possible legal action for libel to try to compel Mesbla to make available all financial information.

3) Contact senior officials at the CVM (Brazil's version of the U.S. SEC) to look into the details of this debt conversion, and the mysterious transfers of property.

The CVM turned out to be unwilling to enforce the regulations regarding voting rights for preference shareholders when dividends are not paid for three years. It generally exhibited a strong preference not to become involved in protecting minority shareholder rights.

As I write, the case is still pending, and wending its way with exquisite lassitude through the Brazilian judicial system.

Two More Losers I'd Rather Forget

Two of our most interesting fiascos took place in China. Both share a similar pattern:

An unrealistic evaluation of a supposedly untapped market.

We bought Forever Bicycle, whose shares traded on the Shanghai exchange, in November of 1993, at what seemed like a remarkably cheap price: $278.

The company caught our attention because bicycles are, and will continue to be for some time, the most popular form of transit in China. Forever Bicycle—perhaps the name should have given us pause—was the second largest operator in what was being construed as a huge, untapped market.

Watch out for "huge, untapped markets"—by the time brokers and bankers are singing the praises of "huge, untapped markets," they're being tapped like a rubber tree in the Amazon.

In this case, the macroeconomic scenario influenced us strongly. China had just opened up its market for B shares—the only kind foreigners can own—and the supply of new B shares was strictly limited. With the hunger on for Chinese shares, we fell into a mental trap:

At this price, we can't lose.

Oh yes we could!

The problem?

In a word: competition. New entrants, lured by all this "untapped potential," began tapping into the market like a family of woodpeckers in heat. Their costs were lower, they had less baggage, and they were able to outsell the former dominant players. The free market worked, in this case, like a charm. And took the wind out of Forever Bicycle's inner tubes.

By going with the incumbent, we came out with egg on our face: by the time we sold out at an average price of $163, we'd taken a hit of $4 million. Not a king's ransom, to be sure. But not chicken feed either. Our only consolation was that we'd learned a lesson:

Keep a hawk's eye on competition waiting in the wings.

We made nearly the same mistake with Shanghai Narcissus—another weirdly named company that should have made us gaze at our own reflections in the pool. Here was another newly listed Shanghai-traded company, a washing machine manufacturer.

Once again, we were impressed by its dominant position in Shanghai.

Also by its low P/E, and its pending joint venture with Whirlpool.

The market liked the new things we did. At the time of the float, the IPO did great right out of the gate.

Our mistake:

Not selling at that point.

Instead, we clung hopefully to the stock as the joint venture with Whirlpool went sour. It finally broke up, a year later, amid much name-calling and finger-pointing. Whatever the blame for the failure of the joint venture, what really hurt Shanghai Narcissus was much more mundane.

1) New entrants into the market.

2) Rising costs for raw materials, steel and PVC.

By the time we got out, with our tails between our legs, we'd dropped $2 million.

Our mistake:

Being ahead in one region is no guarantee of success as a national brand.

By the way, for all this talk of "mistakes," it's important to recognize that not only is nobody perfect, but that mistakes are an integral part of investing. You're never going to always pick winners, and picking losers—in my opinion—should in no way reflect any lack of care or negligence in the selection of investments for a portfolio under management. That said, if you pick too many losers, that will affect your performance, just the same as if you always picked winners.

Winners

You're already familiar with a few of the majors. Here are a few of the minors.

China Overseas Land and Investment Company Ltd.

This was one of the early red chips—People's Republic of China–based companies listed on the Hong Kong exchange. What caught my eye about COLIC—not the name for a Chinese crybaby—was that at the time (summer 1995) it was still a novelty for a Chinese company to be listed on the Hong Kong exchange, particularly a company openly owned lock, stock, and barrel by a state-owned company in China. It was, in short, the original red chip.

In this case, China Overseas Land and Investment Company was transparently and legitimately an investment vehicle for the China State Construction Engineering Corporation, one of the country's largest state-owned construction companies. We understood that its principal activities would be property development and management of large-scale construction contracts, but we didn't know where. When we first began looking into the stock, we'd assumed that they were looking to raise capital in Hong Kong to import back into China.

In the light of subsequent excitement over red chips' vaunted "connections" to the Chinese leadership (*guanxi*), we didn't focus too much on the political factors. Instead, we were more blown away by the P/E, which ranged from an attractive 7 to 8. And we liked the fact that the stock was trading at a deep discount to NAV (net asset value).

But what really clinched the deal for us was the quality of the management. When we talked to the president, he told us that he intended to put most of the money raised in Hong Kong—60 to 70 percent of assets—in Hong Kong, not China.

I asked him why. He didn't bat an eyelash: "Because Hong Kong is more profitable than China."

Rather than being used as a vehicle to suck assets out of Hong Kong and pump them back into China, this company was being operated in a strictly businesslike way. This was a good sign, because it meant that the Chinese were being practical, and weren't just looking to fleece the foreigners by raising money to be indiscriminately dumped into some sinkhole back in the homeland. Or, even worse, to bail out a flagging Chinese state-owned dinosaur.

What people don't get about red chips is that *guanxi* can work both ways:

1) Connections can get you contracts and business.

2) They can also come with strings attached that can reduce operating efficiency.

When the red chip hype shot all these stocks through the roof, we sold COLIC out when its P/E jumped to 14 and 15 and the stock was selling at a steep premium to NAV.

So what did we do right?

Buy on fundamentals, sell on hype.

Lai Sun International Group

When we first bought into this Hong Kong–based diversified company in 1989, some of the management had been getting quite a lot of press as ladies' men and men-about-town. The word was that some of them ran around with models and actresses, as if that somehow meant they couldn't be serious businessmen.

Peter and Franky Lam had started out in what in New York they call the "rag trade"—and had made a name for themselves producing shirts and other garments under the Crocodile label. In a sense, their ascent as tycoons runs parallel to the global rise of Hong Kong in general, because they started out turning out the classic sort of cheap Hong Kong knockoffs that once made "Made in Hong Kong" synonymous with low-grade sludge, and then expanded gradually into the upmarket end of the business. And from there, the world became their oyster.

In 1987 they purchased another company that initially made copies of high-end products similar to those made by the French company Izod under the Chemise Lacoste label, which featured a crocodile. In imitation, theirs were produced under the Crocodile label. But after establishing themselves, they began developing Crocodile as a brand name in its own right, and even launched a highly successful subsidiary, Crocokids, to tap into that Asian perennial, the baby-boom market.

After successfully running and expanding a chain of Crocodile stores, Lai Sun blossomed into one of the largest property developers in Asia. They began building hotels in Pacific Rim cities from Manila to Kuala Lumpur to L.A., where they snapped up a piece of the Regent Beverly Wilshire. They made their off-Broadway debut in New York with the Four Seasons Hotel in Manhattan, designed by I. M. Pei. By the time the Asian Flu hit, they'd hit the big time. They were highly leveraged. And their once-cheap stock was riding high on the hog.

We paid them a courtesy call at their offices at Crocodile House at Connaught Road, in Central Hong Kong—a premier address if ever there was one. The Group, as it had then become known, was moving its garment manufacturing operations out of Hong Kong into China, and was, apart from property development of hotels and apartment complexes all over Asia, even getting into TV. Their Asia TV had acquired the largest Chinese-language program library in Asia.

I was as impressed by the Lam brothers' sobriety and probity in business by day as the gossip columnists were impressed by their nocturnal activities. I liked the way they'd skillfully built on their garment industry expertise, and used it as a springboard to leapfrog into other areas. I also thought they had assembled a first-rate management. Upon leaving their office, while still in the elevator, I turned to my team and said: "Let's go for it. The assets are there, they're doing a good job. Management seems very good. They have their fun, but that's their business."

A good example of buying contrarian. The sentiment was very negative on Lai Sun.

Fast-forward ten years. By now, as the Hong Kong property market has gone stratospheric, the Crocodile brothers are shelling out huge sums for sizable stakes in trophy properties, hotels, shopping malls, apartment complexes. When the stock hit the magic 200 percent over our initial strike price, we sold.

Any share that has quadrupled in value is a prime candidate for taking profits.

As has been proven time and again, "Bears sleep in the winter, and bulls run in the summer, but pigs get slaughtered."

As the Asian Flu sweeps into Lai Sun's home turf, the company comes under heavy scrutiny. As markets plunge, Lai Sun Development, the company's property arm, takes a heavy hit, due to its relatively heavy debt load: 60 percent of equity. As a company spokesperson makes haste to announce that they had sold a major development site only the previous week, and were planning to "reduce its debt-to-equity ratio within six months," the stock hits a record low. It drops 15 percent in a day. And as whispers about "indebted developers" like Lai Sun shove the Hang Seng index down 7 percent in four hours, my interest in Lai Sun is suddenly rekindled.

Now, rumors began circulating that Lai Sun was in some kind of trouble—not surprising, in Hong Kong's perennially overextended property market. They were said to be "quietly considering" offers for their stakes in the Beverly Wilshire and the Four Seasons. They were said to be desperate to raise cash.

What did we do?

Let's just say that what goes around comes around: Lai Sun had become interesting again.

Shanghai Dazhong Taxi Co. Ltd.

Quite simply, one of the best run companies in Shanghai. A lot of other big Shanghai companies were government factories, saddled with big workforces, big overheads, big bureaucracies, and potentially big headaches. But these guys were different: close to the ground. Very much with it. In tune with the public, in tune with the streets. The top brass were mostly former taxi drivers, who had formed their own entrepreneurial company, predicated on grassroots appeal.

Because they'd started driving cabs for a living, they'd learned how to keep costs down and profits up, and how to keep a complex, decentralized operation well organized. The cash flow was also tremendous. We were particularly impressed that they were running a service operation in China, which to put it mildly is hardly famed for the quality of its service economy. These taxi guys were training their staff to be courteous, and efficient. And that training was paying off.

When we visited their principal offices on Nanjing Road in Shanghai, just a few minutes' walk from John Portman's Shangri-La Hotel, I noted that the decorations and decor in general were old and shabby. Gu Hua, the company's vice director for planning and development, dryly explained that they were contemplating moving to a new building, one that they had built for themselves, not for prettier decorations, but to save money on rent.

He noted that the company had lately branched out to launch taxi fleets outside Shanghai, to neighboring major cities in Jiangsu province: Wuxi, Hangzhou, Suzou, Ningbo. All were booming proto-metropoli—and all were ripe for this low-key form of capitalist exploitation. A newly announced government policy of a five-day workweek—intended to force companies to employ more people—had helped them expand their core business immeasurably, because people now had more leisure time, and were more likely to travel by taxi to neighboring cities.

This development should also boost the company's fast-growing car rental business, he said. The company was on top of all developments pertaining to mobility—upward and horizontal—in what had until very recently remained an exceedingly static society.

Their home removal (moving) business was taking off like a rocket. Even the construction of a subway in Shanghai didn't appear to faze the Dazhong Taxi types in the least: "Decreased road congestion," he said mildly, "will help our drivers be more efficient."

They were on top of the latest high-tech developments: they'd even outfitted 600 taxis out of their fast-growing fleet with a GPS (global positioning system) satellite navigation system. And they'd recently launched Dazhong Insurance Company, which in its first year of operation was already showing a healthy profit.

Having branched out into building and managing hotels and other properties, this former taxi company had carefully targeted the Chinese middle- and lower-class hotel customers located near the train stations. They had no interest in going head-to-head with the big chains, which were concentrating on the high-end business market.

The only fly in the ointment?

Escalating administrative and general expenses, which could not be easily passed on to the customer because taxi fares were regulated by municipalities.

Which was why, our source explained, they had diversified in the first place.

Irony: if the taxi drivers had enjoyed a free market, they might have remained taxi drivers.

Electricidad de Caracas

In 1995, we were the sole bidder in a government-sponsored auction for shares in Electricidad de Caracas—the main electricity company of Caracas, the capital of Venezuela. At the time, we'd been investing in Venezuela for about four years, and had become—after a long period of trepidation—fairly comfortable with the environment's pros and cons.

When we'd first gone into Venezuela, it was a disaster from a commercial standpoint. Inflation was high, the government was still populist in orientation, public spending was out of control, and the establishment was proving extremely resistant to change. They were way behind the curve in the general trend in the region toward more market-oriented policies.

The government was refusing to privatize their state-owned enterprises, and all the bureaucrats disguised as businessmen were generally living like spoiled pashas off their oil wealth. They were squandering this wealth, rather than productively investing it in new enterprises. The oil industry of Venezuela, which was providing the wherewithal for much of this indulgence, had been nationalized back in the mid-1970s, in conjunction with the rise of OPEC, and was still caught in a 1970s time warp, when the going thing was the transfer of wealth from North to South, combined with Third World solidarity.

The whole nonaligned movement, of course, collapsed with the downfall of the Soviet Union, and the conclusion of the Cold War. OPEC, meanwhile, had lost so much credibility that rather than being the bane of the consuming countries' existence, it had basically become an irrelevance. Every time OPEC threatened to cut production to raise prices, the world could count on other major producers failing to go along. The result: low oil prices throughout the 1990s, an enormous boon to a gradually integrating global economy. And a major contributor to global warming.

When we first arrived in Venezuela, the place was—on a

macro level—a shambles. But here was another classic case—similar to one prevailing several years later in Russia—where a godawful macro picture provided camouflage for the growth of a number of well-managed, undervalued companies, which because of the macro problems were quite cheap on an asset value (NAV) basis.

So when the shares in Electricidad de Caracas were put out to bid, we were the only players game enough to sign on. We ended up taking about a 10 percent share of the company, at what I don't mind telling you was a very sweet price. In less than two years, the stock doubled.

What did we do right?

Well, looking back on it, I'd say that we took full advantage of an atmosphere of uncertainty, and made an optimistic bet that global forces would, in time, prevail even upon one of the last redoubts of socialism.

Why had we been so confident? Because it was becoming quite clear that even the most stubborn holdouts would have to give way to the new world order, or get lost in the shuffle, something even the labor union leaders and bureaucrats could not, in the end, condone.

Looking at the regional picture, we felt sure that the trend of events in Latin America toward privatization, and more market-oriented private and public policies in general, had acquired a certain critical mass, and enough political momentum to steamroll the nay-sayers.

But we didn't gamble. We made an educated choice based on a set of facts, which showed the following:

1) The P/E ratio was very low.

2) The net assets were worth a great deal more than the market cap of the company.

We weren't heading into that major purchase all starry-eyed, to strike some idealistic blow on behalf of Adam Smith's invisible hand.

Now, shoot ahead a couple of years, to 1998. All of a sudden, the tables have turned. Venezuela has been experiencing high rates of growth and low rates of inflation. The stock market has risen dramatically. Everything is going along swimmingly.

So what do we do then?

We start selling, of course. Quietly, cautiously, but still heavily.

While in Venezuela on that second go-round we visited a fine old shipping company called the H.R. Bolton Company. A fairly large, well-established, family-run company which over the years has diversified into, among other things, the ceramics business.

A nice, young, handsome, tall American was the financial director for the ceramics end of the business. He was intense, hardworking, and clean-cut, and I could tell, disturbed by something that he felt awkward about bringing forward. After sitting through an excellent presentation, which was justifiably upbeat, we made our move to exit, stage right, amid the usual cordial atmosphere of smiles, encouraging words, and rosy projections.

I'd almost made it out the door when this young fellow, overcoming some resistance within himself, threw caution to the winds and whispered in my ear, "Before you go, I'd like to ask you just one question."

Of course, I could hardly fail to oblige.

"Why are you selling our shares?"

I hadn't expected that one. I felt embarrassed. I felt as if I was hurting this nice guy's feelings. And I wasn't sure what to say.

Honestly, I wished I hadn't felt compelled to sell his shares, but the reason was obvious: they had gotten very *expensive,* and we could put that money to better use elsewhere.

So I mumbled something innocuous like, "Well, you know how it is, some of our funds have to sell because we have redemptions. We're buying and selling at different times. It's no reflection on the company . . ." And I edged on out the door, before things became even more awkward.

So why were we selling stock in such a fine company?

Precisely because it was such a fine company!

And since it was a very fine company, and since the whole wide world now knew all about what a fine company it was, and the whole wide world had since fallen in love with Venezuelan stocks, the shares had become a prime candidate for profit-taking.

Of course, what I should have said was: "You must remember that we were buying Bolton when nobody wanted Bolton; when

things were really bad. Now that things are good, it's our responsibility to sell."

I could well recall our first meeting at Bolton, several years before, when the elderly head of the company (whose name, not
surprisingly, is Mr. Bolton) came limping into his own boardroom, leaning on a crutch.

Since he was chairman of the company, I couldn't help but
think to myself: "Is this a reflection of the health of the company?"

Psychologically and physically, the company's position was
quite bad at the time.

So what did we do? We looked at the assets and concluded the
stock was undervalued.

We bought the stock.

Now, five years later, we briefly saw this same guy again, and
he was in the pink of health. I hardly recognized him. He had regained all his old vigor, he was aggressive, he was barking orders, he was on top of the world. Also the stock had jumped up
to very high levels—it had become overpriced.

So what did we do?

You tell me.

The World According to Mark

Things change.

You know, in a nutshell, that's just about it.

The common thread running through nearly all the stories I've
told in this book is the constant of change, and the need to remain—as a manager, as a messenger, as an investor—fluid and
flexible. Markets, like oceans and tides, are a wave phenomenon. The only way to stay on top is to bend your knees, keep
your balance, and surf.

Like surfing, riding the waves of the global markets can be a
blast. Not to mention incredibly profitable. But what we look
for consistently, as a key part of our fundamental analysis, is a
company's, a country's, a region's, and a management's capacity
to *manage change*.

Change of any kind is often greeted with fear by people set in their ways.

If you want to find the companies of the future, look for people who can handle the future.

The greatest changes in my lifetime, I'd have to say, have taken place in the past decade:

1) The end of the Cold War, the decline of Communism, and . . .

2) The globalization of the economy.

"Privatization" may be an ugly word, but it sure is a beautiful concept.

With the demise of the centrally planned and even the mixed economy, markets now rule. This is one change about which many people, from central bankers to bureaucrats to bankers to politicians, tend to feel a little ambivalent. Central bankers don't like it—they can't stand no longer calling the shots. In the new age of the truly free market, all sorts of once-powerful people have seen their authority eroded, probably never to be regained.

As the Asian financial crisis spread around the world, a call came up from some curious quarters to once again "manage" and "control" global markets, to stanch and slow the quicksilver flow of capital across borders, and around the world. One of the most thoughtful and eloquent voices calling for the reinstitution of some form of global control—comparable to the Bretton Woods agreement after World War II—was a famous hedge fund manager, who lent credence to many people's growing fears that without some new world financial "order," there would be chaos and anarchy.

I not only disagree with this view as a matter of philosophy, I'm not at all convinced it could be achieved, as a practical matter.

How in the age of computers and virtually instantaneous data transfer could you possibly levy a tax on the flow of global capital?

This strikes me as an attempt to turn back the clock, to put the genie back in the bottle. However, a restriction on excessive leveraging and derivatives would be a step in the right direction.

But who knows? I might be wrong, and if all these smart people do figure out a way to tax the flow of capital, we'll just have to figure out a way to derive benefit from it.

What many people failed to grasp during the Asian crisis was that it was mainly another hurdle to be crossed before the creation of a truly global free market. The so-called tiger economies had been beneficiaries of Cold War economics, and had flourished economically while becoming sclerotic politically.

So much attention has been paid, in recent years, to the wholesale conversion of dozens of former Third World socialist economies to a free-market model that we've tended to forget how radical a transition it has been for the semisocialist economies of Western Europe and Latin America to adapt to an age of global financial freedom.

Freeing up markets from central planning and government control embraces the Big Bang of the early 1980s that released British markets from red tape and regulation as well as the more recent Big Bang of the late 1990s by which the Japanese belatedly hope to do much the same thing for their own troubled engine, once the glory of the world, now a prostrate patient in need of radical surgery.

The IMF role in the creation of truly free markets across Southeast Asia, where cartels of one sort or another had proliferated, cannot be underestimated.

One of my all-time favorite movies (for reasons that will become clear presently) is Paddy Chayefsky's *Network,* starring the late, great Peter Finch as the newscaster Howard Beale, who one day decides that he's "mad as hell and not going to take it anymore," and Faye Dunaway as the cool, chilly network executive who makes his life a living hell.

In a key scene, Howard Beale's ultimate boss, Jensen, calls the renegade broadcaster on the carpet for attempting to throw a monkey wrench into the works of a pending takeover of the network. In a rage, he castigates Beale for being a man of the past, who's failed to grasp the realities of the new, cutthroat, competitive global environment.

JENSEN: You have meddled with the primal forces of nature, Mr. Beale, and I won't have it, is that clear? You think you have merely stopped a business deal—that is not the case.

The Arabs have taken fifty billion dollars out of this country and *now* they must put it back. It is ebb and flow, tidal gravity, it is ecological balance! You are an old man who still thinks in terms of nations and peoples. There are no nations! There are no peoples! There are no Russians! There are no Arabs! There are no Third Worlds! There is no West!

There is only one holistic system of systems, one vast, interwoven, interacting, multivariate, multinational dominion of dollars! . . .

It is the international system of currency that determines the *totality* of life on this planet! That is the natural order of things today! That is the atomic, subatomic, and galactic structure of things today! And you have meddled with the primal forces of nature, and you will atone! Am I getting through to you, Mr. Beale?

HOWARD (*from the darkness*): Amen.

When *Network* was first released, back in the 1970s, globalization was more of a dread specter, only just coming to pass, and far from the quotidian reality that it is today. Such a trend was widely regarded with fear and loathing by many, if not most, thoughtful people, many of whom could only recognize and feel comfortable in a world made up of sovereign, almighty nation-states, immutable and secure. But also, frequently at war with one another.

What the perennial pessimists failed to foresee was that globalization would occur against the backdrop of falling political barriers like the Iron Curtain, and that its ultimate arrival would as likely usher in an era of greater freedom, political and economic, as a new form of slavery.

One of the most common complaints I hear from people around the world is that our world, as it becomes smaller, is becoming more and more the same. The new "global culture," they say, has deteriorated into a frantic, frenzied scene of a shopping binge, while many once-beautiful, graceful, and traditional cities and landscapes have been paved over to build shopping malls.

I can't really argue with that, particularly not after spending so much time in the high-rise boomtowns now paving the Pacific Rim. But I do believe that the only reliable way for the vast majority of human beings to ever free themselves of materialism—even assuming that this would be a good thing—is for the economies of the world to grow rapidly enough to provide more people with more of what they want than ever before. Because only in an atmosphere of abundance and security will people ever be willing to look beyond the basic necessities, and after that the luxuries, of life.

Many people mourn the passing of the past, and the tyranny of the future.

But I believe that the world is a far better place than it was ten, twenty, or fifty years ago.

One reason for that improvement has been the steady decline in the capacity of central governments, bureaucracies, autocrats, and central planners to control the lives of ordinary people. Under the sway of impersonal free markets, people have a far better chance of making decent lives for themselves, and of engaging in "the pursuit of happiness," than they ever had before.

The story of emerging markets has been, as I've repeatedly said, one of hope and growth.

I've been proud to have been a part of it, over the past ten years. And I hope that just as these markets have grown at a breakneck pace, you too have seen some of what makes these markets so appealing, not merely to me personally, but to thousands of savvy investors: the vastness of their potential, the speed with which they've evolved, the fabulous wealth of opportunities just waiting to be grasped, tapped, and productively promoted.

Ten years ago, I was one of the first American fund managers to fight my way through the Byzantine layers of bureaucracy and red tape that tie up these markets in knots. Today, there are hundreds of emerging markets funds, and instead of millions, billions of dollars invested in them.

These marvelous markets, as they continue to evolve and develop, are likely to be volatile, as recent trends have vividly revealed. But I sincerely hope that after reading this book, you'll no longer view volatility only in negative terms. Volatility can be a good thing, for producers as well as investors. Market ups and downs, even the most violent ones, provide incentives for people to adapt to new environments, and shifting realities. Free markets can be a harsh taskmaster, but as Winston Churchill once said of democracy, the free market may be a lousy system, but it just happens to be the best one we've got.

Passport Control

Well, it looks like I've got a plane to catch.

And a new load of companies to check out tomorrow.

At least you can thank me for saving you from jet lag.

As for me, I'll just push my little brass button and sit back and watch the air show come up on the TV screen at the front of the cabin—which still looks alarmingly like the boudoir of an Arab princess—telling me which way we're headed, and where we're scheduled to land next.

But you know what?

I think I'll just sit here and stare out the window, because if you want the God's honest truth, whichever direction we end up headed, north south east west, really doesn't matter to me anymore. After all these years of roaming around, I've started to like surprises.

Wherever we touch down tomorrow, chances are that it'll be some place well worth the visit, and some place fascinating to explore. I only hope that they've got a gym, and a sauna. And a freely convertible currency. Fair, efficient, liquid, and transparent markets. And a hands-off central bank.

And of course, I almost forgot:

No lousy foreign share premium.

APPENDIX

To those not inclined or prepared to jump on a plane and pay company visits to "kick the tires," the best—and cheapest—sources of information on emerging markets are the general interest business periodicals, ranging from *The Wall Street Journal* to *The Financial Times, The Economist, Fortune, Barron's,* and other publications geared toward investors, which frequently publish special sections on regions, countries, and companies of interest to global investors.

Since many people who actively invest also travel, I cannot stress gaining on the ground experience too much, from paying an always entertaining and often instructional visit to the local stock exchange, to reading local periodicals, to speaking to people one meets in a café, over lunch, or even on line to change money at the bank. Company visits can sometimes be arranged through local brokers who may be interested in gaining even a small or novice investor's business. More rarely, visits may be arranged through a company itself, although gaining entry to corporate offices is by no means guaranteed even to shareholders. Sometimes even to large shareholders.

For the armchair investor curious enough to invest money as well as time in studying foreign markets, I recommend the following sources of timely information—most are print publications, but there are also some Web sites of interest.

For Web and Internet searches—though a word of caution should be inserted as to the uncertain reliability of some Web-based information—most of the stock exchanges mentioned in this book have put up Web sites, as have many of the companies and countries mentioned herein.

One of my personal favorites on the Web is a site maintained by the Bank of New York (address: http://www.bankofnycom/adr), which features depository receipts provided by many different depository banks (including Bank of New York competitors) and is a highly reliable source of up-to-date information on ADRs and GDRs available on major stock exchanges.

Another excellent source is www.apr.com, a site created by J. P. Morgan

By far the best general source for raw emerging markets data, in my opinion, is the International Finance Corporation's IFC Index books (see below). For selection of funds, one of my favorites is Morningstar, which is relatively inexpensive and is consistently well done. The Lipper service is one of the most comprehensive mutual fund information sources. Of the increasing number of newsletters being published on emerging markets, my personal favorite is *The Bank Credit Analyst* emerging markets letter published by the BCA Group in Canada. Others, mainly focused on particular countries or regions, are listed below. I should emphasize that these are purely personal preferences, and in no way reflect the opinions of my employers or colleagues at the Franklin/Templeton Group.

IFC

Monthly updates
Address: http://www.ifc.org

LIPPER:

Monthly fax updates and quarterly analysis
Address: http://www.lipperweb.com/home/def.html-ssi

MORNINGSTAR:

Monthly CD-ROM
Address: http://www.investools.com/cgi-bin/library/msmf.pl

Emerging Markets Newsletters

From BCA Publications Limited:

The BCA Emerging Markets Strategist
The Bank Credit Analyst
The International Bank Credit Analyst
The BCA China Analyst

From Thomson BankWatch Asia: Bank Watch Monthly

Brazil Watch (Orbis Publications)

Business Africa—*The Economist* Intelligence Unit
Central European Business Weekly
Emerging Markets Week

From Institutional Investor Inc.:

Institutional Investor Emerging Markets Week
Institutional Investor Newsletters

From Business Monitor International Ltd:

China and North Asia Monitor
The Emerging Markets Monitor
Indian Subcontinent Monitor
South East Asia Monitor
Southern Africa Monitor
North African Monitor